District Gazetteers of India Series 65

CENTRAL PROVINCES DISTRICT GAZETTEERS

AMRAOTI

(DESCRIPTIVE)

District Gazetteers of India Series 65

CENTRAL PROVINCES DISTRICT GAZETTEERS

AMRAOTI

(DESCRIPTIVE)

Edited By

S. V. FITZGERALD, A. E. NELSON

30 Volumes (In 33 Bindings)

(2nd, Vol. A)

GYAN

Published by

Gyan Publishing House
5, Ansari Road
Daryaganj, New Delhi-110002
Phone: 011-47034999, 9811692060
E-mail: books@gyanbooks.com

Distribution Network
gyanbooks.com
India, USA, Canada, UK, Australia, France

ISBN: 978-93-6208-539-9 (Set) 30 Volumes (In 33 Bindings)
978-93-6208-548-1 (PB)

First Published, 1911

2nd Impression 2024

Printed at: Gyan Press, Delhi.

CENTRAL PROVINCES DISTRICT GAZETTEERS (2nd, Vol. A)
Edited By: S. V. FITZGERALD, A. E. NELSON

LIST OF VOLUMES

S. NO.	ISBN NO.	VOLUME	TITLE	AUTHOR	PRICE	PAGES
			ASSAM DISTRICT GAZETTEERS			
1	9788121285926	1st	Cachar	B. C. Allen	600	300
2	9788121285919	2nd	Sylhet	B. C. Allen	750	378
3	9788121285902	3rd	Goalpara	B. C. Allen	400	203
4	9788121285896	4th	Kamrup	B. C. Allen	675	344
5	9788121285889	5th	Darrang	B. C. Allen	725	364
6	9788121285872	6th	Nowgong	B. C. Allen	560	280
7	9788121285865	7th	Sibsagar	B. C. Allen	675	343
8	9788121285858	8th	Lakhimpur	B. C. Allen	690	347
9	9788121285841	9th	Naga Hills and Manipur	B. C. Allen	580	294
10	9788121285834	10th	The Khasi And Jaintia Hills, The Garo Hills And The Lushai Hills	B. C. Allen	675	363
11	9788121285827	11th	The Sadiya and Balipara Frontier Tract	B. C. Allen	375	190
			BENGAL DISTRICT GAZETTEERS			
12	9788121218672	1st	Angul	L. S. S. O'Malley	340	168
13	9788121259637	2nd	Bakarganj	J. C. JACK	970	194
14	9788121218696	3rd	Balasore	L. S. S. O'Malley	450	228
15	9788121259590	4th	Bankura	L. S. S. O'Malley	1000	199
16	9788121218375	5th	Bhagalpur	J. Byrne	390	194
17	9788121218290	6th	Birbhum	L. S. S. O'Malley	300	150
18	9788121259651	7th	Eastern Bengal and Assam - Bogra	J. N. Gupta	940	188
19	9788121218351	8th	Burdwan	J. C. K. Peterson	450	227
20	9788121259538	9th	Calcutta District Gazetteer - Statistics, 1901 - 02		340	68
21	9788121218313	10th	Champaran	L. S. S. O'Malley	410	205
22	9788121259613	11th	Eastern Bengal District Gazetters - Chittagong	L. S. S. O'Malley	1080	216
23	9788121259552	12th	Chota Nagpur Tributary		130	26
24	9788121259415	13th	The Cooch Behar Gazette: Statistics		1460	292
25	9788121218412	14th	Cuttack	L. S. S. O'Malley	490	248
26	9788121261357	15th	Eastern Bengal District Gazetteers Dacca	B. C. Allen	400	207
27	9788121218436	16th	Darbhanga	L. S. S. O'Malley	360	180
28	9789362089335	17th	Darjeeling	L. S. S. O'Malley	500	248
29	9788121259453	18th	Eastern Bengal District Gazetteers - Dinajpur	F. W. Strong	890	178
30	9788121259392	19th	Faridpur	L. S. S. O'Malley	700	140
31	9788121218474	20th	Gaya	L. S. S. O'Malley	540	270
32	9788121214032	21st	Bihar and Orissa District Gazetteer: Hazaribagh	E. Lister	715	234
33	9788121218337	22nd	Hooghly	L. S. S. O'Malley	680	340
34	9788121218191	23rd	Bengal District Gazetteer Howrah	L. S. S. O'Malley	390	199
35	9788121259293	24th	Eastern Bengal and Assam - Jalpaiguri	John F. Gruning	890	178
36	9788121259279	25th	Jessore	L. S. S. O'Malley	960	192
37	9788121259231	26th	Khulna	L. S. S. O'Malley	1100	220
38	9788121259217	27th	Malda	G. E. Lambourn	670	134
39	9788121267854	28th	Manbhum	H. Coupland	600	313
40	9788121218498	29th	Midnapore	L. S. S. O'Malley	500	252
41	9788121218597	30th	Monghyr	L. S. S. O'Malley	560	280
42	9788121259156	31st	Murshidabad	L. S. S. O'Malley	1250	250
43	9788121259576	32nd	Bengal District Gazetteers - Muzaffarpur	L. S. S. O'Malley	940	188
44	9788121259132	33rd	Mymensingh	F. A. Sachse	960	192
45	9788121259118	34th	Nadia	J. H. E. Garrett	1070	214
46	9788121259095	35th	Eastern Bengal and Assam - Noakhali	J. E. Webster	580	115
47	9788121218450	36th	Feudatory States of Orissa	L. E. B. Cobdenramsay	790	395
48	9788121259071	37th	Pabna	L. S. S. O'Malley	710	142
49	9788121218511	38th	Palamau	L. S. S. O'Malley	380	190
50	9788121218634	39th	Patna	L. S. S. O'Malley	500	250
51	9788121218535	40th	Puri	L. S. S. O'Malley	650	328
52	9788121218757	41st	Purnea	L. S. S. O'Malley	440	220
53	9788121258937	42nd	Rajshahi	L. S. S. O'Malley	1080	216
54	9788121256681	43rd	Bihar and Orissa District Gazetteers: Ranchi	M. G. Hallett	1350	278
55	9788121258913	44th	Eastern Bengal and assam - Rangpur	J. A. Vas	890	178
56	9788121218559	45th	Sambalpur	L. S. S. O'Malley	480	242
57	9788121214056	46th	Santal Parganas	L. S. S. O'Malley	940	308
58	9788121218610	47th	Saran	L. S. S. O'Malley	380	190
59	9788121218658	48th	Shahabad	L. S. S. O'Malley	380	190
60	9788121256704	49th	The Gazetteer of Sikhim	H. H. Risley	960	481
61	9788121218573	50th	Singhbhum, Saraikela And Kharsawan	L. S. S. O'Malley	560	280
62	9788121259439	51st	Eastern Bengal District Gazetteers - Tippera	J. E. Webster	730	146
63	9788121259033	52nd	24 Parganas	L. S. S. O'Malley	1420	284

S. NO.	ISBN NO.	VOLUME	TITLE	AUTHOR	PRICE	PAGES
			CENTRAL PROVINCES DISTRICT GAZETTEERS			
64	9789362081728	1st, Vol. A	Akola (Descriptive)	A. E. Nelson, C. Brown	870	436
65	9789362085481	2nd, Vol. A	Amraoti (Descriptive)	S. V. Fitzgerald, A. E. Nelson	1050	524
66	9789362089267	3rd,Vol. A	Balaghat (Descriptive)	R. V. RUSSELL	430	216
67	9789362083494	4th, Vol. A	Betul (Descriptive)	R. V. RUSSELL	610	306
68	9789362085146	5th, Vol. A	Bhandara (Descriptive)	R. V. RUSSELL	580	292
69	9789362088390	6th, Vol. A	Bilaspur (Descriptive)	R. V. RUSSELL	870	434
70	9789362086044	7th, Vol. A	Buldana (Descriptive)	A. E. Nelson	1090	543
71	9789362089014	8th, Vol. B	Chanda (Descriptive)	R. V. RUSSELL	470	234
72	9789362086938	9th	Chhattisgarch Feudatory State	E. A. De Brett	880	440
73	9789362082961	10th	Chhindwara (Descriptive)	R. V. RUSSELL	550	274
74	9789362089342	11th, Vol. A & B	Damoh (Descriptive and Statistical Tables 1891-1901)	R. V. RUSSELL	830	414
75	9789362081230	12th, Vol. A	Durg (Descriptive)	A. E. Nelson	460	232
76	9789362086037	13th, Vol. A	Hoshangabad (Descriptive)	R. V. RUSSELL	860	430
77	9789362086792	14th, Vol. A	Jubbulpore (Descriptive)	A. E. Nelson	950	474
78	9789362089663	15th, Vol. A & B	Mandla (Descriptive and Statistical Tables 1891-1901)	R. V. RUSSELL	370	186
79	9789362086419	16th, Vol. A	Nagpur (Descriptive)	R. V. RUSSELL	790	394
80	9789362080646	17th, Vol. A	Narsinghpur (Descriptive)	R. V. RUSSELL	510	257
81	9789362084835	18th, Vol. A	Nimar (Descriptive)	R. V. RUSSELL	600	299
82	9789362087737	19th, Vol. A	Raipur (Descriptive)	A. E. Nelson	790	396
83	9789362080264	20th, Vol. A	Saugor (Descriptive)	R. V. RUSSELL	570	285
84	9789362081117	21st, Vol. A	Seoni (Descriptive)	R. V. RUSSELL	460	232
85	9789362084965	22nd, Vol. A	Wardha (Descriptive)	R. V. RUSSELL	600	302
86	9789362083401	23rd, Vol. A	Yeotmal (Descriptive)	R. V. RUSSELL	550	277
87	9789362080325	24th, Vol. I, Pt. I	Gwalior (Text and Tables)	R. V. RUSSELL	980	489
88	9789362087133	24th, Vol. I, Pt. II	Gwalior (Maps)	R. V. RUSSELL	400	198
89	9789362086341	24th, Vol. I, Pt. III	Gwalior (Village List)	R. V. RUSSELL	810	406
90	9789362085467	24th, Vol. I, Pt. IV	Gwalior (Photos)	R. V. RUSSELL	1400	698
91	9789362087393	25th, Vol. II	Indore (Text and Tables)	C. E. Luard	1050	524
92	9789362084422	26th, Vol. III	Bhopal (Text and Tables)	C. E. Luard	540	272
93	9789362086815	27th, Vol. IV	Rewah (Text and Tables)	C. E. Luard	500	250
94	9789362087584	28th, Vol. V, Pt. A	Western States - Malwa (Text)	C. E. Luard	1520	762
95	9789362087300	29th, Vol. VI, Pt. A	Eastern States - Bundelkhand (Text)	C. E. Luard	930	463
96	9789362082169	30th, Vol. VI, Pt. B	Eastern States - Bundelkhand (Tables)	C. E. Luard	830	417
			GAZETTEER OF THE BOMBAY PRESIDENCY:			
97	9788121283441	1st, Part I	History of Gujarat	Ed.: James M. Campbell	3220	644
98	9788121285582	1st, Part II	History of the Konkan Dakhan and Southern Maratha Country	Ed.: James M. Campbell	4200	840
99	9788121285568	2nd	Gujarat, Surat and Broach	Ed.: James M. Campbell	2990	598
100	9788121285544	3rd	Kaira and Panch Mahals	Ed.: James M. Campbell	1690	339
101	9788121285520	4th	Ahmedabad	Ed.: James M. Campbell	1860	372
102	9788121285506	5th	Cutch, Palanpur, and Mahi Kantha	Ed.: James M. Campbell	2390	478
103	9788121285483	6th	Rewa Kantha, Narukot, Cambay, and Surat States	Ed.: James M. Campbell	1450	290
104	9788121285469	7th	Baroda	Ed.: James M. Campbell	3260	652
105	9788121285445	8th	Kathiawar	Ed.: James M. Campbell	3790	758
106	9788121285421	9th, Part I	Gujarat Population - Hindus	Ed.: James M. Campbell	3170	636
107	9788121285407	9th, Part II	Gujarat Population - Musalmans and Parsis	Ed.: James M. Campbell	1520	304
108	9788121285384	10th	Ratnagiri and Savantvadi	Ed.: James M. Campbell	2500	501
109	9788121285360	11th	Kolaba and Janjira	Ed.: James M. Campbell	2550	513
110	9788121285346	12th	Khandesh	Ed.: James M. Campbell	3190	638
111	9788121285322	13th Part I	Thana	Ed.: James M. Campbell	2050	413
112	9788121285308	13th Part II	Thana	Ed.: James M. Campbell	1770	357
113	9788121285285	14th	Thana - Places of Interest	Ed.: James M. Campbell	3290	659
114	9788121285261	15th Part I	Kanara	Ed.: James M. Campbell	2340	348
115	9788121285247	15th Part II	Kanara	Ed.: James M. Campbell	1740	348
116	9788121285223	16th	Nasik	Ed.: James M. Campbell	3490	698
117	9788121285209	17th	Ahmadnagar	Ed.: James M. Campbell	3860	772
118	9788121285186	18th Part I	Poona	Ed.: James M. Campbell	2930	586
119	9788121285162	18th Part II	Poona	Ed.: James M. Campbell	2680	537
120	9788121285148	18th Part III	Poona	Ed.: James M. Campbell	2500	503
121	9788121285124	19th	Satara	Ed.: James M. Campbell	3450	692
122	9788121285100	20th	Sholapur	Ed.: James M. Campbell	2730	547
123	9788121285087	21st	Gazetteer of the Bomaby Presidency: Belgaum	Ed.: James M. Campbell	2570	514
124	9788121285063	22nd	Dharwar	Ed.: James M. Campbell	4200	841
125	9788121285049	23rd	Gazetteer of the Bombay Presidency:Bijapur	Ed.: James M. Campbell	3550	712
126	9788121285025	24th	Kolhapur	Ed.: James M. Campbell	2250	450

S. NO.	ISBN NO.	VOLUME	TITLE	AUTHOR	PRICE	PAGES
127	9788121285001	25th	Botany	Ed.: James M. Campbell	2040	408
128	9788121284981	26th, Part I	Materials Towards a Statistical Account of the Town and Island of Bombay - History	Ed.: James M. Campbell	2500	504
129	9788121284967	26th, Part II	Materials Towards a Statistical Account of the Town and Island of Bombay - Trade and Fortifications	Ed.: James M. Campbell	2690	538
130	9788121284943	26th, Part III	Materials Towards a Statistical Account of the Town And Island of Bombay - Administration	Ed.: James M. Campbell	2450	702
131	9788121284929	27th	General Index	Ed.:R. E. Enthoven	2190	428
			MADRAS DISTRICT GAZETTEERS			
132	9788121258814	1st	Anantapur	W. Francis	1140	227
133	9788121258555	2nd	Malabar	C. A Innes & F. B Evans	3010	602
134	9788121258791	3rd	Bellary	W. Francis	1890	377
135	9788121258777	4th	Statistical Appendix For Chingleput		280	56
136	9788121258753	5th	Coimbatore	K. N. Krishnaswami Ayyar	3420	628
137	9788121232814	6th	Madras District Gazetteers District Gazetteer Cuddapah	C. F. Brackenbury	1120	285
138	9788121258715	7th	Statistical Appendix For Ganjam		370	73
139	9788121256766	8th, Vol. 1st	Godavari District Gazetteer	F. R. Hemingway	650	320
140	9788121256803	8th, Vol. 2nd	Godavari District Gazetteer	F. R. Hemingway	160	83
141	9788121258678	9th	Statistical Appendix For Kistna		640	127
142	9788121258654	10th	Statistical Appendix For Kurnool		270	54
143	9788121258616	11th	Madura	W. Francis	1900	379
144	9788121258579	12th	Statistical Appendix For Madura		740	148
145	9788121258630	13th	The Nilgiris	W. Francis	2190	437
146	9788121234276	14th	Madras District Gazetteers Gazetteer Of The Nellore District Brought Upto 1938		1150	386
147	9788121258517	15th	North Arcot		590	118
148	9788121258494	16th, Vol. 1, Part I	Salem	F. J. Richards	1710	343
149	9788121258593	16th, Vol. 1, Part II	Salem	F. J. Richards	1800	360
150	9788121258456	17th	South Arcot	W. Francis	2400	480
151	9788121258470	18th	Statistical Appendix For South Canara		400	80
152	9788121258432	19th, Vol. 1st & 2nd	Tanjore: Main Volume and Statistical Appendix		2070	401
153	9788121258395	20th	Tinnevelly	H. R. Pate	2740	547
154	9788121258418	21st	Statistical Appendix For Tinnevelly		320	64
155	9788121258371	22nd, 1st & 2nd	Trichinopoly: Main Volume and Statistical Appendix	F. R. Hemingway	2440	487
156	9788121241953	23rd	Vizagapatam District Gazetteer	W. Francis	760	385
			PUNJAB DISTRICT GAZETTEERS			
157	9788121255943	1st	Ambala District 1883-84		620	124
158	9788121255967	2nd	Amritsar		1180	236
159	9788121255981	3rd	Delhi		1300	260
160	9788121256001	4th	Ferozepore		950	188
161	9788121256025	5th	Faridkot		350	70
162	9788121256049	6th	Gujranwala 1893-94		1270	254
163	9788121256063	7th	Gujrat	C. E. Luard	1140	228
164	9788121256087	8th	Gurdaspur 1891-92		1260	252
165	9788121256100	9th	Gurgaon 1883-4		1020	203
166	9788121256124	10th	Hazara	H. D. Watson	2290	458
167	9788121256148	11th	Hissar district and Lohar State		1840	367
168	9788121256162	12th	Hoshiarpur		1420	283
169	9788121256186	13th	Jhang		1070	213
170	9788121256209	14th	Jhelam		1010	202
171	9788121256223	15th	Jalandhar District 1883-84		540	108
172	9788121256247	16th, Vol. XIV-A	Jullundur District, with maps and Kapurthala		1990	398
173	9788121256261	17th, Pt. I	Kangra (Proper)		1450	290
174	9788121256285	17th, Pt. II	Kangra (Kulu, Lahual, Spiti)		1800	357
175	9788121256308	18th	Karnal		1930	386
176	9788121256322	19th	Kohat		1540	307
177	9788121256346	20th	The Lahore District 1883-84		1220	244
178	9788121256384	21st	Ludhiana and Maler Kotla		1680	335
179	9788121256407	22nd	Lyallpur		735	147
180	9788121256421	23rd	Mianwali		1170	234
181	9788121256445	24th	Montgomery	P. J. Fagan	1590	318
182	9788121258364	25th	Multan (1901-02)	E. D. Maclagan	2400	480
183	9788121258708	26th	The Rohtak District 1883-84		980	196
184	9788121258746	27th, Vol. III A	Dujana State 1904		500	16
185	9788121256483	28th	Shahpur District		1780	356
186	9788121256506	29th	Simla District		800	159

S. NO.	ISBN NO.	VOLUME	TITLE	AUTHOR	PRICE	PAGES
187	9788121256520	30th	The Chamba State		2040	408
188	9788121256544	31st	The Chenab Colony 1904		1550	310
189	9788121256568	32nd	Kalsia State		270	53
190	9788121256582	33rd	Suket and Mandi		770	154
191	9788121256605	34th	Phulkian States, Patiala Jind And Nabha 1904		2070	414
192	9788121256643	35th	Simla Hill States		2220	443
193	9788121256667	36th	Sirmur		920	183
			RAJPUTANA DISTRICT GAZETTEERS			
194	9789362088994	1st, Vol. I-A & B	Ajmer-merwara (Text and Statistics Tables)	C. C. Watson	1230	246
195	9789362080882	2nd. Vol. II-A & B	Mewar Residency (Text and Statistics Tables)	K.D. Erskine	1700	339
196	9789362088444	3rd, Vol. III-A & B	The Western Rajputana States Residency And The Bikaner Agency	K.D. Erskine	3590	718
			UNITED PROVINCES OF AGRA AND OUDH DISTRICT GAZETTEERS			
197	9789362087560	Vol. I	Agra	H. R. Nevill	2260	452
198	9789362082466	Vol. II	Aligarh	H. R. Nevill	1300	260
199	9789362089779	Vol. III	Allahabad	H. R. Nevill	2050	409
200	9789362081346	Vol. IV	Almora	H. G. Walton	1670	333
201	9789362085658	Vol. V	Azamgarh	D. L. Drake Brockman	1750	349
202	9789362080547	Vol. VI	Bahraich	H. R. Nevill	1410	281
203	9789362085214	Vol. VII	Ballia	H. R. Nevill	1750	350
204	9789362084668	Vol. VIII	Banda	D. L. Drake Brockman	1750	349
205	9789362086518	Vol. IX	Bara Banki	H. R. Nevill	1720	344
206	9789362084101	Vol. X	Bareilly	H. R. Nevill	1640	327
207	9789362086631	Vol. XI	Basti	H. R. Nevill	1610	321
208	9789362083814	Vol. XII	Benares	H. R. Nevill	2290	458
209	9789362086105	Vol. XIII	Bijnor	H. R. Nevill	1820	363
210	9789362081674	Vol. XIV	Budaun	H. R. Nevill	1890	378
211	9789362086891	Vol. XV	Bulandshahr	H. R. Nevill	2100	419
212	9789362081520	Vol. XVI	Cawnpore	H. R. Nevill	2210	442
213	9789362088031	Vol. XVII	Dehra Dun	H. G. Walton	1710	342
214	9789362088710	Vol. XVIII	Etah	E. R. Neave	1600	320
215	9789362082992	Vol. XIX	Etawah	D. L. Drake Brockman	1390	277
216	9789362082220	Vol. XX	Farrukhabad	E. R. Neave	1620	324
217	9789362083869	Vol. XXI	Fatehpur	H. R. Nevill	1890	377
218	9789362085962	Vol. XXII	Fyzabad	H. R. Nevill	1700	339
219	9789362087997	Vol. XXIII	Garhwal	H. G. Walton	1270	254
220	9789362089892	Vol. XXIV	Ghazipur	H. R. Nevill	1600	320
221	9789362085436	Vol. XXV	Gonda	H. R. Nevill	1650	330
222	9789362080271	Vol. XXVI	Gorakhpur	H. R. Nevill	1890	378
223	9789362086129	Vol. XXVII	Hamirpur	D. L. Drake Brockman	1390	277
224	9789362087638	Vol. XXVIII	Hardoi	H. R. Nevill	1680	336
225	9789362081636	Vol. XXIX	Jalaun	D. L. Drake Brockman	1180	236
226	9789362084309	Vol. XXX	Jaunpur	H. R. Nevill	1750	350
227	9789362084187	Vol. XXXI	Jhansi	D. L. Drake Brockman	1960	391
228	9789362089168	Vol. XXXII	Kheri	H. R. Nevill	1650	330
229	9789362086778	Vol. XXXIII	Lucknow	H. R. Nevill	1760	352
230	9789362088635	Vol. XXXIV	Mainpuri	H. R. Nevill	1740	348
231	9789362080424	Vol. XXXV	Meerut	H. R. Nevill	2170	434
232	9789362081087	Vol. XXXVI	Mirzapur	D. L. Drake Brockman	2430	486
233	9789362085443	Vol. XXXVII	Moradabad	H. R. Nevill	1900	380
234	9789362082763	Vol. XXXVIII	Muttra	D. L. Drake Brockman	2140	428
235	9789362089915	Vol. XXXIX	Muzaffarnagar	H. R. Nevill	2260	451
236	9789362086143	Vol. XL	Naini Tal	H. R. Nevill	1890	377
237	9789362086761	Vol. XLI	Partabgarh	H. R. Nevill	1560	312
238	9789362081124	Vol. XLII	Pilibhit	H. R. Nevill	1570	314
239	9789362084453	Vol. XLIII	Rai Bareli	H. R. Nevill	1610	322
240	9789362088284	Vol. XLIV	Rampur	H. R. Nevill	1170	234
241	9789362083654	Vol. XLV	Saharanpur	H. R. Nevill	2190	438
242	9789362083142	Vol. XLVI	Shahjahanpur	H. R. Nevill	1510	302
243	9789362083623	Vol. XLVII	Sitapur	H. R. Nevill	1590	317
244	9789362089939	Vol. XLVIII	Sultanpur	H. R. Nevill	1330	266
245	9789362080851	Vol. XLIX	Unnao	H. R. Nevill	1530	305

CENTRAL PROVINCES DISTRICT GAZETTEERS

AMRAOTI DISTRICT.

VOLUME A.

DESCRIPTIVE.

EDITED BY

S. V. FITZGERALD

Assistant Commissioner

AND

A. E. NELSON

Superintendent of Gazetteers.

BOMBAY:

PRINTED AT THE CAXTON WORKS FRERE ROAD.

BY G. W. AND A. E. CLARIDGE.

1911.

PREFATORY NOTE.

For the chapter on History and Antiquities we are indebted to the scholarship of Major Haig and for the detailed account of Agriculture to Mr. D. Clouston. Several other gentleman have contributed articles concerning subjects on which they are expert and their kindness has been gratefully acknowledged in the course of the text. The riches of Sir Alfred Lyall's "Berār Gazetteer" of 1870 have been freely plundered and we have made frequent use of the Imperial Gazetteer of India both in the old and the new editions. We have also been particularly fortunate in receiving suggestions from a large number of friends, amongst whom we especially desire to record our thanks to Mr. F. G. Sly, Commissioner of Berār, the Hon'ble Rao Bahādur R. N. Mudholkar, to Mr. F. W. A. Prideaux and Lieut.-Colonel Mauduit, to Mr. C. G. Rogers, Mr. E. C. Rich, Mr. Sorābji Shāpurji and Mr. Narāyan Raghavendra. Mr. Clouston also wishes to mention the assistance rendered by Mr. V. R. Vairāgkar of the Veterinary Department. Rai Bahādur Hīra Lāl, Assistant Superintendent of Gazetteers has, as in previous volumes of this series, been a great support, and excellent clerical work has been done by Messrs. G. Pydiah Nāydu, R. G. Dāmle and Mohammad Nurruddīn. Of the illustrations some are from photographs specially taken for this volume, others from originals kindly lent by Messrs. Williamson and Bartlett, Forest Officers in the Melghāt and by Saiyid Azmat Husain, of Ellichpur.

S. V. FG.
A. E. N.

NOTE.—This Volume is complete in itself and can be used apart from Volume B which collection of administrative statistics.

Errata.

P.	l.				
P. 39	l. 36	for	Nasir-ud-din	read	Nasr-ud-din.
52	6	,,	Niz-amul-Mulk	,,	Nizam-ul-Mulk
61	16	,,	Bijapurs	,,	Bijapuris
138	6	,,	fat her	,,	father
148	9	,,	may be	,,	maybe
211	8	,,	Chanur	,,	Chandur
263	25	,,	clining	,,	clinging
281	11	,,	Mill	,,	Hill
351	6	,,	Hari	,,	Houri
363	headline	,,	Town	,,	Camp
388	10	,,	of	,,	or

AMRAOTI DISTRICT GAZETTEER.

CONTENTS.

APPENDIX.

LIST OF MAPS AND PHOTOGRAPHS.

PARAGRAPH INDEX.

CHAPTER I.—GENERAL DESCRIPTION.

CHAPTER II.—HISTORY AND ARCHÆOLOGY.

Chapter III.—POPULATION.

Chapter IV—AGRICULTURE.

CHAPTER V—LOANS, PRICES, WAGES, MANUFACTURES, MARKETS AND FAIRS, TRADE AND COMMUNICATIONS.

Loans—

CHAPTER VI.—FORESTS AND MINERALS.

Forests—

Minerals—

CHAPTER VII.—FAMINE.

CHAPTER VIII.—LAND REVENUE ADMINISTRATION.

Page

CHAPTER IX.—GENERAL ADMINISTRATION.

APPENDIX—GAZETTEER OF TAHSILS, TOWNS IMPORTANT VILLAGES, RIVERS AND HILLS.

Name of place

Name of place | Page.

Name of Deputy Commissioner.	Period.	
	From	To
D. Cs. North Berār. 1. Mr. T. H. Bullock ...	1853	13-9-1857
D. Cs. North Berār. 2. Capt. Meadows Taylor	14-9-1857	end of Feb. 1858
D. Cs. North Berār. Mr. T. H. Bullock ...	end of Feb. 1858	end of Dec. 1858
3. Captain J. Allardyce ...	Jany. 1859	11-2-1862
4. " J. G. Bell ...	12-2-1862	13-5-1862
5. " J. T. Bushby ...	14-5-1862	Nov. 1863
" J. Allardyce ...	Nov. 1863	2-2-1866
6. Lieut. H. C. A. Szczepanski ...	3-2-1866	1-4-1866
Captain J. Allardyce ...	2-4-1866	Dec. 1866
" J. G. Bell ...	Dec. 1866	12-4-1868
7. " J. Fitz Gerald ...	13-4-1868	12-6-1868
" J. G. Bell ...	13-6-1868	20-4-1870
8. Major H. C. Menzies ...	21-4-1870	11-5-1870
9. Captain D. W. Laughton ...	12-5-1870	20-7-1870
" J. G. Bell ...	21-7-1870	0-3-1871
10. Lieutenant H. de P. Rennick...	7-3-1871	15-3-1871
Major J. T. Bushby ...	16-3-1871	2-10-1872
11. Mr. C. Hordern ...	3-10-1872	8-5-1875
Major D. W. Laughton ..	9-5-1875	6-8-1875
Mr. C. Hordern ...	7-8-1875	11-12-1875
12. Captain K. J. L. Mackenzie ...	12-12-1875	2-4-1876
13. " R. Bullock ...	3-4-1876	4-9-1876
14. Mr. A. J. Dunlop ...	5-9-1876	13-11-1876
Captain R. Bullock ..	14-11-1876	4-1-1877
Mr. C. Hordern - ...	5-1-1877	31-3-1878
15. Mr. H. S. Nicholetts ...	1-4-1878	15-4-1878
Lieut.-Colonel H. C. Menzies ...	16-4-1878	12-11-1878
Major D. W. Laughton ...	13-11-1878	13-1-1879
Lieut.-Colonel H. C. Menzies ...	14-1-1879	24-3-1880
Mr. H. S. Nicholetts ...	25-3-1880	18-11-1880
Major R. Bullock ...	19-11-1880	7-7-1883
16. Lieut.-Colonel F. W. Grant ...	8-7-1883	29-7-1883
" R. Bullock ...	30-7-1883	30-4-1884
" F. W. Grant ...	1-5-1884	31-7-1884
" R. Bullock ...	1-8-1884	14-4-1885
Mr. H. S. Nicholetts ...	15-4-1885	1-5-1885
Lieut.-Colonel R. Bullock ...	2-5-1885	16-2-1886

List of Deputy Commissioners who have held charge of the Amraoti District (concld.)

Name of Deputy Commissioner.	Period.	
	From	To
Mr. H. S. Nicholetts	17-2-1886	19-6-1886
Lieut.-Colonel R. Bullock ...	20-6-1886	14-8-1888
17. Mr. A. Elliott ...	15-8-1888	4-1-1889
Colonel R. Bullock ...	5-1-1889	8-4-1889
Mr. A. Elliott ...	9-4-1889	26-3-1890
18. Captain W. Hastings ...	27-3-1890	15-9-1890
19. Colonel E. J. Gunthorpe ...	16-9-1890	14-3-1893
Mr. H. S. Nicholetts ...	15-3-1893	5-5-1894
20. Mr. H. Godwin-Austen ...	6-5-1894	6-8-1894
Mr. H. S. Nicholetts ...	7-8-1894	1-9-1895
21. Mr. F. W. A. Prideaux ...	2-9-1895	30-9-1895
Mr. H. S. Nicholetts ...	1-10-1895	1-4-1896
22. Mr. A. Lucas, I.C.S. ...	2-4-1896	29-10-1897
23. Captain R. P. Horsbrugh ...	30-10-1897	2-2-1898
Mr. A. Lucas, I.C.S. ...	3-2-1898	21-4-1898
Captain R. P. Horsbrugh ...	22-4-1898	13-4-1900
24. Major R. P. Colomb ...	14-4-1900	10-7-1900
Captain R. P. Horsbrugh ...	11-7-1900	5-3-1901
25. Major R. V. Garrett ...	6-3-1901	10-3-1901
26. Captain D. O. Morris ...	11-3-1901	19-7-1901
Major R. P. Colomb ...	20-7-1901	7-5-1902
Lieut.-Colonel R. V. Garrett ...	8-5-1902	6-3-1903
27. Mr. R. A. Simpson ...	7-3-1903	28-5-1903
28. Major F.R.M.C. de R. Mauduit.	29-5-1903	1-7-1903
Captain D. O. Morris ...	2-7-1903	24-7-1903
Mr. H. Godwin-Austen ...	25-7-1903	28-7-1904
Captain D. O. Morris ...	29-7-1904	30-10-1904
Mr. H. Godwin-Austen ...	31-10-1904	14-4-1905
29. Mr. B. Clay ...	15-4-1905	31-8-1905
Major R. P. Colomb ...	1-9-1905	26-11-1905
Mr. H. Godwin-Austen ...	27-11-1905	14-3-1906
Major R. P. Horsbrugh ...	15-3-1906	30-3-1908
30. Mr. J. T. Chamberlain, I.C.S. ...	31-3-1908	25-11-1908
Lieut.-Colonel F. R. M. C. de R. Mauduit ...	26-11-1908	......

List of Deputy Commissioners who have held charge of the Ellichpur District, with the dates of their periods of office

Name of Deputy Commissioner.	Period.	
	From	To
1. Lieut.-Colonel J. W. Stubbs ...	23-7-1867	23-9-1867
2. Lieutenant H. C. A. Szczepanski...	24-9-1867	14-8-1869
3. Captain H. C. Menzies ...	15-8-1869	14-10-1869
„ H. C. A. Saczepanski ...	15-10-1869	20-11-1870
Colonel J. W. Stubbs ...	21-11-1870	27-5-1870
4. Captain D. W. Laughton ...	28-5-1871	28-8-1871
5. „ K. J. L. Mackenzie ...	29-8-1871	12-4-1872
„ D. W. Laughton ...	13-4-1872	14-4-1872
6. „ A. Farrer ...	15-4-1872	8-7-1872
„ K. J. L. Mackenzie ...	9-7-1872	28-3-1872
7. Major J. T. Bushby ...	29-3-1874	4-4-1874
„ K. J. L. Mackenzie ...	5-4-1876	22-7-1876
8. Captain H. de P. Rennick ...	23-7-1879	23-10-1879
Major K. J. L. Mackenzie ...	24-10-1879	20-7-1889
9. Mr. H. B. Knowlys ...	21-7-1882	11-10-1882
Major K. J. L. Mackenzie ...	12-10-1882	7-4-1882
Mr. H. B. Knowlys ...	8-4-1883	7-8-1883
Lieut.-Colonel K. J. L. Mackenzie ...	8-8-1884	11-7-1886
10. Major R. S. Thompson ...	12-7-1886	13-10-1886
Lieut.-Colonel K. J. L. Mackenzie ...	14-10-1886	1-9-1887
11. Captain J. G. Morris ...	2-9-1887	15-11-1887
Lieut.-Colonel K. J. L. Mackenzie ...	16-11-1887	1-6-1888
12. Mr. R. Obbard, I.C.S. ...	2-6-1888	8-8-1888
Captain J. C. Morris ...	9-8-1888	1-12-1888
13. Mr. H. S Nicholetts ...	2-12-1888	10-4-1890
Colonel H. de P. Rennick ...	11-4-1890	26-4-1891
14. Mr. H. Godwin-Austen ...	27-4-1891	26-7-1891
Colonel H. de P. Rennick ...	27-7-1891	18-5-1892
15. Lieutenant A. G. Davidson ...	19-5-1892	18-7-1892
16. Captain W. Hastings ...	19-7-1892	14-10-1892
17. Mr. F. Wright ..	15-10-1892	15-11-1892
Captain W. Hastings ...	16-11-1892	17-7-1893
18. Khan Bahadur Saiyad Shamsuddin Ali Khan ...	18-7-1893	19-10-1893
Captain W. Hastings ...	20-10-1893	27-1-1894
19. Mr. C. E Biddulph ...	28-1-1894	26-12-1894
20. Captain F. R. M. C. de R. Mauduit ...	27-12-1894	3-1-1895

List of Deputy Commissioners who have held charge of the Ellichpur District (concluded.)

Name of Deputy Commissioner.	Period.	
	From	To
Mr. H. Godwin-Austen ...	4-1-1895	31-8-1895
Captain F. R. M. C. de R. Mauduit ...	1-9-1895	16-9-1895
Mr. H. Godwin-Austen ...	17-9-1895	4-11-1897
21. Lieutenant D. O. Morris ...	5-11-1897	25-11-1897
Mr. H. Godwin-Austen ...	26-11-1897	21-3-1898
22. Mr. R. D. Hare ...	22-3-1898	23-7-1898
23. Rao Bahadur B. K. Joshi ...	24-7-1898	19-11-1898
Mr. R. D. Hare ...	20-11-1898	6-3-1899
24. Munshi Aziz-ud-din ...	7-3-1899	20-3-1899
25. Captain T W. Haig ...	21-3-1899	7-5-1899
" F. R. M. C. de R. Mauduit ...	8-5-1899	17-12-1899
Mr. R. D. Hare ...	18-12-1899	20-12-1900
Captain D. O. Morris ..	21-12-1900	8-3-1901
26. Major R. P. Horsbrugh ...	9-3-1901	10-2-1902
27. Mr. R. A. Simpson ...	11-2-1902	13-11-1902
28. Major R. P. Colomb ...	14-11-1902	9-11-1903
Lieut.-Colonel W. Hastings ...	10-11-1903	24-6-1904
Major R. P. Colomb ...	25-6-1904	21-8-1905
29. Mr. Saiyid Muin-ud-din Khan...	22-8-1905	31-8-1905

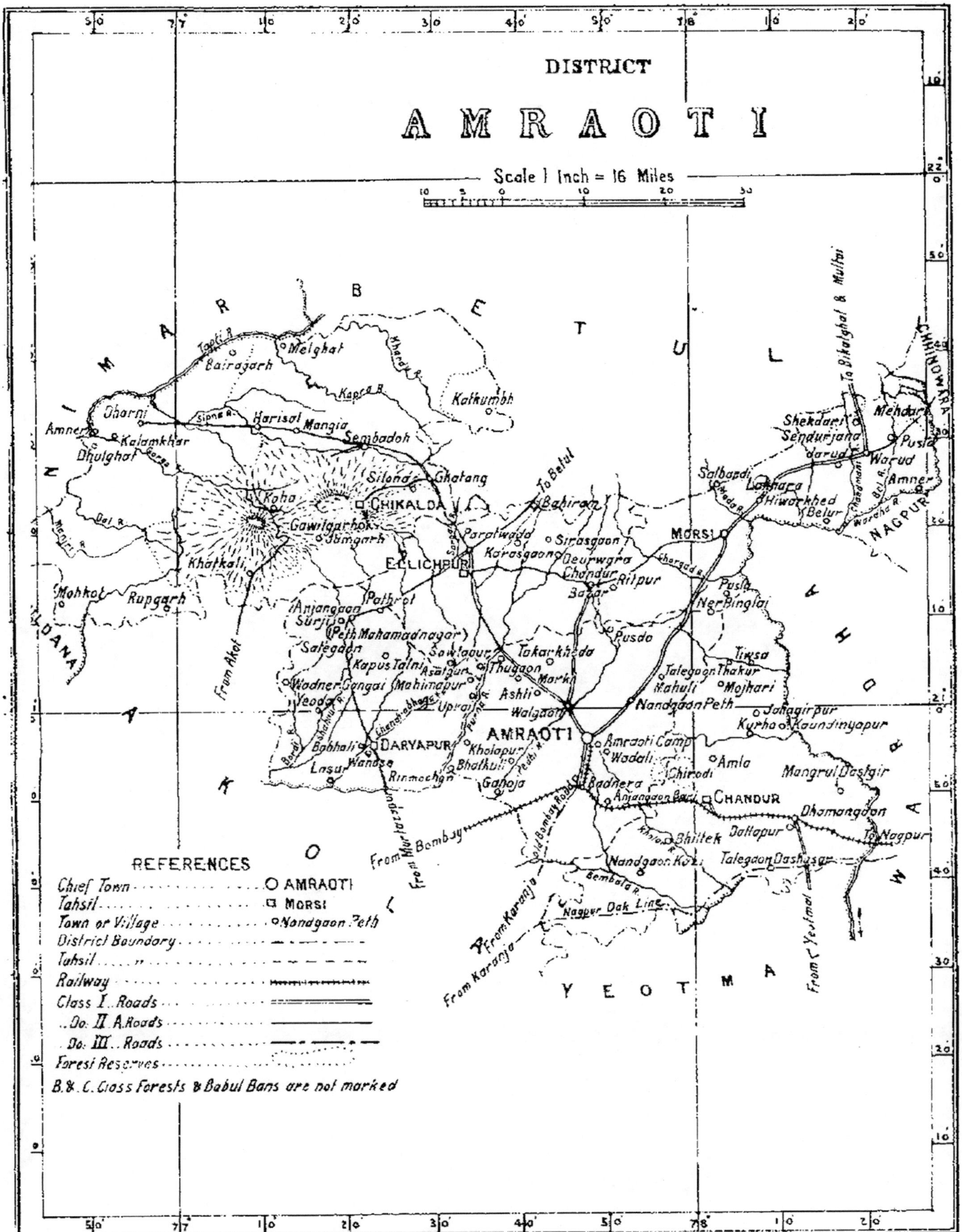
DISTRICT
AMRAOTI
Scale 1 Inch = 16 Miles
NIMAR
BETUL
CHHINDWARA
NAGPUR
WARDHA
YEOTMAL
AKOLA
BULDANA
Melghat
Bairagarh
Tapti R.
Kapra R.
Khandu R.
Katkumbh
Dharni
Amner
Kalamkhar
Dhulghat
Sipna R.
Harisal
Mangia
Sembadoh
Silona
Ghatang
Koha
CHIKALDA
Gawilgarh
Jamgarh
Khatkali
Mohkot
Rupgarh
To Betul
Bahiram
Paratwada
Sirasgaon
Karasgaon
ELLICHPUR
Deurwara
Chandur Bazar
Ritpur
MORSI
Salbardi
Lakhara
Hiwarkhed
Belur
Shekdari
Sendurjana
Warud
Mehdari
Pusla
Amner
To Betul & Multai
Anjangaon
Surji
Pathrot
Peth Mahamadnagar
Sategaon
Kapus Talni
Sawlapur
Takarkheda
Thugaon
Mahimapur
Asatpur
Wadner Gangai
Yeoda
Upirai
Ashti
Markl
Walgaon
Pusda
Ner Pinglai
Pusla
Tiwsa
Talegaon Thakur
Mahuli
Mojhari
Nandgaon Peth
Jahagirpur
Kurha
Kaundinyapur
AMRAOTI
Amraoti Camp
Wadali
Chirodi
Amla
Mangrul Dastgir
DARYAPUR
Babhali
Lasur
Wanosa
Kholapur
Bhatkuli
Rinmochan
Ganoja
Badnera
Anjangaon Bari
CHANDUR
Dhamangaon
Dattapur
Bhiltek
Nandgaon Kazi
Talegaon Dashasar
To Nagpur
From Bombay
From Murtazapur
From Akot
Old Bombay Road
From Karanja
Nagpur Dak Line
Bembala R.
From Yeotmal
REFERENCES
Chief Town .... AMRAOTI
Tahsil .... MORSI
Town or Village .... Nandgaon Peth
District Boundary
Tahsil ,,
Railway
Class I. Roads
Do. II A. Roads
Do. III. Roads
Forest Reserves
B. & C. Class Forests & Babul Bans are not marked

AMRAOTI DISTRICT.

CHAPTER I.

GENERAL DESCRIPTION.

BOUNDARIES AND PHYSICAL FEATURES.

Boundaries and Physical Features.

1. The District of Amraoti stretches from 21° 46′ to 20° 32 N. and from 76° 38′ to 78° 27′ E. and includes the northern and north-eastern portions of Berār. It is divided into two widely different tracts, the first, an expanse of level plain lying in the rich valley of the Pāyanghāt and almost square in outline, but for the long projection of the Morsi tāluk eastwards; the second, a stretch of mountainous country extending along the whole north of Berār, producing little save forest and inhabited by few but aborigines; this is a continuation of the Sātpurā hills and has been known at various times as Banda,[1] Gāngra and the Melghāt. Along the north-western boundary for some distance runs the Tāpti river and on the eastern side the Wardhā, while the Pūrna flows through the midst of the District; to the north are the Nimār, Betūl and Chhindwāra Districts, and to the east the Nāgpur and Wardhā Districts of the Central Provinces; to the south and west the Yeotmāl, Akolā and Buldāna Districts of Berār.

---

[1] In the Ain-i-Akbarī.

The area is 4754 square miles, of which 3123 are in the plain; the population according to the 1901 census is 809,499 persons. The greatest length of the District from east to west is about 120 miles and from north to south about 90 miles. Its name is taken from that of the present headquarters' town and is said to be derived from the temple of Ambā Devī situated there. This derivation, however, is a very doubtful one. There is a village on the Krishna river in the Madras Presidency also called Amrāvati, (the word is the same) which is famous for a collection of sculptures now in the British Museum; and the name is said to mean in Sanskrit the abode of immortality or the Eternal City. Amraoti is also connected with the Hindu god Krishna to whom the river that bears his name is sacred, and it is conjectured that the derivation may be identical. The pronunciation Umraoti, though very common, seems to be a corruption.

Hills.

2. The Gāwīlgarh hills, a part of the Sātpurās, so named from the fortress situated on one of their southern spurs, lie between 20° 10′ and 21° 47′ N. and 76° 40′ and 77° 53′ E., and pass from the Betūl District through the Melghāt tāluk to end at the junction of the rivers Tāpti and Pūrna in Nimār. In the Melghāt the crests of the range attain an average elevation of 3400 feet, the highest point, according to the most recent calculations, being the Bairāt plateau of 3866 feet and Chikaldā and Gāwīlgarh being only slightly lower. The foot hills bordering on the Tāpti have a mean height of about 1650 feet. The range is composed of Deccan trap of the upper Cretaceous or Lower eocene group. The only other range is a low line of trap hills rising in the vicinity of Amraoti and extending eastwards to some distance beyond Chāndur Railway with a general average height of two to three hundred feet above the surrounding country, or about fifteen hundred feet above the sea-level. Spurs from these hills extend northwards for some distance, and the barrenness of the land around them is in sharp contrast with the general fertility.

Bemrose, Collo., Derby.

THE AMBA GATE, AMRAOTI.

3. With these exceptions, the District is an undulating plain of black alluvial soil of a very fertile description, its richest tracts being perhaps those in the neighbourhood of the Wardhā and Pūrna rivers. It is watered by a number of small streams which escape from the Sātpurā hills in the north. The soil near the hills is shallow and requires frequent showers to prevent the crops from drying up. Though containing no large forests, the lowlands in some parts are well wooded. *Bābul bans,* small areas of a few acres or square miles covered with *bābul,* are found all over the District. The mango grows in profusion and small groves are common especially near Ellichpur, but the tree does not, as a rule, attain to any great size.

The Plains.

4. The Pūrna, the largest river of the District, takes its rise in the southern slopes of the Gāwīlgarh hills and flows partly through Ellichpur and partly through Amraoti tāluks till it turns westward and forms the boundary between Murtizāpur and Daryāpur tāluks, passing thence into the Akolā District. The Chandrabhāga, after watering the western portion of the Ellichpur tāluk, flows south-west past Khallār and Daryāpur to join the Pūrna at Dhāmni Khurd in the Daryāpur tāluk; its tributary the Sirpān flows past Ellichpur city which it formerly supplied with water through a now ruined aqueduct. The Shāhnur and the Bordi are affluents of the Pūrna which water the Daryāpur tāluk ; and the Pedhi runs from north to south through the entire length of the Amraoti tāluk. Several considerable streams such as the Chundāmani, the Bel and the Matu cross the Morsi tāluk for a few miles on their way from the hills to the Wardhā. The latter river supplies water to the villages on the borders of the District for over 50 miles. To the north of the Melghāt lies the Tāpti, which bounds the District for about 30 miles and receives, through its tributaries the Kāmda, Kapra, Sipnā and Gargā, a large share of the rainfall of the Gāwīlgarh hills. In former times it was used by the jungle people to provide cheap transport for their timber to Burhānpur.

Rivers.

5. Apart from the Melghāt which has already been discussed, there is little variety in the contours of the District. The height above sea-level of the principal towns and stations is given in the following table:—

Elevations.

Name of Town	Place where height taken.	Height in feet.
Badnerā	Railway Stn. Platform ...	1097
Amraoti City	Do.	1118
Amraoti Camp...	D. C.'s Court house ...	1193
Ellichpur City	Inner Fort, opposite to Nawab's Palace ...	1297
Ellichpur Civil Station ...	Roof Artillery Mess ..	1268
Chikaldā	A village tree	3664
Daryāpur	Library plinth	928
Morsi	Inspection Bungalow plinth	1151
Chāndur	Railway Stn. Platform ...	1083
Dhāmangaon	Do. do. ...	977
Chāndur Bazār	Police Station plinth ...	1205
Anjangaon Surji	Police Station plinth ..	1123

Of these Nos. 1—6 are heights obtained by the Trigonometrical Survey; the remainder by the Public Works Department. Of the tāluks except Melghāt, Morsi shows the greatest altitude, its highest summit, Surya Barād, an outlying spur of the Betūl hills, being 1994 feet above sea-level, while Urwāpathar stands 1716 feet. Both these are in the Mehdari reserve. Chincholi, Kassara, Pusla and Pusli are all over 1500 feet, the rest of the tāluk varying from 1100 to 1400. Chāndur ranges from 1500 feet at Kurha to 967 at Kāzikhed, but the general average is from a thousand to twelve hundred. Ellichpur tāluk varies from 1069 to 1273 and Daryāpur slopes gradually from about

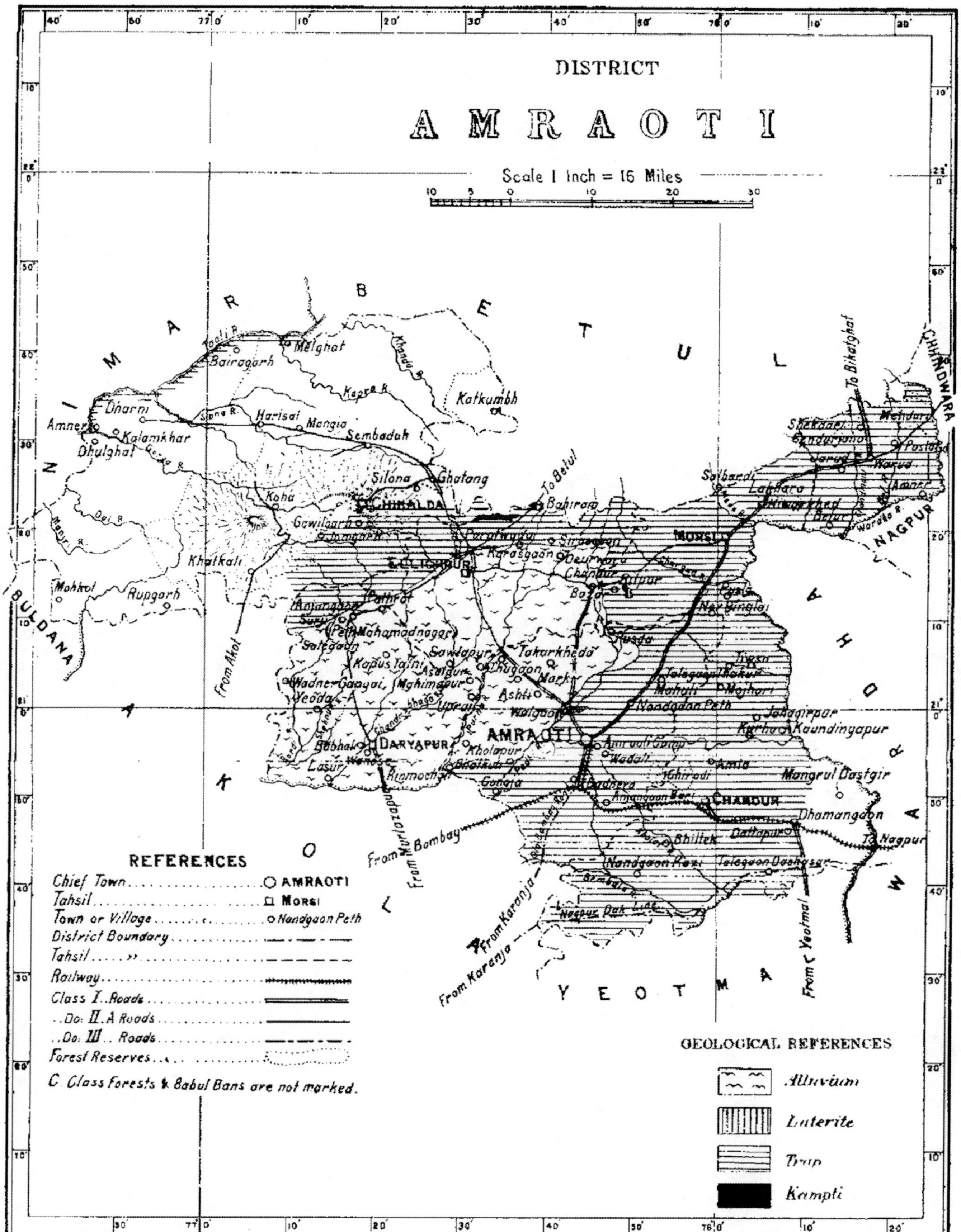

Reg. No. 2691 E. 08 – 460.

Phz., S. I. O., Calcutta.

1100 in the north to about 900 close to the Pūrna. Amraoti shows a wider range of figures, the eastern portion of the tāluk lying in the Amraoti Chāndur hills being upwards of 1400 feet above the sea, while the remainder varies between 1000 and 1300.

GEOLOGY.

(*L. L. Fermor, Imperial Geologist.*)

Geological Formation.

6. Except for two small inliers of Lametā, Gondwāna, and Metamorphic rocks along the northern boundary of this District and occasional patches of laterite, the only geological formations represented are Deccan Trap, and the alluvium of the Pūrna valley. A large portion of the District is occupied by plains, but there are two hilly tracts, both formed of Deccan Trap rocks. These have already been described.

The following is a list of the formations, which will be described in order :—

1. Cotton Soil, etc. (Recent)
2. Pūrna Alluvium (Pleistocene)
3. Laterite
4. Deccan Trap (Cretaceous)
5. Lametās (Cretaceous)
6. Gondwānas (exact horizon unknown)
7. Metamorphics (Archaean).

Cotton Soil.

7. Concerning the cotton soil, A. B. Wynne writes.[1] 'The 'cotton soil or black soil of the Pūrna 'valley, although common enough, 'as is usual in these trappean districts, has no 'geological peculiarity here requiring attention. To its 'development, however, and the fertile nature of soils 'derived from the trap, may be traced doubtless the name 'which this country has obtained as a cotton producing 'district.'

---

1 *Rec. Geol. Surv. Ind.* Vol. II, part I, page 5 (1868).

8. Below the Gāwīlgarh range lies the Pāyanghāt or valley of the Pūrna river, running through the Amraoti, Akolā and Buldāna Districts of Berār, before entering Khāndesh. It is described by Wynne as follows [1] :—

Pūrna Alluvium.

'The valley of the Pūrna possesses but little variety of 'geological interest and is principally distinguished by 'monotonous repetitions of features observable in crossing the 'Deccan from the seaward to this locality, where each hill and '*ghāt* and undulating slope or plain exhibits similar kinds of 'nearly horizontal flows of gray amygdaloidal trap, with here 'and there a bed of harder texture of columnar structure, 'or of bright red bole, or alternations of these; the traps 'sometimes containing numerous zeolites.

'In the river valleys, and where superficial "rain-wash" has 'accumulated, a light brown "kankry" alluvium is associated 'with sub-recent calcareous conglomerate below and black 'cotton soil above, one being quite as occasional and acci-'dental as the other, the conglomerate or concrete being 'perhaps the most persistent along the river courses, the 'brown alluvium or (?) "soda soil" more universal and the 'cotton soil occurring, subject only to the rule that it is 'always uppermost.

'The alluvium of this great plain, although of very 'considerable depth and occupying so large an area, is as 'completely isolated from that of the neighbouring rivers 'as such a deposit can be. A section crossing the 'valley from the Ajanta ghāts, by Edlābād (Khāndesh) 'across the Pūrna river, to the western termination of the 'Gāwīlgarh range, would show the ordinary trap of the 'Deccan, forming the high ground at either end, and an undu-'lating country between, which viewed from above or from 'a distance has a plain-like aspect, but frequently exposes 'the rocks of which it is formed, consisting of the usual traps,

---

[1] *Rec. Geol. Surv. Ind.* II, part I, page 1, (1868.) The words given in brackets in the following quotations are additions to the original.

'here and there covered only by slight detrital accumulations 'of the same kind as those of the Deccan. Except on the 'very banks of Pūrna no considerable quantity of alluvial 'matter would be found, and this does not extend far from 'the river at either side. North and south through Malkāpur '(Buldāna) a different section would be obtained. Here a 'wide space, chiefly on the south side of the Pūrna, is 'occupied by fine brown calcareous alluvium with "kankry", 'and is connected by a narrow neck, at Piprāla, with the 'great alluvial deposit of this valley which in thickness may 'exceed 150 feet; and nothing else, save varieties this, of is 'to be seen in or near the river from Dādulgaon (Akolā) 'on its south bank eastwards up the stream nearly to the '"sangum" or junction of the Phairli river, (Akolā 'District), except two or three small exposures of trap 'in its bed near Piprāla Pulsod (Akolā). . . . The Pūrna 'changes its course from the N. N. E. at the junction 'of the above-named tributary, and thence takes a 'westerly direction:—the alluvium on its south side seldom 'extending beyond an average of ten miles from the river and 'nearly coinciding along its southern boundary with the 'Nāgpur extension of the Great Indian Peninsula Railway, 'while on the north it reaches nearly to the base of 'the mountains. On the east its rather arbitrary and 'indefinite boundary closely approaches the watershed 'of Ellichpur, and bending southward traverses undulating 'country, eventually reaching the flanks of the hills near 'Amraoti.

'All round the margin of this alluvial tract is a belt of 'country that might or might not with propriety be included 'within it, although the surface deposits there do not conceal 'the underlying rock, the exposure of which was taken as 'the chief guide in determining the line of boundary. On 'the north and east, this tract of country is very stony, and 'it may be supposed that streams descending from the moun-'tains and hills have frequently travelled across this space; 'their courses subject to lateral deviation, covering the whole 'of it with coarser fragment brought down by floods at a time 'perhaps when the water of a lake or the sea occupied the 'basin of the finer alluvium and arrested the boulder-'bearing velocity of these mountain streams.

'In every part of the alluvium calcareous conglomerate or 'concrete is of common occurrence. It occasionally contains 'fragments of bone or fossil teeth of ruminants, but although 'sought for, no large accumulation nor even a large fragment 'of these fossils was observed. Yet enough was seen to 'show an identity of the conditions under which these de-'posits and those of the Nerbudda valley were formed. This 'sub-recent conglomerate is very frequent in the stony tract 'above mentioned. It was everywhere searched for worked 'flints but without success, although one flake was found in 'a quite similar deposit, forming the right bank of the Godā-'vari at Paithan in the Deccan, at a considerable distance 'to the south.'

'A deposit of varying thickness (within three feet) and but 'small lateral extent, consisting of fine dazzlingly white sand 'finely laminated, occurs in the alluvial bank of the Pūrna at 'Paruth. It appears to be composed of comminuted or 'disintegrated crystals of felspars with a small admixture of 'clay. It did not appear to be formed of or to contain minute 'organisms, such as foraminfera, and was not elsewhere 'observed.

'Much of this Pūrna alluvium produces efflorescences of 'salts, of soda chiefly, and in many places the wells sunk in 'it are brackish or salt. Over a wide tract on each side of 'the Pūrna river, north of Akolā and thence eastward to-'wards Amraoti, wells are specially sunk for obtaining 'common salt from highly saturated brine.'[1]

'That the alluvium of the valley is of considerable depth 'may be perhaps inferred from the absence of numerous 'exposures of rock, as well as from the depth of nullahs and 'height of the river cliffs. The conglomerate, as usual, 'occurs in its lower portions, but was observed in some

[1] The industry has been prohibited.

'places west of Patulla at different heights in the sections 'exposed. Its constant or frequent occurrence beneath the 'rest of the alluvium would not prove its being contemporaneous in all places, as the trap-rocks, upon which these 'deposits lie, cannot be presumed to have had a surface 'sufficiently even to have permitted this.

Formation of the Alluvium.

9. 'Whether the whole of this alluvium was deposited in 'a lake, or by the river travelling from 'side to side of the valley under other 'conditions than at present obtain, 'does not appear. A former estuarine state of thing 'may be indicated by the salt-bearing gravels, or a large 'salt lake, but the even though interrupted surface of 'the alluvium is against the probability of its having been 'deposited by the Pūrna under present conditions; while 'want of information as to the relative levels obscures 'the possibility of determining whether the rocky country 'about Edlābād may not have formed a natural *bund* 'flooding the country occupied by the alluvium[1]; certainly 'the stream through most of this is sluggish, but it 'seems to be a rather strong assumption, that no greater 'fall than the height of the river banks where it enters this 'rocky tract—perhaps on an average not more than 30 'feet—takes place within so great a distance as extends 'between this and the upper end of the alluvium, about 'south-west of Amraoti.'

Laterite.

10. With regard to the occurrence of laterite in this District W. T. Blanford writes[2]:—

'Two small tracts of laterite are met with, one just 'south of Rithpur, the other about four miles north of 'Amraoti. The latter is the largest and best exposed, some 'good sections of it occurring in the river bank. Above, it is

---

[1] The formation of the alluvial tracts of the Pūrna, Tāpti, Nerbudda, and Godāvari, has been explained recently by Mr. Vredenburg as due to the formation of slight anticlinal axes in Pleistocene times; the rocks being ridged up along these axes so as to impound waters with the formation of lake basins that were subsequently filled up by alluvial deposits. See *Rec. Geol. Surv. Ind.* XXXIII, page 33, (1906).

[2] *Mem, Geol. Surv. Ind.* VI, page 285, (1869).

'gravelly in texture, consisting of the usual small ferruginous 'grains in a red matrix; the grains when broken showing 'concentric structure. Beneath, it is more compact, but 'soft. In one place it was seen to rest on greenish-grey 'mottled mudstone, breaking into small cuboidal fragments, 'with joint surfaces between, so minute that it is impossible 'to obtain a fair fracture. This is probably decomposed 'trap.'

Wynne[1] refers to the following lateritic occurrence :—

'The plateau upon which Chikaldā stands and the 'surrounding summits have a strongly lateritic appearance, 'such as may be seen at Matheran, and other summits of the 'Western Ghāts.'

11. The Gāwīlgarh range of hills is composed, as has already been mentioned, of rocks of the Deccan Trap formation. It is described by Dr. Voysey in the following terms[2]: —

Deccan Trap.

'The principal part of the whole range is formed of com-'pact basalt, very much resembling that of the Giant's 'Causeway. It is found columnar in many places, and at 'Gāwīlgarh it appears stratified—the summits of several 'ravines presenting a continued stratum of many thousand 'yards in length.

'The basalt frequently and suddenly changes into a wac-'ken, of all degrees of induration, and, of every variety of 'composition usually found among trap-rock.'

'In external appearance, the columnar and semi-columnar 'basalt closely resembles that of the Giant's Causeway, 'possessing the same fracture, internal dark colour, and 'external brown crust. It is equally compact and sonorous.— 'Perhaps the basalt of the Gāwīlgarh range, more nearly 'resembles, in every respect, that of the Pouce mountain in 'the Mauritius.'

An interesting feature of this range is the existence all along its southern edge of a marked northerly dip (in places

[1] *Rec. Geol. Surv. Ind.*, II, page 5, (1869).

[2] *Asiatic Researches*, XVIII, page 189 (1833).

as high as 15°) in the lavas of which it is composed. This is a very uncommon occurrence in the Deccan Trap, which is almost everywhere horizontal; it is due to the fault that brings up the Gondwāna inliers noticed below.

With regard to the hill Deccan Trap formation south of the Pūrna alluvium Wynne[1] says :—

The hills and portion of the valley south of the Pûrna river ' have been stated to consist of trap similar to that of the ' Deccan. All the usual varieties of amygdaloid, zeolitic, ' columnar, hard, gray, and softer ashy-looking traps occur, ' their stratification being very perceptible and always nearly ' horizontal.'

Inliers of Gondwānas, Lametās, and Metamorphics.

12. Along the northern boundary of the District, lying partly in Amraoti and partly in Betūl, there are some inliers of the Gondwāna age, concerning which Medlicott and Blanford write in the first edition of the Manual of the Geology of India, page 224, (1879), that along the southern scarp of the Gāwīlgarh Hills :—

' there is, north and north-east of Ellichpur, a line of fault, ' running east-north-east to west-south-west, and having a ' considerable down-throw to the south. Along the northern or ' upthrow side of this fault, sedimentary beds appear in places, ' from beneath the Deccan trap, forming the whole of the ' surrounding country, and extend for a considerable distance ' (in one case for several miles) along the base of the hills. ' These exposures are but 30 miles south-south-east of the ' sandstones in the Tāpti west of Betūl.

' The most western of these inliers occurs about 8 miles ' north of Ellichpur, and extends east and west between 6 ' and 7 miles. For 16 miles to the eastward no sedimentary ' rock is seen in place, but in one spot, 3 miles west of Narha, ' some blocks of sandstone occur, and there may be a small ' outcrop. At Narha, about 22 miles east by north of Ellich- ' pur, the sandstones reappear north of the fault, and extend

[1] *Rec. Geol. Surv. Ind.* Vol. II. page 8.

'for 15 miles. They then disappear again, but two small 'inliers, each about a mile long, occur at short intervals just 'beyond.

'In these inliers Lametā (cretaceous) beds occur imme'diately beneath the basaltic traps, and are succeeded in 'descending order by about 500 feet of strata comprising 'felspathic sandstones, white and brown conglomeratic beds, 'occasional ferruginous beds, and thin layers of white and 'purple shale. It has not been decided whether these rocks are 'of Kāmthi age, or whether they should be referred to the 'Mahādeva series, no distinguishable fossils having been 'found.

'No beds of Barākar or Tālchir age have been detected 'and the base of the sedimentary beds is not seen, whilst an 'attempt to discover coal by boring proved unsuccessful 'Metamorphic rocks appear in one place along the southern 'edge of the sandstone, and are apparently brought up 'between two faults with their throws in opposite directions 'As these faults coincide at each end of the strip of meta'morphics, there is evidence in this instance of two throws in 'opposite directions having taken place along the same line 'of weakness.'

BOTANY.

I. AMRAOTI FOREST DIVISION.

(*Pandurang Narāyan, E.A.C.F.*)

Plants of Village Waste.

13. *Cassia Tora*, locally called *tarotā*, is used in the beginning of the rains as a vegetable, but is a most harmful weed as it comes up in great profusion is not eaten by cattle and does very material damage to grazing grounds by killing the grass. *Cassia auriculata* (*tarwad*), with large yellow flowers, is found in poor soils along the foot of the Sātpurā range and on roadsides the bark is known to possess tanning properties but it is not so used in the District. *Achryanthes aspera* (*agara*) is a very common erect herb, ribbed between angles and much enlarged at the nodes, found generally in *bābul bans*; it has burrs which stick to the clothes; the leaves are used for worship by the

Hindus, and the seed possesses medicinal properties. *Martynia diandra* (*wāgnak*) is found in waste fields, field borders and deserted village sites. *Ocimum sanctum*, basil (*tulsī*), is generally grown for worship in courtyards of Hindu houses and temples as it is held to be sacred. *Tamarix indica* (*jhau*) forms dense thickets in the beds of some rivers. *Indigofera tinctoria*, wild indigo (*unhali*), is generally found in patches on the waste land near villages and roadsides. Both the species of *daturā*, *Datura Stramonium* and *Datura fastuosa* are found on rubbish heaps of villages and near temples; the leaves are used medicinally but the seed is poisonous, producing a species of intoxication, sometimes resulting in death.

Roadside Plants and Garden Trees.

14. *Melia indica* (*nīm*), *Albizzia Lebbek*, (*siris*), *Ailanthus excelsa* (*mahāruk*), *Mangifera indica*, the mango (*ām*), *Melia azadirachta* (*nīm* or *bagain*), *Bassia latifolia* (mahuā or *mohwā*), *Ficus bengalensis* (*bar*) the banyan are commonly planted along roadsides and camping grounds; *Sesbania aegyptiaca* (*saorā*) is grown in betel leaf gardens for supporting the creepers and affording shade. *Moringa pterygosperma* (*shengā* or *sojnā*) is cultivated in the open country; its long drooping, fleshy pods being used as a vegetable. *Feronia elephantum* (*kavit*, wood apple or elephant apple) is less commonly found along field borders. *Dalbergia Sissoo* is cultivated as an avenue tree, and is an import from Northern India. The handsome *Sapindus Mukorossi* (*rithia*) or soapnut tree, is sometimes grown in gardens. The scrambling shrub of *Clerodendron phlomoides* (*takal*), with its pleasant and sweet smelling white flowers, is common in hedges. *Euphorbia Tirucalli* (*thuar*), a plant with a round green stem, full of milk, makes a good hedge.

Forest and Wasteland Trees.

15. Almost all kinds of trees found in other plain Districts of Berār are met with in Amraoti. The following may be mentioned as commonly found. The teak (*Tectona grandis*) grows naturally in the north of the Morsi tāluk, but not to any large size. The *bābul* (*Acacia arabica*) is the most common and one of the most useful trees, thriving

best in deep black soil with a permanent but not excessive bed of moisture in the subsoil. *Dhaorā* (*Anogèissus latifolia*), *tiwas* (*Ougeinia dalbergioides*) and *dhāman* (*Grewia tiliæfolia*) are less common and do not attain any size. *Hiwar* (*Acacia leucophlæa*) with its dirty white bark and sweet smelling white flowers is commonly met with on dry stony soil and waste lands in the open country; the bark is locally used for tanning and the leaves and pods are greedily eaten by wild animals. *Acacia eburnea* (*murmatti*), *Prosopis spicigera* (*saondar*), with pinnate leaves and flowers in slender spikes and pods which when young are used for vegetables, and *hingan* (*Balanites Roxburghii*) are the common associates of the *kuria* variety of *bābul* on poorer soil. *Bauhinia racemosa* (*aptā*) is a common small tree with thin stem and straggling crown, leaves of which are distributed at Dasahra. The white and smooth barked *Terminalia Arjuna* (*kahu*) fringes some of the perennial streams. *Terminalia belerica* (*bahedā*,) with its very evil smelling flowers, grows sporadically, and is generally associated with a stunted form of *Terminalia tomentosa* (*sajad* or *ain*) with black and furrowed bark. The frankincense tree or *salai* (*Boswellia thurifera*) is the characteristic tree of the higher hill slopes in forest tracts. *Pterocarpus Marsupium* (*bījasāl* or *bīja*), much sought for musical instruments and also for cart poles, is found occasionally in Morsi tāluk. *Dalbergia latifolia* (*shīsham*), Bombay black wood, is only found on the outer ranges of the Sātpurā range in the Morsi tāluk; the leaves are used medicinally for cattle. The silk cotton tree *semal* (*Bombax malabaricum*) is found here and there in the open country; its roots are used medicinally; the red flowers serve as food in times of hardship, and the pods furnish silk cotton used for stuffing cushions, &c. Turning now to smaller trees we may mention *palās* (*Butea frondosa*), the roots of which are used for making ropes, the leaves as dining plates among Hindus, and as fodder for cattle, while the red flower yields the dye used during the Holi festival. The wild plum *Zizyphus vulgaris* (*ber*), the stems of which are made into spindles and thorns used for fencing; *Acacia Catechu* (*khair*), a bush which exists in very poor soil; *Celastrus senegalensis* (*bharāti*);

Flacourtia Ramontchi (*gurguti*); *Woodfordia floribunda* (*dhewti*); and the Mysore thorn *Caesalpinia sepiaria* (*chilati*), with its tufted white, red and blue flowers, are commonly found throughout the District.

16. A few clumps of *Dendrocalamus strictus* (*bāns*) are found in the north of Morsi tāluk. *Bambusa arundinacea* (*katang bāns*) has been introduced into some parts of the District.

Bamboos.

17. *Andropogon Martini* (*tikhāri* or *rūsa*) yields a valuable oil and is easily recognised by the bright red colour of its bracts and its characteristic lemon scent; the stems are used for thatching; it is found in some parts of the District but is not common. *Sorghum halepense* (*boru*) or elephant grass grows very thick and high in rich alluvial soils and deserted village sites; *Cynodon dactylon* (*hariāli* or *dūb*), a small perennial grass with creeping stem, rooting at the nodes, yields an excellent fodder grass, especially for horses; it is the best grass for lawns. *Ischaemum laxum* (*sahāda*), is the best fodder grass when cut before seeding at the end of the rainy season, and when fully matured (in March) is useful for thatching. *Ischaemum sulcatum* (*paonia*) is a very thin and soft grass much valued for fodder. *Andropogon contortus* (*kusal*) or spear grass is used as fodder when young and before it has seeded and for thatching when mature. *Andropogon pachyarthrus* (*gondali*), is a grass which has several varieties. It is readily eaten by cattle before the seeds are ripe. *Andropogon foveolatus*, *Silkia Marvel*, and *Iseilema laxum* (*katri*) are also commonly used for fodder. *Ghod sahāda*, *ghod kusli*, *lokhandi*, *bhusi*, *kāns*, &c., do not afford pasturage in years of plenty but are eaten by cattle in years of scarcity.

Grasses.

II. MELGHAT FOREST DIVISION.

18. The botany of the Melghāt jungles is naturally a far more complicated matter and demands for its adequate treatment more space than may fairly be allotted to it in an Amraoti

Melghàt.

District Gazetteer. Detailed information will be found in Mr. Dickenson's Notes on the flora of the Berār Division and in Mr. D. O. Witt's Forest flora of the Berār circle, as well as in Messrs. Dickenson and Bagshaw's working plan of the Bairāgarh and Gugumāl reserves and Sir Dietrich Brandis's Suggestions for the Melghāt Forests. The first mentioned of these books gives particular attention to the Melghāt flora. As to the uses to which the forest tribes of that tāluk turn their surroundings, Mr. Bartlett writes as follows:—'In 'building their huts they use poles and rafters of almost any 'species. The walls are of bamboo mat and the roof of teak 'leaves and grass held down with rough wooden poles. For 'ploughs they prefer *tiwas* (*Ougeinia dalbergioides*) but use most 'hard woods, and poles are usually of *sāj* (*Terminalia tomentosa*), '*dhaorā* (*Anogeissus latifolia*), *tendū* (*Diospyros melanoxylon*), or '*dhāman* (*Grewia tilifælia*). For other implements *dhaurā* is 'mostly used. Their carts are frequently constructed of teak, 'but if other species are conveniently near the village, they 'prefer *tiwas* (*Ougeinia dalbergioides*) or *kusum* (*Schleichera* '*trijuga*) for naves, *dhaurā* for axles and *sīwan* (*Gmelina* '*arborea*) or *thekdā* (*Garuga pinnata*) for the yoke. Ropes are 'made from the fibres of *palās* roots (*Butea frondosa*), the '*mahul* creeper (*Bauhinia Vahlii*), the bark of the *karai* or '*kondarā* (*Sterculia urens*), but green bamboo is generally used 'for all temporary purposes. As fuel they burn the wood 'nearest to hand. In food, however, they utilize a variety of 'forest produce. Of trees, the red fleshy petals of *semal* '(*Bombax malabaricum*) are dried and ground with juāri as 'flour, and the thickened roots of the young trees are eaten 'raw. The chief fruits are those of the *tendū* (*Diospyros* '*melanoxylon*), *chār* (*Buchanania latifolia*), *sakria* (*Zizyphus* '*rugosa*), *ber* (*Zizyphus vulgaris*), *aonla* (*Phyllanthus Emblica*), '*jāmun* (*Eugenia Jambolana*), *sitā kugathal* (*Embelia Ribes*) and '*gūlar* (*Ficus glomerata*). They are eaten raw or cooked or 'dried and ground as flour. The fruits of the *siwan* (*Gmelina* '*arborea*), *bhilāwa* (*Semecarpus Anacardium*), *kusum* (*Schleichera* '*trijuga*) and the kernels of *bahedā* (*Terminalia belerica*) and

Bemrose, Collo., Derby.

BAMBOO JUNGLE ON THE TAPTI.

'*karai* (*Sterculia urens*) are also crushed and eaten. The fruit 'and bulb shaped stem of the wild plantain (*Musa superba*) are 'eaten raw, and the dried corolla of the mahuā (*Bassia latifolia* 'ground as flour is a staple diet. Of the wild yams *gogdu* '(*Ischaemum rugosum*) *bolar*, *kulu* (*Dioscorea daemona*) and '*dhorkakri* (*Coccinia indica*) are the chief. The Korkū varies his 'food with herbs and leaves fried in oil and seasoned with salt, 'chillies, garlic and turmeric. They mostly use the leaves of 'the creeper *kumbeli* (*Vitis tenuifolia*), the *tarotā* (*Cassia Tora*) 'and *koelāri* (*Bauhinia purpuria*), the petals of the beautiful '*kachnār* flower (*Bauhinia variegata*) and the young fruits of 'the *pendrā* (*Gardenia turgida*) and the *chillū* tree (*Cordia* '*Myxa*). The chief fodder grasses of the Melghāt are *sahāda* '(*Ischaemum laxum*) *gondali* (*Ischaemum pachyarthrus*), *kundhā* '(*Ischaemum pilosum*), and *muchhali* or *harali* (*Iseilema Wightii* 'or *Cynodon dactylon*); *kusli* the spear grass (*Heteropogon* '*contortus*) and *rūsa* (*Andropogon Martini stapt.*) are preferred for 'thatching. A grass called *moya* is used for rope making and 'the seed of the two grasses called *saveli* and *bābhajharā* are 'eaten like rice.'

WILD ANIMALS AND BIRDS.

19. Fauna. The District is indebted to the wide difference in character which separates the Melghāt from the plains for its great variety of wild animals, those of the forest and open country being alike met with. The commonest are described below, the vernacular names being those in use locally. In the case of Korkū where two or more names are given the first is that supplied by Mr. H. E. Bartlett, the remainder have been taken from various old Korkū vocabularies by Forsyth, Hislop and others, kindly lent by the Rev. A. Voss of the Korkū mission. The local Urdū and Hindī are the same.

1. The Hanumān monkey or Bengal Langūr, *Semnopithecus vel Presbytes Entelus*, Hindī *langūr*, Marāthī *vānar*, Korkū *pulamsarā*, or *sarā*. This sacred monkey of the Hindus is met with in all parts of the District in fairly large numbers, and causes considerable damage to crops and fruit trees.

On occasion the larger males have been known to attack villagers when in fear of bodily hurt or when scared away from fields or gardens.

2. The Bengal or red Monkey, *Macacus Rhesus*, Hindī *bandar*, Marāthī *mākad*, Korkū *dugi*. Very common throughout the plains and on the Chikaldā plateau of the Melghāt. When caught and tamed it is a very intelligent pet, and beggars use it locally like the organ grinder's monkey in England as a performing animal.

3. The Tiger, *Felis Tigris*, Hindī *bāgh*, *shèr*, Marāthī *wāgh*, Korkū *khātkūla*, *kūla* and *koda* (?), is not found in the plains except as an occasional wanderer from the neighbouring highlands of Betūl and Melghāt. Cases are on record of its being shot in the Mehdari reserve and also at Sālbardī. But in the Bairāgarh and Gugumāl reserves tigers are numerous. *Shikār* however is very difficult, for owing to the precipitous ravines and hill sides beating is almost impossible, while game is so plentiful that tigers can with difficulty be induced to take tied up baits. They are great wanderers, seldom being found to haunt any particular locality for long; man-eating is rare, no case having been recorded for several years. Both these facts are probably to be attributed to the profusion of game just mentioned; water also can be found almost anywhere below the higher plateaux.

4. The Hunting Leopard, *Felis Jubata*, is generally known in Hindī as *chīta* and in Marāthī *chitlā*, though these words which mean spotted are frequently applied also to the Pard and Panther. Sterndale says that the *chīta* catchers know it as *yuz*, calling the other kinds *bibla*. It differs from the ordinary Pard in being marked with single spots, not rosettes of black; is longer in the body and legs and of a thinner build; the claws only partially retractile; has a distinct ruff round the neck, and Sterndale says that the name Leopard originates from this, the animal being supposed to be a cross of lion and pard. It seems doubtful whether it is to be found in this District. The passes taken out by the Nizām's *shikāris*, to trap leopards for his Highness's pack, are valid for all Berār, though their operations for many years have been in practice confined to the tāluks of the old Bāsim district. Probably, however, a few still exist in the north of the Province. The animal is of a very shy and inoffensive nature and his presence might go long undetected, or he might be mistaken for the ordinary pard.

5A. The Pard, *Felis Pardus*, Hindī *chīta bāgh* or occasionally *chīta* (the tiger being *asl bāgh*); Marāthī *tendwā*; Korkū *sanikulā sonorā*.

5B. The Panther, *Felis Panthera*, Hindī *bhorbachchā*, Marāthī *bībat* or *bīwat*, Korkū *kaīrea*. It is still a more or less disputed point whether these are separate species or merely larger and smaller varieties of the same breed. The most striking difference is one of size, the *bīwat* being comparatively a small animal; but the *tendwā* besides being larger is of a heavier and more powerful build, its skin is shorter-haired and the markings are larger and more distinct. Neither species shows very much fear of man; they will walk into villages and pick out their prey with complete unconcern. One was killed in the summer of 1908 almost in the Amraoti civil station, having lifted cattle from Wadali village; at Ghatang dogs have been carried off from the veranda of the dāk bungalow and in Chikaldā a panther has been seen asleep in the middle of the road in broad daylight. The Korkūs tell stories of the animals coming into their huts and lying down by the fire. They are but rarely man eaters though a pard in Chaurākund in the famine year 1898-99 took to this method of livelihood and killed some 20 or 30 people including full grown men before he was disposed of; in the same year one in Katkumbh accounted for several children. The Pārdhis, a tribe of hunters, trap both species in snares made of antelope tendons, and beat them to death.

6. The Common Jungle Cat, *Felis Chaus*, Hindī *jungli billī* Marāthī *rān mānjar*, Korkū *dongar mānjar*, is fairly common chiefly in grass land and scrub forest and lives upon small game. The true jungle cat has a fulvous coat, but owing to village cats growing wild and inter-breeding, specimens of all colours are met with.

7. The Indian Lynx,, *Felis Caracal*, Marāthī *jhuva* or *jhuā*, Hindī *siāgosh*. Very rare and very shy.

8. The Hyæna, *Hyaena Striata*, Hindī *lakrā*, Marāthī *taras*, Korkū *dhopre* or *tarsā*, a cowardly beast but an excellent scavenger; has been known sometimes to carry off a dog or goat or even a small child; when it develops rabies, as it occasionally does, is particularly dangerous by reason of its enormously powerful jaws.

9. The Lesser Civet Cat, *Viverra vel Viverricula Malaccensis* Hindī and Marāthī locally *udbilao*, which is strictly the name for the otter (*Vide infra*). *Billī* and *mānjar* are words used indiscriminately of all small cat-like animals.

10. The Wolf, *Canis Pallipes*, Hindī *bheria*, Marāthī *lāndgai*, Korkū *lendya*, found in small packs of four upwards in the plain tāluks.

11. The Jackal, *Canis Aureus*, Hindī *siār*, Marāthī *aolhā*, Korku *koleā*.

12. The Red Dog, *Canis vel Cuon Rutilans*, Hindī *jungli kuttā*, Marāthī *rān kutrā*, Korkū *dongar sitā* and *ban sitā*, though not found in the plain tāluks is common in the hills. The jungle tribes are said to regard it as a useful friend, for when a pack has pulled down a sāmbhar or other large game, they beat off the dogs with sticks and appropriate the carcase. Hence even the high reward offered will not tempt them to kill it.

13. The Fox, *Vulpes Bengalensis*, Hindī *lomri*, Marāthī *khokad*, Korkū *panmanghā* and *kakri*.

14. The Indian Sloth Bear, *Ursus vel Melursus Ursinus*, Hindī *bhālu*, Marāthī *aswal*, Korkū *bāna*, is extremely common in the hill country and has a great reputation for stubborn combativeness, a reputation which he yearly upholds by causing the death of many who disturb him.

15. The Badger or Ratel, *Mellivora Indica*, Hindī *bijjū*, Korkū *ote bāna*, is found especially in the neighbourhood of Bairāt in the Melghāt.

16. The Wild Pig, *Sus Scrofa vel Cristatus*, Hindī *suar*, and among Muhammadans *burā* or *bad jānwar*, Marāthī and Korkū *dukar* also Korkū *shukadi*, *chukadi* or *sukdi*, is common everywhere, and in old days before the troops were moved from Ellichpur, the local hunt obtained very good pigsticking.

17. The Common Indian Hare, *Lepus Ruficaudatus*, Hindī *khargosh*, Marāthī *sasā*, Korkū *koati*.

18. The Porcupine, Hindī *sei*, Marāthī *sayal* or *shayalu*, Korkū *jekrā*.

19a and *b*. Two kinds of Mongoose, *Herpestes Pallidus vel Griscus*, and *Herpestes Jerdoni* are found, the latter in the neighbourhood of Chikaldā. Hindī *newala*, Marāthī *mungūs*.

20. The Otter, *Lutra Nain*, Hindī *pankuttā*, Marāthī *pankutrā*, both meaning the water dog, Korku *buā*, is found on the Sipnā river.

21. Of horned game the most important is the bison, *Bos vel Gavaeus Gaurus*, Hindī *gaur*, Marāthī *gawa*, Korkū *gohā* or *gowā*. This magnificent beast is gradually recovering under protection from the effects of an epidemic disease which nearly exterminated the herds in 1900. It is found in the Gugumāl hills, the highlands below Bairāt and sometimes north of Raipur.

The District contains three species of deer and four of antelope.

22. The Sāmbhar, *Rusa Aristotelis*, Hindī and Marāthī *sāmbhar*, Korkū *dhak*, *dhakar*. The Marāthī word *rohi* or *rui* which strictly means a female *nīlgai* is applied indiscriminately by both Marāthī and Korkū speakers to the male and female of this species as well as the *chītal* and *nīlgai*. The sāmbhar is found in the Melghāt and is also an occasional wanderer from Betūl into the Morsi tāluk reserves.

23. The Chītal, *Axis Maculatus*, Hindī and Marāthī *chītal*, Korkū *chitli* and *dhakar*. This spotted deer was at one time plentiful in the District, but the Chirodi herd is now carefully preserved. There are also a few at Mehdari.

24. The Jungle Sheep or Barking Deer, *Cervulus Muntjac*, Hindī *junglī bakri*, Marāthī *bekra* or *baikar*, Korkū *ghotari* (a name applied also to the *chinkāra* and the four-horned antelope) *kākar*. The last word is obviously taken from the animal's peculiar bark.

25. The Blue Bull, *Portax Pictus vel Boselephas Tragocamelus*. Hindī and Marāthī *nīlgai* and *rohi* (see sāmbhar), Korkū *nū*. Plentiful in the Amraoti hills.

26. The Black Buck *Antilope Bezoartica*. Hindī male *haran*, female *harnī*, Marāthī male *kalwit*, female *haran* or *harnī* also *hirn* ; Korkū *kutsar* ; is extremely common all over the plains of the District, particularly in the Chāndur tāluk, but is unknown in the Melghāt save as an occasional wanderer from the plains. The horns are not generally very long, though heads up to 23½ inches have been recently obtained.

27. The Chinkāra, *Gazella Bennettii*, Hindī *chinkāra*, Marāthī *kalsipi*, Korkū *ghótari* and *mendhā*, fairly common all over the District. The misnomer 'Ravine Deer' though not correct as to genus is a fairly accurate description of its habits, the rocky slopes of nullahs and valleys in hilly country being its especial haunt.

28. The Four-horned Antelope, Hindī *chausinghā*, Korkū *ghotari*, *bherki*, very common round Chikaldā.

29. There may also be mentioned the common grey squirrel, *Sciurus Palmarum*, Hindī *gilehrī*, Marāthī *khar*, Korkū *tur*, to be seen in myriads all over the District ; *30*, the flying squirrel *Pteromys Oral vel petaurista*, seen in the Melghāt and known by the Korkūs as *Orār*; *31*, the common flying-fox, Marāthī *watawāghul*, whose flesh when boiled is supposed locally to be a good cure for rheumatism; and a variety of other small animals too numerous to detail. To this list may perhaps be added a herd of domestic cattle in the Chirodi reserve which have now become completely wild.

There are numerous kinds of lizards including in the Melghāt the smaller *Biscobra* or *Iguana*, Marāthī *ghorpod*. The legend runs that it was used by soldiers in old time in the attack on walled fortresses. Rope ladders were affixed to it and it was trained to run up walls. When it arrived at the top its grip was so firm that a man could climb the ladder after it. Most of the ordinary varieties of snakes are found, including the cobra (*nāg*), *krait* and the Indian python. In the Tāpti the alligator is fairly common, but on the upper waters of the Pūrna in this District it is not found.

The following note on fishes written forty years ago by Mr. Nicholetts for Akolā is equally true to-day of this District; the best fish, however, are found in the big rivers on the borders, and in the interior fish are scarce. 'We have the '*hohoe*, a species of carp; the *marral*, the best-eating fish in 'our rivers. He is shaped like the ball-head of England, and 'has the habits of the pyke, is a smooth fish of a dark colour. 'The *com*, the *pupta*, the *bām*, a first-rate eating fish; the '*chilwā*, the *sangara* or dog fish. The fish fit for table are the '*hohoe*, *marral* and *bām*.[1]

'The first is well known in India, is of a delicate flavour, 'but bony. The flesh of the *marral* is like that of the cod 'fish, white, and very firm; the *bām* is more of the lamprey 'kind.

'The fishermen are very great adepts at netting. They drag 'with great precision; sometimes they meet with an active 'old stager but by signals they indicate his course to each 'other and will make a capture of a large fish that had 'passed four or five of them in a regular hunt.

In respect to nets Mr. Nicholetts enumerates :—

'The large stationary net, to which the fish are driven down 'by a number of men getting in the water and advancing 'towards the net.

'The drag net used by men, enclosing gradually any pool 'where fishes are known to stop.

---

[1] It should be added that the *chilwā*, if obtainable in sufficient quantities, makes a passable imitation of whitebait.

'A peculiar kind of large shrimping net which is placed 'at the mouth of a rapid where there is little water; the 'mouth of the net is kept open by means of a small stick 'three feet long which falls and lets it shut when the fish 'move it.

'The cast net, similar to the English one.

'The shrimping net, a kind of a bag-like net, fixed to 'three sticks forming a triangle. The fishermen are 'principally Bhoīs.

'The *marral* is constantly shot during the heat of the 'day; they come to the surface and skim about for 'hours; a tree overhanging a pool is the best place to 'shoot from.'

The Birds.

20. The birds of the District include most of the gaily plumaged varieties common elsewhere, such as the golden oriole, the blue roller (or jay), the king fisher and the little green fly-catchers. They also include the 'painted' and 'rock' sand grouse (*Pterocles Fasciatus* and *P. Exustus),* the peacock (*Pavo Cristatus)*, the grey partridge *(Ortygornis Ponticerianus*), the Jungle quail *(Perdicula Asiatica)*, the large grey and rain quails *(Coturnix Communis* and *C. Coromandelicus)*, and the button quail *(Turnix Dussumieri)*. Of water birds the *kulum*, *kūlin* or *kunja*, (Demoiselle crane), known locally as *karkunj* or *kar*, is rare, but we have most of the ordinary varieties of duck and teal, as well as a varied assortment of cranes and other shore birds. In the Melghāt, as might be expected, are many varieties not common in these parts of India, the following having been noted by the well known naturalist, Lieut.-Col. McMaster, in May 1870.

Ochromela Nigrorufa, the black and orange fly-catcher, otherwise only found on the Nilgiris and in Ceylon.

Cyornis Tickelliæ, Tickell's blue redbreast common in Central India.

Myiophonus Horsfieldii, the Malabar whistling thrush, found near Chikaldā.

Hypsipetes Ganeesa, the Ghāt Black *Bulbul*.

Oriolus Ceylonensis, the southern black headed oriole.

Corvus Culminatus, the Indian corby, (the familiar social pest of the plains is *Corvus Splendens*, the grey crow).

Both varieties of green pigeon *Crocopus Phoenicopteryx* and *C. Chlorigaster*, and both the grey and red jungle fowls, *Gallus Sonneratii* and *Gallus Ferrugineus*.

Rainfall and Climate.

21. Rainfall. The District has 13 stations at which rainfall is registered. Two of these, Amraoti and Chikaldā, are under the Meteorological Department and the remainder under the Director of Land Records. Statistics are as follows, those for Dhārni having been taken for the 10 years ending 1906 and the remainder for the 40 years ending 1900 :—

Station.		Rainfall.	Rain days.
Tāluk Amraoti ...	Amraoti Camp... ...	32·84	46·9
	Kholāpur	24·63	40·9
	Badnerā	25·72	42·7
Tāluk Chāndur ...	Chāndur Railway ...	34·83	46·2
	Talegaon Dashsahasra.	29·27	39·2
Tāluk Morsi ...	Morsi	34·76	47·2
	Warud	32·19	46·1
Tāluk Ellichpur ...	Ellichpur Civil Station.	30·58	47·6
	Ellichpur City	29·72	44·7
	Chāndur Bazār ..	28·38	41·9
Tāluk Daryāpur ...	Daryāpur	31·67	42·8
	Anjangaon	24·42	37·5
Tāluk Melghāt ...	Chikaldā	66·42	77·9
	Dhārni	34·6	...

Thus excluding Chikaldā the figures for which are typical only of the higher plateaux, the rainfall is fairly evenly distributed over the District. The value of the rainfall depends more on its distribution than on its extent, its peculiarity being that an average rainfall in the plains of about 25 inches, if received in due season with a good break in the rains to allow of the crop maturing, and with showers later, can produce an ordinary good crop; while a rainfall of 34·36 inches (the average of the last 40 years) may be and sometimes is followed by a year of scarcity. This was the case in 1896-97 when the District average was 36·56, while in the preceding year good crops were harvested though only 26·33 inches had been received. In 1880-81 and 1886-87 the registered fall was 24·22 inches; yet in both these years the crop was a fairly good one, that in the old Ellichpur District in the former year being described as excellent. In 1887-88 there was a record downpour of no less than 60·87 inches which was distributed as follows :—0·74 in April and May; 8·85 in June; 20·55 in July; 7·57 in August; 7·23 in September; 9·33 in October; and 6·60 in the succeeding months from November to March. Of the 36 years ending 1906-07 one only showed a rainfall of less than 20 inches, the 13·2 received in 1899-1900 being followed by a severe famine. In eight years the amount registered was between 20 and 30 inches, and in sixteen between 30 and 40; in seven a total of from 40 to 50 inches was recorded, while in four only was the latter figure exceeded.

22. Climate. In climate as in almost every other particular, the Melghāt is entirely different from the rest of the District. In the plains, though there is no cold weather like that of Northern India, yet the conditions are for the greater part of the year very healthy. Even the scorching heat which prevails in the day time from about the middle of March to the middle of June is to some extent mitigated by the extreme dryness of the air and the coolness of the nights, so that to many constitutions, even European, this is the healthiest of the seasons. In the Melghāt, the sanitarium of Chikaldā, situated on a lofty plateau open to every wind, is for nine months in the year a delightful health resort. One can be out of doors there at midday in early June without serious discomfort, but when once the rains

have set in, the continual mists make the place somewhat depressing. In the valleys of the Melghāt again a different climate prevails, which is regarded with unmixed dislike by both Europeans and natives. It is certainly very malarious so that the camping is considered risky before January, and officials long stationed there generally fall sick. In the summer, though the open country is a trifle cooler than the plains, the more secluded valleys are suffocatingly hot. The evil reputation which this tract has acquired, however, is sometimes said to be only partly deserved, much being attributable not to the climate but to the depressing influence of the surroundings which are neither true forest, nor fully cultivated land.

[1] There are two meteorological observatories in the Amraoti District, one at Amraoti in the plains and the other at the hill station of Chikaldā. The elevation above sea-level of the barometer at the first is 1215 feet and at the second 3642 feet. The first was founded in 1873 and the second in 1876, and thus a series of more than 30 years observations are on record. The year may be divided into the cold season, the hot weather, and the rainy season, the first lasting from November to February and the second from March to about the 2nd week in June, when the rains usually set in and continue till about the middle of October. During the cold weather there is but little cloud and only occasional light falls of rain. In October winds, which during the greater part of the year blow from westerly directions, change to north at Chikaldā and to east at Amraoti. There is however comparatively little air movement during the winter at either station. Temperature frequently falls below 50° at night but there is seldom any frost. The lowest temperature on record is 40·9° at Chikaldā and 40·6° at Amraoti, both occurring in the month of February. In March temperature begins to rise rapidly and the hot weather sets in. The hottest time of the year is May and the early part of June, when the maximum

[1] The remainder of this Note has been supplied by the kindness of Mr. John Patterson of the Government of India Meteorological Department.

thermometer at Amraoti frequently records a temperature of 110°, the mean maximum for the whole of May being 107.7; Chikaldā temperatures are usually from 13° to 14° below those registered at Amraoti. The highest temperatures on record are 115·5 at Amraoti and 103° at Chikaldā. Humidity is very low at this season, averaging only about 26 or 27 per cent. of saturation in April, which is the driest month of the year. As the baric gradients steepen in May owing to the high temperature prevailing in Northern India, winds increase in strength, and from May to September the air movement is at its maximum, the wind velocity at Chikaldā during this period averaging 10 miles an hour. The velocity is not so great at Amraoti. The rainfall of the hot weather is small and is chiefly connected with thunder storms which are frequently accompanied by hail and cause large and sudden falls of temperature. The normal date for the setting in of the rainy season in the District of Amraoti is the 10th June, and from this date on to about the 15th October more than 90 per cent. of the whole year's rainfall is received Humidity is of course very high at this season of the year and in August averages 95 per cent. of saturation at Chikaldā and 82 per cent. at Amraoti. Temperature is very uniform during the rains at Chikaldā and the daily range of temperature averages only 8·3° in July and 7·7° in August; at Amraoti for the same months it is 13·8° and 13·5° respectively. In October winds fall off in strength, rainfall decreases rapidly and after a period of hot steamy weather the cold season gradually sets in. A statement is annexed giving temperature and wind data for five months in 1906, 1907 and 1908. It will be noticed that the wind velocity at Amraoti in May and June in these years was higher than that at Chikaldā, which is unusual.

Statement showing the Mean Maximum, Minimum Temperatures and Wind Velocity recorded at the Amraoti and Chikaldā Observatories during January, April, May, June, November, and December, 1906, 1907, and 1908.

Months.	Mean Maximum.						Mean Minimum.						Mean hourly Wind Velocity.					
	Amraoti.			Chikaldā.			Amraoti.			Chikaldā.			Amraoti.			Chikaldā		
	1906	1907	1908	1906	1907	1908	1906	1907	1908	1906	1907	1908	1906	1907	1908	1906	1907	1908
January	84·6	86 1	84·3	74·8	74·8	74·3	57·6	58 3	56 9	53·8	54 8	53·9	2·6	1·4	5 5	8·3	6·7	6·9
April	107·3	98·1	106·0	94·4	85·9	94·0	76·9	72 9	76 6	72.6	66 7	72 0	5 0	6·8	6·3	8·1	8·2	7·3
May	110·3	107·2	108·2	97·0	93·7	95·4	82·5	77·1	80·3	75·7	71·6	72 7	10·1	7·9	.7·9	8·0	7 3	7·3
June	93·4	99·3	100·0	83·0	86 9	87·2	76·5	77·2	73·1	68 8	68 4	69 2	10 6	10·0	11·5	8·4	7 9	7·4
November	88·6	90·0	86·3	77·6	80·6	81·7	63·5	65·0	60 3	58 7	60 7	53·1	3·1	5·2	4·7	7·5	6 9	6·9
December	84·2	82 6	81·2	72·4	74·4	72·4	59 8	56·1	54 6	53 5	53·4	51·9	2·4	5·3	5·0	*	6·8	6 6

* Figures not available.

CHAPTER II.

HISTORY AND ARCHÆOLOGY.

(*Major W. Haig.*)

HISTORY.

The history of the Amraoti District, which contains both the ancient and the modern capitals of Berār, as well as its most famous fortress, is to a great extent that of the Province itself.

Legendary period.

23. Berār is first mentioned, under the name of Vidarbha, in the Mahābhārata, one of the two great epics of the Hindus. This poem is in no sense history and, as Mr. Vincent Smith says,[1] while of value as a traditional picture of social life in the heroic age does not seem to contain matter illustrating the political relations of states during the historical period. Nevertheless the period covered by the events which form the basis of the poem's story has been conjecturally placed between 1500 and 1000 B.C.

The Mahābhārata.

24. In the Mahābhārata Vidarbha is described as a large kingdom lying to the south of Nishadh or southern Mālwā, and governed, during the time when the Pāndavas were preparing to expel the Kauravas from Hastināpur, by a proud and boastful rājā named Rukmin. The kingdom took its name from its capital, which is identified, both by legend and etymology, with Bīdar in the Nizām's dominions, the capital of the later Bahmanī kings of the Deccan. If credit may be given to this legend the ancient kingdom of Vidarbha must have been far more extensive than the modern Province of Berār.

Rukmin marched with a large army to the aid of the Pāndavas and was hospitably received and royally entertained by Yudhishthira, the eldest of the five princes. At the banquet Rukmin indulged to excess in liquor, and after boasting of his prowess demanded a share of the kingdom of

---

[1] *Early History of India*, page 8.

Hastināpur as the price of his assistance. His arrogance excited the wrath of Arjun, who told him that although he and his brothers were grateful for the proffered aid they could not tolerate his boasting or accept his conditions, and that he might go or stay, as he pleased. Rukmin then transferred his offer of assistance to the Kauravas and was at first well received by Duryodhan, but contrived to irritate his new friends by his overbearing manners and at length arose in great wrath and returned to his own country.

Rukmin had a beautiful sister named Rukmini, who was sought in marriage by the demi-god Krishna but was already betrothed to Sisupāl, the rājā of Chedi. Rukmin refused to allow her to break her troth but Krishna carried her off by force and married her, the wedding ceremonies being performed, according to local legend, at the temple of Ambā Bhawāni at Amraoti. Rukmin, thus thwarted, retired to Bhātkulī, nine miles west of Amraoti, where he passed the rest of his life as a recluse.

Vidarbha was also the scene of the love-story of Nal and Damayanti. Nal, the rājā of Nishadh, and Damayanti, the beautiful daughter of Bhīm, rājā of Vidarbha, fell in love, each with the other's description. Bhīm proclaimed a *swayamvar* at which Damayanti chose Nal from a large number of rājās to be her husband. The marriage was celebrated and Nal carried Damayanti away to Nishadh. The troubles of their married life and their long separation in consequence of Nal's losses at play are related both in the Mahābhārata and in a long Persian poem by Akbar's poet laureate Faizī, the brother of Abu-l-Fazl, but are not connected with the story of Berār.

Abdur Rahmān the Ghāzi.

25. A purely legendary episode is connected with Ellichpur. This is the fable of the *jihād* or Holy War of Shāh Abdur Rahmān the Ghāzi, sister's son to Mahmūd of Ghaznī, which is said to have taken place in the reign of the eponymous rājā Il of Ellichpur. The legend of rājā Il is that he was a Jain by religion and came from the village now known as Khānzamān nagar near Wadgaon. He founded Ellichpur, according

to local *pandits*, in the year *Samvat* 1115, corresponding with A.D. 1058. A wandering Muhammadan *fakīr* is said to have visited his court, and so to have annoyed the rājā by his zeal for Islām as to cause the latter to have his hand cut off. The *fakīr* left India and laid his case before Abdur Rahmān, whose nuptials were then being celebrated at Ghaznī. The youthful bridegroom in his religious zeal stopped the wedding festivities at once and, assembling an army of several thousand warriors, set out for Berār accompanied by his mother the Bībī Malikā-i-Jahān. The Muhammadan legend says that Northern India was then ruled by a rājā named Vaked who had quarrelled with Il and gladly assisted the invader. Il heard of the approach of Abdur Rahmān and sent an army to meet him. The two armies met near Kherlā in the Betūl District and the Musalmāns were at first hard pressed until Abdur Rahmān was inspired by a voice from heaven to cut off his own head. This he did, and then led his whole army against the Hindus, who were routed and pursued as far as Ellichpur. Here the invaders were met by Il himself who, after an obstinately contested battle, was defeated and took refuge in the city. He was brought bound to Abdur Rahmān who urged him to accept Islām, which the rājā refused to do. When asked what he would have done had he been victorious he replied that he would have flayed Abdur Rahmān, stuffed his skin with straw, and burnt it. Abdur Rahmān immediately ordered the rājā to be so treated and 'sent him to be one of the chiefs of hell.' A chronogram pretends to give the date of this event as A.H. 392 (A.D. 1001-02) which does not correspond with the date of the foundation of Ellichpur according to the Hindu legend.

Pachpīriya legends.

26. This fable, absurd though it is, is one of a very well-known class. The parentage of the hero, the incident of the headless horseman, and the fact that the followers of Abdur Rahmān who captured Rājā Il are locally known as the *Pānch Pīr* or *Pachpīr*, connect the story with the well-known *Pachpīriya* legends of the Bahraich District in the United Provinces. When and by whom this particular fable was invented it is impossible

to say, but it is probably later than the period of Bahmanī rule, to which may be assigned the shrine in Ellichpur known as that of Abdur Rahmān. The shrine is probably a tomb erected to the memory of Shujāt Khān, Dilāwar Khān, Rustam Khān and Bahādur Khān, generals of Firoz Shāh Bahmanī who were slain in a battle at Kherlā in 1400. This identification will account for the association of this shrine with one at Kherlā where, according to the legend, the head of the Ghāzi is buried. The Hindu generals mentioned in the legend are eponymous heroes whose names are connected with the names of places in the Amraoti District. Thus we have Bairāt, connected with Bairāt, and possibly also with Bairāgarh in the Melghāt and Rīdh, associated with Rītpur or Rīdhpur, now the headquarters of the Mahānubhāva sect.[1]

Hindu period.

27. The early history of the District, apart from such legends as these, is vague and fragmentary. Berār formed part of the empire of Asoka Maurya who reigned from 272 to 231 B.C., but it is not certain whether it was governed directly by his officers or whether it formed a protected state under chiefs of the Pulinda tribe. Pushyamitra Sunga, commander of the forces of Brihadratha, the last Maurya emperor, having, in 184 A.D., slain his master, founded the Sunga dynasty and towards the end of his reign his heir-apparent, Agnimitra, made war on and defeated the Rājā of Vidarbha, but neither the short-lived Sunga dynasty nor the northern dynasties which succeeded it ever attempted to reconquer Berār, which was shortly afterwards included in the empire established by the Andhra dynasty of Telingāna which originally had its capital at Shrī Kākulam on the lower course of the Krishna. It is probable that the Province was included among the conquests of the Sakas, Pallavas, and Yavanas in A.D. 100 and was freed from their domination in A.D. 126 by the twenty-third Andhra king, Vilivāyakara II. This king was succeeded in 138 by his son Pulumāyi II, while the Saka satrap Rudradāman assumed the government of the western provinces, among which Berār

[1] For a full version of the legend of Shāh Abdur Rahmān see *Journal of the Asiatic Society of Bengal*, Vol. XXL, Part III.

should probably be included. Rudradāman's daughter Dakshamitra was married to Pulumāyi, but the satrap was deterred by no scruples from attacking his son-in-law and reconquering the territory which Vilivāyakara II had conquered from the Sakas, Pallavas, and Yavanas, for he moved his capital from Kolhāpur to Paithan[1] on the upper Godāvari, a step which indicates that he had business in the north-western corner of his kingdom which demanded his attention.

The Rāshtrakūtas and Vākātakas.

28. The Andhra dynasty came to an end about 236 and from that time to 550 the history of the Deccan is a blank, though, as Mr. Vincent Smith remarks, there is reason to believe that the western territory or Mahārāshtra, in which Berār should probably be included, 'was governed by princes of the Rāshtrakūta or Ratta clan'; which, long afterwards, in the middle of the eighth century, became for a time the leading power in the Deccan. We have, however, some trace of a dynasty, that of the Vākātakas, which appears from its grants to have ruled an extensive tract of country, including the whole of Berār. Very little is known of this dynasty, the capital of which was perhaps at Bhāndak near Chānda in the Central Provinces. A short inscription in cave XVI at Ajanta gives the names of seven members of the family, and from other sources we learn that ten rājās the names of all of whom, save two, have been handed down, ascended the throne. It is by means of Pravarasena II, the fifth rājā, that we are able to connect the dynasty with the Amraoti District, for a copper-plate grant of the eighteenth regnal year of this prince relating to 'Charmānka in the Bhojakata kingdom,' *i.e.*, Chammak in the District, has been discovered. The Bhojakata kingdom was perhaps a feudatory state.

The Chālukyas.

29. The Chālukya dynasty was founded about 550 by Pulikesin I, who had his capital at Vātāpi, the modern Bādāmi in the Bījāpur District, and his immediate successors extended the limits of their kingdom so as to include not only Berār but

---

[1] The *Plithana* of Ptolemy.

also many states to the north. In the reign of Pulikesin II, the sixth of the line, the capital was at Nāsik. In the middle of the eighth century Dantidurga, a member of the ancient Rāshtrakūta family, overthrew Kīrttivarman II, Chālukya, extinguished the main branch of the western Chālukyas, and seized the sovereignty of the Deccan, which was held by his successors for two centuries and a quarter. In 973 Kakka II, the last of the Rāshtrakūta kings, was overthrown by Taila II, a descendant of the Chālukyan stock who had his capital at Kaliyāni, now a town in the Bīdar District of the Hyderābād State. Taila II was not able at once to establish his authority in the northern provinces of the kingdom which had been ruled by the Rāshtrakūtas, and during his earlier wars with Vākpati II, Munja, the Paramāra rājā of Mālwā, the Godāvari formed the boundary between the kingdoms of Mālwā and the Deccan, and Berār belonged to the former kingdom; but about 995 Taila defeated and captured the rājā of Mālwā and Berār was brought once more under the sway of the Chālukyas. In the latter half of the twelfth century the power of the Chālukyas was broken by rebellions and towards the end of the century the greater part of their dominions was seized by the Yādavas of Deogiri on the north and the Hoysalas of Dvārasamudra on the south. Berār seems from Baranī's and Firishta's accounts of Alā-ud-dīn Khiljī's raid into the Deccan, to have been the northern province of the Deogiri kingdom, and it appears that Ellichpur, which Baranī calls 'one of the famous cities of the Deccan,' was even then the provincial capital.

The Yādavas of Deogiri.

30. The founder of the Yādava dynasty was Bhillama, a feudatory noble of the Chālukya kingdom who was killed in battle by the Hoysala Tribhuvanamalla Vīra Ballāla II in 1191. Singhana, the third prince of the line, who reigned from 1210 to 1247, established a kingdom which, during his reign and that of his grandson Krishna, rivalled in extent the realms of the Chālukyas and Rāshtrakūtas. The brother and successor of Krishna, Mahādeva Ugrasārvabhauma, who reigned from

1260 to 1271, had a Brāhman councillor, Hemādri, the Hemād Pant to whom are attributed the old Hindu temples of Berār built in the Chālukyan, locally known as the *Hemādpanthi*, style. Hemādri had a protégé, Bopadeva, the son of Keshava, one of the few literary characters whom Berār has produced. He was the author of the *Harilīlā*, the *Satashlokī*, and the *Muktāphala*, a work on Vaishnava doctrines. The grammatical treatise *Mugdhabodha* is also attributed to him. Mahādeva was succeeded by his nephew Rāmchandra, styled Rāmdeo by Muhammadan historians, the last independent rājā of Deogiri.

Muhammadan period. Invasion of the Deccan.

31. In 1294 Alā-ud-dīn, governor of the province of which Kara on the Ganges, 42 miles north-west of Allahābād, was the capital, and nephew and son-in-law of Jalāl ud-dīn Fīroz Shāh Khiljī, the reigning emperor of Delhi, having assembled an army ostensibly for the purpose of punishing a refractory Hindu chief on the borders of his province, suddenly invaded the Deccan without the knowledge or consent of his uncle. His objective was Deogiri, of the wealth of which kingdom he had heard in the course of his forays in Central India. He marched from Kara to Chanderī, and thence across the Sātpurās to Ellichpur, where he halted for two days, explaining his presence by saying that he was one Malik Alā-ud-dīn who had been one of the nobles of the emperor of Delhi, but was now leaving his master with the intention of taking service with the rājā of Rājamahendrī in Telingāna. His story served its purpose and he was not molested at Ellichpur, which he left suddenly at midnight, advancing by forced marches towards Deogiri. It is unnecessary to recount the details of his successful raid. Alā-ud-dīn not only carried off from Deogiri an enormous quantity of plunder, but was strong enough to insist on the assignment of the revenues of Ellichpur and the districts attached thereto, which probably included the whole of the Amraoti District and the rest of northern Berār. Annexation was not attempted, nor were Muhammadans introduced into the administration. Treasure was all that Alā-ud-dīn required

for his immediate needs, and this the adventurer obtained in plenty.

Alā-ud-dīn ascends the throne.

32. Alā-ud-dīn on his return murdered his uncle and ascended the throne of Delhi early in 1296. During his reign Berār was traversed by Muhammadan armies from Delhi marching on expeditions to the Deccan, but we find no special mention of the Province. In 1302 or 1306, according to one account, an expedition under the African Kāfūr Hazārdināri was sent against Deogiri in consequence of Rāmchandra having failed to remit tribute and having allied himself with Rai Karan of Gujarāt, who had refused to send his daughter Deval Devī to Delhi. Rāmchandra and his family were captured and sent to Delhi, but the emperor pardoned him and restored him to his throne, and it does not appear that the arrangement under which Ellichpur and northern Berār remained under Hindu administrators charged with the remission of the revenue to Delhi was disturbed.

Rāmchandra died in 1309 and was succeeded by his eldest son Shankar, who rebelled against Delhi and refused to remit the tribute. In 1312 Kāfūr, now entitled Malik Naib, led an expedition to Deogiri, defeated and slew Shankar, and annexed his kingdom, including Berār, to the empire. The Amraoti District thus came for the first time directly under Muhammadan administration.

Rebellion in Deogiri.

33. Alā-ud-dīn Khiljī died at the end of 1316, and in the confusion which followed his death and the subsequent assassination of Malik Naib, Harpāl, the son-in-law of Rāmchandra, seized Deogiri and ruled it for a short time as an independent king, bringing Berār once again under Hindū rule, but by 1318 affairs at Delhi had been settled and Kutb-ud-dīn Mubārak Shāh, who was then on the throne, marched southwards, attacked Harpāl, captured him and caused him to be flayed, and placed his head above one of the gates of Deogiri. Amraoti thus passed again, with the rest of Berār, into the hands of the Musalmāns, and the province remained nominally under Muhammadan rule and

administration until it was assigned under the treaty of 1853 to the East India Company.

Malik Yaklakī was appointed governor of the reconquered provinces and shortly afterwards rebelled. We are not told what part the officers in Berār took in the rebellion, which was suppressed.

Tughlak Shāh.

34. Kutb-ud-dīn Mubārak Shāh was assassinated in 1321 and the usurper who ascended his throne was defeated and slain before the end of that year by Ghāzi Beg Tughlak, the Turkī governor of the Punjab, who was raised to the imperial throne under the title of Ghiyās-ud-dīn Tughlak Shāh. The expeditions to the Deccan in his reign are not directly connected with the history of Berār, but the resources of the province were doubtless taxed in the effort to furnish supplies for the armies from Delhi. Tughlak died in 1325 and was succeeded by his son, Muhammad bin Tughlak, who in 1339 transferred the capital of the empire from Delhi to Deogiri, which he renamed Daulatābād. It is likely that the importance of Berār, which now adjoined the District in which the capital of the empire was situated, was temporarily enhanced by this change, but Daulatābād did not long remain the capital.

Organization of the provinces of the Deccan.

35. Mahārāshtra was now divided into four *shikks* or provinces, and though the limits of these are not mentioned, it is probable that they corresponded roughly with the four *tarafs* or provinces into which the Bahmanī kingdom was afterwards divided, and that Berār, with its capital at Ellichpur, formed one of them. The land revenue of the whole tract was assessed at seven crores of 'white *tankas*' of 175 grains each, or about £3,500,000. This assessement seems to have been excessive, for we read that the action of the *shikkdārs* or provincial governors in collecting it caused widespread discontent and a partial depopulation of the country. The *shikkdārs* were Malik Sardawātdār, Malik Mukhlis-ul-Mulk Yūsuf Bughrā, and Aziz Himār or Khammār, but the names of their provinces are not given. All were subordinate to Kutlugh Khān, Governor of Daulatābād, whose deputy was

Imād-ul-Mulk, but Kutlugh Khān was recalled very soon after his settlement had been made, and it was then that the oppression of the *shikkdārs* became unbearable. Immediately subordinate to these *shikkdārs* was a class of officials styled centurions, military officers who also performed such civil duties as the collection of the revenue, the prevention and detection of crime, and the maintenance of order.

Rebellion of the *amīrs* of the Deccan.

36. In 1347 Muhammad bin Tughlak marched to Gujarāt to quell a rebellion which had broken out among the centurions of that Province and, having quieted Gujarāt, summoned the centurions of the Deccan, intending to replace those of Gujarāt with them but the officers of the Deccan whose loyalty was not above suspicion feared that they were being called to punishment, and when they had travelled one day's march towards Bahroch, where they had been ordered to assemble, they slew the officers who had been sent to summon them and returned to Daulatābād. Here they rose in rebellion and elected Ismail Fateh the Afghān, king of the Deccan, with the title of Nasīr-ud-dīn[1] Shāh. This news at once brought Muhammnd bin Tughlak from Bahroch to Daulatābād. He defeated the rebels in the field, but the new king took refuge in the fort and Muhammad was unable to capture the place and news soon arrived that rebellion had broken out afresh in Gujarāt, which compelled him to return thither, leaving an army to besiege Daulatābād. This army was defeated and the *amīrs* of the Deccan, on Nasīr-ud-dīn abdicating, elected as their king, Hasan, styled Zafar Khān, who ascended the throne as Alā-ud-dīn Bahman Shāh[2] in 1347.

The Bahmanīs.

37. Bahman Shāh, the founder of the Bahmanī dynasty of the Deccan, which reigned in fact until 1482 and in name until 1526, divided his kingdom into four *tarafs* or provinces, each under the governorship of a *tarafdār* or provincial governor. The provinces

---

[1] So styled by Firishta, Badaoni and the author of the *Burhān-i Maāsir* call him Nasīr-ud-dīn.

2. This was his correct title, as a contemporary inscription and legend on coins show. The fantastic epithets bestowed on him by various historians are connected with foolish stories.

were Berār, Daulatābād, Bīdar, and Gulbargā. We have, unfortunately, very little information as to the details of provincial administration, but it is known that the powers of the *tarafdārs* were very extensive. The *tarafdārs* of Berār, whose headquarters were at Ellichpur, governed a tract of country far larger than the modern province. Its southern boundary was the Godāvari and its western boundary extended beyond Baitālwādi. In this large province the governor was almost independent. He commanded the provincial army, collected the revenues, and made all appointments, both civil and military, including appointments to the command of forts, which were among the most important of all. His duties to the central authority seem to have been confined to the regular remission of a proportion of the revenue and to attending on his sovereign with the army of the province, whenever he might be called upon to do so. We know little or nothing of the administrative divisions of Berār in these early days, but it was probably divided into two principal divisions, one on the north, with its capital at Ellichpur and one on the south with its capital at Māhur. The existing parganas date, almost certainly, from the period of Hindu rule, and the *sardārs* described in the Ain-i-Akbari were perhaps a legacy from the days of the Bahmanids.

Muhammad Shāh Bahmanī, who succeeded his father in 1358, elaborated the organization of the four *tarafs* and gave to each *tarafdār* a distinctive title, the governor of Berār being styled *Majlis-i-Ālī*.

Safdar Khān, governor of Berār.

38. The first governor of Berār under the Bahmanids was a Persian, Safdar Khān Sīstāni. In 1362 he commanded the army of the province in Muhammad Shāh's expedition into Telingāna and was absent from Berār on this occasion for two years. In 1366, while Muhammad Shāh was waging war against Vijayanagar, Bahrām Khān Māzandarāni, deputy governor of Daulatābād, broke into rebellion at the instigation of Kondba Deo, a Marāthā, and several of the nobles of Berār, who were related to Bahrām Khān, were involved in the rebellion with him. The rebellion was suppressed and its

leaders made good their escape into Gujarāt. At this time highway robbery seems to have been rife in the Deccan, for Muhammad Shāh found it necessary to issue special orders to the *tarafdārs* for the suppression of the crime. The remedy was drastic. The malefactors were beheaded and their heads were sent to the capital. Twenty thousand heads were thus collected at Gulbargā, and we may presume that Safdar Khān sent his share.

The provinces were not neglected in the reign of Muhammad I, who toured in one of them every year unless occupied in war, and hunted for three or four months. This information may appear trifling, but it enables us to understand to some extent how Berār was governed in former days and how it was that a kingdom organized as was that of the Bahmanids did not fall to pieces sooner than it did.

Mujāhid Shāh.

39. Muhammad I died in 1375 and was succeeded by his son, Mujāhid Shāh, who made war against Bukka I of Vijayanagar. Safdar Khān was summoned to the capital with the army of Berār and was sent to besiege Adonī. The Hindus were vanquished before this fortress fell and the siege was relinquished. Mujāhid Shāh returned slowly through the Raichūr Doāb, hunting as he went, and Safdar Khān and the governor of Bīdar, knowing his rash and impetuous disposition, exerted themselves to restrain him from running needless risks in his sport. The king wearied of their good advice and, much against their will, ordered them to return to their provinces. The two governors pursued their way slowly and unwillingly, and shortly after their departure Mujāhid was assassinated, on April 17th, 1387, at the instigation of his uncle, Dāud, whom he had offended during the campaign against the Hindus. Dāud hastened to Gulbargā in order to ascend the throne, but Safdar Khān and the governor of Bīdar refused to attend him there and turned aside to Bījāpur, where the royal elephants were. They seized these, divided them between them, and returned to their provinces with them. Dāud Shāh

was assassinated on May 21st, 1378, and was succeeded by his nephew, Muhammad[1] Shāh II.

On the accession of Muhammad II, Safdar Khān and the governor of Bīdar made their submission and hastened to the capital to offer him their congratulations. Early in this reign there was a severe famine in Berār and the Deccan. A school for famine orphans was established at Ellichpur, where the children were brought up in the Muhammadan faith, and special allowances were given in all towns to religious teachers and to the blind.

Salābat Khān, governor of Berār. War with Kherlā.

40. Muhammad II died on April 22nd, 1397, and was succeeded by his elder son, Ghiyās-ud-dīn, who was 17 years of age. In his reign Safdar Khān Sīstāni, the governor of Berār, died in Ellichpur. His son, Salābat Khān, who had been a playfellow of the young king, was appointed governor of Berār in his father's place, with the title of *Majlis-i-Alī*. On June 16th, 1397, Ghiyās-ud-dīn was blinded and deposed, and his brother Shams-ud-dīn was placed on the throne. He, however, was deposed and imprisoned at the end of the year and was succeeded by his cousin, Tāj-ud-dīn Fīroz Shāh. The army of Berār, under Salābat Khān, took part in Fīroz Shāh's campaign against Harihara II of Vijayanagar in 1398-99. The campaign was eminently successful and Fīroz Shāh on his return left Pūlād Khān, another son of Safdar Khān Sīstāni, in charge of the Raichūr Doāb. But on this occasion the absence of the governor from Berār produced disastrous results, for Narsingh Deo, the Gond Rājā of Kherlā, had overrun the province from north to south and occupied it. Fīroz Shāh hastened northwards and, after recapturing Māhur, pressed on towards Kherlā by way of Ellichpur. Here he halted and sent on an army under the command of his brother Ahmad Khān, the Khān-i-Khānān, to punish the Gonds. Ahmad advanced to within a short distance of Kherlā and was met by

[1] Most English writers, in deference to Firishta, who is obstinately mistaken as to this king's name, style him Mahmūd, in spite of the evidence of coins, inscriptions, and other historians. Mahmūd was his father's name.—*Vide Journal of the Asiatic Society of Bengal*, Vol. LXXIII, Part I.

the Gond troops under Narsingh Deo. The Gonds fought with great determination and broke the centre of the Musalmāns, slaying Shujāt Khān, Rustam Khān, and Dilāwar Khān. The right under the command of Ahmad Khān, and the left under the command of Mīr Fazl-ullah Anjū Shīrāzi still stood fast. Fazl-ullah was told that Ahmad Khān had fallen, but wisely forbade his informant to circulate the rumour, which turned out to be false. He then caused it to be proclaimed that Fīroz Shāh had come in person to the relief of his troops and caused the great drums to be beaten. The scattered forces of the Muslims rallied to the sound and Mīr Fazl-ullah and Ahmad Khān managed to join forces and to attack the enemy. Gopāl Rai, the son of Narsingh Deo, was taken prisoner, and the Gonds were pursued with great slaughter to the gates of Kherlā, whither Narsingh Deo arrived only just in time to save his life. Ahmad Khān and Fazl-ullah then besieged the fortress and after the lapse of two months the Gonds offered to surrender on conditions. The Muhammadan generals replied that they had no power to offer terms, and that if Narsingh Deo desired to obtain them it was necessary that he and his chief nobles should make their submission to Fīroz Shāh in Ellichpur, to which place they were offered a safe conduct. This advice was followed, and the rājā swore at the foot-stool of Fīroz in Ellichpur that he and his successors would be faithful liegemen of the Bahmanids as their predecessor had been in the days of Bahman Shāh. Narsingh Deo was dismissed with honour after paying tribute and presenting to the Sultān a daughter who was received into the *zanāna*.

The names of the Muhammadan nobles killed at the battle of Kherlā are worthy of attention for, as we have seen, they probably provided the apocryphal Abdur Rahmān with a local habitation and a name. They were four in number and it appears probable that the requisite tale of five was completed by Salābat Khān, the governor of Berār, for no more is heard of this *tarafdār*, and Fīroz Shāh, immediately before he left Ellichpur for Gulbargā, appointed he gallant Mīr Fazl-ullah Anjū governor of Berār.

Wars with Vijayanagar and Gondwāna.

41. In 1406 Fīroz Shāh was at war with Vijayanagar and the army of Berār under Fazl-ullah was employed in the siege of Bankāpur. The expedition was successful, Bankāpur, with the country surrounding it, was annexed to the Bahmanī dominions, and Fazl-ullah and his army returned to Berār. In 1412 Fīroz Shāh indulged in an apparently purposeless campaign in Gondwāna in which the army of Berār probably took the principal part.

In 1417 Fīroz embarked on a disastrous war against Vīra Vijaya of Vijayanagar. Mīr Fazl-ullah Anjū who, with the army of Berār, played the man in the decisive battle of the campaign, in which the Muslīms were defeated, was treacherously slain by a Kanarese attendant who had been bribed by his co-religionists. The affairs of the kingdom fell into great confusion and nobody was immediately appointed to succeed the gallant *tarafdār* of Berār, but the government of the province was probably carried on by the deputy whom Fazl-ullah had left behind him when he set out on the fatal expedition.

The Khān-i-Jahān appointed governor of Berār.

42. In 1422 Ahmad Khān deposed his brother Fīroz Shāh and ascended the throne in Gulbargā as Ahmad Shāh I. His first care was to bring the war with the Hindus to a successful conclusion, and in the attainment of this object he laid waste the territories of Vijayanagar. After one of his actions he was separated from his army while hunting and nearly fell into the hands of a band of resolute Hindu warriors, but was rescued by Abdul Kādir, a commander of 200 horse and captain of the guard, whose soldierly precautions averted the disaster which Ahmad's foolish behaviour courted. Abdul Kādir's reward was the vacant governorship of Berār with the title of Khān-i-Jahān in addition to the *ex-officio* title of *Majlis-i-Alī*. Abdul Kādir, who held the governorship of Berār for nearly forty years, was the son of Muhammad Isā, the son of Mahmūd, the son of a Turk named Malik Hindūī who received the title of Imād-ul-Mulk from Bahman Shāh, and held under that king

the appointment of inspector-general of the forces. The Khān-i-Jahān was thus a Deccani of Turkī descent.

Ahmad Shāh made peace with Vīra Vijaya and then set out to capture Warangal, which fell into the hands of Abdul Latīf Khān i-Azam, the governor of Bīdar. The king then returned to his capital.

Ahmad Shāh vis ts Ellichpur.

43. In the confusion which followed on the rout of the Muslims at Pāngul affairs in the provinces of the kingdom had fallen into great disorder and the Hindus of the greater part of Berār seem to have risen in rebellion. In 1425 Ahmad Shāh was compelled to march northwards to restore order. After capturing Māhur and Kalam, which had fallen into the hands of the Gonds or Hindus, he marched to Ellichpur, where he halted for a year. His object in making this long halt in the capital of his northern province is said to have been the preparation for the extension of his kingdom towards the north. His brother Fīroz Shāh had sent a complimentary letter with expressions of submission by Mīr Fazl-ullah Anjū to Amīr Tīmur when that scourge invaded India in 1398 and the conqueror acknowledged the letter by bestowing on Fīroz the sovereignty of Gujarāt and Mālwā in addition to that of the Deccan, and Firishta supposes that Ahmad now purposed, if possible, to turn this empty grant to some account. The theory is a most improbable one. Ahmad Shāh, as we shall see, had conscientious scruples against attacking brother Muslims, and to the south of his kingdom lay an unconquered Hindu empire which was both lawful prey and a source of danger in the case of difficulties in the north, and he had very little chance of success against the combined forces of Gujarāt and Mālwā, which would certainly have been joined by Khāndesh. The more reasonable view is that Ahmad was merely strengthening his northern frontier in order to prevent inroads during his southern wars, and to this end he built the fort of Gāwīl and repaired that of Narnāla. These expressions, which are Firishta's, seem to imply that Narnāla was the older fort of the two, but they need not be taken too literally, for

Gāwīlgarh was probably fortified long before the time of Ahmad Shāh. Its name points to its having been at one time like Gaolīgarh in Khāndesh and Asīrgarh (Asā Ahīr Garh), the stronghold of a local Gaolī chieftain before the advent of the Musalmāns. Whatever Ahmad's object may have been Hoshang Shāh of Mālwā disapproved of his preparations, and invited Narsingh Deo of Kherlā, who had been reduced to vassalage by Fīroz, to transfer his allegiance to Mālwā. Narsingh Deo refused to listen to Hoshang who, after consulting Nasīr Khān of Khāndesh, without whose acquiescence he could not afford to act, twice attacked Kherlā and was twice defeated. Ahmad Shāh rendered no material assistance to his vassal and Hoshang's third attempt on Kherlā was more successful. His officers wrested some districts from the Gonds and Hoshang prepared to follow up this advantage by marching on Kherlā in person. Narsingh Deo considered that it was high time to appeal to his suzerain and in 1428 sent messengers to Ahmad Shāh, who had returned to his capital, to ask for help. Ahmad Shāh ordered the Khān-i-Jahān to march to the assistance of Narsingh Deo with the army of Berār and marched northwards in leisurely fashion, as though bent only on sport, until he reached Ellichpur. Meanwhile Hoshang, attributing Ahmad's comparative inaction to fear, advanced on Kherlā and after ravaging the country, sat down to besiege the fortress, boasting that Ahmad Shāh Bahmanī was afraid to meet him in the field. Ahmad Shāh was much incensed when he heard of Hoshang's boast, and at once set forth from Ellichpur to encounter him. While he was yet forty miles distant from Hoshang's army the doctors of religion in his camp approached him, reminded him that no Bahmanid had ever yet declared war on a Muhammadan king and advised him that it ill became him to attack Hoshang in support of an infidel. Following their advice Ahmad Shāh sent an envoy to Hoshang apprising him that Narsingh Deo was a vassal of Gulbargā and requesting him not to molest him. After the despatch of the envoy Ahmad Shāh began to retire and this retrograde movement combined with his spiritless policy confirmed

Hoshang in the belief that Ahmad feared him, and emboldened him to pursue the Deccanis so closely that he halted each evening on the ground which they had occupied in the morning. This insolence transgressed the bounds of even the pious Ahmad's forbearance, and when Hoshang crossed the frontier the doctors of religion were sent away from Ahmad's camp and the Deccanis instead of pursuing their way halted to receive the invaders who advanced without any apprehension of resistance. Ahmad Shāh drew up his forces on the bank of a river, unfortunately not named. The governor of Berār commanded the right wing, Abdullah Khān, a grandson of Ismail Fateh, the left, and Alā-ud-dīn Ahmad, the king's eldest son, the centre. Ahmad Shāh himself, with 2,000 picked cavalry and twelve elephants, lay in ambush far to the left. Hoshang. with no more than 17,000 cavalry, suddenly came upon the Deccanis in a carefully chosen position. He had no choice but to attack them and did so, and while action was at its height Ahmad Shāh suddenly fell upon Hoshang's rear, The army of Mālwā was routed and Hoshang Shāh fled so precipitately that he left the ladies of his harem in Ahmad's hands. Meanwhile Narsingh Deo had heard of his enemy's disaster and, emerging from Kherlā, fell upon the beaten army and completed the heavy tale of slaughter, while Hoshang and the remnant of his forces made the best of their way to Māndū. The loss suffered by Musalmāns at the hands of an unbeliever again aroused Ahmad Shāh's scruples and to console his adversary he returned his ladies to him under a trusty guard, accompanied by a present of many eunuchs. Ahmad then returned to Gulbargā. A less probable account of this campaign represents Ahmad Shāh as the aggressor. According to this account he was preparing to attack Narsingh Deo when Hoshang Shāh marched to the latter's aid. Whichever version be accepted Ahmad Shāh was victorious. He left Berār in 1429 and in the same year transferred his capital from Gulbargā to Bīdar.

War with Gujarāt and Mālwā.

44. In 1430, the daughter of Nasīr Khān, the ruler of Khāndesh, was married to Alā-ud-dīn Ahmad, the eldest son of Ahmad Shāh. The marriage is of local interest for it after-

wards led to a war between Alā-ud-dīn Ahmad and his father-in-law. In the same year Khalaf Hasan Basrī, entitled Malik-ut-Tujjār, who had been one of Ahmad Shāh's earliest partisans, was made governor of Daulatābād. Here his zeal in his master's service brought on a war between Ahmad Shāh of the Deccan and Ahmad Shāh of Gujarāt which lasted for a year and exhausted both sides. In 1433 Hoshang Shāh of Mālwā, taking advantage of the enfeebled condition of the Deccan. attacked and annexed Kherlā, slaying Narsingh Deo. Ahmad Shāh marched into Berār and was on the point of attacking Hoshang when Nasīr Khān of Khāndesh intervened and proposed terms of peace which were accepted by both sides. These terms were that Hoshang Shāh should return to Kherlā and that Berār should remain a part of Ahmad Shāh's dominions. The acceptance of these terms by Ahmad Shāh indicates the extent to which he had been weakened by the war with Gujarāt, for it would have been unnecessary to introduce into the treaty the article relating to Berār unless Hoshang Shāh had been prepared, with some hope of success, to attempt its annexation, and Ahmad Shāh actually gave up all that he was prepared to fight for.

War with Khāndesh.

45. Ahmad Shāh I died in 1435 and was succeeded by his eldest son, Alā-ud-dīn Ahmad Shāh II, who had married the daughter of Nasīr Khān. This lady, in a fit of jealousy, complained to her father that her husband was neglecting her for a Hindu mistress, and Nasīr Khān prepared to invade his son-in-law's dominions. Having obtained the assent of Ahmad Shāh of Gujarāt to his enterprise he began to prepare his way by detaching the nobles of Berār from their allegiance to the Bahmanī king. Nasīr Khān claimed descent from the second *Khalīfa*, Umar-ul-Fārūk, and succeeded in persuading many of the officers in Berār that the one who fell fighting in the cause of the descendants of the greatest of the prophet's successors would receive the reward promised to martyrs for the faith. It is not easy to understand how the officers of Berār were deceived for Nasīr Khān allied himself with infidel Gonds and probably with the Korkūs of the Melghāt also, but many fell into the trap and

formed a strong party in Berār against the Bahmanī king. The campaign did not take place in the Amraoti District but in Buldāna and Khāndesh, whither Nasīr Khān was driven, and ended in the complete discomfiture of the invaders, but before engaging Nasīr Khān, Khalaf Hasan Basrī found it necessary to strengthen the garrison of Ellichpur, in order to prevent the Korkūs from descending on the plains.

War with Vijayanagar.

46. In 1443 the army of Berār was employed, with the armies of the other provinces of the kingdom, in driving Devarāya II of Vijayanagar out of the Raichūr Doāb, which he had occupied, but Berār does not seem to have been settled enough to spare its governor for this expedition, for the Khān-i-Jahān did not accompany the army.

Invasion of the Deccan by Mahmūd of Mālwā.

47. Alā-ud-dīn Ahmad II died in 1458 and was succeeded by his son Humāyūn "the Tyrant" who had hardly ascended the throne when Jalāl Khān and Sikandar Khān, two nobles who had rebelled in the previous reign, again rose. The governor of Berār who had visited the capital for the purpose of offering his congratulations to the new king was employed against the rebels, but was defeated, and the rising was ultimately suppressed by Humāyūn. We hear no more of Berār during this brief and troubled reign. Humāyūn Shāh died in 1461 and was succeeded by his son Nizām Shāh, aged eight. In 1462 Mahmūd Shāh of Mālwā, taking advantage of the new king's youth, invaded the Deccan by way of western Berār. The army of Bīdar was employed in keeping off the rājās of Telingāna and Orissa, who had invaded the Bahmanī dominions on the east, and the armies of Berār, Daulatābād and Gulbargā marched to meet Mahmūd Shāh. A battle was fought at Kandahār about seventy miles north of Bīdar, and the Bahmanī forces were defeated, Nizām Shāh was carried off by his mother to Fīrozābād near Gulbargā while Mahmūd Shāh of Mālwā sacked Bīdar. He had begun to lay siege to the citadel when he heard that Mahmūd Shāh of Gujarāt, to whom Nizām Shāh's mother had appealed for help, had reached the north-western frontier of the Bahmanī kingdom

with 80,000 horse. Mahmūd Gāwān, one of the chief nobles of the Bahmanī kingdom, joined the Gujarātis with five or six thousand cavalry, and continued to raise and borrow troops until he was able to take the field with an army of 40,000 Deccani and Gujarāti horse. He sent 10,000 Deccani horse into Berār to cut off the invader's retreat and marched towards Bīdar with the remainder of his force. Encamping between Bīr and Kandahār he cut off the besiegers' supplies but would not risk a battle, though Mahmūd Shāh of Mālwā could not put more than 30,000 horse into the field. At length the army of Mālwā was starved out and Mahmūd Shāh of Mālwā, after blinding his elephants and burning his heavy baggage, retreated northwards through eastern Berār. He was pursued and harassed throughout his retreat by Mahmūd Gāwān and the ten thousand horse which had been awaiting him in Berār. In order to avoid Mahmūd Gāwān on the one hand and escape Mahmūd Shāh of Gujarāt on the other, he resolved to retreat through the hills of the Melghāt and engaged one of the Korkū rājās of that tract as a guide. After leading him by Ellichpur and Akot the rājā took him into the hills and there intentionally led him astray. In the Melghāt the army of Mālwā perished by the thousand from heat and thirst and by the attacks of the Korkūs, who were instigated by their rājā. When the remnant of the army at length emerged from the wild hill country, Mahmūd Shāh of Mālwā had the Korkū rājā put to death.

In the following year Mahmūd of Mālwā again invaded the Bahmanī dominions and advanced as far as Daulatābād, but retreated on hearing that Mahmūd of Gujarāt was again marching to the support of the Deccanis.

Nizām Shāh died in 1463 and was succeeded by his brother Muhammad III, surnamed *Lashkari* or "the soldier."

War with Kherlā.

48. In 1467 Nizām-ul-Mulk the Turk, who had commanded the left wing in the battle of Kandahār against Mahmūd Shāh of Mālwā, was appointed governor of Berār and was ordered to capture Kherlā, where a Gond prince still owed allegiance to Mālwā.

The army of Berār marched against Kherlā and besieged it and the army of Mālwā, in an attempt to raise the siege, was signally defeated. Kherlā fell, but two Rājputs of the place approached Nizām-ul-Mulk under the pretence of making their submission to him and assassinated him. They then attacked his attendants and were put to death. The two officers next in authority to Nizām-ul-Mulk were Yūsuf Adil Khān[1], afterwards the founder of the Adil Shāhi dynasty of Bījāpur, and Daryā Khān the Turk. These nobles argued that the desperate enterprise of the two Rājputs could not have been undertaken otherwise than at the instigation of some of the inhabitants of Kherlā and a massacre of these unfortunates, with their wives and children, followed. Yūsuf and Daryā left a force to hold Kherlā and returned to Bīdar with the body of their late leader. Muhammad Shāh approved of their action and bestowed Kherlā upon them in jāgīr. Mahmūd Shāh of Mālwā now sent an embassy to Muhammad Shāh and reminded him of the treaty between Ahmad Shāh Bahmanī and Hoshang Shāh of Mālwā, in which it was stipulated that Kherlā should belong to Mālwā and Berār to the Bahmanids. He besought Muhammad Shāh not to be a breaker of treaties, or the means of stirring up strife between Musalmāns. Muhammad Shāh returned to him a dignified reply by Shaikh Ahmad the *Sadr*, and Sharīf-ul-Mulk. He thanked God that no one of the race of Bahman had ever been known to break a treaty and reminded Mahmūd Shāh that when the affairs of the Bahmanī kingdom were in confusion after the accession of the boy-king Nizām Shāh it was Mahmūd himself who had broken faith by invading the Bahmanī dominions. As for Kherlā, he said, he had no need of such fortresses. In every corner of the empire of Karnāta, which was still in the hands of the infidels, there were many fortresses like Kherlā, and since these were ready to his hand he had no wish to deprive a brother Musalmān of his fortresses. A new treaty was concluded whereby either sovereign bound himself

[1] There is some conflict of authorities here. Some historians give the name of Yūsuf Adil Khān the Deccani, a much less distinguished person, but a bitter enemy of Yūsuf Adil Khān *Sawai*, as he was called. On the whole the account given in the text is the more probable.

by the most solemn oaths not to molest or invade the dominions of the other, and Kherlā, which had been annexed to Berār, was handed back by Muhammad Shāh to the king of Mālwā.

Fateh-ullah Imād-ul-Mulk.

49. The governorship of Berār seems to have remained vacant for a few years after the death of Niz-āmul-Mulk the Turk until, in 1471, Fateh-ullah Imād-ul-Mulk was made governor. This *amīr* is worthy of special notice, for he founded the Imād Shāhi dynasty, which reigned in Berār for a period of eighty years. He was a Brāhman of Vijayanagar who was captured by the Musalmāns in 1422 early in the reign of Ahmad Shāh I, and was bestowed on the Khān-i-Jahān, who was appointed governor of Berār immediately after the conclusion of the campaign, and was brought up as a Musalmān, but never forgot his Brāhman descent or his native land. More than sixty years after his capture when, as governor of Berār, he strengthened the fortifications of Gāwīlgarh, he adorned the northern gate, afterwards known as the Delhi gate, with representations of the emblem of Vijayanagar, the *ganda-bherunda*, a fabulous two-headed bird which was said to prey upon elephants, and these representations still remain, almost as clearly cut as when Fateh-ullah set them up as his boast that though a Musalmān and the faithful servant of a Musalmān he was by blood a twice born Brāhman and a native of the great Hindu empire of Vijayanagar. Fateh-ullah had spent all his service, if we except temporary periods of absence in the field, in Berār and was a very fair instance of the strength and the weakness of the provincial system of the Bahmanī kingdom. He seems to have been sincerely attached to the province, despite his pride of race and descent, and to have been at the same time a faithful servant of the Bahmanids. In his later years, when troubles gathered thick and fast around the head of the descendant of Bahman Shāh and when the provincial governors were driven rather than tempted to rebellion, he was regarded as the Nestor of the Deccan, and his entire freedom from party prejudice was displayed in his grief and anger at the unjust execution of Mahmūd Gāwān, a foreigner, and in his unwaver-

Bemrose, Collo., Derby.

LARGE DARWAZA, GAWILGARH.

ing friendship for Yūsuf Adil Khān Sawai another foreigner, who differed from him in religion, being a staunch Shiah while Fateh-ullah was an equally staunch Sunnī.

Berār suffered, with the rest of the Deccan, from the terrible two years of famine in 1473, and 1474, and most of those who escaped death from starvation fled to Mālwā and Gujarāt. In the third year rain fell, but prosperity was slow to return, for there were few left to till the soil and the wanderers returned by slow degrees.

Redistribution of provinces.

50. In the campaigns of Muhammad III in Orissa, Telingāna, and the Peninsula, Fateh-ullah, with the army of Berār, bore a share. In 1480, before these campaigns had been brought to a close, the four provinces into which the Deccan had been divided by Bahman Shāh were subdivided into eight. Berār was divided into the two new provinces of northern Berār, named Gāwīl, and southern Berār, named Māhur, the whole of the Amraoti District being included in the former, which remained under the governorship of Fateh-ullah Imād-ul-Mulk, while Khudāwand Khān the African was made governor of Māhur. At the same time the powers of the provincial governors were much curtailed. Many parganas of the provinces were made *khās* and were administered by officers appointed direct by the crown, while the governors were allowed to appoint a commandant only to the chief fort in each province, all other commandants of forts being appointed direct by the king. These belated reforms caused much dissatisfaction among some of the *tarafdārs*, but the faithful Fateh-ullah, though stripped of half his province, seems to have taken no exception to them. The malcontents, however, entered into a conspiracy against Mahmūd Gāwān, the author of the reforms, and compassed his death in 1481. Muhammad III who was their dupe discovered his minister's innocence when it was too late and bitterly repented his action. Fateh-ullah Imād-ul-Mulk and Khudāwand Khān, with the troops of Berār, left the royal camp and encamped at a distance of two leagues from it. When asked the reason of this move Fateh-ullah boldly replied that when so old and

faithful a servant as Mahmūd Gāwān could be murdered on the lying reports of false witnesses nobody within the king's reach was safe. The wretched king, now smitten with remorse, sent a secret message imploring them to return that he might take counsel with them regarding the punishment of those who had brought Khāja Mahmūd to his death, but Fateh-ullah and Khudāwand Khān replied that they would shape their conduct on that of Yūsuf Adil Khān, who was then absent on a distant expedition. Yūsuf was at once recalled and joined Fateh-ullah and Khudāwand Khān. The three *tarafdārs* then entered the royal camp and made their demands. They did not succeed in bringing the ringleaders of the conspiracy to punishment, but Yūsuf obtained the province of Bījāpur, which enabled him to make provision for the followers of the deceased minister. Shortly after this the *tarafdārs* were dismissed to their provinces.

Disaffection of the *tarafdārs* of Berār.

51. Fateh-ullah and Khudāwand Khān were recalled from Berār shortly afterwards in order that they might attend Muhammad III on a progress through the Province of Bījāpur. They obeyed the summons, but both on the march and in camp placed a distance between themselves and the royal camp, and saluted the king from afar when he marched. In this manner the armies reached Belgaum, whence the *tarafdārs* were ordered to accompany the king to Goa and the Konkan, which they refused to do. Yūsuf Adil Khān, however, marched to the aid of Goa, then besieged by Rājashekhara of Vijayanagar, while Muhammad III marched to Fīrozābād. Fateh-ullah and Khudāwand Khān refused to accompany him any further, and returned to Berār without leave. Muhammad felt their defection deeply, but dared not resent it, for he knew that their mistrust of him was justified, and that civil war would but hasten the disruption of his kingdom.

Accession of Mahmūd Shāh.

52. Muhammad Shāh died of drink on March 23rd, 1482, and was succeeded by his son Mahmūd Shāh, a boy of twelve ; all power in the capital was held by Malik Hasan Nizām-ul-Mulk, the principal enemy of the late Mahmūd Gāwān who

was now minister of the kingdom. Fateh-ullah Imād-ul-Mulk, on visiting the capital to congratulate the young king on his accession, was made titular minister of the kingdom, his son Shaikh Alā-ud-dīn being appointed his deputy in northern Berār, but the intrigues and massacres of the capital were not to the veteran's taste, and he returned to Ellichpur without having exercised the duties of his post at the capital.

Malik Hasan Nizām-ul-Mulk was assassinated before 1485 and affairs in Bīdar went from bad to worse. The young king showed a precocious bent towards debauchery and the administration passed into the hands of Kāsim Barīd, a Turk. The *tarafdārs*, well aware that all orders issued were the orders of Kāsim Barīd, ignored messages from the capital, and were practically independent, attending only occasionally with their armies when summoned to do so. This attendance only accentuated the humiliation of the nominal ruler, whose splendour was utterly eclipsed by that of the armaments which the *tarafdārs* brought into the field.

Fateh-ullah Imād-ul-Mulk independent.

53. In 1490 Malik Ahmad, the son of Malik Hasan Nizām-ul-Mulk, having founded Ahmadnagar and made preparations for securing his independence, invited Yūsuf Adil Khān of Bījāpur and Fateh-ullah Imād-ul-Mulk of Gāwīl to join him in assuming the style and insignia of royalty. The compact was sealed by the consent of each of these three provincial governors, and each had the *khutbā* read in the mosques of his kingdom in his own name, omitting that of Mahmūd Shāh Bahmanī. Henceforth these rulers will be known by the titles Yūsuf Adil Shāh, Ahmad Nizām Shāh, and Fateh-ullah Imād Shāh, though Yūsuf and Fateh-ullah appear to have been very chary of using the royal title.

The supremacy of Kāsim Barīd in the capital had, however, convinced Fateh-ullah of the necessity for some decisive step, and the veteran statesman had already prepared himself for possible opposition by improving the defences of Gāwīlgarh and Narnāla.

Although Fateh-ullah had declared himself independent he still regarded himself, to some extent, as a vassal of the

Bahmanī king. Thus, in 1494, when a rebel named Bahādur Gīlāni, who had established himself on the western coast of the Deccan, committed in Gujarāt excesses, which caused Mahmūd Shāh of that country to demand his punishment at the hands of Mahmūd Shāh Bahmanī, Fateh-ullah Imād Shāh, together with Yūsuf Adil Shāh and Ahmad Nizām Shāh, responded to his old master's appeal and aided him against the rebel, who was defeated and slain after a long and arduous campaign. But the aid thus rendered differed from the submissive attendance of the *tarafdārs* for the Sultāns did not attend in person but sent contingents.

Combination against Bījāpur.

54. In 1504 Yūsuf Adil Shāh, who was a Shiah, had the *khutbā* read in the mosques of the Bījāpur kingdom after the Shiah fashion, he being the first Muhammadan ruler in India to make this public profession of the Shiah faith. Amīr Barīd who had succeeded his father, Kāsim Barīd, in that same year sent notices in Mahmūd Shāh's name to Fateh-ullah Imād Shāh, Khudāwand Khān of Māhur, and Sultān Kulī Kutb-ul-Mulk, who had been appointed governor of Telingāna and had established himself at Golconda, asking them to combine to stamp out the heresy. The result of the appeal was curious. Sultān Kulī Kutb-ul-Mulk who was himself a devoted Shiah, responded to it at once, apparently on the ground that Yūsuf Adil Shāh's act was a more pronounced declaration of opposition to Bahmanī traditions than his mere assumption of independence, and possibly from the motive which led Innocent XI to advise James II to moderate his zeal for the propagation of Roman doctrine and practice in England. Fateh-ullah Imād Shāh, and Khudāwand Khān on the other hand, though both were professed Sunnīs, showed very clearly their disinclination to act against their old ally, and excused themselves. As to what followed there is a conflict of authority. Firishta says that Amīr Barīd was much perplexed by the contumacy of the two chiefs of Berār and applied to Ahmad Nizām Shāh for aid which was promptly rendered. Alī bin Aziz-ullah Tabātabāi, whose dates do not agree with those of Firishta,

though he is clearly referring to the same incident, writes that Mahmūd Shāh, on becoming aware of Fateh-ullah Imād Shāh's refusal to take the field against Yūsuf Adil Shāh, marched into Berār, whereupon Fateh-ullah, who was no more willing to take up arms against the Bahmanid than against Yūsuf, made his submission to him. Firishta's account is to be preferred, for he was, though sometimes misinformed, always impartial, whereas the author of the *Burhān-i-Maāsir* was an uncompromising partisan of the Nizām Shāhi kings and also, strangely enough, a strenuous supporter of the fiction that Mahmūd Shāh was as independent a king as any of his forefathers. Moreover, immediately after its account of these events, the *Burhān-i-Maāsir* goes wildly astray in its references to Fateh-ullah Imād Shāh and Yūsuf Adil Shāh. The following is the true account of what happened. Amīr Barīd with Mahmūd Shāh, Sultān Kulī Kutb-ul-Mulk, Ahmad Nizām Shāh, and Fakhr-ul-Mulk the Deccani marched against Yūsuf Adil Shāh, who, finding that his external foes and the Sunnīs in his own kingdom were too strong for him, left Fakhr-ul-Mulk the Turk to hold Gulbargā and the surrounding country, sent his infant son Ismail with Kamāl Khān the Deccani to Bījāpur, and made the best of his way, with 5,000 horse, to the territories of his old friend Fateh-ullah Imād Shāh, closely pursued by the allies who followed him almost to the gates of Gāwīlgarh. Fateh-ullah was again greatly perplexed. He would not give up the refugee, he would not fight for the Shiah religion, and in no circumstances would he draw the sword against the Bahmanī king. He therefore despatched Yūsuf Adil Shāh to Dāud Khān of Khāndesh, while he proceeded to make terms with the invaders of Berār. His methods are a fair example of the astuteness which he seems always to have brought into play in the interests of justice and toleration. He sent envoys to Ahmad Nizām Shāh and Sultān Kulī Kutb-ul-Mulk to apprise them of his view of the quarrel which was that Amīr Barīd, well known, he said, as 'the fox of the Deccan,' was not actuated in his persecution of Yūsuf Adil Shāh by religious scruples, but merely desired to gain possesion of Bījāpur. Should he attain his object, the old diplomatist added, the position of those who held the other provinces of the kingdom would not be enviable, for Amīr Barīd already held the Bahmanī king in the hollow of his hand and wanted but an addition to his territorial possessions to make him supreme in the Deccan. This entirely correct view of the situation impressed itself on Ahmad Nizām Shāh and Kutb-ul-Mulk, who at once returned to their provinces without even going through the form of bidding Mahmūd Shāh farewell. The Sultān of Berār was now free to deal with the Sultān of Bīdar. He represented to Mahmūd that there was nothing to be gained by prosecuting the war and that the wisest course was to proclaim that Yūsuf was pardoned and to return to Bīdar. Mahmūd Shāh was inclined to accept this counsel, but Amīr Barīd did not intend to let Bījāpur slip through his fingers so easily and was about to carry Mahmūd off to besiege Bīdar, but meanwhile Yūsuf Adil Shāh had heard of the retreat of Ahmad Nizām Shāh and Kutb-ul-Mulk and returned with all haste from Burhānpur to Gāwīlgarh. He now took the field against Mahmūd Shāh, or rather against Amīr Barīd, who, perceiving that he was no match for Yūsuf and Fateh-ullah in combination, hurriedly retreated to Bīdar, leaving Berār in peace.

Death of Fateh-ullah Imād Shāh.

55. The date of the death of Fateh-ullah Imād Shāh is variously given as 1504 and 1510. The latter seems to be a mistake. His age when he was taken from Vijayanagar in 1422 is not given, and we are merely told that he was then a boy. Assuming his age to have been ten years he must have been 82 years of age at the time of his death. Fateh-ullah was succeeded by his son Alā-ud-dīn Imād Shāh, of whom Firishta contradictorily says that he was the first of the dynasty to use the royal title. There can be little doubt that his father used it occasionally, certainly in his correspondence with Yūsuf Adil Shāh and Ahmad Nizām Shāh, to whom he would not have admitted himself to be inferior, but it is likely that he refrained from using it in correspondence with the Bahmanī king.

56. The early part of Alā-ud-dīn's reign is obscure. According to one authority he quietly succeeded his father, but according to another he was a prisoner in the fort of Rāmgiri, in Telingāna, at the time of his father's death, in the power of Amīr Barīd and remained in captivity until he was rescued by one of the sons of Khudāwand Khān of Māhur. On his release Alā-ud-dīn is said to have proceeded at once to Gāwīlgarh and to have assumed the government of his father's kingdom, while Mahmūd Shāh Bahmanī, at the request of Yūsuf Adil Shāh, conferred upon him his father's title of Imād-ul-Mulk. This story is improbable. In the first place the dates are all wrong, for Fateh-ullah is represented as having died before 1500, whereas he was certainly alive in 1504, and in the second place it is highly improbable that Fateh-ullah, who had, as we have seen, great power and influence in the Deccan would have left his son—his only son so far as we know—in the hands of his greatest enemy, 'the fox of the Deccan.' The more probable story is that which represents Alā-ud-dīn Imād Shāh as quietly succeeding his father in Ellichpur.

Alā-ud-dīn Imād Shāh.

57. In 1508 Burhān Nizām Shāh succeeded his father Ahmad in Ahmadnagar at the age of seven. The administration of that kingdom was in the hands of Mukammal Khān, who had been Ahmad's minister, and the Deccani nobles of the State, whose predominance was distasteful to the 'foreigners,' *i.e.*, the Persian and Turkī soldiers of fortune who always formed a political party of their own in the Deccan. The foreigners conspired to overthrow the Deccanis, and on the failure of their plot fled from Ahmadnagar with 8,000 horse and took refuge with Alā-ud-dīn Imād Shāh in Ellichpur. They found no difficulty in persuading him that the affairs of Ahmadnagar were in hopeless confusion and that the conquest of that kingdom would be an easy task. Alā-ud-dīn, without waiting to consider how far the interests of the fugitives had coloured their story, collected his troops from Gāwīlgarh and Ellichpur and marched for the frontier. Mukammal Khān was prepared and met him. After a severely con-

War with Ahmadnagar.

tested battle victory declared itself for Ahmadnagar, and Alā ud-dīn with the army of Berār fled to Ellichpur. The army of Ahmadnagar followed up its victory and laid waste the greater part of south-western Berār, pressing Alā-ud-dīn so hard that he deserted his country and fled to Burhānpur, where he besought Adil Khān III, the ruler of Khāndesh, to use his good offices in the cause of peace. Adil Khān of Khāndesh and his doctors of religion brought about a peace, but quarrels soon broke out afresh.

The affair of Pāthri.

58. Burhān Nizām Shāh's grandfather, Malik Hasan Nizām-ul-Mulk, was descended of a Brāhman family which had held the hereditary office of *kulkarni* or patwāri [1] in Pāthri, near the Godāvari river. For some reason or another, probably the proselytizing zeal of one of the Bahmanī kings, the ancestor of Hasan had fled from Pāthri and taken refuge in the Hindu kingdom of Ahmadnagar. Malik Hasan, whose original name was Tīma Bhat, had been captured, like Fateh-ullah Imād-ul-Mulk, in one of the campaigns against Vijayanagar, and brought up as a Muslim. When he attained to power, and the governorship of a province to the border of which his ancestral home was adjacent, his relatives flocked from Vijyanagar to Ahmadnagar and urged his son, Ahmad Nizām Shāh, to include in his dominions the town of Pāthri, which lay on the southern border of Berār. Mukammal Khān wrote, by command of Burhān Nizām Shāh, proposing that Alā-ud-dīn Imād Shāh should cede Pāthri to Ahmadnagar in exchange for a richer pargana. Alā-ud-dīn refused to listen to this proposal and began to fortify Pāthri. Mukammal Khān then complained that the establishment of a military post so close to the frontier would give rise to depredations on the part of the more lawless members of the garrison and consequent hostilities between Ahmadnagar and Berār. Alā-ud-dīn paid no heed to the protest, completed his fort and returned to Ellichpur. In 1518 Mukammal Khān, under the pretence that Burhān Nizām Shāh wished to enjoy the cool air

1. In this case probably the Despāndya *watan* of the pargana.

of the hills above Daulatābād and visit the caves of Ellora, collected a large army and marched in a leisurely way to Daulatābād, whence he made a sudden forced march on Pāthri. The town was taken by escalade and the army of Ahmadnagar possessed itself of the whole pargana. Burhān having attained his object returned to his capital leaving Miyān Muhammad Ghorī, an officer who had greatly distinguished himself in the assault, to govern the pargana with the title of Kāmil Khān. Alā-ud-dīn Imād Shāh was not strong enough to resent this aggression at the time, and though it rankled in his memory he suffered himself to be cajoled six years later by Mullā Haidar Astrābādi, an envoy from Ahmadnagar, into an alliance with Burhān Nizām Shāh, who was then engaged in an acrimonious dispute with Ismail Adil Shāh regarding the possession of the fortress of Sholāpur. In 1524 a battle was fought at Sholāpur and Alā-ud-dīn, whose army was opposed to a wing of the Bījāpurs commanded by Asad Khān of Belgaum, was utterly defeated and withdrew by rapid marches and in great disorder to Gāwīlgarh, forsaking his ally. Burhān Nizām Shāh was defeated and forced to retreat to Ahmadnagar.

Pāthri recovered. War with Ahmadnagar and Bīdar.

59. Alā-ud-dīn Imād Shāh now perceived his error in allying himself with Burhān, and Ismail Adil Shāh, anxious to weaken Ahmadnagar as much as possible, persuaded Sultān Kulī Kutb Shāh in 1527 to aid Alā-ud-dīn in recovering Pāthri. The allies succeeded in wresting Pāthri for a time from Burhān, but he entered into an alliance with Amīr Barīd of Bīdar and marched from Ahmadnagar to Pāthri, the fortifications of which place, in the course of a cannonade of two months' duration, he succeeded in destroying. The place fell again into his hands and once more the pargana was annexed to Ahmadnagar and bestowed upon some cousins of Burhān Nizām Shāh who still adhered to the faith of their fathers. Burhān was not disposed to regard the recapture of Pāthri as a sufficient punishment for Alā-ud-dīn, and having captured Māhur occupied southern Berār. He now turned his eyes towards Ellichpur and formed the design of annexing the whole

of Berār to his kingdom. Alā-ud-dīn, who had been deserted by Sultān Kulī Kutb Shāh, was in no position to face the allied armies of Ahmadnagar and Bīdar. He, therefore, fled from Ellichpur to Burhānpur and sought assistance from Mīran Muhammad Shāh of Khāndesh. Mīran Muhammad responded to the appeal and marched with his unfortunate ally into Berār. The armies of Berār and Khāndesh met the allied armies of Ahmadnagar and Bīdar in battle and were utterly defeated. We are not told where this battle was fought, but it was probably not far south of Ellichpur, towards which place the invaders had marched from Māhur, and may have been in the immediate neighbourhood of the town. Burhān Nizām Shāh now held practically the whole of Berār and captured 300 elephants and the whole of Alā-ud-dīn's artillery and stores. Alā-ud-dīn and Mīran Muhammad Shāh fled to Burhānpur and thence sent a message to Bahādur Shāh of Gujarāt, imploring his assistance. Bahādur Shāh snatched at the opportunity of interfering in the affairs of the Deccan and in 1528 sent a large army by way of Nandarbār and Sultānpur towards Ahmadnagar, and also entered Berār. Burhān Nizām Shāh was much perturbed by the appearance of this formidable adversary on the scene. He made a wild appeal for help to Bābar, not yet firmly seated on the throne of Delhi, and more reasonable appeals to Sultān Kulī Kutb Shāh of Golconda and Ismail Adil Shāh of Bījāpur. The former was engaged in warfare with the Hindus of Telingāna and professed himself unable to send assistance, but Ismail sent 6,000 picked horse and much treasure. Bahādur Shāh entered Berār on the pretext of restoring Pāthri and southern Berār to Alā-ud-dīn, but having seen the country he desired it for himself and made no haste to leave. This was very soon perceived by Alā-ud-dīn, who repented of his folly and ventured to suggest to Bahādur Shāh that the Ahmadnagar kingdom should be the theatre of war. He promised that if Bahādur Shāh would conquer that kingdom for him he would resign the kingdom of Berār. Bahādur Shāh accepted the offer and advanced against Burhān Nizām Shāh, who was now encamped on the plateau of Bīr. Amīr Barīd fell upon the advancing foes and slew two or three thousand of the Gujarātis. This enraged Bahādur Shāh, who sent 20,000 horse against Amīr Barīd. The battle soon became general, and the Deccanis were defeated and fled to Purenda. Being pursued thither they again fled to Junnār, while Bahādur Shāh occupied Ahmadnagar. Here he remained until supplies, which the Deccanis cut off, became scarce. He then marched to Daulatābād and left Alā-ud-dīn Imād Shāh and the *amīrs* of Gujarāt to besiege that fortress while he encamped on the plateau above it. Burhān Nizām Shāh now made a fervent appeal to Ismail Adil Shāh for further assistance. Ismail replied with expressions of goodwill, sent five hundred of his most efficient cavalry, and expressed regret that the hostile attitude of the rājā of Vijayanagar prevented him from leaving his capital. Burhān wanted the prestige of Ismail's presence with his army, not a regiment of cavalry. In the circumstances he did the best he could, collected all the troops that could be raised between Junnār and Ahmadnagar, and ascended into the Daulatābād plateau. Here a battle was precipitated by the incautious valour of Amīr Barīd, and although the issue hung for some time in the balance, the Deccanis were again defeated. The problem now was not an equitable decision of the dispute between the kings of Berār and Ahmadnagar, but the expulsion of an inconvenient intruder who was strong enough to upset entirely the balance of power in the Deccan. Burhān Nizām Shāh opened negotiations with Alā-ud-dīn Imād Shāh and professed himself ready to restore all that had been captured by him. Alā-ud-dīn and Mīran Muhammad Shāh were now as apprehensive as their former enemies of Bahādur Shāh's intentions and approached Khudāwand Khān, the latter's minister, with a request that his master would leave the Deccan. Khudāwand Khān replied that Bahādur Shāh had not come uninvited, and that if the Sultāns of the Deccan composed their differences all would be well. The intimation was sufficient. Alā-ud-dīn Imād Shāh sent his surplus supply of grain to the defenders of Daulatābād and returned to Ellichpur. Bahādur Shāh and Mīran Muhammad Shāh decided that they would do well to return to their capitals before the rains rendered both the country and the rivers impassable. They retreated after stipulating that the boundaries of Berār and Ahmadnagar should remain *in statu quo ante bellum*, that the *khutbā* should be read in both kingdoms in the name of Bahādur Shāh and that both Alā-ud-dīn and Burhān should pay a war indemnity. Mīran Muhammad Shāh, after his return to Burhānpur, called upon Burhān Nizām Shāh to fulfil his obligations by restoring to Alā-ud-dīn Pāthri and Māhur and all the elephants and other booty which had been captured near Ellichpur. Burhān's reply to this message was to return to Mīran Muhammad some elephants which had been captured from him, on receiving which Mīran Muhammad desisted from urging on Burhān the fulfilment of his compact with Alā-ud-dīn.

War with Golconda.

60. This was not the last campaign in which the warlike but unfortunate Alā-ud-dīn was engaged. Sultān Kulī Kutb Shāh of Golconda, who had proclaimed himself independent in 1512, was for many years troubled by a Turk entitled Kivām-ul-Mulk who had been appointed by Mahmūd Shāh Bahmanī governor of eastern Telingāna and resisted Sultān Kulī's claims to dominion over that tract. He maintained a guerilla warfare for years, with intermittent encouragement from Bīdar and perhaps from Berār also, until he was defeated by Sultān Kulī at Gelgandal when he fled and took refuge with Alā-ud-dīn Imād Shāh in Berār. Sultān Kulī sent an envoy to Berār to demand the delivery of the fugitive and also the restoration of certain districts of south-eastern Berār which in the time of the Bahmanids had belonged to Telingāna. On Alā-ud-dīn's refusal to satisfy these demands Sultān Kulī marched northwards and Alā-ud-dīn marched from Ellichpur to meet him. A battle was fought near Rāmgiri and the Berāris were utterly defeated. Alā-ud-dīn fled to Ellichpur and Sultān Kulī possessed himself of the disputed territory and returned to Golconda. Unfortunately the date of these operations is not given, but it appears probable that they took place after the departure of Bahādur

Shāh of Gujarāt from the Deccan. The date of the death of Alā-ud-dīn Imād Shāh is not certain, but he probably died in 1529 and was succeeded by his son Daryā Imād Shāh.

Daryā Imād Shāh.

61. The early years of Daryā Imād Shāh's reign were uneventful and his kingdom enjoyed a much needed rest. In 1554 Husain Nizām Shāh succeeded, not without opposition, to the throne of Ahmadnagar. His younger brother, Abdul Kādir, was induced to make a fight for the throne but was overcome and took refuge with Daryā Imād Shāh, under whose protection he remained until his death. Shortly after Mīran Abdul Kādir's flight Saif Ain-ul-Mulk, who had been commander-in-chief of the army of Ahmadnagar in the latter part of the reign of Burhān Nizām Shāh and on his death had espoused the cause of Abdul Kādir, became apprehensive lest Husain Nizām Shāh should punish him for his defection, and fled to Ellichpur, where he took refuge with Daryā Imād Shāh. He did not remain long in Berār but took service under Ibrāhim Adil Shāh of Bījāpur, who interested himself in plots to dethrone Husain Nizām Shāh. Ibrāhim's interference brought about a war between Bījāpur and Ahmadnagar and Husain sent a Brāhman envoy named Viswās Rao to Daryā Imād Shāh to ask him for aid. Daryā sent 7000 cavalry to his neighbour's assistance and Husain then advanced to Sholāpur, which place Ibrāhim was besieging. In the battle which ensued the armies of Ahmadnagar and Berār were on the point of fleeing when Ibrāhim Adil Shāh was attacked by doubts of the loyalty of Saif Ain-ul-Mulk, who commanded a large body of his cavalry, and suddenly returned to Bījāpur, leaving the allies in possession of the field. Husain then returned to Ahmadnagar and sent the cavalry of Berār back to Ellichpur.

Alliance with Ahmadnagar.

62. After the death of Ibrāhim Adil Shāh I in 1557 Husain Nizām Shāh persuaded Ibrāhim Kutb Shāh of Golconda to join him in an attempt to capture Gulbargā and the

eastern districts of the Bījāpur kingdom. The attempt failed owing to Ibrāhim Kutb Shāh's distrust of his ally, and Alī Adil Shāh, who had succeeded to the throne of Bījāpur, resolved to revenge himself on Husain Nizām Shāh, who sought strength in an alliance with Daryā Imād Shāh. In 1558 the kings of Berār and Ahmadnagar met at Sonpet on the Godāvari where Daulat Shāh Begam, Daryā's daughter, was married to Husain, Sonpet receiving the name of Ishratābād in honour of the event.

Invasion of Ahmadnagar.

63. Meanwhile Alī Adil Shāh had formed an alliance with Ibrāhim Kutb Shāh and Sadāshivarāya of Vijayanagar and in 1560 these allies invaded the dominions of Ahmadnagar. Husain Nizām Shāh's trust lay in Alī Barīd Shāh of Bīdar, Daryā Imād Shāh of Berār, and Mīran Mubārak II of Khāndesh. Unfortunately for him influences had been at work to break up this alliance. The Khān-i-Jahān, brother of Alī Barīd Shāh, was friendly with Alī Adil Shāh and had entered the service of Daryā Imād Shāh, whom he dissuaded from joining Husain Nizām Shāh. He then led an army of 5,000 cavalry and infantry from Berār into the Ahmadnagar kingdom and laid waste those northern tracts which lay out of the way of the more powerful invaders from the south. Against this force Husain Nizām Shāh sent nearly 3,000 horse under Mullā Muhammad Nīshābūri. The army of Berār was utterly defeated and the Khān-i-Jahān, ashamed to return to Berār, joined the army of Alī Adil Shāh. Jahāngīr Khān the Deccani now became commander-in-chief of the army of Berār, and had an easier task than his predecessor, for by this time the members of the southern alliance had closed round Ahmadnagar and left Daryā Imād Shāh's army little occupation but that of plundering a defenceless country. The allies, however, quarrelled. Ibrāhim Kutb Shāh, who had gradually been drawn into sympathy with Husain Nizām Shāh, withdrew rapidly and secretly to Golconda, leaving behind him a small force which joined Husain. Jahāngīr Khān with the army of Berār also went over to Husain who was enabled, by this accession of strength, to cut off the

supplies of Alī Adil Shāh and Sadāshivarāya, who were besieging Ahmadnagar. Sadāshivarāya, who perceived that he had been drawn by Alī Adil Shāh into no easy undertaking, was now in a mood to entertain proposals of peace, and when Husain Nizām Shāh sued for peace he agreed to retire on three conditions, one of which was that Jahāngīr Khān, whose activity in intercepting the supplies of the besiegers had caused much suffering among them, should be put to death. Husain was base enough to comply and the commander of the army of Berār was assassinated. Fortunately for Husain his father-in-law was either too weak or too poor spirited to resent this act of gross ingratitude, and the kingdom of Ahmadnagar was by these shameful means, freed of its invaders. Daryā Imād Shāh did not long survive his disgraceful acquiescence in his servant's death. He died in 1561 and was succeeded by his son, Burhān Imād Shāh.

Burhān Imād Shāh.

64. We have no certain information of the age of Burhān when he succeeded his father. He is described as a boy or a young man, but he was not too young to resent the murder of Jahāngīr Khān, for when Husain Nizām Shāh and Ibrāhim Kutb Shāh invaded the territory of Bījāpur in 1562 and Alī Adil Shāh and Sadāshivarāya of Vijayanagar marched against them, Burhān not only refused to respond to Husain's appeal for assistance but prevented Alī Barīd Shāh of Bīdar from joining him. Husain Shāh then abandoned the siege of Kaliyāni, in which he was engaged, and sent his ladies and heavy baggage to Ausa. The kings of Ahmadnagar and Golconda now found themselves opposed by Alī Adil Shāh of Bījāpur, Sadāshivarāya of Vijayanagar, Alī Barīd Shāh of Bīdar, and Burhān Imād Shāh of Berār, and advanced to meet them, halting within twelve miles of their camp. On the following day Husain and Ibrāhim advanced against the enemy, the former making the camp of Sadāshivarāya and the latter that of Alī Adil Shāh, Alī Barīd Shāh, and Burhān Imād Shāh his objective. When they were well on their way heavy rain fell, and Husain's artillery and elephants stuck fast in the mire. Any further advance was out of the question, and Husain

returned to his camp with only forty out of seven hundred guns. Meanwhile Murtazā Khān with the Marāthā officers of Bījāpur had been sent by Alī Adil Shāh to warn the allies to prepare for battle. On his way he came upon the abandoned guns of Husain Nizām Shāh, and learnt that Husain had returned to his camp. Murtazā informed his master of what he had found and Alī Adil Shāh and Sadāshivarāya sent troops to take possession of the guns. After securing the guns these troops fell in with the forces of Ibrāhim Kutb Shāh, attacked them, and defeated them. Ibrāhim reformed his beaten army in rear of Husain Nizām Shāh's camp and made a stand which enabled Husain Nizām Shāh to come to his aid. The troops of Bījāpur and Vijayanagar were repulsed, but Husain Nizām Shāh was much dispirited by the result of the day's fighting and by Ibrāhim's failure, and on the following day, when the armies of Bījāpur, Vijayanagar, Berār and Bīdar advanced to the attack, he and Ibrāhim Kutb Shāh fled in the direction of Ahmadnagar, leaving their camps in the hands of the enemy. At Ausa they separated, Ibrāhim returning to Golconda, whi e Husain retired on his capital, followed by the allies. Husain did not venture to defend his capital but, having provisioned the fortress, fled onwards to Junnār. When the allies sat down to besiege Ahmadnagar the Hindus of Vijayanagar committed great excesses, destroying mosques and other buildings and ravishing Muhammadan women. Alī Adil Shāh had good reason to be ashamed of his allies, and thinking that a march would give them less opportunity of misbehaving themselves than the comparative leisure of a siege, persuaded Sadāshivarāya to leave Ahmadnagar and to pursue Husain Nizām Shāh to Junnār, but before the allies left Ahmadnagar Burhān Imād Shāh and Alī Barīd Shāh, disgusted with the insolence of the Hindus, retired to their own kingdoms. On Burhān's return to Berār he was seized and imprisoned in Narnāla by Tufāl Khān the Deccani, one of his own *amīrs*, who henceforth exercised regal functions in Berār. Tufāl Khān refused to join the confederacy of the Muhammadan Sultāns of the Deccan which was formed in 1564 for the purpose of overthrowing the power of Vijayanagar and Berār had, therefore, no share in the decisive victory of Talikota. Tufāl Khān's refusal to join the Muhammadan league may be attributed to his sense of the insecurity of his position as an usurper, to apathy, to Hindu sympathies, or to the view that the power of Vijayanagar could always be usefully employed for the maintenance of the balance of power between the Muhammadan kingdoms of the Deccan, but the refusal, whatever the motive may have been, brought much trouble and suffering to Berār.

Invasion of Berār.

65. In June, 1565, Husain Nizām Shāh died and was succeeded in Ahmadnagar by his son, Murtazā Nizām Shāh I, who persuaded Alī Adil Shāh to join him in invading Berār in order to punish Tufāl Khān for his refusal to join the league against Vijayanagar. The allies invaded the kingdom from the south and south-west and devastated it with fire and sword as far north as Ellichpur, destroying all standing crops. They remained in Berār, wasting the country and slaughtering its inhabitants until the approach of the rainy season, when Tufāl Khān approached Alī Adil Shāh with an enormous quantity of treasure and besought him to use his influence to induce Murtazā to retire. Alī undertook the task and succeeded in persuading Murtazā, on the pretext that the rains would render marching and campaigning on the black cotton soil of Berār a difficult task, to retire to Ahmadnagar, while he himself returned to Bījāpur.

Annexation of Berār by Ahmadnagar.

66. The unfortunate little kingdom was not, however, destined to enjoy a long rest. In 1572 Changīz Khān, Murtazā Nizām Shāh's minister, brought about a meeting between his master and Alī Adil Shāh at which the two kings entered into a treaty under the terms of which Murtazā was to be allowed to annex Berār and Bīdar without hindrance from Bījāpur while Alī was to be allowed to appropriate so much of the dismembered kingdom of Vijayanagar as should be equal in revenue to those two kingdoms. Ibrāhim Kutb Shāh was left out of the arrangement. In the same year

Murtazā Nizām Shāh, in pursuance of the treaty, encamped at Pāthri and prepared to invade Berār. A pretext was not wanting. He sent Mullā Haidar of Kāsh to Tufāl Khān to call him to account for keeping Burhān Imād Shāh in confinement. Tufāl Khān was ordered to release his king, to be obedient to him in all things, and to refrain from interfering in the government of Berār. The letter concluded with a threat that disobedience would entail punishment and with three couplets warning Tufāl Khān against undertaking a task which was beyond his power. Tufāl Khān was much alarmed by this message and took counsel of his son, Shamshīr-ul-Mulk, who had a reputation for valour and was astute enough to detect Murtazā's object. The solicitude for Burhān Imād Shāh, he said, was a mere pretence, and Murtazā's object was the annexation of Berār to Ahmadnagar. He bade his father take heart, assuring him that the resources of Berār were equal to those of Ahmadnagar, which was not the case, and advised him to send Murtazā's envoy back unanswered. Murtazā, as soon as he heard of Mullā Haidar's dismissal, marched from Pāthri towards Ellichpur, and Shamshīr-ul-Mulk, who commanded the advanced guard of the army of Berār, marched to meet him. The site of the battle is, unfortunately, not recorded, but the armies must have met either in the Amraoti District or the Akolā District. Shamshīr-ul-Mulk fell upon the advanced guard of the army of Ahmadnagar and defeated it. Changīz Khān threw forward reinforcements and Shamshīr-ul-Mulk called upon his father for support. Tufāl Khān at once marched to support his son and Changīz Khān, being apprised of the approach of the main body of the army of Berār, sent forward Khudāwand Khān, Jamshīd Khān, Bahrī Khān, Rustam Khān, and Chandā Khān to the support of the African *amīrs* of Ahmadnagar, on whom the brunt of the fighting was falling, and followed them in person with Murtazā's guards and three thousand mounted 'foreign' archers, who were evidently regarded as the flower of the army of Ahmadnagar. The battle soon became general. Changīz Khān, who had as his body-guard five hundred of his own followers, spared no efforts to win the day. With his own hand he cut down Tufāl Khān's standard bearer, and the army of Berār was routed. Tufāl Khān and his son fled to Ellichpur and Changīz Khān returned with 270 captured elephants to the camp of Murtazā Nizām Shāh, who no longer made any attempt to conceal the real object of his enterprise. He did not hasten in pursuit of his defeated enemy or attempt to gather at once the fruits of victory, but remained in his camp and issued *farmāns* to all the Hindu revenue officials of Berār informing them that they had nothing to fear, and that if they would tender their allegiance to him they would find him a lenient and sympathetic master. The descendant of a line of Brāhmaṇ patwāris knew with whom he had to deal. The hereditary Hindu officials cared little for Burhān, Tufāl, or Murtazā but much for the blessings of peace, and they were not slow to perceive which was the stronger side. They hastened to the camp of the invader, where they were received with honour and whence they were dismissed with rewards and promises. Murtazā Nizām Shāh, having thus made sure his foothold, advanced on Ellichpur, whereupon Tufāl Khān and Shamshīr-ul-Mulk, whose power had been so utterly broken in the field that the respite afforded to them by Murtazā's delay had profited them nothing, fled into the Melghāt. Through the hills and jungles of this tract they were pursued for six months at the end of which time they found themselves hemmed in by the forces of Ahmadnagar in a position whence no outlet was apparent. The invader refrained from pressing his advantage and Tufāl Khān succeeded in extricating himself and escaped to Burhānpur. Murtazā, having pursued him as far as the Tāpti, sent a letter to Mīran Muhammad Shāh II, king of Khāndesh, threatening to invade his country if the fugitives were harboured. Mīran Muhammad sent the letter, without comment, to Tufāl Khān, who at once understood that he could find no asylum in Khāndesh and returned by an unfrequented road to Berār. At the same time he sent a letter to Akbar, then seated on the throne of Delhi, saying that he regarded himself as one of the emperor's soldiers and Berār as a province of the empire, which had been invaded by the Deccanis. He sought, he said, the appointment of warden of the marches and asked for assistance, promising to surrender Berār to Akbar's officers when they should arrive. Akbar was not at this time prepared to undertake an expedition to the Deccan and no immediate answer was returned to Tufāl Khān's effusion. Meanwhile both Tufāl Khān and his son Shamshīr-ul-Mulk now separated were hard pressed by Murtazā and were fain to seek the protection afforded by stone walls. Tufāl Khān shut himself up in Narnāla while Shamshīr-ul-Mulk sought refuge in Gāwīlgarh, and Murtazā Nizām Shāh laid siege to Narnāla. Meanwhile Tufāl Khān's letter had reached Akbar's camp in Gujarāt and one of the emperor's *amīrs* wrote to Murtazā Nizām Shāh saying that Tufāl Khān, having submitted to the emperor, was one of his vassals and that Murtazā would do well to desist from harassing him, and that Berār, which was a province of the empire, should be evacuated at once. This absurdly bombastic message was treated with the contempt which it deserved and both Narnāla and Gāwīlgarh were closely besieged. The former fell before the end of the year, and Tufāl Khān and Burhān Imād Shāh fell into Murtazā's hands. Shamshīr-ul-Mulk on hearing of the fall of Narnāla and the capture of his father surrendered Gāwīlgarh to Murtazā's officers on condition that his life should be spared. Murtazā Nizām Shāh sent Burhān Imād Shāh, Tufāl Khān, Shamshīr-ul-Mulk, and all their relatives and attendants, to the number of about forty souls, to a fortress in the Ahmadnagar kingdom where, after a short time, they all perished. We have various accounts of the manner of their death and in one passage it is hinted that they may possibly have died a natural death, but the sudden, simultaneous, and convenient extinction of so large a number of obnoxious persons cannot have been fortuitous. Another story is that the whole party was confined in a small room and the windows were shut upon them, the result being a tragedy similar in all respects to that of the Black Hole of Calcutta, save that in this case there were no survivors. Elsewhere it is said that the whole party was strangled or smothered individually.

The Black Hole story appears to be the most probable, but whichever story is true the fact remains that the Imād Shāhi dynasty was utterly extinguished in 1572[1] and that Berār became a province of the Nizām Shāhi kingdom of Ahmadnagar.

Berār a province of Ahmadnagar.

67. Murtazā apportioned the districts of Berār to his nobles, and now wished to return to Ahmadnagar and enjoy the fruits of victory, but Changīz Khān incited him to further exertions. Alī Adil Shāh, he said, was occupied with the siege of Bankāpur, and the opportunity of gaining possession of Bīdar, to which as well as to Berār, his treaty with Bījāpur entitled him, was too good to be lost. Murtazā was thus persuaded to march against Bīdar, and while he was thus employed affairs in Berār took a new turn. Mīran Muhammad II of Khāndesh seized the opportunity of harassing an inconveniently powerful neighbour, and, as soon as Murtazā Nizām Shāh was engaged with Bīdar, set up the son of Burhān Imād Shāh's foster mother as king of Berār alleging that he was a son of Daryā Imād Shāh and sent the pretender to the frontier of Berār with 6,000 horse. Many adherents of the extinct family either believed the fable or were willing to adopt any pretext for maintaining the independence of Berār, and rose in rebellion, driving the officers of Murtazā Nizām Shāh from their military posts. The rebels numbered eight or nine thousand, and their activity was a serious menace to the stability of the newly established authority. Khudāwand Khān and Khurshīd Khān, the two officers who had been appointed to administer Berār, sent a message to Murtazā Nizām Shāh inploring him to return. The king recalled Changīz Khān, who had preceded him to Bīdar, despatched Saiyid Murtazā Sabzawāri with 8,000 horse to Berār and followed him with the main body of the army. Changīz Khān returned from Bīdar by forced marches and begged the king to make a short halt in order that the

[1] There is a discrepancy as to this date. From the detailed account of the siege of Narnāla it appears that the fortress did not fall until 1574, but the date of its fall is also given in a chronogram which works up to 982=1572 A.D.

troops might rest. Murtazā Nizām Shāh refused to listen to the proposal and pressed on. Mīran Muhammad Shāh, who was hovering on the border of Berār, ready to make a descent as soon as Murtazā Nizām Shāh should be safely out of the way, was much disconcerted by his adversary's activity and fled in haste to his fortress capital of Asīrgarh. The army of Ahmadnagar now invaded and laid waste Khāndesh and Asīrgarh was on the point of falling into their hands when Mīran Muhammad Shāh bought off Murtazā Nizām Shāh with a large sum of money. Murtazā Nizām Shāh now returned to Berār where, in the course of a complicated intrigue connected with the invasion of Bīdar, he poisoned Changīz Khān in 1574. He then returned to Ahmadnagar and in 1575 appointed Saiyid Murtazā Sabzawāri governor of Berār. The new governor was assisted in his administration of the province by a large number of *amīrs*, the chief of whom were Khudāwand Khān the *muwallad*,[1] Jamshīd Khān, Bahrī Khān Kazilbāsh, Rustam Khān the Deccani, Chaghtai Khān the Turkmān, Tīr Andāz Khān Astrābādi, Shīr Khān Tarshīzi, Husain Khān Tūni, Chanda Khān the Deccani, and Dastūr the eunuch.

Rumours of invasion from the north.

68. In 1576 it was reported that Akbar was preparing to invade the Deccan. Murtazā Nizām Shāh, now sunk in sloth and debauchery, made a feeble and confused effort to take the field. He was better served in Berār than he deserved. Bahrām Khān, who was commandant of Gāwīlgarh under Saiyid Murtazā Sabzawāri, put the fortress into a state of thorough repair and has left a record of his zeal in an inscription on the bastion which bears his name. The chronogram in the inscription gives the date A.H. 985 equivalent to A.D. 1577. Fortunately these precautions were unnecessary, for Akbar's journey was no more than a trip from Agra to Ajmer and back, and Ahmadnagar and Berār were left for a time in peace. The rumour of danger from the north had, however, galvanized the wretched

[1] *I.e.*, a man of foreign descent born in the Deccan of an Indian mother.

Murtazā Nizām Shāh into something like activity, and early in 1578 Saiyid Murtazā Sabzawāri was summoned to Ahmadnagar in order that he might parade the army of Berār before the king. This effort to secure military efficiency in the frontier province had most unfortunate results. Murtazā Nizām Shāh's unworthy favourite Sāhib Khān, a Deccani, grossly insulted one of the foreign officers of the army of Berār, with the result that the old quarrel between the foreigners on one side and the Deccanis and the Africans on the other was renewed. A fight followed in which the king identified himself with the Deccanis, whereupon most of the foreign officers left his service and entered that of Golconda and Bījāpur. In the confusion which followed Salābat Khān grasped the reins of government and Murtazā Nizām Shāh was left powerless. He attempted to recover possession of Sāhib Khān and bespoke the good offices of Saiyid Murtazā Sabzawāri to this end, but the Saiyid was unable, and probably unwilling to save the wretch and Sāhib Khān was ultimately slain by Khudāwand Khān, one of the *amīrs* of Berār. Salābat Khān was now regent of Ahmadnagar and Saiyid Murtazā Sabzawāri retained the governorship of Berār. In 1584 Salābat Khān sent an order to Jamshīd Khān Shīrāzi, who has been already mentioned as one of Saiyid Murtazā's officers, directing him to join an embassy which was about to leave Ahmadnagar for Bījāpur. As the order had not been countersigned by Murtazā Nizām Shāh, Jamshīd Khān replied that he could not obey it without the sanction of his superior officer, Saiyid Murtazā. The latter was much annoyed by Salābat Khān's assumption of the right to communicate an order to Jamshīd direct, and refused to permit Jamshīd to leave his post in Berār. The quarrel reached such a point that Saiyid Murtazā Sabzawāri assembled the army of Berār and marched towards Ahmadnagar with the intention of overthrowing Salābat Khān, but the *amīrs* at the capital intervened and brought about a temporary peace, and Saiyid Murtazā returned to Berār. Towards the end of the same year the quarrel was renewed and Saiyid Murtazā of Berār again marched on Ahmadnagar. Salābat Khān advanced to meet him, defeated him, and pursued him through Berār, and Saiyid Murtazā and his lieutenant fled by way of Burhānpur to the court of Akbar. Meanwhile Shāhzāda Burhān, a brother of Murtazā Nizām Shāh, had been persuaded by a party in Ahmadnagar to make an attempt to dethrone Murtazā and seize the throne. The plot was frustrated by Salābat Khān and Burhān was forced to flee in the guise of a *darvesh* to the Konkan whence he reached Gujarāt and joined Akbar's court.

Mughal raid on Berār.

69. Akbar now resolved to attempt the conquest of the Deccan and ordered his foster-brother, Mirzā Azīz Kūka entitled Khān-i-Azam, who was then governor of Mālwā, to assemble the army of Mālwā and march against Ahmadnagar, taking Burhān with him. Salābat Khān replied by sending 20,000 horse to Burhānpur. Mirzā Muhammad Takī who commanded this force, succeeded in attaching Rājā Alī Khān of Khāndesh to the cause of Ahmadnagar despite an attempt by the Khān-i-Azam to secure his adherence to the imperial cause. The Khān-i-Azam's expedition was delayed by a quarrel between him and Shahāb-ud-dīn Ahmad Khān, the governor of Ujjain and Mirzā Muhammad Takī and Rājā Alī Khān carried the war into the enemy's country and encamped over against the Khān-i-Azam at Handia. The Khān-i-Azam was unwilling to risk a battle, but by a rapid night march eluded the Deccanis and entered Berār by a circuitous route. The Mughal horse plundered Ellichpur, hastened thence to Bālāpur, and before the Deccanis, who had turned back from Handia to meet them, could come up with them, retreated by way of Nandarbār into Mālwā. Rājā Alī Khān then returned to Burhānpur and Mirzā Muhammad Takī to Ahmadnagar. Akbar did not at once pursue his project of adding the Deccan to his empire and Berār had peace for a few years.

Accession of Ismail Nizām Shāh.

70. In June, 1588, Murtazā Nizām Shāh, who had attempted to destroy his son Mīran Husain by setting fire to his bedding, was, in return, suffocated in his

bath by the prince, who succeeded him as Husain Nizām Shāh II. Husain II was put to death after a reign of less than two months and the *amīrs* of Ahmadnagar raised to the throne Ismail, the son of the fugitive Burhān. Jamāl Khān, who had been one of Saiyid Murtazā's lieutenants in Berār, was now regent in Ahmadnagar. He belonged to the heretical sect of the Mahdavīs and in the name of Ismail Nizām Shāh, who was too young to understand theological disputes, established their religion in Ahmadnagar with the result that the kingdom became a refuge for most of the Mahdavīs throughout India. The *amīrs* of Berār were much annoyed by the spread of the heresy and in 1589 released Salābat Khān, who had been imprisoned by Murtazā Nizām Shāh in Kherlā, and induced him to lead them against Ahmadnagar, while Ibrāhim Adil Shāh II of Bījāpur invaded the kingdom from the south. Jamāl Khān defeated the *amīrs* of Berār at Paithan on the Godāvari, then the southern boundary of the Province, and the Bījāpurīs at Ashtī. Salābat Khān made his peace with Jamāl Khān and returned to his jāgīr to die.

Burhān's first attempt to gain his kingdom.

71. In 1590 the time was ripe for the invasion of Berār and the Deccan by Akbar. The *amīrs* of Berār were disaffected and disgusted with the heterodox doctrines now fashionable at the court of Ahmadnagar and the elevation to the throne of the young Ismail, the son of the emperor's protégé Burhān, furnished Akbar with a pretext for aggression. He offered Burhān as many troops as he should consider necessary for the purpose of gaining the throne of his ancestors, now unjustly held by his son, but Burhān had no desire to reign at Ahmadnagar as Akbar's puppet and declined the proffered aid. Akbar then bestowed upon him the pargana of Handia in jāgīr and gave him letters to Rājā Alī Khān of Khāndesh, who was ordered to render him all the assistance in his power. Burhān took up his quarters at Handia and issued letters to the principal officers and landholders of Berār and the rest of the Ahmadnagar kingdom reminding them that he was their lawful king and exhorting them to

be faithful to him. These letters were well received and Burhān received many assurances of loyalty and offers of assistance, including one from Jahāngīr Khān the African, warden of the northern marches of Berār. Burhān now entered Berār, with a small force of horse and foot which he had collected, by way of the Melghāt, but Jahāngīr Khān had repented of his promise, and attacked and defeated the small army, forcing Burhān to retire to Handia in great disorder. From Handia he went to Burhānpur where he sought assistance from Rājā Alī Khān who received him kindly and not only promised him aid but invoked the aid of Ibrāhim Adil Shāh II of Bījāpur who, smarting under the recent defeat of his forces by Jamāl Khān, readily sent an army northwards. Jamāl Khān again defeated the Bījāpurīs but had not recovered from the fatigues of the fight when he heard that the nobles of Berār had declared for Burhān, who was on the point of entering Berār.

The story of the campaign which followed need not be recounted in detail here. Burhān and Rājā Alī Khān defeated and slew Jamāl Khān at Rohankhed in the Buldāna District and captured the young Ismail. The whilom protégé of Akbar now ascended the throne of Ahmadnagar as Burhān Nizām Shāh II, and appointed Nūr Khān governor of Berār.

The Mughals invited to Ahmadnagar.

72. Burhān died on April 29th, 1595, after a troubled reign of rather more than four years, and was succeeded by his elder son Ibrāhim Nizām Shāh, who had been previously passed over in favour of his younger brother Ismail on the score that his mother was a negress and his personal appearance unkingly. The affairs of the State were now in the utmost confusion. Rival factions contended at the council board while Ibrāhim Adil Shāh on the south and Akbar on the north prepared to invade the kingdom. Ibrāhim Nizām Shāh after a reign of less than four months was slain in battle with the Bījāpurīs, and a faction attempted to raise to the throne Ahmad, son of Shāh Tāhir, who had pretended to be the

son of Sultān Muhammad Khudāwand, one of the sons of Burhān Nizām Shāh I. But the circumstances of Shāh Tāhir's birth had already been secretly investigated, and there were those at the capital who knew the details of the inquiry and published them. Nevertheless the impostor's faction held the field for a time, and when they were hard pressed in Ahmadnagar they sent a message to Sultān Murād, Akbar's fourth son, and implored him to come from Gujarāt to their aid. Murād had a general commission from his father to attempt the conquest of Berār and Ahmadnagar whenever the time should seem propitious and at once made preparations to invade the Deccan. Meanwhile, however, an unexpected quarrel in the camp of those who opposed the impostor's claims enabled Miyān Manjhū, his chief supporter, to emer from Ahmadnagar and attack them. He defeated them on October 1st, 1595, and, deeming himself now strong enough to dispense with foreign aid, began to regret his invitation to Murād. Murād, however, was already on his way and when he reached the borders of the Ahmadnagar kingdom with the Khān-i-Khānān, Abdur Rahīm and Rājā Alī Khān of Khāndesh, Miyān Manjhū leaving Ansār Khān, in whose charge was Chānd Bībī, in command of Ahmadnagar, fled with his protégé Ahmad to Ausa, where he attempted to raise an army and to enlist the aid of Ibrāhim Adil Shāh II and Muhammad Kulī Kutb Shāh of Golconda.

Cession of Berār to Akbar.

73. Chānd Bībī soon asserted her supremacy in Ahmadnagar and had Bahādur, the infant son of Ibrāhim Nizām Shāh, proclaimed king in place of the impostor set up by Miyān Manjhū. The imperial army meanwhile closely besieged Ahmadnagar, and though Sultān Murād did not succeed incapturing the city he was only bought off by a treaty of peace concluded in April, 1596, one of the conditions of which was the cession of Berār to the empire. On the conclusion of peace Murād occupied Berār which thus became once more, after the lapse of two centuries and a half, an appanage of the crown of Delhi. After the withdrawal of the imperial

army Bahādur Nizām Shāh was seated on the throne of Ahmadnagar while the pretender Ahmad was provided for by the Sultān of Bījāpur.

During the early days of the Mughal occupation of Berār the old capital, Ellichpur, lost some of its importance. In the first place its distance from the Ahmadnagar frontier and from the high road between Hindustān and the Deccan, which ran through the western corner of Berār, rendered its selection as a military capital impossible, and in the second although Berār had been ceded to the empire by treaty the fortresses of Gāwīlgarh and Narnāla were held by *amīrs* of Ahmadnagar and the slothful Murād was not anxious to besiege them. He therefore made Bālāpur his principal military post, and built himself a palace at a village about twelve miles west of that town.

Death of Murād and fall of Ahmadnagar.

74. Hostilities with Ahmadnagar were renewed by an attempt to seize Pāthri, and on February 8th, 1597, the Khān-i Khānān was defeated at Sonpet on the Godāvari by the troops of Ahmadnagar aided by contingents from Bījāpur and Golconda. On the following day, however, he retrieved his defeat and put the allied Deccanis to flight. Having returned to Jālna, his headquarters, the Khān-i-Khānān ordered the despatch of troops to Gāwīlgarh and Narnāla, but Murād now interfered, and announced his intention of taking the field against Ahmadnagar, and when the Khān-i-Khānān insisted that the fortresses of Northern Berār should first be reduced Murād wrote to his father and complained of the Khān-i-Khānān's apathy. In 1598 that officer was recalled and Abul Fazl was sent to the Deccan in his place with orders to reduce Gāwīlgarh and Narnāla, which duty he carried out. He failed, however, to send aid to the Mughal governor of Bīr who, having been defeated and wounded in the field, was besieged in that fortress, and reported to Akbar Abul Fazl's failure to come to his aid. Akbar now recognised that the only officer capable of managing affairs in the Deccan was the Khān-i-Khānān, whose only

fault was his intolerance of the slothful and drunken Murād. The difficulty was solved by the death of Murād in 1599 at Shāhpur, his palace near Bālāpur, from the effects of drink and incontinence. Sultān Dāniyāl, Akbar's youngest son, was now sent to the Deccan under the tutelage of the Khān-i-Khānān. In the same year (1599) Ahmadnagar was captured by the Khān-i-Khānān and Asīrgarh by Akbar and Sultān Dāniyāl became governor of Khāndesh—now renamed Dāndesh—Berār and Ahmadnagar.

The Ain-i-Akbarī.

75. A detailed account of Berār was added to the Ain-i-Akbarī in 1596-97, immediately after the treaty of Ahmadnagar under which the province was ceded to the empire, and as the Mughal officers cannot have had time, before the account was written, to settle the province and readjust boundaries of its administrative divisions we may regard this description as an account of the province as it was administered by the Nizām Shāhi and Imād Shāhi kings, and probably also by the Bahmanids. It was divided into thirteen *sarkārs*, or revenue districts, of which the largest and richest was Gāwīl, which contained forty-four parganas and corresponded roughly with the Amraoti District. Some of its parganas lay beyond the present limits of the District, *e.g.*, Sirson (Murtizāpur), Māna, Kāranja Bībī, Mānba, Pāpal and Kamargaon, now in the Akolā District, Ner Parsopant in the Yeotmāl District, and Arvī and Ashtī in the Central Provinces. The District was assessed at rather more than 28 lakhs of land revenue and 2½ lakhs of *suyārghāl* or assignments for the pay of troops. Amraoti, not being a pargana town, is not mentioned. Ellichpur is described as 'a large city and the capital' and Gāwīlgarh as 'a fortress of almost matchless strength' containing a spring at which weapons of steel were watered. Against two of the parganas of the Melghāt we find such entries as '100 cavalry, 2,000 infantry—Gonds,' which indicate that the Korkūs of the Melghāt, described by Abul Fazl as by the Deccani historian and by British administrators of a later day as 'Gonds,' were duly assessed for military service.

6

Malik Ambar.

76. After the imprisonment of Bahādur Nizām Shāh in Gwālior in 1599, Malik Ambar the African, the most powerful remaining adherent of the Nizām Shāhi dynasty, raised to the throne Murtazā Nizām Shāh, the son of Shāh Alī, one of the sons of Burhān I., and established him in the fortress of Ausa. It is unnecessary to pursue through all its details the story of the long conflict which Ambar carried on with the *amīrs* of the empire, but reference will be made to the struggle so far as it affected the Amraoti District.

In 1605 Sultān Dāniyāl died of drink in Burhānpur and in October of the same year Akbar died and was succeeded by his eldest son, Salīm, who assumed the title of Jahāngīr.

In 1610 Malik Ambar recaptured Ahmadnagar, which had been held for the emperor by Khāja Beg Mirzā Saffavī, and overran nearly the whole of Berār which for the greater part of Jahāngīr's reign was more often in the hands of Malik Ambar than in those of the imperial officers. So far as the land revenue was concerned the administration was probably *do-amlī* each party collecting what it could, but the Mughals regarded Burhānpur as their chief stronghold in the Deccan, and though a military post was usually maintained at Bālāpur their hold in Berār can have been but slight. In 1617 Sultān Khurram, Jahāngīr's third son, was appointed to the command of the troops in the Deccan, and on the arrival of this energetic prince the imperial cause revived and the Mughals strengthened their hold on Berār. Sultān Khurram was recalled later in the year and received the title of Shāhjahān.

Malik Ambar occupies Berār.

77. In 1620 Malik Ambar drove the Mughals from Berār and occupied not only that Province but Khāndesh also. Shāhjahān was now sent to Burhānpur with a large force. He relieved that city, which was beleaguered by the Deccanis and drove the latter through Berār, pursuing them as far as Khirkī[1] which place he laid waste after defeating

[1] Afterwards named Aurangābād.

Malik Ambar in the field. Berār was thus once more in the hands of the Mughals. In 1622 Shāhjahān rebelled against his father, drawing into rebellion with him Darāb Khān, the governor of Berār. After extensive operations in Hindustān and Gujarāt the prince was pursued by his brother Parvez through Berār to Māhur, whence he fled to Golconda. The Deccanis, in spite of Shāhjahān's rebellion, effected no lodgment in Berār, which remained in the hands of Parvez, who appointed Asad Khān Māmurī governor of Ellichpur. In 1624, however, Yākūt Khān the African marched through Berār and besieged Burhānpur, but fled when he heard of the approach of the Khān-i-Khānān and Parvez who had been temporarily transferred to Bengal in consequence of Shāhjahān's appearance in arms in that Province.

Treachery of the Khān-i-Jahān.

78. In 1625 Shāhjahān submitted to his father and was pardoned, and in 1626 Parvez, now governor of Berār and the Deccan, died in Burhānpur of colic and epilepsy brought on by excessive drinking. In the same year Malik Ambar died, in the eightieth year of his age, and his place was taken by his son Fateh Khān. Later in the same year Umdat-ul-Mulk Khān-i-Jahān, who had been sent to the Deccan in consequence of the renewed activity of Murtazā Nizām Shāh and Fateh Khān, sold the Bālāghāt of Berār to the Deccanis for twelve lakhs of rupees. This treasonable bargain did not directly affect the Amraotī District, but it must have thrown the affairs of the whole province into great confusion.

Jahāngīr died on November 9th, 1627, and in the course of the ensuing disputes regarding the succession, the affairs of the Deccan fell into great confusion, and between the Khān-i-Jahān, who was plotting with the enemy entirely for his own hand and other imperial officers who favoured the cause of Shahryār, Shāhjahān's youngest brother, the fortunes of the Mughals in Berār and the Deccan were at a very low ebb.

Accession of Shāhjahān

79. Shāhjahān ascended the imperial throne in Agra on February 15th[1] 1628, and was thereafter free to attend to the affairs of the empire. At the beginning of his reign the Khān-i-Jahān was still governor of Berār and Khāndesh, but his bargain with the Deccanis was disturbed for the officers of Murtazā Nizām Shāh evacuated the Bālāghāt in obedience to an imperial *farmān*. The Nizām Shāhi commandant of Bīr alone held out and the Khān-i-Zamān was sent against him. When this officer advanced Murtazā Nizām Shāh sent a force of 6,000 Marāthā horse under Sāhujī Bhonsla to threaten his line of communication with Burhānpur and this force operated in the northern tāluks of the Amraoti and Akolā Districts and in Khāndesh. Unfortunately for the schemes of the Deccanis the commandant of Bīr surrendered, and Daryā the Rohilla, who held a jāgīr in the Amraoti District, fell upon Sāhujī's Marāthā horse and dispersed them. The Khān-i-Jahān was now summoned to court and deprived of his title, whereupon he fled to the Deccan and entered the service of Murtazā Nizām Shāh and on Murtazā refusing to surrender him Shāhjahān set out for the Deccan at the end of 1629, reaching Burhānpur early in 1630, where he was joined by Irādat Khān who had been appointed governor of Berār, Khāndesh, and the Deccan in the place of the disgraced Khān-i-Jahān. In the campaign which followed Shāhjahān's arrival at Burhānpur the Deccanis were driven from the Bālāghāt of Berār which they had again occupied, but it does not appear that the Amraoti District was the scene of hostilities unless the village of Talegaon, which was captured and burnt by the Deccanis, were Talegaon Dashāsar. The war lasted until the fall of Daulatābād in 1633, but the Mughals had now advanced well into the Deccan and though the Amraoti District, with the rest of Berār, suffered severely from demands for supplies for the forces in the field it was freed from the curse of war within its borders.

---

[1] So the *Pādishāh-nāma*. The *Muntakhab-ul-lubāb* has February 14th and the *Tuzāk-i-Jahāngīri* March 5th.

80. In 1630 the rains failed completely in Berār and the Deccan and partially elsewhere, and this calamity, combined with the heavy tax which the war had placed upon the tracts which it most affected, produced one of the most severe famines ever known in Berār. 'Buyers were ready to give a life for a loaf, but seller was there none. The flesh of dogs was sold as that of goats and the bones of the dead were ground with the flour sold in the market, and the punishment of those who profited by this traffic produced yet direr results, men devoured one another and came to regard the flesh of their children as sweeter than their love. The inhabitants fled afar to other tracts till the corpses of those who fell by the way impeded those who came after and in the lands of Berār, which had been famous for their fertility and prosperity, no trace of habitation remained.' This account, taken from the official record of Shāhjahān's reign, is obviously hyperbolical, but cannot be dismissed as entirely imaginary. Berār had suffered much from protracted hostilities during which it had been the prey of hostile armies which had little respect for the rights of property, and the measures of relief undertaken were utterly inadequate.

Famine.

81. On November 27th, 1634, Shāhjahān issued a *farmān* reorganizing his territories in the Deccan. Hitherto the three *sūbahs* of Khāndesh, Berār, and the conquered districts of Nizām Shāhi dominions had formed a province under one provincial governor, whose headquarters were usually at Burhānpur. Under Shāhjahān's redistribution scheme those parganas of the *sarkār* of Handia which lay to the south of the Nerbudda were transferred from Mālwā to Khāndesh and Berār. Khāndesh, and the districts taken from Ahmadnagar, were formed into two *sūbahs* or divisions, the Bālāghāt on the south and the Pāyanghāt on the north. This arrangement dismembered, for a time, the old province of Berār, for the line dividing the two new *sūbahs* followed the line of the edge of the plateau of the Bālāghāt, running, approximately, from Rohankhed on the west to Sāwargaon on the Wardhā river, on the east.

Redistribution of Deccan provinces.

The Amraoti District was thus included in the Pāyanghāt division, the *sūbahdār* of which was the Khān-i-Daurān, while Sipahdār Khān, a valiant soldier, was subordinate to him at Ellichpur.

82. This scheme of reorganization was very soon amended.

The Deccan provinces again redistributed. Aurangzeb.

In 1636 Shāhjahān appointed his third son, Aurangzeb, to the viceroyalty of the Deccan, where the possessions of the empire were redistributed into four *sūbahs* or divisions—(1) Daulatābād and Ahmadnagar, the nominal capital of which was Daulatābād, while Aurangzeb resided at Khirkī, which he renamed Aurangābād, (2) Telingāna which included those tracts of north-western Telingāna, which had been annexed to the empire, (3) Khāndesh, the administrative capital of which was Burhānpur, while its principal military post was Asīrgarh, and (4) Berār, the capital of which was Ellichpur, 'in the neighbourhood of which lay the fortress of Gāwīl, situated on the crest of a hill and noted for its great strength.' Each of these divisions was governed by a *sūbahdār* in immediate subordination to Aurangzeb as viceroy, and the Khān-i-Daurān was retained as *sūbahdār* of Berār, with Sipahdār Khān as deputy governor in Ellichpur.

83. In 1637 the Khān-i-Daurān with Sipahdār Khān and

Campaign in Golconda and Gondwāna.

the army of Berār undertook an expedition through the northern district of the kingdom of Golconda, where they collected tribute and thence they marched through the *sarkār* of Paunār to besiege Nāgpur, which was held for Kokiya, the Gond ruler of Deogarh. The army of Berār was joined by Kībā, the Gond ruler of Chānda and Nāgpur was taken. It was probably at this time that the *sarkār* of Deogarh was added to the province of Berār.

In 1642 Shāh Beg Khān, a commander of 4,000 horse, was appointed *sūbahdār* of Berār in place of the Khān-i-Daurān and two years later Allāh Vardī Khān was made a commander of 5,000 horse and received Ellichpur in jāgīr on the death of Sipahdār Khān.

84. Early in 1658 Aurangzeb left the Deccan in order to participate in the contest for the imperial throne which ensued on the failure of Shāhjahān's health, and in 1659 having worsted his competitors he gained the prize. He appointed Rājā Jai Singh to the viceroyalty of the Deccan and made Irij Khān *sūbahdār* of Berār. In 1675 Irij Khān was removed to make way for the Khān-i-Zamān, but in the following year he was reappointed *sūbahdār* of the province.

Accession of Aurangzeb and siege of Golconda

In 1680 Sambhājī, the son of Shivājī, overran Berār and did much damage, especially to the standing crops, and after passing through Berār he plundered Burhānpur and burnt seventeen of its suburbs in the short period of four days which elapsed before he was driven off.

In 1685 Irij Khān died and Husain Alī Khān was appointed to succeed him as *sūbahdār* of Berār. He governed the province through a deputy, Razī-ud-dīn Khān, who died in 1686 and was succeeded by Muhammad Momin Khān, a relative of Irij Khān. In the same year Husain Alī Khān died and Mahābat Khān was appointed *sūbahdār* of Berār in his place, Muhammad Sādik being appointed his deputy. Husain Alī Khān's unexpected death was a misfortune for the province for he is mentioned as one who excelled his fellows in valour and leadership, and as a well-wisher of the people, a speaker of the truth and an upright man. Such men were not common in the Deccan in the days in which he lived.

In the same year, while the siege of Golconda was in progress, Berār was called upon to supply material of war and cattle. In 1687, after the fall of Golconda, Aurangzeb appointed his youngest son, Muhammad Kām Bakhsh, *sūbahdār* of Berār. At some time after this the prince was relieved of his appointment, for towards the end of 1697 he was again appointed to the governorship and Mīrak Husain was appointed as his deputy. In 1698 Askar Alī Khān the Hyderābādi was appointed *sūbahdār* in place of the prince.

85. In 1699 Rājārām, who, since the death of his brother Sambhājī, had been continually a fugitive from the imperial troops, collected

Marāthā raids.

a large army and appeared in Berār with the avowed intention of conquering the province. His troops, after the fashion of Marāthā armies, laid the country waste and destroyed towns and villages, and he succeeded in enlisting the aid of Bakht Buland, the Gond rājā of Deogarh, who notwithstanding his acceptance of Islām, was but a lukewarm adherent of Aurangzeb. Bedār Bakht, the eldest son of prince Muhammad Azam, was sent against the disturbers of the peace, and drove them from Berār.

In 1702 Lutf-ullah Khān was appointed *sūbahdār* of Berār with Ghāzi-ud-dīn Khān Fīroz Jang, father of Asaf Jāh, as his deputy, but Lutf-ullah died before he could reach Ellichpur and the deputy succeeded as *sūbahdār* and Sarandāz Khān was appointed deputy. The latter was removed in 1703 and Rustam Khān, who held the post until the end of Aurangzeb's reign, was appointed in his place. In 1704 the Marāthās were again active in Berār and Fīroz Jang marched northwards from Ellichpur in pursuit of Nīmā Sindhia.

Accession of Bahādur Shāh.

86. On March 4th, 1707, Aurangzeb died at Ahmadnagar and was shortly afterwards buried at Rauzā, afterwards called Khuldābād, near the caves of Ellora and about seven miles from Daulatābād. The usual conflict for the throne followed the death of the emperor and victory finally declared for Shāh Alam, the eldest surviving son, who ascended the throne under the title of Bahādur Shāh. Fīroz Jang at first held Berār for prince Muhammad Azam by whom he was transferred, as *sūbahdār*, to the Province of Gujarāt, but the cautious *amīr* was a lukewarm partisan and readily made his peace with Bahādur Shāh who confirmed him in his appointment in Gujarāt.

Towards the end of 1707 Zūl-fikār Khān Nusrat Jang was viceroy of the whole of the Deccan, and it was now that the officers of the imperial army first began to enter into regular agreements with the Marāthās for the payment of the blackmail known as *chauth* and *sardeshmukhī*.

Bemrose, Collo., Derby.

NAU GAZ TOP, GAWILGARH FORT.

Accession of Farrukhsiyar.

87. Bahādur Shāh died in 1712 and was succeeded by his eldest son, Muizzuddīn who took the title of Jahāndār Shāh. On his death the two Saiyid brothers of Bārha, who were now all-powerful at Delhi, raised to the throne Farrukhsiyar. It was in his reign, in 1718, that the imperial court first disgraced itself by formally acknowledging the claim of the Marāthās to *chauth* and *sardeshmukhī*. In consideration for refraining from ravaging Berār and the other five *sūbahs* of the Deccan these freebooters were to be allowed to collect for themselves one-quarter of the revenue under the name of *chauth* and in addition to this a further proportion of one-tenth under the name of *sardeshmukhī*, which was regarded as a recompense for the trouble and expense of collecting the *chauth*. It was the imperial recognition of these claims which laid the foundation of that system of government known as *do-amlī*, afterwards to prove so ruinous to Berār, which has been admirably described by Sir Alfred Lyall: 'Wherever the 'emperor appointed a *jāgirdār* the Marāthās appointed another 'and both claimed the revenue while foragers from each side 'exacted forced contributions so that the harassed cultivator 'often threw up his land and helped to plunder his neighbour.'

Plots of the Saiyids and accession of Muhammad Shāh.

88. It is not necessary to follow in detail the course of the intrigues of the Saiyid brothers at Delhi. After deposing Farrukhsiyar and setting up two nonentities to succeed him, they raised to the throne in 1719 Raushan Akhtar, who took the title of Muhammad Shāh. In 1720 they hatched a plot against Asaf Jāh Nizām-ul-Mulk, son of Ghāzi-ud-dīn Fīroz Jang; and sent him as *sūbahdār* to Mālwā in the hope that he would either be disgraced in the vain attempt to quell the disturbances which they fomented against him or would rebel. To their disappointment he was joined by all the men of importance in Mālwā and also by his uncle Iwaz Khān, *sūbahdār* of Berār. Alam Alī Khān, the nephew of the Saiyids, who was viceroy of the Deccan, now appointed Anwar Khān *sūbahdār* of Berār but he too joined Asaf Jāh. The plot of the Saiyids failed. Asaf Jāh met their

nephew, Alam Alī Khān, at Bālāpur and there defeated and slew him. He then returned to Delhi and was appointed *sūbahdār* of Gujarāt while his son Ghāzi-ud-dīn Khān Fīroz Jang was appointed to Mālwā. In 1722 he received news that his Province of Gujarāt and his son's Province of Mālwā were overrun by the Marāthās, and he therefore obtained permission to leave Delhi for the purpose of expelling the intruders. While he was setting the affairs of Mālwā in order he learnt that Mubāriz Khān the *sūbahdār* of Hyderābād, whom he had believed to be devoted to his interests, had been bribed by the Saiyids with the promise of the viceroyalty of the Deccan to take up arms against him and was even then marching to meet him. At the same time he heard that his son Fīroz Jang, who held the post of prime minister of the empire as his deputy, had been superseded in Delhi.

Asaf Jāh obtains the Viceroyalty of the Deccan.

89. He therefore set out for the Deccan to meet Mubāriz Khān, whom he defeated and slew at Shakarkheldā [1] in the Buldāna District on October 13th, 1724. The date is an important one in the history of Berār and the Deccan for the battle of Shakarkheldā established the virtual independence of the Deccan under the Nizāms of Hyderābād. Neither Chin Kilīj Khān Nizām-ul-Mulk nor any of his successors at Hyderābād ever assumed the style of independent sovereigns, but they settled questions of succession among themselves, made all appointments in the six *sūbahs* of the Deccan and behaved in all respects as independent rulers with the exception that their coin bore the name of the reigning emperor and that the imperial recognition of each succession was purchased by large presents and professions of subservience. Shortly after, if not before, the death of Asaf Jāh the Bhonsla rājās of Nāgpur were recognized as *mokāsadārs* or assignees of the Marāthās' share of the revenues of Berār, and they maintained their collecting officers in the province under the *do-amlī* system already described until the conclusion of the second Marāthā war in 1803.

[1] Renamed Fatehkheldā by Asaf Jāh to commemorate his victory.

In 1738 Raghujī Bhonsla took advantage of the absence of Asaf Jāh in Delhi to invade Berār, and defeated and slew Shujāt Khān the *sūbahdār* in the neighbourhood of Ellichpur. It was probably at this time that the fortresses of Gāwīlgarh and Narnāla, which were held by the Bhonslas, except for a short period, until the end of the third Marāthā war, passed into his possession.

Disputes regarding the succession in Hyderābād.

90. On June 2nd, 1748, Asaf Jāh died on the bank of the Tāpti river on his way from Burhānpur to Daulatābād, and was succeeded in the Deccan by his son Nasīr Jang. In 1750 Nasīr Jang was succeeded by his brother Salābat Jang who on the death of Saiyid Sharīf Khān Shujāt Jang in June, 1752, appointed Saiyid Lashkar Khān Nasīr Jang to the vacant appointment of *sūbahdār* of Berār. In the same year Ghāzi-ud-dīn Khān, the eldest son of Asaf Jāh, having been appointed by the emperor Ahmad Shah viceroy of the Deccan, advanced as far as Aurangābād to secure his heritage, but in Aurangābād he died suddenly, from cholera according to one account, but according to another from poison administered by or at the instance of Salābat Jang's mother. Salābat Jang spent the rainy season of 1753 in Aurangābād where Saiyid Lashkar Khān *sūbahdār* of Berār, who had now received the title of Rukn-ud-daulah, was appointed *vazīr* of the Deccan, which appointment he resigned after a few months, leaving the finances of the State in a deplorable condition. Ghāzi-ud-dīn Khān, in order to attach the Marāthās to his cause, had assigned to them the revenues of all the northern districts of the Deccan and Raghujī Bhonsla, on the pretext of Ghāzi-ud-dīn's promise, had collected and retained the whole of the revenue of Berār. One of the first acts of Samsām-ud-daulah, who had succeeded Rukn-ud-daulah as minister, was to send against Raghujī an army which succeeded in forcing him to disgorge five lakhs of rupees—an utterly inadequate share of his plunder. In 1754 Raghujī Bhonsla died and Rukn-ud-daulah returned to Berār as *sūbahdār*. He was displaced in 1756 in favour of Mīr Nizām Alī, the brother of Salābat Jang, who on his

appointment as *sūbahdār* of Berār received the title of Nizām-ud-daulah. Nizām-ud-daulah now marched into Berār, where his presence was required, and encamped at Ellichpur. While he was halting here Bāpu Karandiya, Bhonsla's lieutenant, invaded the province and advanced as far as Borgaon where Nizām ud-daulah met and defeated him. The treaty of peace which was concluded was not, however, sufficiently stringent in its terms to prevent the Marāthās from continuing their depredations in Berār.

Accession of Nizām Alī and civil war

91. In 1761 Nizām-ud-daulah, who had already received the titles of Asaf Jāh and Nizām-ul-Mulk, deposed his brother and became ruler of the Hyderābād State. In 1763 he appointed Ghulām Saiyid Khān governor of Berār, but removed him in 1764 to Daulatābād and replaced him in Berār by Ismail Khān the Afghān.

In 1773 Zafar-ud-daulah, who had been engaged in suppressing a rebellion in Nirmal and had pursued some of the rebels into Berār, conceived the idea that Ismail Khān was harbouring them. He wrote to him accusing him of treason and Ismail sent an indignant reply. The correspondence between the two *amīrs* became so acrimonious that Ismail, as a precautionary measure, strengthened the fortifications of Ellichpur, whereupon Zafar-ud-daulah reported to Rukn-ud-daulah, Nizām Alī's minister, that the governor of Berār was meditating rebellion and asked for permission to march against him. Rukn-ud-daulah, who did not doubt Ismail's fidelity and was loth to see the resources of the State frittered away in civil war, returned no reply to this request, and Zafar-ud-daulah, either taking his silence for consent or affecting to believe that the urgency of the case was sufficient to justify him in acting on his own responsibility, invaded Berār and in June besieged Ismail in Ellichpur. On hearing that the conflict which he had tried to prevent had broken out Rukn-ud-daulah hastened to Ellichpur and patched up a temporary peace between the two disputants.

Affairs at Nāgpur. Overthrow of Ismail Khān in Berār.

92. In 1775 Nizām Alī, taking advantage of the existence of a strong party opposed to Mudhojī Bhonsla in Nāgpur, sent Ibrāhim Beg against him, and himself advanced as far as Ellichpur. Mudhojī, unable to cope at the same time with his foreign and domestic enemies, obtained a cession of hostilities by causing Gāwīlgarh and Narnāla to be surrendered to the Mughal officers and submitted himself, with his son Raghujī, to Nizām Alī in Ellichpur. Here the wily Marāthā, by the humility of his demeanour, succeeded in obtaining better terms, and in consideration of his agreeing to co-operate with the Nizām's troops in suppressing the Gonds, Gāwīlgarh and Narnāla were restored to him. At the same time Nizām Alī's eldest son, Alī Jāh, was appointed *sūbahdār* of Berār. Ismail Khān was in disgrace. Rukn-ud-daulah, who had befriended him, had been killed and his place had been taken by Ismail's former enemy, Zafar-ud-daulah. Before Rukn-ud daulah's death Ismail Khān, fearful of the effect of Zafar-ud-daulah's intrigues at court, had left Ellichpur without leave and presented himself before Nizām Alī. This breach of official etiquette was made the pretext for his degradation and he was informed that a jāgīr had been assigned to him in Bālāpur and that he had been degraded to the position of governor of that District. The message delivered to him was purposely made as galling as possible. He was ordered to vacate Ellichpur and appear before Nizām Alī and was advised that his surest avenue to favour was to apply for an interview through Zafar-ud-daulah. The headstrong Afghān refused so to humiliate himself, and on this refusal being reported to Nizām Alī, Zafar-ud-daulah was sent against Ellichpur, and was closely followed by Nizām Alī himself. Ismail Khān marched out of Ellichpur and attacked Zafar-ud-daulah with great determination, but though the vigour of the attack threw the enemy into confusion for a time, the garrison of Ellichpur was no match for the army of Hyderābād. Ismail Khān was surrounded and overpowered and when he fell his head was severed from his body and sent to the Nizām. Nizām Alī marched on, and on May 14th encamped at Ellichpur and made a pilgrimage

to the shrine of Abdur Rahmān. Zafar-ud-daulah was rewarded for this victory with the title of Mubāriz-ul-Mulk. Bahrām Jang was appointed Alī Jāh's lieutenant in Berār, Saiyid Mukarram Khān was appointed Dīwān of the province, and a Hindu, Shām Rao, was made *faujdār* of Ellichpur.

Attempt to oust the Marāthās.

93. In 1783 Bahrām Jang was removed from his appointment in Berār and was succeeded by Zafar-ud-daulah's son Ihtishām Jang. Zafar-ud-daulah had died in the meantime and his title was bestowed upon his son. The second Zafar-ud-daulah was intent on breaking the power of the Marāthās in Berār and was preparing to besiege Gāwīlgarh and Narnāla and expel the Marāthā revenue collectors from Berār when Mudhojī Bhonsla became aware of his designs and complained to Nizām Alī that the governor of Berār was meditating the violation of treaty agreements. Zafar-ud-daulah was therefore removed and Muhammad Kabīr Khān, one of the jāgirdārs of the province, was appointed in his place. In 1790 Muhammad Kabīr gave way to Salābat Khān, the elder son of Ismail Khān. In 1792 Buhlūl Khān, Salābat Khān's younger brother, was appointed *sūbahdār* of Berār and Aurangābād. Buhlūl was a debauchee with a taste for architecture and spent all the revenues which his able Dīwān, Khāja Bahādur, could squeeze out of the province on his pleasures and his hobby. He was summoned to Hyderābād and ordered to render an account of his stewardship, which proved to be so unsatisfactory that he was thrown into prison, where he remained for some years, and officers were sent to search his house in Ellichpur. If they expected to discover hoarded money they were disappointed for Buhlūl had spent the money as he received it.

Disturbance in Ellichpur and siege of Gāwīlgarh.

94. The deputy governor of Berār in 1801 was Gangārām Narāyan, who in that year caused an *émeute* in Ellichpur. He introduced a new tax apparently for the purpose of augmenting his private income, and attempted to levy it from all the habitants of the town alike, including soldiers and other

customary exemptees. The malcontents rose and attacked the fort of Ellichpur. When they burst in, the wretched Gangārām threw himself on their mercy and promised never more to offend them. Thus were the people satisfied and the power and prestige of the government held up to scorn.

On December 5th, 1803, General Arthur Wellesley, having defeated the Marāthās at Argaon on November 29th, arrived at Ellichpur on his way to Gāwīlgarh, which was held for Raghujī Bhonsla by the Rājput Benī Singh. On the 7th Wellesley marched to Deogaon, below the southern face of the fort, sending Colonel Stevenson and his division by a route about thirty miles in length through the hills with the object of attacking the fort from the north. From the 7th to the 12th Stevenson's division suffered great hardships, dragging the heavy ordnance and stores by hand over roads which the troops themselves made for the occasion. On the 12th Stevenson occupied Labāda, a village, now deserted, on the *col* which connects the Gāwīlgarh hill with the Chikaldā plateau, and just north of the fort, near the present cemetery. On the night of the 12th Stevenson erected two batteries opposite to the north face of the fort, where the principal attack was to be delivered and on the same night Wellesley's division erected a battery on a hill under the southern gate, the Pīr Fateh *darwāza*, but this battery was of little use save to distract the enemy's attention from the attack on the north face, for the heavy iron guns could not be moved to the top of the hill, and the brass guns produced but little effect. On the morning of December 13th all the batteries opened fire on the fort, and by the night of the 14th the breaches in the northern face were practicable and all arrangements had been made for storming the place. The storming party consisted of the flank companies of His Majesty's 94th Regiment and of the native corps in Stevenson's divisions and was commanded by Lieutenant-Colonel Kenny of the 1st battalion of the 11th Madras Native Infantry (now the 81st Pioneers). It was supported by the battalion companies of the 94th and Lieutenant-Colonel Halyburton's brigade, Lieutenant-Colonel Macleane's brigade being in reserve, and the attack was delivered at 10 A.M. on the 15th. At the same time Wellesley delivered two attacks from the south. One was directed against the southern gate, the attacking party consisting of the 74th Highlanders, five companies of the 78th Highlanders and the 1st battalion of the 8th Regiment of Madras Native Infantry (afterwards the 8th Madras Infantry) under the command of Lieutenant-Colonel Wallace of the 74th, and the objective of the other party, which consisted of the remaining five companies of the 78th Highlanders and the 1st battalion of the 10th Regiment of Madras Native Infantry (afterward the 10th Madras Infantry), under the command of Lieutenant-Colonel Chalmers, was the north-western gate.

These two attacks from the south were destined merely to distract the enemy's attention from Stevenson's attack on the north, unless it should be found possible to blow the gates in. Neither of the two gates was blown in, but Chalmers' column was able to perform a useful service for it arrived at the north-western gate at the same time as a detachment sent forward by Stevenson, whose first attack had been successful, to establish communication with Chalmers, and in time to intercept considerable numbers of the enemy who were flying from that detachment through the gate. Chalmers was thus enabled not only to enter the outer fort without difficulty, and thus join forces with Stevenson for the attack on the northern face of the inner fort, but also to destroy large numbers of the fleeing enemy.

Fall of Gāwīlgarh.

95. The next task of the besiegers was to effect an entrance into the inner fort, the wall of which had not been breached, and some ineffectual attempts were made to force an entrance by the Delhi gate which is the strongest gate in the fort and is exceedingly well provided with flank defences on the Indian system of fortification. A place was then found where it was possible to scale the wall and Captain Campbell, with the light company of the 94th, fixed the ladders, escaladed the wall, and opened the Delhi gate to the storming party. After

Bemrose, Collo., Derby.

THE OUTER FORT, GAWILGARH.

a brief resistance the fort was in the possession of Wellesley's troops, but the slaughter of the enemy was very great, especially at the gates. The bodies of the *kilādār* and Benī Singh were found amidst a heap of slain within the Delhi gate. Some of the Rājputs, and among them these two officers, had attempted to perform the rite of *jauhar* before sallying out to meet their assailants, but fortunately the work was clumsily done, for of twelve or fourteen women only three were found to be dead and a few others wounded. The survivors were treated with respect and were well cared for.

The British losses were very small, considering the nature of the operation. Among the British troops three officers were wounded, of whom two, Lieutenant-Colonel Kenny already mentioned, and Lieutenant Young of the 2nd battalion of the 7th Madras Native Infantry died, and five rank and file were killed and fifty-nine wounded. The casualties among native troops were eight killed and fifty-one wounded. Lieutenant-Colonel Kenny was buried at Ellichpur and Lieutenant Young near the spot where he fell. Around the latter's grave the Chikaldā cemetery wall is built.

General Sir Jasper Nicolls in his diary praises the personal bravery of Benī Singh and the *kilādār*, but adds that they did not seem to be able to frame any regular plan for the defence of the inner wall, or to have infused much of their own spirit into their sepoys. It is, indeed, evident from the insignificance of the besiegers' losses, that the victories of Assaye and Argaon had awed the troops of the Marāthās, and the defence of the fort was far from being resolute. The difficulties with which the attacking force had to contend arose principally from the nature of the country. Stevenson's arduous march through the hills has already been described. Of this feat Wellesley wrote: 'the troops in his division went 'through a series of laborious services, such as I never before 'witnessed, with the utmost cheerfulness and perseverance.' Wellesley's own division was less severely tried, but the erection of a battery on the hill under the southern gate must have entailed much heavy labour, and their operations on

15th must have been most exhausting, even to the Highlanders of the 74th and 78th Regiments, for the approaches to the fort from the south are exceedingly difficult.

Treaties of Deogaon and Anjangaon.

96. Two days after the fall of Gāwīlgarh a preliminary treaty was signed at Deogaon, Wellesley's headquarters, by which Raghujī Bhonsla agreed to withdraw from the plains of Berār to the east of the Wardhā river, retaining, however, the fortresses of Gāwīlgarh and Narnāla, and the Melghāt. This treaty, which was described by the Governor-General in a private letter to his brother as 'wise, honourable, and glorious,' was followed by another with Sindhia, signed on December 30th at Anjangaon in the Daryāpur tāluk. These two treaties brought the second Marāthā war to an honourable conclusion.

Civil and Military adminstration.

97. Rājā Mahipat Rām, who had commanded the subsidiary force supplied by the Nizām for the second Marāthā war, was rewarded with the governorship of Berār, but intrigued against the minister in Hyderābād, was degraded, and then openly rebelled against the Nizām. After giving some trouble he took refuge with Holkar, in whose dominions he was assassinated. In 1806 Rājā Govind Bakhsh succeeded him as *sūbahdār* of Berār and Aurangābād. In 1813 Vithal Bhāgdeo of Karasgaon, who has left as a monument of himself in his native town a fort of fine sandstone, was appointed deputy governor of Ellichpur. Throughout these changes Ṣalābat Khān held a large jāgīr at Ellichpur for the purpose of maintaining the Ellichpur brigade, consisting of two battalions of infantry and 1600 horse which were reported by the Resident Mr. (afterwards Sir Henry) Russell in 1817 as being among the best troops in the Nizām's army. The infantry battalions were incorporated in the Hyderābād Contingent. Salābat Khān's jāgīr was resumed from his son Nāmdār Khān in 1832.

98. The District was not affected by the war of 1817-18, but the Peshwā, after his defeat by Lieutenant-Colonel Adams at Siwanī in the Yeotmāl District, fled northwards through the District into the Sātpurā hills.

Third Marāthā war, Pindāri war, Treaty of 1822, and the Assignment.

The treaty of Deogaon had left the Melghāt with its two fortresses in the hands of the Bhonslas and the tract served as a refuge and stronghold for rebels and outlaws, the most notorious of whom was Sheikh Dullā, whose depredations in the hills, and excursions into the richer plains extended over some years. The District was not the scene of any important action during the Pindāri war, though it had suffered from the ravages of these marauders. The wall which surrounds the town of Amraoti was built in 1807 as a protection against their inroads, and there was some local fighting for the *khūnāri* ('bloody') wicket in this wall is said to be so called from 700 persons having fallen in a fight close to it in 1818.

In 1822, after the conclusion of the Pindāri war, a fresh treaty was made whereby the tracts lying to the east of the Wardhā were ceded to Nāgpur, and the Melghāt, with its fortresses, Gāwīlgarh and Narnāla, was restored to the Nizām. By the same treaty the claims of the Marāthās to *chauth* were extinguished, but this provision benefited Berār little, for extravagance and maladministration at the capital led to the farming out of the province to usurers, and these extortioners reduced it to a condition of great misery, which was enhanced by the famine of 1833.

In 1853 the District, with the rest of Berār, was assigned to the East India Company in satisfaction of the debt due on account of arrears of pay disbursed to the Contingent and as security for the pay of that force in future.

99. The troubles of 1857 scarcely affected Berār, and Tāntia Topī who attempted, by forcing his way through the Melghāt, to escape from Hindūstān into the Deccan was turned back. Meadows Taylor who was Deputy Commissioner during a portion of this time praises

The Mutiny and the treaty of 1861.

the loyalty of the Melghāt Rājās in repelling emissaries sent by the mutineers to raise the Deccan. In 1858 the fortress of Gāwīlgarh was dismantled, and in 1861 the treaty of Assignment was revised, the Nizām receiving several advantages in return for his staunchness in the Mutiny.

Administration since the Assignment. Progress since Mutiny.

100. When the province first fell into the hands of the Company it was divided into two districts, South Berār (the 'Bālā Ghāt') with its headquarters at Hingoli and North Berār with headquarters at Buldāna. The latter district included the whole Pāyanghāt valley, that is to say the present Amraoti District, the northern half of Akolā and part of Buldāna. After the Mutiny Hingoli with the neighbouring country was restored to the Nizām, and the province reconstituted into East Berār with headquarters at Amraoti, and West Berār with headquarters at Akolā. In 1864 the Yeotmāl District, at first called the South-east Berār and later the Wūn District, was separated from Amraoti and in 1867 the Ellichpur District, which at first included the tāluk of Morsi, subsequently restored to Amraoti, was formed. In 1903 the treaties of Assignment were superseded by an agreement under which the Nizām leased Berār to the Government of India in perpetuity in return for an annual rent of twenty-five lakhs, and the administration of the Province was transferred from the Resident at Hyderābād to the Chief Commissioner of the Central Provinces. After this transfer, in 1905, the Districts of the Province were redistributed and the Ellichpur District was once more amalgamated with Amraoti, while the Murtizāpur tāluk was transferred from Amraoti to Akolā.

Since 1857 the history of the District has been the record of a steady increase of prosperity, which received a sudden stimulus from the American Civil War, which increased the demand for Indian cotton, and was only temporarily checked by the season of scarcity in 1896-97 and the famine of 1899-1900.

ARCHÆOLOGY

The Amraoti District is poor in archæological remains, the only monuments of interest being the hill fort of Gāwīlgarh and a few buildings in Ellichpur.

Gāwīlgarh

101. It is impossible to say when the Gāwīlgarh hill was first fortified, but its name points to the fact that it was at one time, like Gaolīgarh in Khāndesh and Asīrgarh (*Asā Ahīr Garh*) near Burhānpur, a stronghold of Ahīr or Gaolī chieftains, and a legend exists to the effect that these chiefs had a mud fort on this hill. No part of the existing fort can be traced back to a period anterior to 1425, when it is said, by Firishta, to have been built by Ahmad Shāh Walī, the ninth king of the Bahmanī dynasty. It was subsequently repaired and improved by Fateh-ullah Imād-ul-Mulk, the first independent king of Berār, in 1488, and by Bahrām Khān, commandant of the fort under Saiyid Murtazā Sabzawāri, in 1577. The most conspicuous of the remains upon the hill is the ruin of the great *masjid* which stands upon the highest point towards the south side of the plateau. The mosque, which is visible from the Berār valley for a great distance, has seven arches in its facade and was three bays deep from front to back. All along, above the arches, runs an overhanging cornice of simple design, three-fourths of which have been destroyed. Each end of the facade is flanked by a projecting square pier; but these, instead of being surmounted by *minārs*, as elsewhere, carry above the roof most elegant little square canopies or *chhatrīs* with deep cornices, rich brackets, and perforated *jālī* or screen-work in each of their four sides. The *chhatrī* from the south pier is missing; that on the north remains, but is damaged. A flight of steps descend from the mosque to the great square courtyard before it, the pavement of which is now nearly all up. A high wall, with niches at intervals, encloses the courtyard, having a great gateway on the east and smaller entrances on the north and south. From the great eastern gateway a deep flight of

steps leads down to the ground without, but at some later period a tomb has been built before this, and with its flanking walls, encloses an area before the steps and prevents access to the entrance, save through the tomb. A small amount of blue tiling has been used on the face of the mosque. The mosque is unfortunately in a ruinous condition. The whole of the western wall, which contained the *mihrābs* and was supported by buttresses, has fallen away down the steep hillside and has carried with it portions of the north and south walls and one entire range of the domes, so that only fourteen domes now remain. A small and substantially built mosque stands on the edge of a large tank, a short distance to the north-east of the great mosque. There are a few old iron guns in the fort, two of which are of considerable size. The most interesting monuments in Gāwīlgarh are two gateways, the *Delhi darwāza* between the inner and the outer fort, and the *Pīr Patha*[1] *darwāza*, the south-western gate of the fort. Above the latter are the remains of an inscription, much weatherbeaten, for it has borne the full force of the south-western monsoon for more than four centuries, which tells us that Ulugh Imād-ul-Mulk, that is to say Fateh-ullah Imād-ul-Mulk, rebuilt with the old stones in the year H. 893 (A. D. 1488) the *jāmi masjid* above the tank, in the reign of Mahmūd Shāh Bahmani. This inscription evidently refers to the repairing of the great mosque, the western wall of which had probably even then given away, owing to the steepness of the slope of the knoll on which it is built. The Delhi gate has a group of sculptured symbols on its face, above the archway. In the centre is a palmtree, and on either side of this and below it a lion *passant*, looking inward with a small elephant below each paw. Above the lion, on each side, is an eagle displayed, double-headed, holding in each of its beaks a small elephant. This bird is the fabulous *ganda bherunda*, one of the symbols of the Vijayanagar empire of Southern India. The

[1] So called locally. The word is probably *Fateh*.

Bemrose, Collo., Derby.

NORTH END OF GREAT MOSQUE, GAWILGARH.

occurrence of this symbol enables us to determine the builder of the gate, for Fateh-ullah Imād-ul-Mulk was a Brāhman of Vijayanagar who was captured in childhood by Ahmad Shāh Walī and was brought up as a Musalmān. His extensive repairs to the fort, were a preparation for his declaration of independence in 1490.

In the western face of the fort is a fine bastion with the following inscription :—

'In Gāwīl Bahrām built a bastion
'The like of which the eye of time hath not seen,
'He carried it to such a height
'That the planet Saturn takes his ease in its shelter.
'When I pondered over the date of its construction
'(It was found in the words) "That bastion of Bahrām is completed."'

The chronogram gives the date (A.D. 1577), wrongly given in the Berār Gazetteer[1] as A.H. 453 (A.D. 1061) at which period there were certainly no Musalmāns in the Deccan. Bahrām Khān was commandant of Gāwīlgarh under Saiyid Murtazā Sabzawāri, Murtazā Nizām Shāh's governor of Berār, and the fort was repaired in 1577 owing to the prevalence of a rumour that Akbar was then marching on Berār. What is known as the outer fort of Gāwīlgarh, which lies between the *Delhi darwāza* and the deserted village of Labāda, was probably built by the Bhonsla rājās of Nāgpur, who held Gāwīl from the first quarter of the eighteenth century until 1822. On one of the battlements there is an inscription in Sanskrit or Marāthī, probably the latter. This has not yet been deciphered, but a careful study of the stone itself would probably lead to a successful decipherment, for the Nāgarī or Bālbodh letters are well and carefully formed, though they are so lightly incised in the rough granite that it would be a matter of great difficulty to obtain a satisfactory impression.

---

[1] Pages 143, 144.

Ellichpur.

102. The shrine at Ellichpur which bears the name of Abdur Rahmān Shāh the Ghāzi, the legendary history of whom has already been discussed, has no architectural merit and cannot be assigned to any date earlier than A.D. 1400. It is probably the tomb of the officers of Fīroz Shāh Bahmanī who were killed in an expedition against Kherlā in that year. There are remains of other buildings at Ellichpur, but none is of archæological interest.

CHAPTER III.

POPULATION.

STATISTICS OF POPULATION.

Statistics.

103. The present Amraoti District was constituted in 1905 of the old Amraoti and Ellichpur Districts with the exception of the Murtizāpur tāluk. The last census was held in 1901 and as under the various heads it gives most commonly District not tāluk totals, statistics for the present area are extremely difficult to obtain.[1] Moreover, the wide difference in character that separates the Melghāt from the plains must always make generalizations as to the whole District deceptive.

Among the Districts of the Central Provinces and Berār Amraoti stands third in respect of population and sixth in respect of size. The following table shows the figures by tāluks; and the comparison with the rest of the Provinces:

	Square miles.	Population.	Average density per Sq. M.
Amraoti Tāluk	672	175,557	261
Morsi ,, ...	622	143,734	231
Chāndur ,, ...	855	192,805	226
Ellichpur ,, ...	469	146,035	311
Daryāpur ,, ...	505	114,698	227
Melghāt ,, ...	1,631	36,670	22
Amraoti District	4,754	809,499	170
,, ,, excluding urban areas	...	... ...	133
,, ,, excluding Melghāt but including urban areas	...	......	247
,, ,, excluding both Melghāt and urban areas	...	......	209
British Districts C. P. and Berār ...	...	......	120

Daryāpur with 210 persons per square mile shows the highest rural density of any tāluk.

[1] In this section italics will be used for district totals which include and ordinary type for those which exclude Murtizāpur.

The District contains according to the census nineteen towns and 2,033 villages of which 43 have over 2,000 inhabitants and 1,214 less than 500; 448 are uninhabited. The towns are as follows:—

Amraoti Tāluk.

Amraoti ...	34,216
Badnerā ...	10,859
Kholāpur ...	5,373
Amraoti Camp.	5,295
Balgaon Jāgīr	5,284

Ellichpur Tāluk.

Ellichpur ...	26,082
Paratwāda or Ellichpur Civil Station ...	10,410
Karasgaon ...	7,456
Shirasgaon Qasbā ...	6,537
Chāndur Bazār	5,208

Morsi Tāluk.

Morsi ...	8,313
Warud ...	7,179
Sendurjana ...	6,860
Ner Ping'ai ...	5,408

Chāndur Tāluk.

Chāndur Railway	5,700
Mangrul Dastagīr	6,588
Talegaon Dashāsar	6,220
Dattāpur ...	5,187

Daryāpur Tāluk.

Anjangaon, 8,783.

The total urban population is therefore 176,958 or 21·85 per cent. of that of the District, a proportion only exceeded in Nāgpur. Many of the so-called towns are almost entirely agricultural in character, while one or two large villages omitted from the list, such as Daryāpur 4389 with its suburb Wanosā 915, have a considerable mercantile population. There are only four municipalities, namely, the two Amraotis and the two Ellichpurs; but each of the tahsīl headquarters in the plain, as well as Dattāpur, possesses a cotton market committee which exercises some of the functions of a municipality, so far at least as the cotton market and its surroundings are concerned.

Of the various towns there is little of importance to note. Eleven have increased and eight decreased in population since 1891; the decrease is most remarkable in Sendurjana 31·7 per cent.; Ner Pinglai 21 per cent. and Anjangaon 17 per cent. All these are largely agricultural in character; while the increase is most notable in commercial towns, Dattāpur having risen from 3225 to 5187 (60·8 per cent.), Chāndur Railway 4794 to 5700 (nearly 19 per cent.), and Chāndur Bazār, in spite of its unfavourable position with regard to communications, from 4974 to 5208 (5·7 per cent.). The total urban population has, however, risen only by 5928 persons, *i.e.* less than 3 per cent. Further details will be found under the separate headings in the Gazetteer Appendix. A characteristic feature of Amraoti, as indeed of every Berār District, is the number of large villages, no less than 2·68 per cent. of the whole number having over 2000 inhabitants, a proportion not elsewhere exceeded in these Provinces; and 6·48 per cent. having between 1000 and 2000, a proportion only exceeded in Akolā and Buldāna.

Growth of population.

104. A census of the District has been taken on four occasions. For the first (1867) only provincial totals are now obtainable; but in 1881, 1891, 1901 the figures for the present area were 778,167; 849,604; and 809,499 respectively. The first decade was one of uninterrupted prosperity while the second was broken by the two severe famines of 1897-98 and 1899-1900. The increase and decrease require no further explanation. A comparison of tāluk totals suggests nothing of importance. As we might expect, Ellichpur and Daryāpur being far removed not only from the railway but from any through line of communication, have decreased steadily but slowly throughout: while the other tāluks increased in the first period and fell off in the second. The loss in numbers appears to have been most heavy in the Melghāt where it amounted to not less than 21·7 per cent. of the whole population. Largely, no doubt, this figure is due to the rigour of the famine and the extreme difficulty of administering relief in a wild and mountainous country to a backward and diffident population: but the decrease does not signify sheer loss of life. Much of it is traceable to emigration, both temporary and permanent, to the richer tracts of Nimār and Berār, and part to the absence of

temporary immigrants whom the forests ordinarily attract from neighbouring areas. Something also must be allowed for the temporary road gangs at work in 1891 who had no successors in 1901.

Population and Cultivation.

105. The proportion of net cropped area per head of population in 1891-92 was 1.93 acres; in 1901-02 it had risen to 2.14; and in 1906-7 to 2.24 on the last census population, a higher figure than is given for any other District in these Provinces. At the last census *650,784* persons were returned as dependent upon agriculture while *6691* were supported in various ways by pasturage. As the returns show, the District is almost entirely an agricultural one, for besides those returned as directly engaged on the soil, who by themselves are more than two-thirds of the population, there are many minor occupations of an agricultural nature. Village servants, for instance, who number with dependents *13,695* : patels and patwāris not shown as agriculturists, with their dependents, *5725* and *2708* respectively ; hay grass and fodder sellers *3489* ; and several other descriptions are all connected with agriculture. Probably, it will be no great over-estimate to say that seven out of every eight persons in the District are in one way or another immediately dependent on the care and cultivation of the soil.

Other pursuits.

106. It is natural that with so large a rural population no other pursuit should show figures of much interest. The staple crop is cotton, and we find accordingly that *33,465* persons are engaged in or dependent on the preparation of cotton (and silk) for the market, of whom *16,239* belong to cotton mills and gins and *10,115* are hand loom weavers. Piece goods and tailoring further support *8634*. No other trades show figures of much interest though we may note the totals *4536* bankers and moneylenders, with *10,018* moneylenders' and shopkeepers' servants as indicative of the amount of money in circulation; and goldsmiths *9560* and liquor sellers *6207* as giving some indication of the margin which the people manage to devote to mere luxuries.

Migration.

107. In 1901 just over *87* per cent. of the population were shown as having been born within the District: of the remainder *46,697* came from other Berãr Districts and may be treated as the natural shifting of population inside the Province. No less than *125,355* are returned as born in the Central Provinces, an enormous total due no doubt partly to the higher wages of labour in Berãr and to the facility for coming into it from other parts of the Central Provinces: the same explanation holding true of the *11,187* from Rãjputãna and *13,441* from the United Provinces. Large numbers of casuals known as "Pardesīs" drift down from Upper India to this neighbourhood, sometimes in search of employment and sometimes, it is to be feared, with very good reasons for quitting their native country. Bombay also, with which Amraoti is closely connected by the cotton industry and the railway and by a common language, has given *17,343* persons. Further explanation of the figures is not forthcoming, nor are statistics available of the emigration from Amraoti which has also undoubtedly been very large.

Diseases.

108. All the original Settlement Reports speak of cholera and small-pox as the two great endemic scourges of the District, and some also make reference to malaria. Of the progress of the latter it is impossible to speak with any certainty, for Hospital Assistants are given to describing all fevers as malarial and the statistics are therefore open to suspicion. It seems probable however that there has been of recent years a great decline in the prevalence of this complaint; and it appears to be a general opinion that excepting the Melghãt, where a specially virulent type prevails, the District is as a whole tolerably immune, though in a mild form malaria is common toward the close of the rains. Cholera to-day cannot be described as endemic. In only four recent years, namely, 1896, 1897, 1900, 1901 was it in any degree severe. Two of these were famine years and in a third the people had not fully recovered from the effects of famine; in 1896 it appears probable that

the disease was imported by religious pilgrims returning from a fair. Indeed the disease referred to by the Settlement Officers was probably not what we now call cholera, but some less acute bowel complaint. Such troubles are still fairly common every year in the beginning of July, and in August a few cases of dysentery occur. The most popular explanation, adopted by Major Elphinstone in his Daryāpur Settlement Report, ascribes them to the Berār custom of storing juāri, the staple food, in earthen pits called *peos* where it becomes very damp and mouldy at the commencement of the rains. Medical investigations, however, do not completely bear out this theory. Statistics show deaths from dysentery and allied diseases as very much more common in Berār than in the Central Provinces. But very considerable allowance must be made for the greater completeness of Berār vital statistics as well as for the tendency of police and village officers to reduce all cases of death to a few simple causes; and in Amraoti District it would certainly be a mistake to say that bowel complaints were unusually common. In general the District is admittedly a very healthy one both for Europeans and Indians in spite of the fierce heat prevalent in the summer months. It has been said that not a single authentic case of enteric has ever been known in Berār; and though this is doubtless an exaggeration, it is certainly true that this malady is extremely rare.

Vaccination in Berār (excepting the Melghāt, where it is said, though statistics are not available, to be somewhat backward) has been a great success and the Amraoti District in particular has of recent years been remarkably free from small-pox. Not only has there been no severe epidemic, but in only three years 1896, 1905, 1906 did the number of deaths reach one hundred. This excellent result is due largely to the active co-operation of village officers in the spread of vaccination; for the Vaccination Act does not apply except in the four municipal towns. The District is divided into circles, two for each tāluk, and the vaccinator visits every village in his circle. The patwāri prepares a list of children to be vaccinated and the names are entered in a register by the vaccinator. As a general rule the protection afforded is fully understood and people are perfectly willing to accept it. These remarks of course do not apply to the jungle tribes of the Melghāt, among whom registers are not maintained, reliance being placed rather upon personal influence. The latest statistics for the plains show an annual proportion of 33·76 persons protected per 1000 of population.

Amraoti appears to have escaped plague until 1902 when there were 39 cases. In 1903-04 there was a severe outbreak; the deaths in the old Amraoti District numbered over 9000 and those in Ellichpur nearly 3000. This was followed by two years in which the mortality was less than one thousand, a second serious epidemic occurring in 1906-07 with 6000 deaths. In 1908-09 the disease was again virulent, carrying off 2800 persons. Amraoti city alone lost 3100, 1100 and 996 lives in the three epidemics respectively.

Language; Marāthī.[1]

109. The principal language of the District is Marāthī, which is spoken by 627,000 persons, or 70 per cent. of the population. The form of the language locally used is that known as the Berāri dialect and is closely related with that which Marāthī assumes in the Deccan. The difference between the two forms of speech is slight and they gradually merge into each other in Buldāna. Long vowels, and especially final ones, are very frequently shortened, and there is a strong tendency among the lower classes to substitute *o* for *ava* or *avi*; thus *zol* for *zaval*, near; *udoīā* for *udavilā*, squandered. An *a* is very commonly used where the Deccan form of the language has an *è*, especially in the termination of neuter bases, in the suffix *nè* of the instrumental, and in the future. Thus *asa*, so; *sāngitla*, it was said; *dukra*, swine; *asal*, I shall be. *I* is very often interchanged with *è* and *ya*; thus *dila*, *dèlla* and *dyalla*, given; initial *è*, is commonly pronounced as a *ye*; thus *èk*, and *yèk*, one. The Anunāsika is very commonly dropped, or, occasionally replaced by an *n*; thus *karu*, to do; *tyāmule* therefore; *tun* thou. This is, however, the case in the Deccan also. The cerebral *n*

[1] Mr. Hira Lāl, Asst. Gazetteer Superintendent, has kindly supplied the note on Languages.

is always changed to the dental *n*; thus *kon*, who; *pāni*, water. *L* and *n* are continually interchanged in the future tenses; thus *mī mārīn* and *mārīl*, I shall strike. *V* is very indistinctly sounded before *i* and *e* and is often dropped altogether. Thus *isto*, fire; *īs*, twenty; *yel*, time. This fact accounts for occasional spellings such as *Vishvar*, God. The neuter gender is thoroughly preserved only in Marāthī and Gujarāti, but the distinction between it and the masculine is weakened in the Berāri dialect. *Mānsa*, men, is a neuter plural, but it is frequently combined with an adjective in the masculine gender; thus *tsāngle mānsa*, good men. In verbs the second person singular has usually the form of the third person; thus *tū āhe*, thou art, for *tū āhès*. In the present tense *a* is substituted for *è* in the terminations of the second person singular, and the third person plural; thus *tū mārta*, thou strikest; *te mārtat*, they strike. The habitual past is often used as ordinary past; thus *to mhanè*, he said. In the Ellichpur tāluk two small dialects Zadpī and Koshti are spoken but they do not materially differ from the prevailing language of the District. A peculiarity of Zadpī is the substitution of the cerebral *l* for a cerebral *d* when preceded by a vowel; thus *gholā*, a horse. The genuine cerebral *l* is commonly pronounced as *r*; thus *kār*, famine. A further characteristic of Berāri Marāthī as distinguished from the purer tongue spoken farther west is the large vocabulary which, in the course of Muhammadan dominion in Berār, it has borrowed from Urdū.

110. Other Languages. Among other languages Urdū is spoken by 66,000 persons or 8 per cent. of the population. This is the largest figure in any District of the Provinces. The same is the case with Mārwāri which has 13,000 speakers in the District. Urdū is spoken by Musalmāns, while Mārwāri is spoken by trader immigants from Rājputāna. The number of Hindī speakers exceeds that of the other three Districts of Berār put together by 2,000, there being 35,000 in this District forming 4 per cent. of the population. These are all immigrants from the north. It is impossible to draw any distinction between the Urdū and Hindī

locally spoken. Except among a few Persian scholars in Ellichpur the language is the same whichever alphabet is used; and this fact is recognised locally by the term *Musalmāni bāt* which covers both tongues. Almost the whole of the Korkū population of Berār is concentrated in this District or more specifically in the Melghāt tāluk; and it looks somewhat curious that there should be 27,748 speakers of the Korkū language against the tribal strength of 27,051. But this is probably due to the fact that Nihāls, the drudges of the Korkūs, also speak their language. Originally the Nihāls had a distinct language of their own which is now very rapidly disappearing. Nothing is known as to its affinities, and the few who still speak it do so with so large an admixture of Korkū and Marāthī words that it has become difficult to obtain any definite knowledge. Gondī is spoken by 24,399 persons, exceeding the number of Gonds by 1154. This may be explained by the fact that Gondī is also used as their speech by Pardhāns. Korkū and Gondi belong to different families of aboriginal languages, the former to Mūnda and the latter to Dravidian stock. The Rev. John Drake has written an excellent Korkū grammar which may be consulted for details. The phonetical system is broadly the same as in Santāli. There are two genders, one denoting animate beings and the other denoting inanimate objects. They are, however, often confounded. There are three numbers, the singular, the dual and the plural. Number is only marked in the case of animate nouns. The suffix of the dual is *king* and that of the plural *kū*. It is interesting to see that the dual is used to denote a married wife as in Santāli, *e. g.*, Tumta-king, that is, Tumta's wife. Adjectives do not change for gender, number or case. Comparison is effected by putting the compared noun in the ablative. It is a well-known fact that the Mūnda verb is not a verb in the strictest sense of the word. Every form can be used as a noun, an adjective and a verb. The principal dialects have a separate particle, the so-called categorical *a*, by simply adding which any word may be turned into a verb. Thus Santāli *dal-ket* is the base of the past tense of the verb *dal*, strike. It can also be used as a noun or as an adjective; thus *dal-ket-ko*, those who struck; *dal-ket-har* 'the struck having man,' 'the man who struck.' If we add the categorical *a* this form is changed into a real verb; thus *dal-ket-a*, (he) struck him. Korkū does not possess any such thing as a categorical *a*. The same form is, without any difference, used in the different functions. Thus, *ing-ken-tol-ing* means 'me-to binding me,' 'binding me.' If we use this form as a noun, we may, for instance, add the suffix of the locative; thus *ing-ken-tol-ing-en*, 'me-to binding-me-in,' 'in binding me.' The same form can be used as an adjective and as a verb; thus, *ing-ken-tol-ing koro*, 'me-to binding-me man,' 'a man who binds me;' *dich*, *ing-ken bang tol-ing*, he me-to not binding-me, he does not bind me. The negative particle is *bang* or *he-bang* which sometimes precedes and sometimes follows the principal verb. *Bang* can be inflected as a verb, but in the past tense it is more common to add *dun* to the base. Among minor languages may be mentioned Gujarāti with 6000 speakers, Telugu with 4000, and Banjāri with 2000. The former two are spoken by immigrants from Gujarāt and Telingāna respectively and the last by wandering pack-bullock traders of whom Berār possesses a very large number.[1]

RELIGION.

Statistics of Religion.

111. The figures of religion show that Hindus constitute 84 per cent. of the population, Muhammadans 8 per cent. and Animists 5 per cent. In 1901 the District had also 5252 Jains, and 1127 Christians. The proportion of professed Animists is large as compared with other Berār Districts, owing to the inclusion of the Melghāt. The Hindu religion of Berār is in no way different from that of the rest of Mahārāshtra, and it would be difficult if not impossible to calculate its precise indebtedness to the pantheism of the Aryan invaders, the local animistic fetish worship of early tribes, and the philosophical and moral revivals of Buddha and the Jains.

[1] The information about the Marāthī and Korkū languages has been principally taken from Dr. Sten Konow's Vols. on the Marāthī and Mūnda languages, edited by Dr. G. A. Grierson in his Linguistic Survey of India Series.

Probably the strongest element has been the latest, that of the Brāhmanic counter reformation. Among Brāhmans and other high castes the Vedas, Purānas and Shāstras carry the same authority as elsewhere in the Deccan. Among Kunbīs and other Sūdras, and among the more completely Hinduized castes below the Sūdras, the same deities, the same temples and shrines, the same beliefs, rites and observances will be found. As throughout India, the popular dogmas are a mixture of gross superstition, metaphysical speculation and high religious philosophy. Among the lower castes Islām has had some slight influence, though it is easy to exaggerate this. The spread of Islām in Berār probably dates from 1294 A.D. when Alāuddīn made his first expedition to the Deccan. Strict upholders of the faith are to be found among those who can claim descent from the invaders, but in the villages laxities have crept in. 'Here, as 'elsewhere in India, the Musalmān villager has borrowed 'or inherited from his Hindu neighbour or ancestor many 'practices which precisians would condemn as superstitious.'[1] One may compare the customs of Goanese Christians. Living side by side with his Hindu brethren in the same or the next village, sharing property in the same land, and forming a part of the same family with them, it would have been impossible for the Musalmān convert completely to cast off his old religious customs and ideas. The women especially are offenders. A Musalmān woman who had not made an offering to the small-pox goddess, would feel that she had deliberately risked her child's life.

Village deities.

112. As usual each village has a number of petty deities at whose shrines worship is offered on special occasions. 'Of all the gods 'of the Hindu pantheon Mahādeo and Māroti (Hanumān) 'probably receive the most attention.'[2] Mahādeo or Siva is represented by his symbol the Linga or phallus, typical of reproduction. A representation of his sacred animal, the

---

[1] Draft Imperial Gazetteer of Berār, page 23. [2] *Ibidem.*

bull Nandī, is usually placed before him. 'The cult of Siva,' says Dr. Barnett,[1] 'affects the two poles of society. He 'is favoured by many high class Brāhmans and ascetics who 'are devoted to metaphysical studies; for the history of Siva 'in this connection shows him growing from a wild moun-'tain-devil, patron of goblins and thieves, into a mystic 'sorcerer-god, and thence into a type of the Yogīs and cog-'nate orders of philosopher-saints. For the same reason he 'is popular with the lowest classes; the Yoga system in its 'practical side is largely based upon vulgar ideas of magic 'and Shamanism, and hence many of its professors have 'always been vulgar charlatans, and worse.' Māroti is the monkey-god whose shrine is found in every village. 'If a 'large number of temples and shrines were any test of the 'popularity of a god, Māroti would certainly bear off the palm.' He is represented by an image of a monkey coloured with vermilion. The face of the image must always be to the south because *Lankā* (Ceylon) is situated on the south of India. Māroti's services to Rāma as related in the Rāmāyana were great and many. He acted as his spy, and fought most valiantly in the great expedition against Rāwan the demon king of the island for the recovery of Sīta. The exploits of Māroti are favourite topics among Hindus from childhood to age, and paintings of them are common. On Saturdays people fast in his honour. Vermilion mixed with oil is applied to the image, a garland of *rui* (*Calotropis gigantea*) flowers placed on its neck and urad grains on its head. In almost every village of Berār in connection with Siva stands closely united, his son Ganesh, locally known as Ganpati, as presiding over the troop of deities attendant on Siva. Ganesh is represented by a figure, half-man and half-elephant, in a sitting posture, with a large belly. He is called Lambodar, 'pendant-bellied.' He is the god of good luck and of learning and remover of difficulties and obstacles. He is addressed by orthodox Hindus at the commencement of all undertakings, and at the opening of all compositions. Even the

[1] Hinduism (Religions Ancient and Modern Series), page 40.
[2] Old Berār Gazetteer, page 208.

yearly account books commence with his sacred symbol and with the phrase 'Shrī Ganeshāya namah' (I bow to the illustrious Ganesh). Khandobā is also held in much reverence by Kunbīs, as also by Dhangars and many lower castes. The Wāghyas beg in the name of Khandobā and the Murlī girls are dedicated to him. In many houses there is a small silver image of the god, mounted and sword in hand, before which on the Champā Shastī is waved a copper platter bearing cocoanut, jaggery, turmeric and sixteen small lamps made of wheaten flour. His votaries also offer him brinjals and onions, his favourite diet, which they may not use themselves before this day. The black dog of Khandobā is also worshipped. Sunday is the day sacred to this deity (who is also known as Mārtand), and alms are solicited on this day in his name.

Other village deities.

113. The favourite incarnation of Devī is probably Bhawāni, to whom large temples at Amraoti and Māhur are dedicated, and in whose service the Gondhalīs are enrolled. She is worshipped for the nine days, Bhawāni Naorātra, preceding the Dasahra, the idol being placed on a basket crowned every day with fresh flowers. The basket rests on a pot full of water, and for the whole period of nine days a light is kept burning on a stand before the image. On the tenth day or the Dasahra, the head of the village slays a buffalo in remembrance of the victory of Devī over the demon god Mhaisobā or Mahishāsur. On this day also an unmarried girl used to be placed beside the image of Bhawāni and worshipped, the ceremony being possibly a relic of the 'left-handed ritual' of the *panchmākār*. Bhawāni is also worshipped on the new and the full moon.[1] Sītalā or Māta Mai is the goddess of small-pox. She is represented by a few stones rubbed with vermilion and worshipped only during an attack of small-pox. Cooked rice and curds are offered to the goddess when the small-pox has subsided. Sometimes fowls or goats are sacrificed to her. Meskai is a deity enshrined on the boun-

[1] Berār Census Report, 1881 page 45.

dary of a village. He-buffaloes are sacrificed to her annually on Dasahra day. She must be propitiated at the time of marriage by the offer of turmeric and vermilion, the remainder of the former article being brought home and applied to the bride or bridegroom. 'Mhaisobā is a buffalo god known 'to live under the water of large rivers, and requiring propitia- 'tion; Wāghdeo must be appeased by those who run risks 'from tigers; Satwai is a goddess who cures children; and 'Marai Māta regulates the spread of cholera in accordance with 'the attentions which she receives. A heap of stones daubed 'with red, under a tree fluttering with rags, represents Chindia 'Deo, or the divinity of tatters; if you present a rag in season 'you may chance to get good clothes.'[1] Asra is the goddess of water inhabiting tanks, rivers and wells. She is represented by a stone rubbed with vermilion. Chānd Shāh Walī, or Chānd Khān Walī as he is also called, is a Jinn who resides in mud forts. He is enshrined in a platform over which a white flag waves. The flag must be renewed on the day of Dasahra by the village patel, otherwise stones are thrown on the houses at night time by the annoyed *walī* and the safety of the village is endangered. The story goes that Chānd Shāh Walī was a great magician in times gone by. He used to take away the daughter of a king for days together and nobody knew who took her away and where she was taken. The king, therefore, offered a great reward to the man who would detect the thief. It is said that one aspirant instructed the princess to take with her some cotton and to throw its pieces on the way while she was being thus rudely abducted. The magician was thus traced and brought before the king who ordered him to be buried alive in the foundation of a mud fortress. The wizard besought the king for his life and the courtiers also interceded for him, but the king was inexorable. As his last prayer the magician requested that the king should do something whereby his name would be perpetuated. The king granted his request and ordered that on every Dasahra day a new flag should be raised near the village *chāwri* to perpetuate

[1] Berār Gazetteer 1870, page 190.

Bemrose, Collo., Derby.

GALLERY IN FRONT OF THE AMBA TEMPLE, AND ENTRANCE, AMRAOTI.

the magician's memory. The tradition is reminiscent of the Arabian Nights and even the name of the magician is typically Muhammadan; and that the *walī* should have become a Hindu god honoured at Dasahra is but one of many instances that might be given to show the intermingling of the lower forms of the two faiths. The tomb of Chilam Shāh Walī at Amraoti Camp is an object of reverence to both alike: so are also the shrine at Uprai, the rock of Bairam, and the Makbarā of 'Dūlha Rahmān,' the mythical headless Ghāzi of Ellichpur. In many villages of the District will be found the grave of some local ascetic who made himself dear to the villagers. To the Hindus he is a *guru* and they paint one side of his tombstone vermilion and do *pūjā* in his honour accordingly; but to the Musalmāns he is a *pīr* and the other side is therefore whitewashed and covered at the Great and the Lesser Id with a cloth of bright green.

114. Among Hindus the sights and occurrences of the early morning are believed to foreshadow the fortunes of the day 'The 'sight of a corpse or of flesh is a lucky omen, except with 'Lāds and Sonārs. To Gosāwis and Bairāgis, salt, earth 'and a potter are inauspicious, but not to other castes: while 'a Brāhman with his headcloth on his head and his caste 'marks painted brings good luck, but if he should be encoun'tered bare-headed, misfortune is the result. A married 'woman is lucky to meet; a widow unlucky. A pot full of 'water is a good thing to see; an empty pot is not so. If a man 'has a twitching in his right eye the omen is good, but not so 'if it occurs in his left eye: while with the woman the case is 'reversed. A sweeper bearing nightsoil is a lucky man to 'meet: a Teli with an oil pot is unlucky. Should a spider 'cross one's hand it is a good omen, but a house lizard falling 'on one's body is bad. A single sneeze when a person is 'speaking denotes bad luck to him, but an additional sneeze 'will change it. A deer, blue jay, peacock, or ichneumon on 'the left hand side are all harbingers of good; as are also a 'mongoose, a cow with calf, and an ox; but woe to the man

Omens.

'whose path is crossed by a crow, a jackal, or a cat, or who 'hears a dog howling, or an owl hooting. A wild parrot perching 'on the head or shoulder, the sound of joyful music, dreaming 'a good dream, or meeting a corpse borne by four men are 'all omens of good import; while a lamp falling, a man's *pagrī* 'or a woman's toe ring coming off, or a ringdove entering 'the house are events fraught with evil consequences. If a 'ringdove enters the house, the occupants forsake it for three 'days: on the third day a cow is brought into the house, and 'food and alms are given to Brāhmans, after which it is again 'habitable.'[1] If a child is born with the umbilical cord round its neck like a halter it is believed that he ended his former life a prisoner in some jail; the analogy to the possible method of his last death is obvious.

Magical ceremonies.

115. When a village is threatened by an epidemic of cholera the people raise a public subscription and purchase a he-buffalo. It is worshipped by the village patel and taken round the village The patel then sacrifices the animal in the name of Marai (goddess of cholera) in the presence of all the villagers. The head is buried on the boundary of the village. Till the worship is complete no fire should be kindled in the village. People will also cook their food outside the inhabited portion of the village. Another device to avert an epidemic of cholera is that a widow Māngni is dressed in yellow cloth and marked with turmeric and *kunku*. She is seated in a small cart newly prepared for the occasion and taken round the village. A spinning wheel, a winnowing fan and similar things are placed in the cart. She is sent out of the inhabited portion of the village and she must live in the fields for one whole night. She is considered a Marai and the villagers will not allow the personated Marai Māta to enter their village. The idea in giving her a spinning wheel and other things is to keep her engaged in domestic work and not to allow her leisure for playing havoc in the village. A

[1] Berār Census Report, 1881, page 45.

method of divining whether rain will fall or not in vogue among cultivators, especially Kunbīs, is that on the day of Akshaya-tritiya the enquirer will arrange nine clods of white earth in the name of the asterisms and on top of the clods place an earthen pot full of water. He worships the earthen pot in the name of his deceased ancestor and examines the clods of earth next day. If any of them remains dry it is believed that in the asterism, the name of which the clod bears, there will be no rain. But as the pot is naturally porous, the omen has every chance of being favourable. Another device is that on any Sunday in the month of Poush a pot full of milk and rice is placed on fire and the direction in which the milk boils over will be the direction from which the next monsoon should be expected. If a river is in flood and the safety of a village situated on its bank seems to be endangered, the patel with his wife will go to the river and propitiate the river goddess by the offer of turmeric, *kunkū*, and a *cholī*. He will then commence measuring the waters of the flood by *pailīs* to cause the flood to subside.[1]

The Mānbhao Sect.

116. The Mānbhaos are a small sect of Hindus whose chief seat and place of pilgrimage is at Ritpur or Ridhpur in the Morsi tāluk, though they have also an establishment near Poona; and the 'Jai Kisnya' sect in the Punjab is said to be a branch of the same rule. There is even, it is said, a *math* in Kābul. Their first *achārya* is said to have been Nāgdeo Bhat, who is supposed to have been born in A.D. 1236, and the name is also given of Kisn Bhat, the spiritual adviser of a rājā who ruled at Paithan about the middle of the fourteenth century. His followers believe him to have been the demi-god Krishna, returned to earth. His doctrines repudiated a multiplicity of gods, and the hatred and contempt which he endured arose partly from his insistence on the monotheistic principle, but chiefly from his repudiation of the caste system. He inculcated the exclusive worship of Krishna as the only

[1] Compare our English saying, "measuring the Atlantic with a thimble."

incarnation of the Supreme Being, and taught his disciples to eat with none but the initiated, and to break off all former ties of caste and religion. Such is the legendary origin of the order, but from recent scientific enquiries (vide Imperial Gazetteer Vol. XXI, p. 302) it appears that the founder's name was Chakradhara, and that he was a Karhāda Brāhman who about the middle of the 13th century was regarded as an incarnation of Dattātreya. The oldest composition in the Marāthī language, the 'Līla Charitra,' is claimed as the work of a member of this order. It is written in prose and is divided into two portions, a Shruti containing lives of two Mahants Prashānta and Chakradhara, and a Smriti containing biographical notices of the kings of Deogiri from Singhana down to Rāmchandra Yādava A.D. 1210-1309. There are also other ancient Manbhao writings including an interesting account of the religious sects prevalent in the early fourteenth century. The head of the sect is a Mahant, with whom are associated a number of priests. The sect is divided into two classes, celibates and *gharbaris*, or seculars. Celibacy is regarded as the perfect life but matrimony is permitted to the weaker brethren. The celibates, both men and women, shave all hair from the head and wear clothes dyed with lamp-black. The lower garment is a waist cloth forming a sort of skirt, and is intended to typify devotion to the religious life and consequent indifference to distinctions of sex. Marriage being contrary to strict rule, they inform their *guru* and get his consent before entering upon it. The ceremony is performed in strict privacy inside the temple. A man is wont to signify his choice of a spouse by putting his *jholī* or beggar's wallet on hers: if she lets it remain there, the betrothal is complete. A woman may signify her desire by weaving a pair of garlands, with one of which she crowns the image of Krishna, and with the other her intended spouse. He may reject the offer if it so pleases him. The marriage ceremony is very quiet and unaccompanied by processions or rejoicings. Widow re-marriage is allowed. Mānbhaos evince a great respect for animal life. They all quit their villages at Dasahra, on account of the he-buffalo sacrifice, and remain in the fields until it is over; when questioned in respect to every-day slaughter in towns and large villages they have no answer to give. They will neither cut nor break down a tree, large or small. They are prohibited from drinking for three days of the water of the village where a man has been murdered or poisoned, or killed by falling down a well; obviously a salutary observance.

The dead are buried in salt, usually in a sitting posture though sometimes the corpse is laid in the grave on one side with feet to the south, head to the north and face to the east. The Mānbhaos still proselytise, but restrict their missionary efforts to good castes. Mahārs, Māngs, Chambhārs, Lohārs, Telis, Dhobis, Musalmāns and some other castes low in the social scale are excluded.

Brāhmans hate the Mānbhaos who have not only thrown off the Brāhmanical yoke themselves, but do much to oppose Brāhman influence among the villagers. The ridiculous tale of Kisn Bhat's magic cap by which he assumed a likeness to the god Krishna, and of the artifice by which the cap was taken from him bears the mark of its origin. It is possible, of course, as has been suggested, that Kisn actually did marry a Māng woman to show his contempt for caste, just as Luther after renouncing his vows married a nun: but it is far more probable that the story was invented as a basis for the spiteful derivation of Mānbhao from Māng and *bhao* (brother). The name is really a corruption of Mahā Anubhava (great understanding) and is so spelt in all the documents of the sect. The Mānbhaos are respectable and respected and a *guru* is often taken from among them in preference to a Brāhman or Gosāwi. They are however a declining body numbering only 2566 in Berār in 1901 as compared with 4111 twenty years previously.

Worship of Shāh Dāwal.

117. Reference has been made above to the mingling of Hindu and Muhammadan forms of faith among the lower classes in Berār. The most noteworthy example of this is furnished by the cult of Shāh Dāwal. Dāwal, tradition says, was a

Mahār and Shāh or Malik a Madāri *fakīr*; they came according to the story from Hindustān together some two hundred years ago, and lived together like Nānak and Farīd, the Hindu and Muslim disciples of Kabīr. At their death they were buried together in the same tomb at Uprai in the Dāryāpur tāluk. Among Kunbīs, Telis, Bhois, Dhangars and similar castes the worship of Dāwal Malik is frequent. The custom is to pray before the shrine previous to any enterprise or when any gift is particularly desired. Persons wishing to make a pilgrimage to the tomb of the saint dress themselves in a single white cloth marking its borders with red ochre. A bottle gourd is split in two and one half serves as a begging bowl. A wallet is also attached to two small sticks of *ber* tree which are held on the shoulder. The first alms of grain must be begged at the house of a Mahār or a Māng with the words "Dām, Dām, Dām Sāhib" and then only can the worshippers receive alms from the higher castes. Cakes are prepared from the flour of the grain so collected. Cooked food is begged from all comers irrespective of caste and creed and eaten at the spot (Uprai) where it is believed to convey no pollution. But this is a rule which obtains also in several of the best known Hindu temples. Indeed it would be impossible to carry on the worship of a great shrine where all castes meet without some such relaxation of caste observance. The worshippers put on also iron hand-cuffs and walk on foot from their houses to the saints' tomb as a mark of humility. The *fakīr* who officiates as a priest at the tomb breaks them and receives a fee of five annas for so doing: he also gives the worshippers a drink of jaggery and water. After return it is usual to sacrifice a goat and give a caste feast. A Mahār after his marriage should go with his bride to offer worship at the shrine.

Muhammadans.

118. Muhammadans number about 67,500 persons, and are strongest in the towns of Amraoti, Ellichpur, Paratwāda, Morsi, and Daryāpur. The Vaidyas are a class of Hindu converts to Islām. They perform the marriage ceremony secretly by

walking round a marriage post and then have the *nikāh* pronounced by the Kāzi. Momins (weavers), Satranjīwālas (carpet-makers), Bāgwāns (gardeners) are all Muhammadans but have continued their Hindu endogamous groups. They will on no account marry outside their circle and retain still a few Hindu marriage customs. These are all low classes of Muhammadans and will not eat food cooked by a Teli, Dhobi, or Lohār. They will also throw away their earthen pots if touched by a member of these castes. Beef also is not eaten.

119. Of the eight hundred thousand persons in the District at the last census, 1127 were Christians, 705 being natives of India and the rest Europeans and Eurasians. The Church of Rome claims the greater proportion of these having 626 members of whom no less than 580 are natives, the Anglican Communion coming second with a total of 323, of whom 70 are natives, though there is no definitely Anglican mission. The Presbyterians and Methodists have 38 converts each, the former having 4 and the latter 3 other followers ; there are eleven Baptists, of whom six are natives. No other sect is found, though 63 persons of whom 52 are natives have not returned a denomination and should probably be placed to the credit of the Korku and Alliance Missions, both undenominational bodies, who account also for many of the converts to the Church of England.

Christians.

As the Church of Rome is by far the most successful in the District so also it was the earliest to commence work, the Rev. Father Thevenet having visited Ellichpur in 1848, before the province came under British Administration. He was the pioneer of Christianity throughout Berār and in the neighbouring portions of the Nizām's dominions and the Central Provinces ; and his labours continued for nearly forty years. At the present day the Mission is under the Roman Catholic Bishop of Nāgpur and comprises four parishes in Berār, all of which have their headquarters in this District ; namely Chikaldā, Ellichpur, Amraoti and Badnerā. The priests, of whom there are six, belong to the order of St.

Francis of Sales, and are mainly drawn from the diocese of Annecy in France. The original centre for Berār was Akolā, but in 1874 Father Thevenet built a Chapel dedicated to St. Francis Xavier and bungalow at Amraoti, and in 1884 the headquarters were moved here. In 1886 representations having been made to Father Thevenet of the need for a school for European children, the Convent of Daughters of the Cross was opened. The Chapel has been enlarged to a Church of imposing dimensions and there is a fine convent building and a presbytery. The Sisters maintain a European school teaching up to the Final Standard for boys and to the Middle Standard for girls with 48 pupils, and a native school with 23 pupils, also an orphanage for native girls, a school in the city for high caste girls and dispensaries for the poor. They greatly distinguished themselves both in the famine of 1900 and by the prominent part they took in combating the great outbreak of plague at Amraoti in 1903 and they visit various other places in the District, especially Badnerā, Ellichpur and Chikaldā, where they have a branch station. There is a Church of St. John the Evangelist at Badnerā, the priest of which place also visits Akolā, Shegaon and various other stations both in and out of Berār. At Ellichpur there is a church of the Sacred Heart and the headquarters of a Mission amongst the Mahārs of this and neighbouring Districts; a namesake and nephew of the first Father Thevenet is in charge. It was from Ellichpur in 1874 that attempts were made to evangelize the Korkūs, but these failed and it was not till 1899 when the mission had been established at Chikaldā for three years that the great famine gave the Fathers a second chance. A few families and some orphans were then gathered together and formed into a village of about 160 souls to which the name of Marianpur was given. A Chapel of Saint Ann was consecrated. The first efforts however at the evangelization of the Korkūs had been not by a missionary but by an officer of Government Mr. J. Mulheran, who about 1860 was deputed to make a survey of the Melghāt and to report on its inhabitants. During his tour he used freely to preach to the jungle tribes;

and he appealed to the bishop of Calcutta to despatch a missionary for the work. However, before his appeal could be met, he died suddenly. In 1870 the Rev. H. Haden and his brother were appointed but stayed only a short time, being relieved in 1874 by the Rev. H. Norton. A short sketch of the Korkūs as well as a Korkū grammar and several translations into that tongue were compiled by the Rev. E. F. Ward, who settled at Ellichpur in 1885. In 1889 the Korkū and Central India Hill Mission, organized by the energies of Lieut.-Colonel Oldham (of the Hyderābād Contingent) took over from the Rev. A. Norton the work which he had carried on since 1874. The mission is not sectarian, its preachers being laymen drawn from the English, Lutheran and other communions. It did excellent work in the famine of 1896-97 and was specially praised in the Commissioner's famine report. As a permanent legacy from the famine there remained 3 orphanages and a leper asylum. The latter remains and the former have been consolidated into two, one for boys at Khudāwandpur near Ellichpur, and the other for girls at Chikaldā. Primary schools have been opened and an Industrial school at Khudāwandpur in which carpentry, smith's work and tailoring are taught. The mission has also branches at Ghatang, Dhārni and Duni as well as in the Betūl District.

The Christian and Missionary Alliance is an American Society which has been in the District for about fifteen years and has stations at Amraoti, Chāndur and Daryāpur. Like the Korkū Mission it is non-sectarian. The United Free Church of Scotland has a mission whose headquarters are in Wardhā under the Revd. D. Revie. It is chiefly remarkable in Berār for the honourable part which ordained converts have played in its work. The founders were the Rev. Nārayan Sheshādri, D.D., and the Rev. Sidobā Misal, the latter of whom settled in Amraoti about 1870, where he was succeeded in 1888 by the Rev. Timothy Sheorām; and in 1906 the Rev. P. A. Yardi was ordained. The last report shows 54 baptized Christians; an increase of 10 since the census, and there is a primary school for boys with 130 pupils and for girls with 30.

Amraoti is in the Anglican diocese of Nāgpur, and the

Chaplain of Berār has his headquarters here with outstations at Badnerā, Chikaldā and Ellichpur. There are churches at Amraoti and Ellichpur and Government cemeteries at these two places and at Chikaldā and Badnerā.

CASTE.

120. The most numerous castes in the District are Kunbīs who constitute 24 per cent. of the population, Mahārs 14 per cent. and Mālis 9 per cent. The cultivating castes are the Kunbīs, Marāthās, Mālis, Gaolīs, Bāris, Telis and a few Dhangars and others. The titles of Deshmukh and Deshpāndia are borne by families who held pargana or subpargana revenue offices under native rule. The latter are generally Brāhmans, but the former are almost coming to be regarded as a separate caste; and it is quite usual for a man on being asked his caste to reply not Marāthā or Kunbī or Māli but simply Deshmukh, the historic title conveying more distinction than the commonplace terms of every day. The primitive tribes are represented by the Gonds (23,245), Korkūs (27,051) and Kolīs (6903). Sonārs number 9589 and Sutārs 9628. Chambhārs (9193), Mahārs (105,306) and Māngs (17,325) are out-castes and their touch is considered by higher classes of Hindus to convey pollution. The descriptions which follow are founded on information supplied by members of these castes. They vary in some respects from other published accounts; but how far the differences are due to real local variations or to the ignorance or prejudice of the informants it is impossible to say.

Principal castes.

121. Brāhmans number about 21,500 persons or 3 per cent. of the population. Though not very strong numerically yet they are by far the most influential caste owing to their hereditary priestly influence. Of the Marāthā Brāhmans the majority are Deshasthas, although a considerable minority belong to the Konkanastha and Karhāda divisions. The word Deshastha literally means residents of the country and the name is given

Brāhman.

to the Brāhmans of that part of the Deccan which lies above the Ghāts. Most of the Deshasthas pursue secular professions and are writers, accountants, merchants, etc. The posts of village patwāris are almost monopolised by them. As their name indicates, the original home of the Konkanasthas is the Konkan or the narrow strip of low-lying country from Broach to Ratnāgiri, between the Ghāts and the sea. The immigration of Konkanasthas into Berār probably dates from the time of the Konkanastha Peshwās (1714-1818) whom they followed as accountants, clerks, etc. They are also known as Chitpāvan or Chittapāvan, the story being told that Parasurām, enraged at the ungrateful conduct of the Brāhmans of his day who refused to attend the *shrāddha* of his father, provided himself with Brāhmans by restoring to life some corpses which he found floating on the sea off the Konkan coast after a shipwreck. The story is indignantly denied by many modern Chitpāvans as it is thought that the part played in it by a corpse is an insult to the dignity of the caste ; but the fair, sometimes almost ruddy complexions, blue eyes, and light hair which are their distinguishing features, seem to point to some such arrival from overseas. The Karhāda Brāhmans are so called from Karhād, a town at the meeting of the Krishnā and Koynā rivers. Another suggested explanation of the name is that it refers to the mountain country ; the high summits which separate the home of the Kokanastha Brāhmans on one side from the tableland of the Deshasthas on the other. The Karhādas are charged with having in former times offered human sacrifice, and even the murder of Brāhmans to propitiate their deities. The accusation is said by them to be an invention of some Deshastha Brāhman. Whatever room there may be for comment on the religion of the Karhādas, they are quite equal to the Kokanasthas and Deshasthas in every other respect. Besides the above three divisions which in practice are endogamous, the Marāthā Brāhmans are divided into Rigvedīs and Yajurvedīs who eat together but do not intermarry. The Yajurvedīs are the followers of the white Yajus and are further subdivided into two branches, called Kānvas and

Mādhyandinas. The Kānvas are so called on account of their adopting the Kānva recension of the white Yajus. The Mādhyandinas derive their name in the same manner from the Mādhyandina branch of the white Yajus. They attach great importance to the recital of the Sandhyā prayer at noon, *i.e.* after 11 A.M. But the Rigvedīs might perform the mid-day prayer even at sunrise. As a class the Marāthā Brāhmans are well-to-do, their abilities leading them to success in almost every profession. Hindustāni (or Pardesī) and Gujarāti Brāhmans are also met with. The former are generally employed as office peons or in similar unskilled work, and the latter as traders. In the villages the Brāhman's exclusiveness is naturally modified. Brāhman patwāris are more or less subordinate to Kunbī patels, and they with the schoolmasters and others in small villages, if they wish for any but the most limited society, must seek it among castes considerably lower than their own.

Rājput.

122. Rājputs number 12,672 persons and constitute 2 per cent. of the population. The Rājputs of Berār may be divided into two classes (1) those who are originally of foreign origin having come here before the Assignment to take military service with one or other of the petty powers who infested the land; and (2) those who have assumed the name of Rājputs, but are really of humbler birth. Bais Rājputs occur in every taluk, being most plentiful in Chāndur and Daryāpur. Their original home is Baiswāra in Oudh. The Rāthor Rājputs are most numerous in the Amraoti and Ellichpur tāluks, and come chiefly from Mārwār. The Rājputs are mainly engaged in cultivation.

Wāni or Baniā.

123. The Wāni or Baniā castes, like the Rājputs, are chiefly of foreign origin. They number 16,264 or 2 per cent. of the population. Wānis, being strangers in the land, are generally distinguished among Berāris by the name of their country or their sect. Hence such entries in the Census Lists as Mārwāri or Gujarāti on the one hand; and Lingāyat or Jain on the other. The Wānis

are the chief traders in Berār. The village Wāni is a much abused individual but he is as a rule a quiet peaceable man, a necessary factor in the village economy. They are as a class respectable members of society and a large amount of commercial wealth passes through their hands.

124. The Kunbīs number 193,255 or 24 per cent. of the population. They are overwhelmingly the most important caste in the District, and the Kunbī has come to be the accepted type of all Marāthā cultivators. He is in the apt words of the Nāgpur Settlement Report "a most patient plodding mortal with a cat-like affection for his land" and the majority of agricultural holdings are still in possession of Kunbīs. Their husbandry though careful and good of its kind is extremely conservative and they are more chary than most castes of accepting new ideas. One may occasionally find a wealthy Kunbī who has taken to moneylending, and they are seldom seen in complete poverty, even though always ready to resort to the moneylender.

Kunbī.

Though now a peaceable folk they have furnished even in recent times very daring dacoits, and one sometimes sees it suggested that in old days the armies of Shivāji and of the Peshwās and Bhonslas were recruited mainly from Kunbīs and similar castes who took to a warlike life; and that this is the origin of the Marāthā caste. However this may be, a similar process is even now going on for the Tiroles, the highest division of Kunbīs, to which most of the Deshmukhs and many of the leading patels belong, are to-day on the borderland between the two castes. One rung of the ladder of social advancement is to provide oneself with a Rājput origin, and the Marāthās accordingly claim to be Kshattriyas while the Tiroles derive their name from Therol in Rājputāna. But the ordinary Kunbī is confessedly a Sūdra, and the pretensions just described are regarded with extreme suspicion both by pure Rājputs and by the Brāhmans who are the ultimate arbiters. In religion the Kunbī is a worshipper of Māroti, Mahādeo, Ganpati and Vithobā, but especially of the first-named. He is also a firm believer in the efficacy of omens and of all manner of forms and ceremonies and goes in great dread of ghosts.

125. The Gaolīs number 16,353 and constitute 2 per cent. of the population. The Lingāyat Gaolīs are found in the tāluks of Amraoti, Morsi, Ellichpur and Chāndur and are subdivided into Nagarkar and Wazarkar divisions. Among the Wazarkar Gaolīs the bridegroom is brought to the village of the bride and married there. It is customary among them to marry some twenty or thirty couples under one *mandwā* at one and the same time, possibly from motives of economy.

Gaolī.

126. Dhangars number 17,826 persons constituting 2 per cent. of the population. They are hereditary herdsmen corresponding to the Gadarias of Northern India, and ranking socially below Kunbīs, Gaolīs, and similar castes. Their highest subcaste known as Bangi Dhangars have now developed into a separate caste called Hatkar or Hatgar. The Ain-i-Akbarī calls them 'an indigenous race for the most part proud and refractory.' They were in military employ and therefore claim a higher status than Dhangars. At a Dhangar marriage a Brāhman officiates and the ceremony is performed after the Marāthā ritual. On the third day of marriage they boil wheat and serve it to the assembled guests. This is called *Pānchgāt*. They bury their dead with leaves of *akao* plant strewn over the face of the corpse, but those who die in a specially honourable way, a woman in childbirth or a man in battle, are burned after the manner of high-caste Hindus. Each caste fellow is expected to bring some cooked food to the mourner's house, and when all have assembled they will take food with him. On the eleventh day a caste feast is given. The mourner seats himself on the ground and each guest should drop a pice in his lap. The pice are counted and the number of guests is roughly ascertained as the basis for preparing food. This ceremony is called *Vahti*. They sometimes claim Khandobā or Khande Rao, the chief

Dhangar.

who overcame Mallā and Māni, the oppressors of the Brāhmans, as their caste-man and progenitor. They have a special ceremony called *Vari* in the month of Poush. The image of Khandobā is placed in a brass plate and the Dhangars all in a body beg alms from other people of their village. Cakes are prepared from flour of the grain received in alms and the spirit of Khandobā takes possession of one of them who exhibits the usual signs of demonolepsy especially that of unnatural strength. The caste has a tribal council headed by an elder called Mehtar. At the time of marriage a mark should be affixed to his forehead as a token of respect. He is entitled to receive a sum of three or four annas at every marriage and should give in return a caste feast once a year. It is said that a Dhangar will not scruple to eat the carcase of his sheep or goat dying a natural death. It will be a pollution for him to sit on a camel or a creaking swing or to wear shoes which may touch the ankles of his feet. This caste is traditionally held to be most successful in the education of its watch dogs. The pups are taken from the mother and suckled by an ewe, which at first is held down and soon takes to them as to its own offspring. The dog when grown never leaves the flock, nor does it shrink from defending it against the attack of any animal.

Korkū.

127. The Korkūs are of Kolarian origin and are strongly represented in the District. In language and general type they are said to be identical with the Kols and Santāls; but the habits of the Korkūs of the Tāpti valley, says Forsyth, are a great advance on those of the Korkūs inhabiting the Mahādeo hills further east. The Korkūs who first came to Berār found the Nihāls in possession of the Melghāt hills. Gradually the latter caste lost their power and became the village drudges of the former. The Nihāls are now fast losing their language also; the younger generation speak Korkū or Marāthī. The Nihāls were once much addicted to cattle lifting, but they have held this propensity in check of late years. The Korkūs are divided into the following classes:—Mawāsi or Bhowavaya, Bawaria, Rūma

and Bondoyas. The term Mowâs signifies the troubled country,[1] and the subcaste ranks the highest probably on account of the gentlemanly calling of armed robbery formerly practised by its members. The names of the other subcastes also seem to be territorial but their exact meanings are not known. They have also *gotras*, the story running that their ancestors were assembled by the gods and that to each was assigned the name of the object—animal, tree or whatever it might be—near which he took up his position. Another tale is that the Korkūs were defeated in a great battle and that the objects in question are those behind which they succeeded in hiding themselves. In either case the legend is a typical example of the way in which totemistic clan names have been clothed in a Hindu respectability. 'I believe,' says Mr. Ballantyne, once a Forest Officer in the Melghāt, 'that the Korkūs were originally 'worshippers of the sun and moon; their most solemn oath is 'by the sun and in the act of worship they turn their faces 'towards it, and point to it with their hands. But now-a-days 'their whole creed is so much tainted with Hinduism that their 'original beliefs are well nigh lost.' In support of this opinion it may be mentioned that the Korkū word for god (*Gomaj*) is also the word for sun and moon; and that on the side of their memorials to the dead which faces east they invariably carve a representation of those bodies. Mr. Ward, indeed, who spent many years as a missionary in these hills and was one of the few who have made a detailed study of their inhabitants, is far more categorical. 'Their chief objects of worship,' he says, 'are the sun and moon whom they regard as male and 'female deities. But they do not, so far as I have been able 'to learn, offer regular or special worship to those celestial 'bodies. Once in a great while, however, in the month of 'April, a goat or a fowl is sacrificed to the sun while the face 'is turned to the east.' 'As a whole," he continues, 'their 'particular hopes and fears seem to lie in the direction of the 'local deities nearer at hand. They build no temples nor

---

[1] The derivation is not by any means certain; a less complimentary theory connects the word with the mahuā tree, whose flowers form an item of Korkū food and whose liquor they are given to consuming rather freely.

'fashion images, after the manner of the Hindus but daub red 'paint on certain stones in or about the village and the adjacent 'forest, and endow them with the names of their divinities. 'Thus *Dongar gomaj*, god of the hills and forests; *Kulla gomaj*, 'god of the tiger; *Mutiyā gomaj*, special village god or penates; '*Hardolī gomaj*, the cholera god; *Māta gomaj*, goddess of small 'pox; besides *Pānchi gomai*, *Kur gomai* and the Hindu god 'Hanumān.' Many of those are but Korkū names for deities that have been adopted by the low caste Hindu in other parts of India; *Kulla gomaj* for instance is simply *Wāgh deo*; and *Māta gomaj*, *Marai Māta*; the Hindu god Mahādeo tends more and more to fill the principal place in the Korkū theogony. As a rule the Korkūs bury their dead. 'A year or so after the 'decease of a person of note, a ceremony called *sidolī* is per-'formed which much resembles the Irish custom of waking 'the dead. A memorial post is carved the next day and planted 'under a mahuā tree where those in memory of the same kin or '*got* (Hind. *gotra*) have been planted before. These posts are 'called in the Korkū language *mundā*; are two to three feet in 'height and about 6 inches square at the base. They are always 'pointed at the top, often arrow headed and usually rudely but 'elaborately carved on the four sides. The carvings consist 'of representations of the sun and moon, men on horseback, 'dancers, apes, peacocks, fowls, crabs, spiders and trees, besides 'zig-zag scrawls, scollops, flutings and cuneiform cuts.' With the exception of the man on horseback which may be an emblem of the sun, Mr. Ward finds no special significance in any of these figures. It is believed, however, that they may be a record by totems of the family and ancestry of the deceased. The post itself is suggestive of phallic worship, and the rude cut of the sun and moon is not without its significance in this connection. The Korkūs are also worshippers of the dead (ancestors *Pitar*); and the ceremony above referred to as *sidolī* appears to be one also known by the name of *phuljāgni*[1] and to be intended more as a species of ghost-laying than anything else. The ceremony has all the usual accompaniments of primitive necromancy, the elaborate formalism by which, for instance, five

[1] The word is connected with the verb *jagne* to wake.

bits of bamboo or five crabs' legs represent the dead man's limbs. It probably varies very much from village to village according to the fancy of the local Bhumka and dancing and intoxication are the only unaltering elements in the performance. The following account[1] of the Korkūs by Mr. P. S. Agnihotri, formerly Clerk of Court in Ellichpur, is sufficiently interesting to be quoted at length. 'They 'are ugly in appearance, (though with rare exceptions) and 'in their manner less sophisticated than the people of Berār; 'their language is Korkū but Hindī is also common among 'them. Their villages are built in two equal rows flanking a 'straight street, and are placed half a mile or more away from 'water. They wear very dirty clothes; sometimes only a *dhotī*, 'and a rag on the head; and the poorest keep a fire in their 'houses beside which, when they have cooked and eaten their 'food, they lie down to sleep at night, wearing nothing but a '*langotī*: their women also wear such *langotīs* and sleep close 'to the fire. In a large family, when the food is ready, they 'sometimes divide it into equal portions; but they have also a 'custom by which it is placed in a heap in their midst, and they 'sit with their backs to it each reaching out a hand behind him 'for what he requires without looking at it. They are flesh-'eaters but will not touch cocks or sparrows; in spite of the 'uncertainty of their food they are stronger and stouter than 'the people of the plains. They do not, like the Berāris, 'protect their crops with a fencing of thorns, or by throwing 'stones from a sling; but camp out in the open till the corn is 'ready for use. They surround their fields with bamboo 'matting and think to frighten away wild beasts with scare-'crows of rags and wood placed at intervals. They build high 'platforms in their fields with roofs called *malās* and in these 'they live, lighting a fire there and cooking their food. In the 'middle of the field, two logs of wood tied together with small 'pieces of bamboo between them, and worked by a rope, are 'made to give a clapping noise and to scare wild animals. 'After the threshing is over they take the corn to

[1] Freely translated from the Marāthī.

'villages and give it to the money-lenders in return for money 'borrowed at the rate of 24 or 32 seers of corn to the rupee '(*i.e.* 100 to 150 per cent. interest). Sometimes this money had 'only been lent two months before the harvest; and thus the 'moneylenders get the whole crop into their possession and 'the Korkū seldom keeps more than a two or three months' 'supply. Few Korkūs are rich; and those few in stores of 'corn rather than in money. Their system of heaping '*kadba*, etc., in the fields differs from that of Berār where it is 'stacked close to the village and a thorn hedge put round it; 'the Korkūs store it on a platform in their fields resembling a '*malā*. Outside the village one may find a hut with some 'painted logs thrust in the ground; these are their gods. They 'worship also the goddess Devī, and offer to her rice, lemons 'and wild flowers with cooked meat; a goat is her sacrifice; 'and at night also in their houses they worship her. On the 'third day of the month Ashvin a great festival begins. They 'assemble together by night, and some dance and sing. Pre-'sently one of their number becomes possessed by a spirit; he 'trembles and breathes heavily, the hair of his head stands up 'and his look grows wild. The inspiring deity is *Baitāl* (a 'demon) or *ghoting*. Next, anyone afflicted with grief or pain 'asks the possessed a remedy therefor. The latter takes some 'juār or rice in his hand and throws over him, uttering incanta-'tions; the sufferer picks up the grains. After this has been done 'two or three times, he is told to retire, and the man possessed 'presently falls headlong to the ground and the god leaves 'him. At holiday time the people of the village assemble 'together and dance, singing Korkū songs, beating on a drum 'called *dholkī* and blowing a pipe called *pungī*. Their women 'too assemble together in one place for the dance. They wear 'each two or three brass anklets on their feet and to the clang 'of these they keep step. The *dholkī* beater stands in the 'midst and they dance round. Another man stands by playing 'the *pungī*, and both men and women adorn themselves with 'bunches of wild flowers in their ears. As in Berār they 'have a custom by which the bridegroom lives with and 'works for his father-in-law; and such a bridegroom is called '*lamjhanā*. After a fixed period, sometimes twelve years, 'is over, he marries the woman for whom he has worked; but 'even within that time while he lives in her father's house, 'he is allowed the rights of a husband. If a man marries a 'woman without serving for her then he or his father gives 'to her fat her an ox as well as a sum of money agreed 'upon. This gift is called *pejā*. In like manner if a 'Korkū woman is found to be living with a man of 'another caste, ten or twenty of her caste fellows will go to 'his house and demand *pejā*; and will beat him if they do 'not get it. If a woman not known to be of loose character 'should lapse from virtue, she is taken by the *panch* to a river 'is rubbed with cowdung and urine, washed in the river and 'shaved. Then when her father or husband has provided a 'caste dinner and much liquor has been drunk, she is again 'considered clean.'

Among them the village priest is expected to ward off and cure diseases, and to defend them from wild beasts. If a tiger come near the place, he indents on the villagers for a he-buffalo, or a cock, and a few small iron nails. At midnight he goes round the village boundary, with one hand leading the animal, and in the other carrying the nails. These he drives into the ground, and sacrifices the victim. This rite ought, he considers, to keep off the tiger for a whole year. The power of magic they hold to be imparted by a tree of knowledge. The aspirant takes counsel with other wise men and then bathes, a very unusual observance among Korkūs. After this he wanders alone in the jungle for three days and nights, plucking leaves from the trees with his teeth, after the manner of a goat. Among the trees are serpents; if he fears them, or put forth his hand, he will surely die. But if his faith and courage fail not, he will light upon the tree of knowledge. Then he returns to his village, bathes and offers a goat. Thus until his teeth drop out he becomes endowed with the power of magic.

Impure classes.

128. The impure castes are Mahār, Māng and Chambhār. The old local religion as might be expected survives more markedly among

these castes than among those higher in the social scale, although the Brāhmans have impressed the mark of their creed upon the more important occasions of life. The auspicious day for marriage is ascertained from the village Joshi, a Brāhman, who receives a fee for his information. And although some peculiar custom may here and there be kept up, as when a Mahār bridegroom drops a ring into a bowl of water, which the bride picks out and wears, or when a Chambhār bride twice or thrice opens a small box which her future spouse each time smartly shuts again, still the ceremony is conducted as far as possible according to the ordinary Hindu rites. Furthermore as the Joshi will not come to the marriage it can only take place on the same day as a marriage among some higher castes, so that the Mahārs may watch for the priest's signal and may know the exact moment at which the dividing cloth (*antarpat*) should be withdrawn, and the garments of the bride and bridegroom knotted, while the bystanders clap their hands and pelt the couple with coloured grain.

Mahār, Māng and Chambhār.

129. Mahārs or Dheds number 105,300 persons constituting 14 per cent. of the population. They are divided, they say, into "twelve and a half" subcastes, each of which is endogamous. Of these, one division is called Somas or Somavanshi, and claims to have taken part with the Pāndavas against the Kauravas in the war of Mahābhārata and subsequently to have settled in the Mahārāshtra. After the Somas Mahārs other important divisions are the Lādwan or Lādsi, the Andhwan, the Baone and the Kosre. The word Baone is sometimes said to be a corruption of Bhawāni, and the sept claims to rank highest among the caste. As a *balutedār* on the village establishment the Mahār holds a post of great importance to himself and convenience to the village. The knowledge gained in his official position renders him a referee on matters affecting the village boundaries and customs. To the patel, patwāri and the big men of the village he acts often as a personal servant and errand runner, for a small cultivator he will also at times carry a torch or act as

escort. To the latter class however the Mahār is an indirect rather than a direct boon, inasmuch as his presence saves them from the liability of being called upon to render the patel or the village personal service. For the services which he thus renders as *pāndyawār* the Mahār receives from the cultivators certain grain dues. When the cut juāri is lying in the field the Māhars go round and beg for a measure of the ears, *bhīk pailī.* But the regular payment is made when the grain has been threshed. A chief duty performed by Mahārs is the removal of the carcases of dead animals. The flesh is eaten and the skin retained as a wage for the work. The patel and his relatives however usually claim to have the skins of their animals returned; and in some places where half of the agriculturists of the village claim kinship with the patel, the Mahārs feel and resent the loss. The village Mahārs take a prominent position in the Dasahra sacrifice (see page 151).

The Lādsi Mahārs also called Bunkars in the Ellichpur tahsīl, are worshippers of Shāh Dāwal, the Baones of Narāyan Deo, and the Kosres of Chānd Shāh Wali. A Lādsi or a Kosre Mahār will be polluted if a dog or a donkey dies at his house. He will have to throw away the earthen pots of his house and provide a caste feast before readmission into the caste. A Baone Mahār will be similarly outcasted if a cat enters his house and he will have to undergo the same penalties; and the Somavanshi have a corresponding aversion to pigs. The women of Somas Mahārs draw the end of their *lugdā* over the right shoulder, those of Lādsi over the left. The women of Somas and Baone have glass bangles on both hands but those of Lādsi and Kosre have glass bangles on the left hand and *kathil* bracelets (*māthas*) on the right hand. Lādsi and Kosre women will not wear nose-rings while those of Somas and Baone have them.

Māngs number 17,325 or 2 per cent. of the population. The subdivisions in the caste are Ghātole hailing from Melghāt, Pungīwālas who play on the fife and Daphlewālas on the tomtom. The Berāri Māngs make baskets of bamboo and use a knife known as the *khāl* while the Dakhanī Māngs will not touch this knife, and work with date-palm leaves. Māngs are socially inferior to Mahārs, whose food they can eat. They eat the leavings of other people. They beg during an eclipse. Rāhu the demon who swallows the moon and thus causes her eclipse and his companion Ketu were both Māngs, and it is to appease them that grain is given to their caste men. A Māng is the born enemy of the village Mahār whose grain dues are many times his own and are much more certain of collection and who disdains to beat the drum in his funeral procession.

The Chambhārs are a leather working caste, their number in the District being about 9200 or 1 per cent. of the population. The Harale (or Marāthe) Chambhārs claim the highest rank. When Mahā Munī's supply of hides ran short Haralya, the primeval Chambhār, rather than disappoint Mahādeo, stripped off a piece of his own skin to make the god shoes withal. In religion they are devoted to Mahādeo, whom they worship on a Sunday in the month of Shrāwan. The *sādhu* who acts as their *guru*, makes a visitation once in every four or five years.

The other important divisions are the Mochīs of northern origin and the Dabgars. The Dabgars are tanners and formerly used to prepare the receptacles for storing *ghī*. The Harale Chambhār dyes leather, and makes shoes, *mots*[1] and *pakhāls*.[2] He will not use untanned leather, nor will he work for Mahārs, Māngs, Jīngars, or Kolīs. If one of these buy a pair of shoes from him he asks no indiscreet questions but he will not mend the pair as he would for a man of higher caste.

130. The most common criminal castes of the District are the Pārdhis, Kaikāris, Bhāmtas, Māng-Gārodis and Takāris; though Banjārās, Rāmosis and many other wanderers of doubtful reputation are also met with. These classes at least have a bad

Criminal tribes.

---

[1] A *mot* is the large leathern bucket and funnel used for drawing water from a well.

[2] A *pakhāl* is a waterman's goat-skin in which he carries water.

reputation, but in many cases their propensity to crime has decreased, if not vanished, and they have settled down to respectable callings. Pārdhis[1] are frequently classed with Takāris (Takenkars) as if they were a tribe of much the same kind but are now quite distinct. Pārdhis have two subdivisions, Phāns Pārdhis and Langotī Pārdhis. The Phāns Pārdhis take their name from the Phāns (noose) which they use in catching birds and animals. They lead a nomadic life and live under tents. They do not normally commit crime. The Langotī Pārdhis derive their name from wearing the *langotī* (a strip of cloth about two feet long and six or eight inches broad, passed between the legs and the ends tucked in to a waist-band before and behind) because of their fear that a *dhotī* if worn might become soiled and therefore unlucky. The Langotī Pārdhis are also called Gaon Pārdhis and are further subdivided into Chauhān, Ponwār and and Solankī, all three being names of well-known Rājput clans. As a rule they marry girls from another class, thus a Chauhān would marry a Ponwār girl and so on. In religion, besides worshipping their ancestors, they worship goddesses who are now identified with the Hindu goddess Devī but who are known in the caste by different names. Chauhāns worship Ambā, Ponwārs worship Marai Māta, and Solankīs Kāli or Kālanka. The pīpal tree is held specially sacred. The chief religious ceremony at which many gather together, is Deo Karia which is performed in the month of Chait. The idol of Kālanka Bhawāni is taken to a tree two or three miles from a village and placed with its face to the east. In front of it a fire-place of earth is made, on which wheaten cakes or sweetmeats are prepared in a large fry-pan. These are taken barehanded out of the boiling oil by any Pārdhi who is possessed by the goddess. A young buffalo or a goat is brought to the spot and stabbed in the left side of the neck; the idol is besmeared with the blood which spouts out, and the worshippers then taste it themselves. The animal is then killed. To the north of the idol a small mound is raised. On

---

1 Reference, Mr. Sewell, D.S.P. of Amraoti, Appendix I to Kennedy's Criminal Tribes.

the third day, by which the flesh has all been eaten, the skull of the animal is placed on the mound, *ghi* and country liquor is poured on it, and fire is applied. This burnt offering closes the ceremony. These are the meetings at which ways and means for committing crime are discussed as well as caste disputes settled, and results of past offences related. In committing burglary they do not take any pride in the hole they make, nor have they any particular mode of breaking through walls from which the work could be recognised as theirs. They sometimes will dig nearly through a wall, leaving only a thin partition against which the leader will carefully listen before finally bursting through. Then when a hole is made big enough to get through, the leader strikes a match which he holds between finger and thumb, with his fingers stretched out so as to form a shade, and holding this in front of him so that his features are shielded, he has a good survey of the room before entering. Pārdhis do not as a rule injure the people they attack in committing dacoity. If all goes well and the victims give no trouble, then they do not hurt them, but they are quite ready and if people resist, they will not hesitate to beat them. If an accomplice reveals the names of others he is outcasted and it is said that he can only be admitted into the caste on drinking a little of his wife's urine. The penalty for nearly every offence is a fine of so much liquor; that resulting from a man's sin is drunk by men and that paid up by the women is drunk by the women. The lobe of the left ear of both men and women guilty of adultery is cut with a razor. A Pārdhi guilty of sexual intercourse with a prostitute is punished as if he had committed adultery. Like all such people Pārdhis have their ordeals and omens. One test is as follows. An accused person having taken oath is told to take out a rupee and a knife from a vessel of water placed within a space marked off with a circle called a *kund*. He delivers these to the *panch*. There is no direct manifestation, but if the man be guilty he will be afraid to touch the knife as his conscience tells him the goddess will punish him if he does. Another test is for the accused to take a knife and going into water up to his chest or neck to take the oath of the goddess. Yet another is for two men to stand within circles drawn in the sand of a river bank and about seven bamboos distance from one another. Accused stands near one of them while a friend goes into the water. Accused touches one man and runs to the other, touches him and returns. When the accused touches the first man the friend dives under water and if he can remain below the surface till accused finishes the run, the latter is judged as innocent, but if not, then he is guilty; accused is then expected to vomit blood and die. There is also the ordeal of the red-hot axe-head. If a woman is suspected of adultery some pīpal leaves are placed on her hand and a red hot axe on them. If she is burnt, or refuses to stand the test she is pronounced guilty. A favourite omen with them is the simple device of taking some rice or juāri in the hand and counting the grains. An even number is lucky; an odd number is unlucky. If dissatisfied with the first result a second or a third pinch is taken and the grains counted. A winnowing basket or a mill stone falling to the right when dropped on the ground is lucky, as is also a flower falling on the right side from the garland with which they crown their goddess. The Phāns Pārdhis never use the railway; and are forbidden the use of any conveyance whatever. The Gaon Pārdhis are polluted if their women happen to throw their *lugdās* on the roof of their house. They generally keep an earthern pot for washing clothes and any cattle touching this pot are polluted and must be sold away or given in charity at once. It is said that Chauhān women will not ride in a cart, drink liquor or wear red cloth. Ponwār women may not ride in a cart, but may drink liquor; and they will not touch gold or eat anything which lives in water.

Bhāmtis or Bhāmtas number 653 persons in the District, their total number being 1697 in Berār. Their ordinary rural avocations are the making of rope and twine and the preparation and sale of gunny bags, but most of them are noted as bazar or railway thieves and pick-pockets. There is no limit to the Bhāmti's field of operations; he is said to travel and work all over India. But he confines his attentions almost entirely to railways, markets, temples and fairs, in fact anywhere where crowds collect, though he is not averse, while making a road journey, to plying his calling among fellow-travellers. The railway however is the most lucrative, and safest field for his activities. The numerous disguises he makes use of, and the variety of methods he has recourse to for accomplishing his purpose, make him difficult to recognise. Both sexes are early trained to follow the profession of crime and soon become experts. Children are first taught to pilfer shoes, cocoanuts, etc., and are liberally chastised for want of proficiency in the course of their education. The women are as adept as the men, and boys are expert at removing ornaments off the persons of children. These juvenile thieves entice their victims away to a quiet spot, by displaying sweetmeats, copper coins or grasshoppers tied to a thread, and then relieve them of their ornaments.

Another more distinctly criminal division are the **Māng-Gārodis.** They generally travel about with small *pāls*, taking their wives and children, buffaloes and dogs with them. They are under the orders of a headman, who is distinguished by his wearing a red cloth or shawl in addition to the short drawers (*chaddī*) and fringed waist clothes (*kāchha*), which form the ordinary male attire. They never do a hard day's work. Begging, performing childish conjuring tricks before villagers, trading in barren half-starved buffaloes and buffalo-calves, sometimes in country ponies, are their ostensible means of subsistence. They also purchase from Gaolīs barren buffaloes which they are said to be able to make fertile, returning them when pregnant for double the purchase money; and they shave buffaloes for villagers. Men, women and children are habitual thieves and pilferers. They specialize in stealing agricultural produce from and grazing their animals in ryots' fields; remonstrance is met with abuse and often violence. The women steal in the day and the men at night, the former being very clever at pilfering clothes put out to dry, picking pockets in bazars, sneaking fowls, shoes, and other things.

The Takāris[1] take their name from the verb *tākne*, to reset or rechisel. They mend handmills (*chakkīs*) used for grinding corn, an occupation however which is sometimes shared with them by the Langotī Pārdhis. The Takāri's avocation of rechiselling grinding stones gives him excellent opportunities for examining the interior economy of houses, the position of boxes, cupboards, etc., and gauging the wealth of the inmates. They are the most inveterate house-breakers and dangerous criminals. A form of crime which the Takāri indulges in, in common with many other criminal classes, is that of decoying into a secluded spot outside the village, the would-be receiver of stolen property and robbing him of his cash—a trick which carries a wholesome lesson with it.

Finally may be mentioned the Kolhātis, a criminal tribe who numbered at the last census 215 in the District, chiefly in the Daryāpur tāluk. They are nomads, the men of the tribe being thieves, while the women are hereditary prostitutes. The information which the latter obtain from their admirers is communicated to their husbands and made use of in their depredations.

Social Life and Customs.

Names of villages.

132. The long Muhammadan dominion has left its mark deep in the nomenclature of the District, large numbers of villages bearing Islāmic names. Instances of such are :—Afzalpur, Aurangpur, Ilāhiābād, Ashrafpur, Adampur, Azmatpur, Ismailpur, Khānzamān nagar and Peth Muhammadābād. Among villages named after trees or plants may be mentioned Chinchpur from *chinch* (a tamarind), Kekatpur from *kekat* (a flower), Ghosali from *ghosali* (a creeper), Ghol from *ghol* (a vegetable), Palāskher and Palāsmandal from *palās* (*Butea frondosa*), Borī from *bor* (plum), Umari from the *umar* tree, Kāranjā from the *karanj* plant, Kumbhi from *kumbhi* (a plant), Nimkhed and Nimbori from the *nīm* tree, Mochkhed from *moch* (a plantain), Amla from *ām* (mango), Pimpalgāon from the *pimpal* or *pīpal* tree, Mogrā from the *mogrā* plant, Lashnāpur from *lasan* (garlic), Yerandgaon and Yerandī from *yerandī*

[1] Musalmān Takāris are not classed as a criminal tribe.

(castor seed), Sirasgaon from the *siras* tree. Some are named after animals as Ghuikhed from *ghui* (an insect), Titiwa from *titiwa* (a bird), Shidorī (from an insect generally found in the rainy season). Harnī is from *harn* (an antelope). Dhāmangaon means the village of the water-snake, Mānjarkhed, the abode of cats, and Mhaispur, the town of the buffalo.

A few villages are named after deities as Asrā (a Devi), Krishnāpur, Tuljāpur, Rāmgaon. Among miscellaneous names may be mentioned Ghotā (an ankle), Godri (a latrine), Dahīgaon (*dahī* curds), Budhli (a cruse of oil), Dongargaon (*dongar*, a hill).

The village. In former times.

133. Just as in mediæval Europe the village blacksmith, the miller and other artificers were provided for by the field work of the remainder, and the parson got his tithes; so in former times a Berār village had its *balutedārs* who were entitled at harvest time to their *hak;* a share in return for their services of the crop that had been raised by the cultivators. They might in a fully equipped village be as many as twelve in number, and include (1) the carpenter, Wadhi; (2) the blacksmith, Khāti; (3) the Gārpagāri, a person who by white magic was supposed to be able to ward off hail storms from the crop; (4) the Mahār or village menial; (5) the Chambhār or leather currier; (6) the potter, Kumbhār; (7) the barber, Mhāli; (8) the washerman, Warthi; (9) the Gurao whose business it is to clean the temple; (10) the Joshi or Brāhman priest and astrologer; (11) the Bhāt or bard and (12) in villages with Musalmān inhabitants, the Mullah who officiated at their ceremonies and performed the *halāl* of animals killed for food. The carpenter made and repaired field tools and the wooden stools used at marriages; the blacksmith the iron work of ploughs and carts. In former times at *Gal Pūja*, the hook-swinging festival, it was his duty to force the iron hook into the muscles of the devotee's back. The Mahār besides being a watchman castrated young cattle; and a Mahār woman acted as midwife. The Mahāli at marriages was a torch

bearer; or led the bridegroom's horse; or escorted the patel's daughter to her husband's house. The Warthi spread white cloths for the bridegroom's relations to walk on. The Gurao beat the drum at the time of worship in the temples. The Joshi prepared the almanac, pointing out lucky days for marriages, for ploughing, for seed time and harvest, calculated eclipses, drew up horoscopes and officiated at marriages and funerals. At the last and at all village festivities the Bhāt attended and recited, may be invented, the genealogy of his host. The Mullah in the absence of the Kāzi was the spiritual guide of the Muhammadans.

But besides its *balutedārs*, a prosperous village might have also ten *alutedārs*. These represent a later stage of economic development, for notions of ownership have begun to appear in the village. They get no share of right in the crops but are paid like a modern workman for what they do. They are (1) the Sonār or goldsmith who assayed coin paid to Government and made ornaments; (2) the Jangam or Lingāyat *guru*; (3) the Māng who beat the tomtom at marriages and performed various menial services; (4) the Shimpī, or tailor; (5) the Teli or oilman; (6) the Kolī, or water carrier (whence our Anglo-Indian word "cooly"); (7) the Gosāwi, a village ascetic living by alms; (8) the Korki or piper and snake-charmer; (9) the Bāri, the cultivator and seller of *pān*; (10) the Gondhali, or drummer.

The system, if system it may be called, was probably simple enough in practice; but with the vast economic development of the last fifty years it has gone the way of all such primitive arrangements, and retains its place only as a memory An atmosphere of romance has gathered about it, and its details are dwelt on in a manner which would speedily have made them unworkable, had they had any but a traditional reality. To-day they are impossible. The village blacksmith has become a stamp-vendor, or a publican, the Shimpī leaves his work to speculate in cotton, and the village Brāhmans have taken to the higher education and departed to the nearest town to seek a living. Even the low caste Mahār is moving with the rest, and will be found to vie with Kunbīs in the care of the soil, and perhaps to have become a prosperous landholder in some other village than his own. The *ghāgar* in which the village women carry their household water is being replaced by the ubiquitous kerosine oil tin, and even the 'three card trick' is not unknown.

To-day the most striking feature of the country-side is its monotonous prosperity. The level plain stretches out to the horizon without an acre of waste land, its flatness relieved only by the mango trees scattered here and there, which lend a touch of variety to the view even at the close of the hot weather. The people speak of their cultivated fields as "the jungle," but the only trees therein are a few *bābul* and mango, and almost the only wild things, the antelope, of which large herds levy toll on the fatness of the harvest. On one side, may be, a line of scrub marks the course of some half-dry nullah, and on rising ground, if there be any rising ground, beside it, the trees grow thicker, and a cluster of brown roofs and mud walls declare the village. As one approaches it the thing most conspicuous is probably the *garhī* or fort, a great square erection of mud with projecting towers at the corners: reminiscent of the uglier aspect of times not very long gone by, when 'Free Companies' of Pindāris and dacoits roamed through Berār and treated the villager with scant consideration, To-day the walls are tumbling down and the site taken up perhaps by a primary school, or a police station, perhaps by the houses of the leading inhabitants; or these may be grouped around it. Among them will be one somewhat more conspicuous than the rest. It will have two stories and a flat sleeping place on top; its front will be whitewashed, and its verandah *(baithak, otā)* and gallery ornamented, perhaps with blackwood carved in primitive fashion before carving became a lost art in Berār, perhaps with more modern twisted iron railings and corrugated roof. This should be, if it has not passed into the hands of the Mārwāri moneylender, the house of the Patelki family; and like all the better houses it will have a small enclosure attached to it. In this part of the village too will be the *chāwrī* or office of the patel and patwāri which is also the village club, a *musāfirkhāna* or traveller's rest house, and any Government buildings that the place boasts of. The chief temple too will probably be there, its dedication being a joint one either to Māroti and Vithobā or Mahādeo and Ganpati; also perhaps a mosque if there are sufficient Muhammadans to support it. Further away will be the *gothān*, an open space used as a cattle stand; perhaps a market place; and separated by these from the houses of the better class the Mahārpeth or quarter of the village servants, over which flies a strip of white or red rag to warn high caste folk away from this place of defilement. On the outskirts will be the wells, that for the low caste being in a different spot to the rest; one or two small shrines of Māroti or *lingas* of Mahādeo; and the trees and shapeless heaps of stone daubed red which represent the village gods and low caste deities, relics of earlier animistic belief. Last of all is the *idgāh*, its scrupulous whiteness as strange a contrast to the prevailing dirt, as is the faith for which it stands to the rude superstitions which in this part of India have been grafted upon it.

Villages in this District are large, a hundred houses with six hundred inhabitants being a usual figure, while many can boast of a population numbered by thousands. The large majority of the inhabitants, including the patel, will probably be Kunbīs; though villages of Mālis, Bāris and similar castes are not uncommon. There are one or two Brāhmans and a few Muhammadans; in some places Muhammadan villages may be found. The usual low caste village servants are there. A number of Pardesīs make up the foreign element; and are employed as casual labourers on such jobs as watching the crops and scaring away wild beasts. Commerce will be represented by the Mārwāri moneylender, the local equivalent of the Irish "gombeen man"; or perhaps by a few Rohillās or Afghāns whose objects are the same though their methods are somewhat more violent and their dealings pettier.

Of the old village community little remains. Those parts of it necessary to government have been upheld—the patel, the patwāri, the menial servants. But the *balutedārs* no longer exist; a Gārpagāri here and there gets a precarious livelihood from such as still believe him; the Bhāt is still in great request at marriages and adoptions; the Joshi and the Mullah have probably obtained *inām* fields—we may almost say 'glebe land' on which to support themselves and the worship they perform. But the Mahār alone, the lowest of all the twelve, can enforce his right to a share in the harvest.

All that is picturesque in village life centres now round the patel. He is, as mentioned elsewhere, the representative of the village in its dealings with Government: he is also in internal matters its acknowledged head, and on four important occasions in the year its leader in the relation with the Gods. His privileges are summed up as being the *Mān* and the *Pān*, or in one word *Mānpān*. The latter are sundry presents of *pānsupāri* and cocoanut and services of a ceremonial nature on such occasions as the marriage of his daughter: the former the position taken by him at the four great festivals of Holī, Dasahra, Tulsilagna and Polā. At Dasahra a *helā* or male buffalo is provided at the village expense for a solemn sacrifice to Durgā Devī. It is taken in procession up to the *jhandā* or flag in front of the *chāwri* where in former days it was slaughtered by the patel with his own hand. Now he makes merely a ceremonial cut and the Mahārs who complete the work carry away the body and eat it. At Holī the patel and Joshi meet; and make an invocation to the *Rākshas* or demons in whose honour it is held. It is then the patel's privilege to light the sacred pile; and he likewise provides the *gulāl* or red powder and the other accessories of the festival. Tulsilagna is the marriage ceremony of the sacred basil plant, which is performed once a year by the patel and the Joshi and signalises the commencement of the auspicious season for matrimony.

But the occasion of the patel's greatest importance is the Polā: and as it is also the festival of all others most typical of this part of India, it deserves a fuller description. It is a religious holiday held on the new moon day of Shrāwan or Bhadrapad, after the ploughing and sowing has been done, by the cultivator in honour of his greatest helper the bullock. On that day all the bullocks of the village will be gaily painted in various colours and their horns and necks covered with garlands. They assemble in one place, where stands the *gudī* a sacred "maypole" of the patel; the Mahārs beating drums in front of it, and a twisted rope of *mol* grass covered with mango leaves being stretched from it to a smaller pole on the right. This rope is known as the *toran* and is dedicated to Māroti. Under this stand the patel's bullocks, which should be a pair without spot or blemish, all white or all red, according to the custom of the village. To the left of the pole a long line is formed of the other bullocks, those of the Patelki family first, then a pair chosen to represent the Deshmukh, a pair to represent the Sarkār, the Patwari's pair and finally those of the other villagers. Bitter indeed are the disputes as to precedence on these occasions, and by no means the less so that the village does not always recognise as patel the man whom Government has appointed, and sometimes takes this opportunity to restore the precedence of a senior member of the family. All now do *pūja* to the pair of bullocks under the *toran*. At a given signal from the patel, his pair are led forward, the *toran* is broken and the remaining pairs follow in order through the place where it has been. With this procession the ceremony ends, but no bullock can be put to work this day; for once in the year they are free from their masters.

When the patel dies, there will be great excitement in the village. Probably the *watan* or right to succeed to the office in not held by one family alone but divided among several in different proportions. These different families are known as the *khels* or *taksīms* of the *watan*; the test of a *khel* being the observance by its members of *sūtak* and *devak* or common mourning and religious rites. They will now vie with one another to produce a successor to the deceased; and even within each *khel* different candidates will appear against one another in a fashion that makes it easy to realise how the word *bhaobandi* (the affection of kinsmen) has come to be the local synonym for deadly hatred. Each will produce a genealogical tree twenty or thirty generations long with infinite ramifications, and will be prepared to swear to the truth of it though he bought it from the Joshi or the Bhāṭ or from some wandering *sādhu* not so very long before. But the cultivators of Berār are peaceable enough and though agricultural riots are frequent, it is but seldom that serious damage is done.

Games and amusements.

134. The villager has few amusements beyond his family; the village gossip in the *chāwri* or the temple, a weekly trip to the nearest market, an occasional visit to a *jātra* or religious fair such as that at Bairam, or more rarely a pilgrimage to a shrine of more than local celebrity. Occasionally a troupe of Nats or Gopāls (strolling acrobats) visit a village, and the people collect to see the exhibition. The boys have their games, *Gilli danda*, (Marāthī *Witi Dāndu*), *Lonpāt*, and *Ardāh Purdāh*. The first is not unlike the English 'Bat Trap and Ball' or 'Tipcat.' A small stick is placed with one end projecting over a hole in the ground; one player strikes it smartly with a longer stick, and the others then endeavour to catch it in mid-air. If any of them does so, he has his innings and the former striker joins the field. *Lonpāt* is a kind of Tom Tiddler's Ground or Prisoner's Base, and is generally played by moonlight. The ground is marked out in squares to each of which a boy of the defending party is posted. Their opponents then try to pass through these squares and back again without being touched. If they do so they win the game. *Ardāh Purdāh* may be compared to "Blind Man's Buff," or perhaps to "Forfeits." The players form equal sides and a curtain is held up between them. One boy then hides close up to the curtain; and the opposite party is asked to guess his name. If they reply correctly he is blindfolded and sent off on some errand, the fun of the game consisting in watching him stumble over and knock his head against the various obstacles placed in his path. Girls have their dolls and play at housekeeping, as they do all the world over, and their amusements are naturally more of an indoor nature. Deshī Kasrat, an Indian 'Swedish exercise,' has been introduced in the schools; and in one or two also cricket. Among men, the games most in favour are *chausar* (a kind of draughts) and cards. Races of trotting bullocks

are held on Til-Sankrānt and wrestling matches, very much of the "catch-as-catch-can" order, on Nāg-Panchamī. Cock fighting and also ram fighting are favoured by the lower classes; and among Gaolīs he-buffalo fighting on Diwāli is a common diversion. The beasts are fed up beforehand with *sarkī* (cotton seed) and green grass and on the day of the contest are given *tāri*, *gānja* and other intoxicants. Cricket, tennis, and similar games are only played where they have been introduced by English officials, in the large towns, among the police and in a few schools.

Leading Families.

135. The most distinguished landholder in the District is the Mahārāja of Jaipur who holds near Ellichpur (as he does also in various other parts of India) land granted to his ancestor the famous general and astronomer Jai Singh by Aurangzeb in recognition of services in the field. The estate is known as Jaisingpurā and is *inām* land. The story goes that Aurangzeb issued a *sanad* to Jai Singh granting him all the land on which his army halted for any considerable time, and the Jaipur family accordingly have such estates scattered all over India. His Highness of course is an absentee, and the resident aristocracy of the District falls into four well defined classes: the Jāgirdārs and others, chiefly Muhammadans, connected with former rulers in Ellichpur; the Rājput chieftains of the Melghāt; the Deshmukhs who are mostly Marāthās, and the Deshpāndes who are all Brāhmans. Besides these there are a few families of merchants and others who have become prominent under British Rule. Very few of these can show anything exciting in their annals or any personage of historical distinction. The story especially of the ex-pargana officers is the story of a class and an institution rather than of great characters or single houses. As a class, they usually refer their *sanads* to the time of early Mughal Emperors, and especially to Aurangzeb; though the offices which they hold are probably much older. As a class, they weathered

Leading families.

the stormy period of *do-amlī* government, to be placed with the arrival of British Rule on political pensions (*rusūm, lawāzimā)* in perpetuity; and as a class they are repidly losing, through the excessive subdivision of these pensions, all the importance that they once possessed.

The Deshmukhs: Daryāpur.

136. Probably the most substantial as well as the best known of the Deshmukh families in the District are those of Daryāpur, Jarūd and Ellichpur. The first are Marāthās, but claim, as so many leading Marāthā families do claim, to have come here from Rājputāna 'in the time of Alamgir;' an assertion in which there is nothing very improbable; for in the general upheaval of that Emperor's Marāthā wars new men on both sides were bound to come to the front and his armies are sure to have left colonists throughout the Deccan. They received a grant of the Daryāpur pargana, which contains 113 villages, in Deshmukhi and quickly became zamindars in addition. At various times they appear to have occupied a position of considerable dignity under both the Nizām's and the Bhonsla's governments, and to have attained at least a partial independence of the local tālukdārs and Sūbah officials. Bahādur Rao, their greatest representative, who seems to have held sway early in the 19th century, had the honour of a palanquin at the expense of the Nizām's Government with a guard of 50 soldiers from the same quarter as well as 50 from the Bhonsla; and used to travel in state to Nāgpur and Hyderābād to present in person the accounts of his pargana. He built at a cost of about a lakh of rupees the great *wāda* or family seat at Daryāpur, which is one of the best houses in the District and contains some very handsome carving. The present head of the family, Bhagwantrao Shankarrao Deshmukh, is his grandson. He has been a Special Magistrate for 28 years and was invested a few years back with second-class powers: he has sat on the District Board ever since its beginning 23 years ago, and in many other ways has helped forward the administration of the

District which he was invited to represent in the Delhi Darbār of 1903. A brother Nāgorao is also on the District Board while a third is Tahsīldār of Amraoti. The family was formerly one of the wealthiest in Berār : and though much of its *inām* land has been made *khālsa* at successive settlements, and an unfortunate lawsuit not yet finally closed has eaten away its revenues, is still very well off. One village Sivar Buzurg containing 572 acres 13 *gunthās* is held on *pālampat* tenure at a fixed tribute of Rs. 321 per annum ; the *lawāzimā* amounts to Rs. 848-2-3, and there is *khālsa* land of 912 acres 7 *gunthās* paying Rs. 2108-11-9 Government land revenue. Bhagwant Rao calculates his total yearly income as being between nineteen and twenty thousand rupees. He holds also the Patelki and *patwāripan* of several villages, but these offices are purely of an honorary nature and the work is done by others.

137. The Ellichpur Deshmukhs are Brāhmans and claim to have obtained their *watan* before the establishment of the Mughal rule in Berār having come from Bīdar in the time of the Bahmanī kings. Probably because their pargana was the headquarters of the province they never appear to have attained to such power as the Daryāpur family, though at least as wealthy. One village is held by them in jāgīr free of payment, and as they also possess a large amount of *khālsa* land scattered in 27 different villages, and a *lawāzimā* which amounts in all to Rs. 4291-11-6 the family may be said to be in a flourishing condition in spite of a debt of Rs. 15,000 on one half of the estate. The property is divided, one share being in the hands of Vyenkat Hanmantrao and the other of Vithal and Harīhar, sons of Mādhorao.

Ellichpur.

138. Like the Daryāpur family the Deshmukhs of Jarūd in the Morsi tāluk are Marāthās and claim to have come originally from Udaipur in Rājputāna. The present head of the family is Rao Sāhib Anand Rao Tukārām who received his title in

Jarūd.

Bemrose, Collo., Derby.

TOMB OF SHAH ABDUR RAHMAN GHAZI, ELLICHPUR.

recognition of services rendered during the famine of 1899-1900, and of his habitual liberality to deserving institutions both in his own neighbourhood and elsewhere. He is both Deshmukh and Mālik Patel of Jarūd receiving a *lawāzimā* of Rs. 120 for the former and Rs. 136 for the latter office. He holds land in Berār paying Rs. 4500 a year Government land revenue and in addition is malguzar of two villages in the Kātol tahsīl of Nāgpur and of seven in the Gwālior State. He pays Rs. 175 income tax on *sāhukāri* dealings and a share in a cotton gin, and estimates his annual income at not less than a lakh of rupees. The estate is, not unnaturally, free from debt. The Rao Sāhib maintains *sadāvart*—free alms to all that choose to ask—at Jarūd and in the famine established a poor-house for 500 people at his own cost. He is chairman of the Warūd Bench of Honorary Magistrates and a member of the Tāluk Board.

The Kāle family of Warūd.

139. Near neighbours of the Jarūd Deshmukhs are the Kāle family of Warūd, who though they have never held pargana office may be mentioned here as a Marāthā family of standing. They are descended from one Sivāji Rao who came from Satāra about the year 1760 at the request of the Bhonsla Rājā and settled here. He is said to have taken part in Marāthā raids towards Bengal and to have held rank as first class Sirdār in the Nāgpur Darbār. Of his two sons Vithalrao the elder settled at Betūl in the Central Provinces while the younger Malhārrao came to Berār; and the family is proud of having held office as Honorary Magistrates for three generations, Vithalrao, Malhārrao, Tukārām and Mārtandrao, the eldest son and grandson of Malhārrao, having all exercised jurisdiction; while Bājīrao, a brother of Tukārām, is a member of the District Board. The family is a large one with many branches, but the Berār half of it at least is joint, and holds property both real and personal valued at five lakhs of rupees and bringing in not less than thirty thousand rupees a year. In addition there is a moneylending business managed by Bājīrao.

The Deshpāndes. Anjangaon.

140. Of the Deshpānde families there are also several of considerable position, but few that can lay claim to any historical importance. That of Anjangaon is descended from one Vithūjī Narāyan who settled in Anjangaon and founded Surji, building the village fort and rampart there in 1697 A.D. Shāmji Deshpānde fought valiantly in the wars of the Nizām and the Marāthās and successfully defended his village against a Pindāri raid. Balwantrao was the head of the house at the time that the representatives of Sindhia and the East India Company met at Anjangaon, and is said to have exerted himself in the interests of peace. His services and hospitality were recognised by both sides and a copy of the treaty presented to him, but this together with *sanads* from the Emperor Aurangzeb and from various Nizāms was destroyed in the fight between the Nawāb of Ellichpur's troops and those of the Munsif of Akot, which took place here in 1850. Of the present members of the family Yeshwantrao is a Special Magistrate, as were also his father and grandfather before him, the former subsequently becoming Tahsīldār of Bālāpur. Raghupatrao, who is now 58 years of age and is regarded as the head of the family, has also been for many years a Special Magistrate. He is a great student of poetry and himself a poet. His *lawāzimā* is drawn on his behalf by his son Govind, and amounts to Rs. 819-13-2. Yeshwantrao draws Rs. 34-6-2 and a third branch of the family represented by Gayābai widow of Pralhād has Rs. 727-1-8. No information has been obtained as to the financial condition of the family except the statement that their *inām* fields were made *khālsa* in 1863-64 by the Inām Investigation Officer. They may however be taken to be fairly well-to-do.

Ellichpur.

141. But the most important Deshpānde family in Berār is that of Ellichpur whose present head is Rao Sāhib Purushottam Bhagwant. Like his father, the late Rao Bahādur Bhagwant Rao, the Rao Sāhib is a second class Magistrate and vice-chairman of the Ellichpur City municipality, a brother Narhar Rao being also a municipal member. The family is a Brāhman one and

claims descent from one Rāmajī and his son Nārorām who came to this District and settled in it in the reigns of Shāh Jahān and Aurangzeb. They received various grants of land and of the Deshpānde *watan*, the earliest being dated A.D. 1656. At the present day the Deshpānde's allowance is Rs. 3410-4-9. The estate consists of *inām* and *khālsa* lands, and each of the three branches into which the family has been divided enjoys an income of about Rs. 15,000 per annum.

142. A position somewhat similar to that of the Deshmukhs and Deshpāndes in the plains was occupied in the Melghāt by the Rājās of the six parganas, Maklā, Dhulghāt, Jāmgarh, Mohkot, Khatkali and Rūpgarh. Living in a poorer country they have never been quite so wealthy but being inaccessible they have attained in the past to far greater independence. Their history is more stirring and the insertion of a clause in their *sanads* establishing primogeniture has given them a chance of stability which the pargana families of Berār unfortunately lack. All these chiefs claim to be of Rājput or Chhatri extraction, the Rājā of Maklā being descended from a certain Bijairao, the Mohkot Rājā from Gambhīrrao and the other four from Garudrao. It is said that in 1598 three years after the close of the Mālwā war, the Emperor Akbar turned his attention to his new dominions and called for volunteers to populate the devastated parganas. Among others the three adventurers just named came forward and offered to settle the rude tract known as Gāngra, the western and southern parts of the present Melghāt tāluk. The Emperor was pleased to accept their services and sent them forth with the hereditary rank of Rājās, bearing letters commendatory to the Governor of Mālwā, Shābash Khān Omdād-ul-Mulk enjoining his assistance. Having reached their destination they set about their work, and to help them called in the services of a wealthy zamīndār named Gondāji. This man (the Solon of the legend) introduced cultivators and when frightened by the pestilential climate they fled back to the plains, he resorted with great success to the cautery as a

The Melghāt Rājās.

cure for malaria. The work prospered and the Emperor was so satisfied that he granted jāgīrs to the adventurers in perpetuity, enjoining on them to uphold order and maintain the peace, and generally to do the duties of a good king. We may hope that they obeyed him for their history for nearly three centuries is a complete blank covered only by lists of names and by *sanads* from Alamgīr which expert opinion pronounces forgeries. But the existence of certain *metkari* tenures along the northern border of Berār (lands held either for the maintenance of police *chaukīs* or as blackmail) together with the undoubted blackmail from the Akolā treasury to the Mohkot Rājā leave some doubt upon the matter. Certainly their first appearance in authentic history is a sufficiently turbulent one, for in 1809 a family quarrel between Khushāl Singh of Maklā and his uncle Jait Karn assumed such dimensions that the latter called in the aid first of the Bhonsla Rājā and subsequently of the Nawāb of Ellichpur, and the whole country was devastated. Eventually however the Rājā won the day and obliged his uncle to take refuge in Ellichpur. From about 1812 to 1818 the history of the Melghāt is bound up with the history of Sheikh Dullā, a daring Pindāri leader. Sheikh Dullā was a young Muhammadan brought into the Melghāt as a personal attendant by Khushāl Singh but the attractions of the freebooter's life were too much for him and abandoning the service of Khushāl Singh he joined a Pindāri gang and soon became one of the most daring and elusive of raiders. Being thoroughly at home in the Melghāt he found it easy to evade pursuit, and it is not difficult to imagine that the local Rājā found the temptation to share in the booty and to connive at his escape irresistible. In 1813, however, his depredations in the neighbourhood of Poona roused the Peshwā to action and a force was despatched to follow him into the Melghāt. Sheikh Dullā himself escaped but Khushāl Singh and his brother being suspected of complicity were seized and in 1814 the whole tract was annexed by the Peshwā. The Rājā and his brother soon escaped and there ensued a period of war between them and the Peshwā's representative whereby entire parganas are said to have been depopulated. In 1816 the Peshwā's force was recalled to Poona, but in 1817 Khushāl Singh was seized by the Nawāb Salābat Khān of Ellichpur, and the Melghāt was annexed to Berār under the sovereignty of the Nizām. Khushāl Singh died two years after his deposition. Jangu Singh, the heir of Khushāl Singh, continued to share in the depredations of Sheikh Dullā upon the Berār valley, till in 1818 the latter met the usual fate of the freebooter and was stabbed to death by an old member of his own gang, who had been sent by some British troops to persuade him to surrender. The information about the position of the Rājās after the annexation in 1814 is very meagre but they appear to have lived the life of outlaws and freebooters till the death of Sheikh Dullā in 1818. Thenceforward they were constantly striving to recover what they had lost by their misconduct. An enquiry into their claims was made in 1840 by Captain Johnston and the Nawāb Jani, and a further inquiry in 1867 by the orders of Sir Richard Temple, Resident at Hyderābād, on the occasion of demarcating the forest reserves. It was at this second enquiry that the Rājās' rights were established on the basis on which they have subsisted to this day. Compensation for the loss of forests and forest rights was ordered to them in the shape of annual cash payments; one-third of the estimated profits on forest produce being divided into two shares, one for the Maklā Rājā who had kept his teak forest in excellent condition and was the greatest loser, one for the other five. In addition the previously vague extent of their jāgīrs was finally settled, their police stipends fixed by Captain Johnston were raised, and the *nazars* or presents made them by their feudal dependents were made voluntary. The *metkari* lands and the blackmail already alluded to were dealt with, the former being made *khālsa* and the latter abolished; the Rājā of Jāmgarh also received Rs. 1500 per annum in extinction of the right which had been granted him to receive grazing tax. Particulars of the Rājās' villages and allowances as finally fixed are given in the following page.

Name.	Jāgīr villages.	Compensation on account of Jāglia cess.	Compensation on account of Forest dues.	Compensation on account of grazing tax.	Police stipend.	Total.
1	2	3	4	5	6	7
		Rs. a. p.	Rs. a. p.	Rs. a. p.	Rs. a. p.	Rs. a. p.
1. Rājā Khuman Singh of Maklā.	1 Maklā. 2 Punjāra. 3 Sumet. 4 Kara. In lieu of the first 3 villages, given up in the State-forest reserve, he has been allowed. 1 Kot Chikhli. 2 Nandūra. 3 Jamber. 4 Kotā. 5 Lawadā.	2,000-0-0	7,809-14-1	... ..	3,600-0-0	13,409-14-1
2. Rājā Tārā Singh of Dhulghāt.	1 Lukto. 2 Kunjoli. 3 Rain Gohan. 4 Chendo. 5 Susardah. 6 Dhulghāt. 7 Tutumbah. 8 Bowur. 9 Palaskunda Buzrug.	1,727-4-0	1,561-15-7	......	1,800-0-0	5,089-3-7
3. Rājā Dān Singh of Jāmgarh.	1 Durmodoh. 2 Chuniamal. 3 Jamri. 4 Sakri. 5 Kuredah. 6 Ambapatti. 7 Takia. 8 Gurguti. 9 Futteypuri.	500-0-0	1,561-15-7	1,500-0-0	1,200-0-0	4,261-15-7
4. Rājā Mangal Singh of Jītgarh.	1 Anor. 2 Rohunkirki. 3 Salone. 4 Kawardeo.	100-0-0	1,561-15-7	......	600-0-0 Rs. 548-6-0 received in lieu of cesses from Akola District.	2,261-15-7
5. Rājā Jām Singh of Khatkali.	... ..	338-0-5	1,561-15-7	......	1,800-0-0	3,700-0-0
6. Rājā Ganpat Singh of Rūpgarh.	... ..	38-0-5	1,561-15-7	......	1,200-0-0	2,800-0-0

143. In 1870 the Maklā Rājā was found to have taken up his residence in Ellichpur. Three of his villages, Maklā, Punjāra and Sumet, had been included in the reserved forest, and owing to the irksome restrictions introduced by the Forest Department the Rājā found existence at Maklā intolerable. His case was represented to the Government of India and in 1872 he was given the five villages of Kot Chikblī, Nandūra, Jamber, Kotā, Lawadā in lieu of these three villages. On sentimental grounds he was allowed to retain possession of the plateau of Maklā, where his ancestral house and magnificent old mango groves were situated

Exchange of villages by Maklā Rājā.

144 No change was made in the position of the Rājās till 1884 when the police arrangements came under consideration. So long as the Melghāt was confined to the simple Korkū, the somewhat primitive police system maintained by the Rājās did well enough; but the opening of the tract by roads attracted traders and moneylenders, and the system broke down. The personality of the Rājās was in itself enough to bring the system into disrepute. They took no personal pride or interest in their position; many of them led dissolute lives and bore evil reputations. Crime was neither reported nor detected; there was no adequate security for person or property. In 1885 three of the Rājās had been deprived of their jurisdiction, two more had been suspended and only one (the Rājā of Khatkali) was in charge of his range. Matters were brought to a head by the depredations of Tantia Bhīl. Several dacoities were committed in the Melghāt and the Rājās absolutely failed either through indifference or sympathy to cope with the situation. A special force of the regular police had to be posted in Melghāt and the local officers were unanimous in favour of making the change permanent. This was accordingly done. The Rājās' connection with the police was terminated and payments made to them on this account ceased. As an act of grace however such part of the payment as had been considered to be the personal allowance of the Rājās was continued to them during their lifetime.

Changes in the police system.

Position of the tenants in jāgīr villages.

145. The Rājās have always been treated as absolute proprietors of all the land within their jāgīrs and no steps have ever been taken to confer any rights on the tenants. In 1871, when the proposals with regard to the exchange of certain villages with the Maklā Rājā were submitted, the Government of India enquired what steps were being taken to prevent the existing tenants in the villages surrendered becoming mere tenants-at-will of the Rājā; but it was pointed out by the Resident that owing to the shifting nature of the cultivation in the Melghāt it was inevitable that in course of time all the tenants would become tenants-at-will and it was urged that, land being plentiful and cultivators few, the Rājā's self-interest would prevent his dealing harshly with the tenants. The tenants therefore all hold their land entirely at the will of the Rājā and no rights of occupancy or transfer have been granted to them. In 1876 it was decided in consequence of the indebtedness of some of the Rājās to place their holdings on the same footing as a service grant in the plains, to protect them that is to say from alienation and subdivision; and the question of issuing *sanads* defining the Rājās' rights was raised. Their issue however was delayed, and it was not till 1896 that all the Rājās had received them. The form of *sanad* is given below;[1] it will

---

1. SANAD granted to Raja son of of in the taluq of the District by under the authority of the Government of India.

I. (1) The Jagir villages of :—
(Name of village or villages)
Acres Guntas .
Total ...

Aggregating an area acres and guntas in the taluqs of the District in Berar, as laid down within the boundaries shown within the boundaries shown upon the survey map of the taluq of (year) on sheet nos : annexed and also the money allowances[1] specified in the margin, are hereby granted, subject to the conditions hereafter stated, to you Rājā son of and to your successors in the Raj to the following order of succession so long as any such successors are forthcoming.

	Rs.	A.	P.
1. Compensation on account of Iaglia Cess ...			
Compensation on account of Forest dues ...			
Compensation on account of grazing dues ...			

be observed that the title of Rājā is used, and therefore definitely recognised by the Government of India. It is not recognized however as conferring any hereditary precedence; and does not even convey the right to a seat in Darbār, only two of the Rājās being at present Darbāris. An exemption in perpetuity from the provisions of the Arms Act has been granted to them with their retinues; and in this respect as well as in the vague social deference customarily paid them their status has been recognised as somewhat higher than that of ordinary jāgirdārs or deshmukhs. In the event of a dispute as to heirship the jurisdiction of the civil courts would apply but in addition to this the Chief Commissioner's sanction to all successions must be obtained. In spite however of the

(2) For the purpose of these jagirs and of the allowances for Jaglia cess and forest dues, the order of succession to Raja and all subsequent incumbents shall be as follows:—Namely—that on the death of any incumbent, he shall be succeeded in the enjoyment of these jagirs and of these allowances by such one of the male persons, (if any then in existence) descended by birth or adoption through males only from Raja as would be preferred according to the rules governing the succession to ordinary private property, and that when according to these rules several such persons stand on an equal footing, the law of primogeniture shall apply.

II. This grant is given on the following conditions, on failure of which it shall be liable to forfeiture, namely—

(1) That the said jagir and the said allowances, viz. the Jaglia cess and compensation for forest dues, being service grants shall on no account be alienated by the said Rājā or his successors either by sale or mortgage or in any other manner without the previous sanction of the Resident in writing.

(2) That the tenure of the grants hereby confirmed shall be entirely dependent on the loyalty to the British Government of the said Rājā and his successors.

(3) That in all cases of succession the confirmation of the Resident shall be obtained.

III. That the abkari revenue of all the villages held in jagir by the Raja or his successors shall belong absolutely to Government.

IV. That the jagirdar shall be considered the proprietor of all forest trees and forest produce in the land hereby confirmed to him, subject always to the condition that any timber or other forest produce removed beyond the limits of the jagir shall pay such dues and be very definite recognition which has been accorded them, the present status of the Rājās is not an enviable one. The Pax Britannica has deprived them of the excitements of gang robbery with violence which formerly relieved the tedium of life for so many of their rank; it has even deprived them of their control over the local police. But it has not yet brought the more solid advantages of civilization into their jungle fastnesses. Shut off from the world so long as they continue to live in the home of their fathers, they have nothing to do but to draw the allowances which Government has granted them and manage their small jāgīrs as best they may; and it is little wonder if the monotony of such an existence is occasionally varied by an incident such as that which

---

subject to such rules as regards transit as the resident may from time to time prescribe.

V. That in the event of Government constructing road or railways within the limits of the lands hereby confirmed to the jagirdar, compensation for any land or for forest produce on such land required for such roads or railways shall only be payable in respect of land actually under cultivation at the time the land is taken up for such purpose or for any inhabited village site in whole or in part or any *bona fide* improvement proved to have been made at the expense of the jagirdar.

VI. That no transit dues of any description shall be leviable by the jagirdar.

VII. That the jagirdar shall maintain in good order and in their proper positions all the boundary marks of his jagir, and that if after the granting of this sanad any boundary marks on the ground are found at any time not to coincide with the position given to them on the map, it will be incumbent on the jagirdar for the time being to erect boundary marks of approved pattern on the places assigned to them according to the map, and that on failure to do so after due notice has been given by the chief revenue authority of the District, it shall be within the power of the chief revenue authority of the District to cause the said boundary marks to be erected and to recover the cost of the same from the jagirdar in the manner prescribed by law for the recovery of arrears of land revenue.

Given under my hand and the seal of my office with the sanction of the Governor-General in Council, this the of

(year to be given in words).

Signed

Resident.

Bemrose, Collo., Derby.

VIEW OF THE MAHADEO HILLS FROM CHIKALDA.

brought one of their number within the grip of the law only a short while past. The most notable occasion in their history is recorded in Meadows Taylor's autobiography. In 1857 they all appeared before that officer and offered their services in keeping out the mutineers from Berār; and the writer records that not one of them failed in the duty for which they had volunteered. Apart from this none of the Rājās have as yet attained to any eminence either in the Melghāt or elsewhere, though the late Rājā Khumān Singh of Maklā and Kot Chikhli appears to have been a man of some dignity and force of character. He was the owner of two very good houses in Chikaldā; and it is hoped that his successor at present a minor may receive such a training as will fit him to fill and perhaps to improve on the position that he occupies. The remaining Rājās are all illiterate and their affairs deeply involved. The names and residences of the present Rājās are as follows :—

1. Rājā Bharat Singh Khumān Singh of Maklā or Kot Chikhli resides at Kot and at Chikaldā.

2. Rājā Bhoran Singh Tāra Singh of Dhulghāt has his residence at Rānigowhān.

3. Rājā Gumān Singh Mangal Singh of Mohkot resides at Salwan.

4. Rājā Ratan Singh Lakshman Singh of Jāmgarh resides at Raipur.

5. Rājā Ratan Singh Benī Singh of Khatkali resides at Mankari.

6. The Rūpgarh Rāj is now represented only by the two widowed Rānīs Lāl Kunwar Dhaokal Singh, and Gendā Ganpat Singh who are each paid an allowance of Rs. 30 per mensem from the Chikaldā sub-treasury.

Kalamganā Jāgīr.

146. Of the former revenue administration and government in the remaining seven parganas of the Melghāt we have no certain information though it seems that revenue officials of the Nizām were

stationed in the Melghāt, and we may suppose that the Rājās held some vague and indefinite authority over the wild tribes in the parganas nearest to them as well as over their own. The parganas of Narnāla and Gāwīlgarh would naturally be under the sway of the *kiledārs* or military castellans of those fortresses; but in the latter at least as well as in the neighbouring parganas a position of great strength was held by the family now represented by Umrao Singh Ganu Singh. They were patels of some fifty villages and jāgirdārs of Kalamganā Khurd, but were not as is commonly said *kiledārs* and are in no way related to the *kiledār* family of Gāwīlgarh whose present head resides at Bhainsdehi in Betūl. There is no definite information forthcoming as to their origin though we may suppose them to have formed part of the original Rājput settlement placed by Aurangzeb in fort Gāwīl and to have maintained throughout a pure descent uncontaminated by marriage with the jungle tribes. Though not *kiledār* the representative of the family was one of the defenders of Gāwīlgarh against the Duke of Wellington, and had held the jāgīr village of Kalamganā Khurd from time immemorial. The jāgīr descended without break to his grandson in whose time it was forfeited for his non-appearance before the Inām Commissioner in 1870. In 1889 however it was restored and the land revenue which had been collected in the interval was paid to the jāgirdār. The present holder is a Darbāri but has no other distinction.

Izāra villages.

147. In 1896 it was proposed to compensate Ganu Singh, the jāgirdār of Kalamganā, for (1) the losses sustained by him on his patelkī rights (including rights in mango and mahuā produce) in consequence of the inclusion of certain villages in the Chikaldā State forest: (2) the losses consequent on the forest produce from his jāgīr village of Kalamganā having to pay dues at the Melghāt forest *nākas*. Compensation in the form of land rather than a money annuity was suggested in the interests of the family, as the experience of the Melghāt Rājās had shown the danger of money grants for which no work was required. Accordingly the two villages of Dongar-

kherā and Kalamganā Buzurg, which adjoin the jāgīr village of Kalamganā, were leased to Ganu Singh at a nominal rent of Rs. 10 per annum for 30 years. On the expiry of the lease which will fall at the close of the year 1925-1926, no compensation for improvements will be claimed, but only permission to remove jāgīr forest produce from Kalamganā Khurd, free of dues, or in lieu thereof a payment, not exceeding Rs. 100 a year, for such term as Government may levy dues on forest produce removed from the jāgīr.

Muhammadans. Khatīb and Kāzi.

148. One of the most interesting survivals of Muhammadan rule in Berār is the provision that has been made for establishment of the faith of Islām. As is well known, that religion recognises no priesthood in the accepted sense of the term but entrusts to various classes of laymen the duties usually performed by priests in other communities. The maintenance of public worship is the business of the State and those who conduct it are civil officers of Government. The Mullah, the Maulvi, the Muezzin have each their rôle assigned to them, but the two most important offices are those of the Kāzi and the Khatīb. The former is one who conducts the services in the mosque and at the *idgāh,* both of which places he is supposed to maintain in repair, performs the *nikāh* or marriage ceremony, settles points of what may be called ecclesiastical law, and is the general referee and arbitrator of his people. For each of his various services he receives a fee. The Khatīb is a more distinctly religious officer, his duties being confined to preaching the *khutbā* (a mixture of "Bidding Prayer" and sermon), leading the devotions of the congregation and distributing alms. He is also expected to deliver lectures on religious subjects. In most places the two offices are held by one and the same man, but where there is a large Muhammadan community they are separate. In Berār a Kāzi serves a circle of Muhammadan villages, frequently those of a pargana, and both offices enjoy in addition to the offerings of the faithful service grants of *inām* land. These have been given to them under *sanads* of

various Delhi Emperors and Nizāms of Hyderābād; and when British Rule was introduced there was much uncertainty as to the light in which the land so held should be regarded. The Inām Investigation Officers were in favour of treating it as given for personal maintenance; and this view was at first accepted with the consequence that the *inām* might be divided up as an inheritance, and further on failure of direct heirs of the grantee would revert to the Crown. The law however does not appear ever to have been enforced and on a petition of Saiyad Amjad Husain (see below) to be allowed to succeed his father-in-law Saiyad Madār Baksh in the *ināms* attached to the Kazāt of Anjangaon Surji and other places, the Government of India reversed the rule and directed that the fields to an amount calculated to bring in Rs. 300 per annum should be regarded not as personal maintenance but as *inām ba-sharte khidmat* or service grant. They are now therefore treated as endowments attached to the office of Kāzi. They cannot be divided and so long as the service for which they are given is performed, and the land is not alienated, they will not be resumed by Government or made *khālsa*. The service may be personal or by the appointment of a Naib Kāzi who acts as a curate-in-charge. In spite of this provision and of the customary dues which they receive, the Kāzi families are by no means well-to-do. As might be expected, the two most prominent in the District are those of the Khatīb and Kāzi of Ellichpur, the former being represented at the present day by Saiyad Azmat Husain and the latter by Saiyad Muhammad Hanīfuddīn. Saiyad Hanīfuddīn's family are Husainī Saiyad and claim descent from one Shahābuddīn Walī who emigrated from Kantur in the time of the emperor Muhammad Tughlak A.D. 1325-1351 to Daulatābād. In the reign of Aurangzeb his descendant Muhammad Sharīfuddīn received a grant of the Kazāt and Khitābat of Daulatābād and Khuldābād and these offices have remained with his decendants. His grandson of the same name migrated to Ellichpur by reason of a famine; and by the favour of Nizām Alī Khān of Hyderābād in 1182 A.H. (1768 A.D.) obtained the office of Kāzi and the title of Khān under a *sanad* of Shāh Alam. Saiyad Mohīuddīn, the grandfather of the present Kāzi, was the author of a religious work entitled 'Hidāyat ul Anwar.' The multiplication of departments under British Rule has meant that various services such as registration, control of bazars and the like for which in old days the Kāzi used to draw fees have passed from his hands; but he still enjoys an *inām* bringing in Rs. 300 annually; and a total income from all sources of Rs. 1000 by his own calculation. The family of the Khatīb is also Husainī Saiyad and claims to have come to Berār with the mythical Shāh Abdur Rahmān Ghāzi in the person of his chief of staff Saiyad Abdul Malik. Having arrived here, however, they settled down to more peaceable occupations and turned from Ghāzis to Muezzins and Khatībs of the Royal Mosque, prospering at the hands of various Mughal Emperors and others down to modern times. Saiyad Muhammad Khalīl in particular was regarded as a saint and as such invited by Nizām Alī Khān, who ruled in Hyderābād from A.D. 1763-1803, to adopt his son, it being considered a great honour even for a prince's son to be adopted by so holy a man. The same Nizām at the Iduzzoha in 1754 A.D. when acting as Governor of Berār on behalf of his brother invested the Khatīb with the Robe of Honour which his descendants still wear at the Idulfitr and Iduzzoha. It consists of a long white gown embroidered with green, a belt similarly embroidered in pink and a *sarpech* of green worked in silver; and though now much worn with age, must when new have been a wonderfully handsome garment. The late Khatīb Khān Bahādur Saiyad Amjad Husain was famous as the author of 'Tārīkh Amjadi,' a history of Berār in Persian and of other works both in prose and verse and in addition to being a second class Magistrate was a man of great position in the city. His influence among his own community was such that both Sunnīs and Shiahs accepted his leadership, and when he preached would worship in the mosque side by side. His brother Saiyad Muhammad Husain was a *Yunāni Hakīm* of note. In days when European medicine was less easily obtainable than now, he was frequently consulted by English officers, and his dispensary received a monthly grant-in-aid from municipal funds. As has been already mentioned, the late Khatīb on the death of his father-in-law Saiyad Ghulām Ahmad, otherwise known as Madār Baksh, succeeded to the Kazāt of no less than six parganas which had been held by the deceased and to the property attached to them. A long correspondence ensued as the upshot of which a large proportion of the land was allowed to remain *inām* and was made 'service grant' attached to the office of Kāzi. Saiyad Amjad Husain left three sons who have divided the duties but enjoy the inheritance in common, the eldest being Kāzi of Anjangaon Surji in addition to the Khitābat and the other two taking the remaining Kazāts of their father. The total landed estate of the family is 990 acres 27 *gunthās* of which 491 acres 3 *gunthās* are *inām* land. The income of the family from all sources including a small political pension is estimated by Saiyad Azmat Husain as nine thousand rupees a year and there is no debt. The Khatīb is a member of Ellichpur City municipality and a Bench Magistrate.

The Nawābs of Ellichpur.

149. The Nawāb family of Ellichpur whose history for the century preceding the introduction of British Rule is the history of the province itself, is now extinct. It is represented however through women by Daud Khān and Yunas Khān sons of Tālemand Khān, and these gentlemen still enjoy something of the consideration as well as part of the property belonging to the old family. They are free from debt and have an income of about Rs. 9000 a year arising chiefly from *khālsa* land. Daud Khān is a member of the municipality and a Bench Magistrate. The family is of Sulemānzai Pathān extraction, and first appears in the Deccan in the reign of Nasirjang (1748-1750), by whom Shādi Khān and Nasīb Khān, horse dealers from Jaipur, were appointed to the command first of a hundred then of a thousand lances and were given a jāgīr in Berār. From mere adventurers they rose to high importance, and from their descendants the governors of Ellichpur were principally chosen. Muhammad Ismail Khān rose to a command of 7000 horse and, having

distinguished himself in the battle of Udgir against the Marāthā forces in the year 1760 was appointed in 1762 by Nizām Alī Khān to the Governorship of Berār. A bullet in the thigh during that battle had lamed him for life, and he was allowed the privilege, by no means a common one, of remaining seated in full Darbār. He was also granted by the Nizām a palanquin, a royal fan of *yak's* tail, a banner, a drum and other honourable distinctions, as well as the jāgīr of Bālāpur, his cousin Hayāt Khān receiving Daryāpur, Karasgaon and other places. As Sūbahdār, he did much to beautify Ellichpur and in particular founded the fine old palace of the Nawābs, a building which is said to have cost three lakhs of rupees. Its courtyards and halls are now in a very tumble-down state, though some good carving and stone work are still to be seen. Part of it is used to-day as a school and part is inhabited by the present representatives of the family. Ismail Khān also constructed the walls of the city, using, it is said, the materials of Rājā Il's Jain temples, and retaining for ten years the whole revenues of his sûbah for the purpose. Whether as seems probable he actually aimed at an independent principality or as the *Nūr-ul-Berār* has it, the Wazīrs Zafar-ud-Daulā and Rukn-ud-daulā succeeded in poisoning their master's mind against him, the Nizām became suspicious of his old friend and lieutenant. Marching into Berār he took the fort of Amner on the Wardhā river from the Bhonsla and advanced against Ellichpur. At Ner Pinglai Rukn-ud-daulā was murdered, and at Deori the Nizām halted, the Nawāb's forces being only four miles away. Here (still following the vernacular account) Zafar-ud-daulā sent a message to Ismail Khān offering to mediate with his sovereign, an offer which was contemptuously rejected. The armies met at Katsura between Ner and Ridhpur, and the Ellichpur forces were routed: the Nawāb fighting with his usual gallantry, was slain. It is noteworthy as disposing of the allegations of treachery on the part of Zafar-ud-daulā that it was at that officer's mediation that Salābat Khān and Bahlol Khān, the sons of the dead man, were invested with their father's honours and jāgīrs. The former lived to make himself very useful to Wellesley, finding supplies for his army and himself fighting with his troops under the General's orders in the campaign against Gāwīlgarh. He is said to have placed his son Nāmdār Khān under Wellesley's special protection : as the local historian somewhat enigmatically says 'General 'Wellesley adopted Nāmdār Khān and gave him the name 'of General Duke.' The latter on attaining manhood was remarkable for nothing but his spendthrift habits : and with his nephew the direct line of the Nawābs expired in 1846. Portraits are still in existence of Ismail Khān, his son and grandson, which might well serve, so marked is the gradual stultifying of the features, as an illustration to Gibbon's famous words on the rise and decline of oriental dynasties. The present family are descended from a sister of Nawāb Ismail Khān. Khān Bahādur Manewar Khān was at the time of the Ināmi Commission confirmed in his jāgīrs for his lifetime only : and on the succession again passing through a lady they were resumed and made *khālsa* ; by this tenure accordingly Daud Khān and Yunas Khān at present enjoy them.

The Jāgirdārs.

150. The three most important jāgirdāri families in the District are those of Saiyad Riyāsat Alī of Asadpur, Saiyad Kāsim of Nāndgaon Peth and Mīr Ahmad Alī of Kharala. Of these Mīr Ahmad Ali who is a retired Special Magistrate, has no co-sharers. He estimates his estate at about five lakhs of rupees, his income from land and moneylending at Rs. 25,000 a year and his expenditure at about Rs. 15,000. Including with the jāgīr, *khālsa* land which he has himself purchased he is a holder in eighteen villages. His great-grandfather Mīr Akram Alī who was the founder of the family received the jāgīr for military service to the Nizām, and both Akram Alī and his successor Akbar Alī had the title of Khān. Ahmad Alī has two sons Husain Alī and Riyāzat Alī who will eventually succeed him. Saiyad Kāsim, who lives at Nāndgaon Peth, is the head of a family which holds the jāgīr of four small villages near that place and is also wealthy. The third

Bemrose, Collo., Derby.

DULA DARWAZA, ELLICHPUR CITY.

jāgīr, that of which Riyāsat Alī is the most prominent representative, was probably in the beginning the largest of the three as the estate of which two villages (Shāhpur and Raipur) are now jāgīr and the rest *khālsa* lies in both the Daryāpur and Ellichpur tāluks. It was granted by Nizām Alī Khān Asafjah-us-Sāni in the year 1177 Hijri (A.D. 1776) to Mīr Wājid Alī, Khān Bahādur for gallantry in battle, but is now very much subdivided, no less than fourteen persons being enumerated as having either shares in or allowances from the estate. Mehdi Alī, Hāfiz Alī and Muhammad Alī, who are brothers, hold one half of it and reside in Daryāpur tāluk; Zulfikr Alī and Riyāsat Alī (with the remaining sub-sharers) hold the rest. In all the estate consists of 876 acres 38 *gunthās* jāgīr and 2720 acres of *khālsa* land. The total income is estimated at Rs. 40,000 and the total expenditure at Rs. 25,000. Riyāsat Alī jāgirdār has a medal of the Royal Humane Society for bravery in saving life from drowning, and both he and Muhammad Alī are Honorary Magistrates. Finally may be mentioned the jāgīr of Mahuli in Amraoti tāluk which was granted (as an exception to the usual practice) by the British Government for conspicuous services during the great Mutiny. The ancestors of the family were jāgīrdārs in Ellichpur and Vaka-i-Nigars in the time of Aurangzeb, but in modern times the founder of their fortune has been Mīr Dilāwar Husain who took service in the Hyderābād contingent and rose to be Risāldār Major of the 2nd cavalry. In the action at Banda in 1858 his valour won him the Order of Merit and he received also the title of Sirdār Bahādur. He met his death in battle at Chichamba, a village in His Highness the Nizām's Dominions in 1859 while fighting against a band of Arab and Rohillā marauders[1] and in the next year the jāgīr was granted to his two sons 'in perpetuity 'or for so long as the British Administration in the H. A. D. 'shall continue.' Both these sons in their turn entered the army, the younger Mīr Akbar Alī becoming a Risāldār and the elder Mīr Bakshish Alī a Risāldār Major and like his

[1] See Major Burton's 'History of the Hyderābād Contingent,' page 232, 243.

father a recipient of the Order of Merit. The present jāgirdār Mīr Mazhar Alī (a grandson) resides at Hyderābād; and his one son is the sole heir to the estate. The land of the village amounts to 2618 acres 23 *gunthās* free of all assessment to Government.

Other families.

151. But perhaps the most influential of the Muhammadan families is that of the late Nawāb Mīr Fateh Alī Khān who was a jāgirdār in the Aurangābād District of the Nizām's territory as well as a large property holder in Akolā and Amraoti; in the latter city he was a Special Magistrate and the recognised leader of the Muhammadan community. His estate and something of his influence have descended to his two sons Mīr Mehdi Alī Khān and Mīr Turāb Alī Khān. The ancestor of the family was Nawāb Mīr Najāf Alī Khān Bahādur Mushīr-ud-daulā Zulfukār Jang, who came to the Deccan with the first Nizām and captured the great fort of Asīrgarh. Of gentlemen who have risen to affluence under British Rule may be mentioned the Honourable Rao Bahādur R. N. Mudholkar and Mr. M. V. Joshi, the leaders of the local bar, both of whom have large houses in Amraoti Camp. The former is a well-known authority on questions connected with the economic development of the country. The most prominent Mārwāris are Fatehlāl Sāligrām the local head of the great house of Shrīrām Sāligrām at Dattāpur and Shrīnarāyan Rāmbilās, the proprietor of the firm of Dhanrāj Pokarmal in Amraoti. Both these gentlemen are Honorary Magistrates; and the latter's family were the first bankers on a large scale in Berār. Dhanrāj Sāhu, indeed, the founder of the family, was murdered by the enraged populace in 1255 Fasli (A.D. 1845) being suspected of having made a corner in grain after a failure of the monsoon. His grandson, Rao Sāheb Rāmbilās Pokarmal, however, gained his title for his many public spirited acts; and the family are at present much respected. Of the village patels one of the best known is undoubtedly Raibhān of Assegaon who in a tenure of office extending from 1861 to 1903 (in which year he relinquished in favour of his son) has done much for the improvement of his village and neighbourhood and has given

several of his family to the service of the State. The Rājput family which holds the patelkī of Tālegaon Thākur and surrounding villages is also very well-to-do: perhaps its best known member is Thākur Chandrabhān Raoji, Deshmukh and patel of Mojhari. He is a very substantial landed proprietor and gin owner and rendered excellent service in time of famine.

CHAPTER IV.

AGRICULTURE.

(*D. Clouston, M.A., B. Sc., Deputy Director of Agriculture.*)

Soils.

Classes of soil.

152. The geological formation of the District is Deccan trap with intratrappean beds of shale, sandstone and limestone which are exposed in places. From the disintegration of the trap and the less prominent layers of non-cystalline rock can be traced the various classes of soil of this tract, varying from the very fertile deep loam of the plains, commonly known as black cotton soil, to the thin red soils of the plateaux resting on partially decomposed trap. The rivers Pūrna in the west and Wardhā in the east with their numerous tributaries, together with the undulating nature of the District, provide a natural system of drainage, which is very favourable to the cultivation of the staple crops—cotton and juāri, which only thrive well on well drained land. The soil is largely a deep black loam, which cakes into a solid mass in the beginning of the dry weather, and cracks freely in all directions later. These fissures run to a depth of several feet and give the soil a reticulated appearance; hence the statement that "black cotton soil ploughs itself." The depth of the black cotton soil varies from a thin covering to a stratum of unknown depth. It reaches its greatest depth in the valleys into which it has been washed as a fine silt from the higher lands. The richest soil of the District is the alluvium of the Pūrna valley lying north of the railway. This soil locally known as *thet* or *awal kāli* is of fine texture, very retentive of moisture, becomes sticky when wet, cracks freely in the dry weather and is comparatively heavy to work. The largest stretches of it are found in the north of the Daryāpur tāluk, in the west of the Amraoti tāluk, in the south-west of Morsi, the east of Chāndur and round about the town of Ellichpur. In different places it is known under

different names such as *chiknī*, which means a sticky soil, *gaohāri*, a wheat soil, and the like. It is very fertile, and well suited to the cultivation of all the different crops grown in the District. As it is mainly found in low-lying or level areas, however, its retentivity sometimes results in water-logging in years of excessive rainfall. In such years cotton grown in this soil suffers badly, while in years of short but well distributed rainfall, the same soil will give a bumper crop. Owing to this tendency of the soil to retain too much moisture during the rains and to retain that moisture late in the season, it used to be largely devoted to wheat. But within the last thirty years wheat has often done badly owing to the failure of the late rains, and the cultivators now grow cotton or juāri in preference to it in this class of soil; or if wheat is grown at all, it is generally in rotation with these. The large rise in the price of cotton has also stimulated the growth of this crop. The area under wheat has decreased from 8·8 per cent. of the total cropped area in 1876 to 4·6 per cent. in 1907; while the area under cotton has, within the same period, risen from 36 to 50 per cent. of the cropped area. The black cotton soil of the plains rests on a layer of marl of a light yellow colour. The water-bearing stratum is generally very deep. In the rich tract of the Daryāpur tāluk it varies from 40 to 80 feet. The water of the wells in such tracts is often brackish owing to the presence of certain soda salts; and it was at one time customary in Berār to utilize the water of these wells for the manufacture of salt. Black cotton soil containing a small percentage of lime in a finely powdered state is known as *kāli*. If there is a still higher percentage of lime present in the form of nodules about as large as peas, the soil is known as *morandi*. These soils containing lime are lighter to work than pure black cotton soil, are less retentive of moisture and less fertile. Sandy soil found on the banks of rivers and streams is known as *retāri*. A shallow stony soil found on high-lying places and producing only inferior grasses and brushwood is called *bardī*. The thin layer of red soil overlying trap rock or *muram* on the plateaux is known as *lāl matti*; a soil subject to scouring is called *khardī*.

A shallow hilly soil interspersed with stones and boulders is known as *gotār* and the patches of greyish coloured marly soils which occur in certain fields, and which are very wet owing to the subsoil being impervious to water, are known as *chopan*. An alluvial soil formed from deposits of silt is called *mali* or *gārwat*. A soil containing much saline matter is designated *khārwan*. A hard shallow *muram* soil of only a few inches in depth is known as *murmati kharkī* or *khairati*. Land when irrigated from wells is known as *motasthal bagāyat* and as *pātasthal* when irrigated from a channel or *pāt*. Land in close proximity to a village is known as *akhar*, and the light coloured soil of such land is known as *pāndhri*. The colour is supposed to be due to the chemical changes which take place in black soil when impregnated with much fermentable organic matter. *Pāndhri* is the soil *par excellence* for garden cultivation.

Berār system of soil classification.

153. By the Berār system of soil classification for land-revenue assessment, there are three main classes of soils, viz., black soils, red soils and grey soils. The factors that lessen or increase the productive power of a soil are considered and a certain value attached to each, the standard for comparison being that of a soil of standard quality. A table is then prepared showing how far any combination of these factors causes a particular soil to differ in productive capacity from soil of standard quality. Fields are not classified as having particular kinds of soil, but are valued at so many annas as compared with soil of sixteen anna quality.

Cultivators. Cultivating castes.

154. With the exception of the Melghāt the standard of cultivation of this District is high. This is evident from the care with which both field and garden crops are cultivated. The best cultivators are of the Kunbī, Māli and Bāri castes. The typical Kunbī is a quiet hard-working unassuming man, who though not very intelligent, is a good and successful practical farmer. Formerly when the caste system was more rigid, the Kunbī cultivated dry crops only, while the Māli attended to garden crops including flowers, vegetables and fruit, and the Bāri to his betel vines. Each was considered expert in his own particular branch of cultivation. The

barriers that separated these cultivating castes have to some extent broken down, and the Kunbī no longer altogether neglects garden cultivation, nor the Bāri and Māli the cultivation of ordinary field crops. Of these castes cultivation is the hereditary occupation. As the population increased, and the competition in other industries grew keener, other castes have been compelled to take up farming as an occupation. Among these are found cultivators who, though they take less kindly to farming than the hereditary farming castes, are often more enterprising than the latter, and for that reason some of them have become successful cultivators. Farm labour is largely done by the poorer Kunbīs and by Mahārs and Muhammadans.

LIVE STOCK.

Speaking at the time of the Mutiny, Captain Meadows Taylor says, 'The Province of Berār contains the finest draught cattle in India.' It is impossible to say to what particular herd he referred, but it is interesting to know that for army transport and battery purposes bullocks of the Khāmgaon breed were employed not so many years ago. In this District there are three fairly distinct breeds of cattle:—(1) the Umardā or Gaorāni breed, (2) the Khāmgaon breed, and (3) the Ghāt or Pahāri breed. Of these, Umardā cattle are considered the most suitable for the plains, but the Ghāt cattle do better in the hilly tracts.

Umardā breed.

155. The Umardā breed is divided into two well defined types which are said to differ in colour only. The colour preferred depends upon the taste of the village cultivators. One village swears by white and purchases and breeds white animals in preference to any other colour; another village prefers red. Mixed colours arising from crossing are not liked. The Umardā bullock is of medium size and is white or red in colour. The body is compact; the head is well placed and broad between the eyes; the forehead is slightly concave, the horns are of medium size; the muzzle is broad and usually dark in colour; the nostrils are large; the neck is short and thick with a rather small dewlap; the back is

straight and the hump of ordinary size. The animal is well proportioned, active and keen-spirited. The breed is very hardy, and a pair will trot from 30 to 40 miles a day. Cattle of this breed are common in Amraoti, Ellichpur, Daryāpur and Chāndur tāluks. A pair of Umardā bullocks will fetch from Rs. 125 to Rs. 200.

Khāmgaon breed.

156. Khāmgaon cattle are seen mostly in Daryāpur tāluk where the soil is deep and heavy to work. The Khāmgaon is the largest and strongest of the Berār breeds, and is therefore well suited for heavy work on black cotton soil. The typical Khāmgaon bullock is a big bony animal with a coat of mixed colours; the general colour is red or tanned red mixed with white, the red generally occurring in round spots which give the animal a mottled appearance. His hoofs, muzzle, horns and inside of the ears are of a chocolate colour; forehead is broad and slightly convex, the muzzle fine and the hump well developed; horns are of medium length and rather thick at the base. When allowed to grow naturally they grow straight out almost in a line with the forehead with an expansion of about 2½ feet. But the owner almost invariably alters their curvature by cutting slits in them near the base when the animal is still young. The slit is cut round the outside of the base of the horn, so as to make them curve round over the top of the head, so that the distance between the horns at the points and the base is about the same. At times this operation is carelessly carried out with the result that the horns become quite unsymmetrical. The height of a good Khāmgaon bullock is 52 inches behind the hump; his length from head to tail is about 6 feet, and his girth about the same. He is round in the barrel and altogether a strong, massive animal. For that reason he used to be much in favour in the army for transport or battery purposes. As a trotter he is inferior to the smaller but more active Umardā bullock, and his hoofs are softer and do not stand the tear and wear of the road so well, of which fact the light colour of the hoofs is an indication. The Kunbī cultivator, who prefers the smaller but hardier breeds, speaks derisively of Khāmgaon cattle as the *pochat* breed, by which he means the breed that cannot stand fatigue. As a strong draught animal he is particularly well

Bemrose, Collo., Derby.

UMARDA BULLOCK.

Bemrose, Collo., Derby.

BULLOCK OF THE KHAMGAON BREED.

suited for areas where the soil is heavy to work. A pair of Khāmgaon bullocks costs from Rs. 150 to Rs. 250.

Melghāt and other breeds.

157. The smallest breed of the District is the Melghāt or *Pahāri* breed. The Melghāt bullock is a hardy, active animal particularly well suited for the conditions of that hilly tract. They vary much in colour, but the predominant colours are red, white, and mixed red and white. The forehead is straight with a vertical depression midway. The limbs are strong and well apart. The pelvis is rather lean and narrow and the dewlap small. When purchased young and brought to the plains where they are well fed, bullocks of this breed attain to a larger size than they do in their native hills. A pair of these bullocks will fetch from Rs. 80 to Rs. 150. In addition to these, cattle of many other breeds are imported into Berār, such as Arvī cattle from Wardhā and Mālwīs from the Hoshangābād side, and much inter-breeding has gone on, more especially between the Arvī cattle and the Umardā breed.

Deterioration and scarcity of cattle.

158. It is often stated that the cattle of this and other Districts of Berār have both deteriorated and become much more costly within the last forty years. This has not been definitely proved. There are still good cattle all over Berār and the prices do not seem to have risen much within the last four decades. In the Berār Gazetteer of 1870 the prevailing prices at that time were stated to range from Rs. 115 to Rs. 132 per pair. At the present time the price of an average pair of Umardā bullocks would be between Rs. 120 and Rs. 150. The fact remains, however, that at the present time cultivators in Berār are doing very little to improve their cattle. The ordinary ryot feeds his working bullocks fairly well, but neglects his cows and young stock, which for the greater part of the year subsist on the dry and unnutritious grass of the grazing areas. No selection is made of breeding bulls; the cows of the village herd are allowed to be covered by immature and inferior bulls. That old custom of keeping Brahmani bulls in the villages which was so common in former days, and which

helped to maintain the quality of the stock, has fallen somewhat into disfavour, consequent on the great amount of mischief done by these privileged animals to the village crops. The only large stock owners and breeders of this District are the Gaolīs of the Melghât, whose aim is to rear as many animals as possible, rather than to improve any particular breed by careful attention to selection. There are no important cattle shows held in the District by means of which a taste for cattle breeding and rearing could be encouraged.

Cattle rearing.

159. Ever since the beginning of the great boom in cotton cultivation, more and more of the waste land formerly available for pasture has been brought under cultivation, and the cultivator has, in consequence, been compelled to reduce the number of his cattle and to provide a daily supply of fodder for his working bullocks. In 1870 there were in the District 12 bullocks, 12 cows and 4 buffaloes for every hundred acres of cultivated land as compared with 9 bullocks 5 cows and 2 buffaloes, respectively, at the present time. It is undoubtedly the case that here as in other parts of Berār, the demand for working bullocks now exceeds the local supply, and that breeders from the Nerbudda valley, Wardhā, Khāndesh and the Nizām's dominions, are finding a ready sale for their bullocks at good prices in Berār markets. This is as it should be; the cultivator of Amraoti under present conditions finds that it pays him better to cultivate cotton than to rear cattle, and it is questionable whether any system of land administration could be devised which would enable him to rear all his own cattle with profit to himself while the price of cotton remains as high as it is.

Cattle-breeding.

160. Cows are kept for breeding, rarely for producing milk. They are poor milkers, the maximum yield of a good cow being about three seers a day; but the ordinary animal does not give enough milk to nourish her calf properly. The price of a cow varies from Rs. 10 to Rs. 40. Nowadays the ryot finds it difficult to rear cattle. If within reach of forest grazing areas he gets a permit from that Department and sends his cows

and young stock there in March for grazing. There they remain under the charge of graziers who charge a fixed rate per head. In October they are brought back again to his village to subsist for the remaining six months on whatever grass they can pick up. For the whole period of twelve months the feeding is poor and is certainly not conducive to the improvement of the breed. The principal breeding ground of the District is the Melghāt. Here there is some grazing in the jungle all the year round, though water is scarce in the dry weather. The breeders of the east and centre of the tāluk have commonly to drive their herds north to the Tāpti valley in the hot season. The chief breeders are Gaolīs, though there are also herds owned by the local Korkūs and by Baniās, Kalārs, Telis and Muhammadans from the Khandwā side, many of whom have settled in the Dhārni circle in the Tāpti valley. Grazing being plentiful and cheap, cattle-breeding is a paying industry in that tract. The grazing dues paid to the Forest Department are 6 annas per head per annum for herds belonging to large graziers and half that sum for those of cultivators. During the day herds of about 200 cows may be seen grazing under the charge of one or two graziers, and at night they are driven to an open place in the jungle where the grazier has his hut, and where they rest in safety, as no tiger or panther will usually attack any animal of a combined herd. The calves, except in rare cases, get all the milk. No serious attempt is made to improve the breed, the cows get nothing but the comparatively dry and unnutritious grass which they pick up, and are allowed to be covered by any one of the three or four inferior bulls with the herd. The male calves when about a year old are sold in the plains of Berār or in the Nimār District. The chief markets for Melghāt cattle are Ellichpur, Bairam and Dhārni.

Grazing areas.

161. The want of sufficient grazing land is one of the greatest difficulties with which the cultivators of the District have to contend. On paying the necessary fees cattle owners can send their cattle to C class forest, *i.e.*, grazing ground set apart for this purpose; but the area is very inadequate. The northern parts of the Morsi, Ellichpur

and Daryāpur tāluks, the western part of Chāndur and the eastern part of Amraoti tāluk take advantage of some larger forest blocks; but in the rest of the plain portion of the District the area for grazing is confined to the few acres of waste land and to the narrow strips of uncultivated land that form the borders of fields. These strips locally known as *dhūrās* have under the stress of competition been gradually brought under cultivation and are now too narrow to be of much value. The pasture lands and forests of the plain tāluks are in consequence much overgrazed.

Working life of a bullock.

162. Bullocks are put to easy work when three years of age; after the age of four they are able to do full work. The working life of a bullock varies from twelve to sixteen years, according to the kind of treatment it gets. Bullocks kept steadily at well work last a much shorter time than those kept for dry-crop farming. For well irrigation a pair is not supposed to last for more than five or six years if worked continuously.

Buffaloes.

163. There are two breeds of buffaloes in the District, the Gaorāni or Nāgpurī breed, and the Mālwā breed. The former are distinguished by their long horns that sweep back over the neck; the Mālwā breed is smaller and their horns shorter and slightly crumpled. Buffaloes are kept by Gaolīs for the production of milk and *ghī*. Herds of from 60 to 80 are kept in the Sātpurās. In towns where they are kept for milk, they are fed on juāri stalks and cotton seed—one cow buffalo being allowed from two to three seers of cotton seed daily. Male buffaloes are but little used for draught purposes, and the bull calves are therefore neglected and many of them die before coming to maturity. The price of a good cow buffalo is Rs. 75.

Ponies.

164. The Berār ryot has no taste for pony breeding, the ordinary pony seen in the villages being a poor specimen. The well-to-do ryot prefers to travel in a cart or *rengī* drawn by bullocks. The price of a good pony is about Rs. 50.

165. The local donkey is of a very small but hardy breed, and varies in price from Rs. 7 to Rs. 25 each. The milk is not commonly drunk, but is sometimes given to children as it is supposed to be very digestible. Mule breeding is not practised.

Donkeys.

166. Sheep are kept only by the Gadaria or shepherd caste. Herds of goats are kept by this and other low castes of Hindus and by Muhammadans. The three breeds of sheep are the Taperkāne, the Batkāne and the Fulkāne. The Taperkāne sheep has long ears and is generally jet black in colour, while the Batkāne breed has small ears and is generally mixed black and white. The Fulkāne breed is said to be a cross between the other two. They have reddish brown ears with white tips. Sheep are kept for the production of wool and mutton. The wool which is used for making coarse blankets is shorn annually in the cold weather, the weight of each fleece bring from one to one and a half pounds. Goats are principally reared by Dhangars for their flesh and milk. Pigs are kept by Gonds and Gowāris who consider pork a luxury.

Sheep, goats and pigs.

167. Epidemics among cattle are very common, and as no care is taken to segregate diseased animals at the first appearance of an outbreak, infection spreads fast in a herd. The diseases most prevalent in the District are rinderpest, foot-and-mouth disease, malignant sore throat and pleuro-pneumonia. Other bovine ailments such as hoven, diarrhœa and dysentery are common. Rinderpest is a disease common to all cattle but young buffaloes epecially are liable to it. An animal attacked by it generally dies within a week : should it live for ten days, there is good hope of its recovery. The curative measures adopted by the owner are to feed the animal on *ghī*, mūng pulse, and rice water and to invoke the help of the goddess Mātā. Inoculation for rinderpest is recommended but not yet practised to any great extent in the District. Foot-and-mouth disease is very common. The animal attacked by it is made to stand in mud, and *dikāmāli* or the resin of *Gardenia lucida*, boiled in linseed or til oil, is

Diseases.

rubbed on the sores of the feet. If there are ulcers on the tongue, they are treated with alum powder. Should the hoofs split, the animal becomes lame for life ; but the disease is not often fatal.

Weeds and fodder grasses.

168. The cultivation of the District is as a whole perhaps cleaner than that of any other part of Berār. The most troublesome of all weeds is *kūnda* (*Andropogon punctatus*) which may be seen growing in its characteristic roundish patches in cultivated fields, and which the cultivator may be seen laboriously digging up with his *kud lī* (pick) during the hot weather. When green it is relished by cattle. *Kāns* grass (*Saccharum spontaneum*) is equally troublesome, but is not so widely spread. It is chiefly found near the foot of the hills but is not so common here as in the northern Districts of the Central Provinces. *Nāgarmothā* (*Cyprus pretensis*) is a most pertinacious weed infesting garden and *akhar* land. *Nāgri* grass (*Arthraxon lanceolatum*), an inferior grass of spreading habit; *paonia* or *sirput* (*Ischaemum sulcatum*), a tufty grass which grows to a height of two feet; *pāndhar* (*Chloris barbata*) a coarse tufty grass growing in wet places are also common weeds in cultivated fields, but can be removed without much difficulty at the time of weeding with the *khurpī*. *Agāra* (*Achryanthes aspera*), whose flowers stick to the clothes like burs, and the leaves and seeds of which are used medicinally, is a very common weed on the borders of fields. Wild *san* hemp *(Crotalaria retusa)* and *sheora*, a species of *Alysicarpus*, are the two commonest leguminous weeds found in cultivated fields. There are also certain shrubs which become very troublesome weeds. *Yelātari (Dichrostachys cinerea)* with its tassel-like flowers, *saondar (Prosopis spicigera)* which may be recognised by its grey rough bark and flowers in slender spikes, *ruī* or *akan (Calotropis gigantea)* and at times *bābul (Acacia arabica)*, *hiwar (Acacia leucophlea)* and other shrubs become troublesome weeds. The roots of some of these go to a depth of 4 ft. or more, and the work of uprooting them at that depth is a heavy one. The cultivator commonly checks their growth by digging up the roots that are in the first six inches of soil. The natural grasses of the *ramnās* and village grazing grounds are those that have adapted themselves to the soil and

climatic conditions of these areas. The hardier and coarser grasses generally flourish at the expense of the finer varieties. The coarser varieties include those already mentioned as common weeds in cultivated fields, as well as *mote kusli* or spear grass, (*Heteropogon contortus*) a coarse grass used mainly for thatching, *tikhāri* or *rūsa (Andropogon Schœnanthus)* from which a fragrant oil is extracted and *mushad (Iseilema wightii)*. The best grasses are *paonia*, the marvels *mothā marvel (Andropogon caricosus)*, and *lahāni marvel (Andropogon annulatus)*, *sahāda (Ichæmum laxum)* and *dūb* grass (*Cynodon dactylon.)*

STATISTICS OF CULTIVATION.

Occupied and cropped area.

169. For the purpose of showing the agricultural progress of the District, the year of the revision settlement 1894-95—may be taken as the starting point. In 1894-95 the village area excluding state forests was 1,930,056 acres, of which the area occupied for cultivation was 1,795,125 acres. During the 14 years ending 1907-08 the village area increased by 138,873 acres and cultivation extended by 106,668 acres. The expansion of these areas has been obtained by the contraction of both the state forests and the unoccupied culturable waste lands. The net cropped area in 1894-95 was 1,714,345 acres, but in the famine years of 1896-97 and 1899-1900 it decreased by 26,944 and 267,098 acres respectively. In 1900-01 there was a rise to 1,742,280 acres and in 1906-07 the highest figure during the last 14 years, namely 1,810,171 acres, was reached, but there was a fall in 1907-08 to 1,777,167 acres. Amraoti has the fourth largest cropped area in the combined Provinces, being exceeded by the two Berār Districts of Yeotmāl and Akolā and the Chhattīsgarh District of Raipur. The double-cropped area of the District is very insignificant, the average area double cropped during the last seven years having been 656 acres.

Fallows.

170. Of the area occupied for cultivation in 1907-08, a total of 124,626 acres or 6 per cent., was under new and old fallows, the new fallow being 99,971 acres and the old fallow 24,655 acres. Owing to the unfavourable seasons the new fallow has

increased in recent years. In 1894-95 the area under old fallow was 26,897 acres but has now fallen to 24,655 acres, or by 8 per cent. Owing to the cotton boom of late years the cultivator sows his field with cotton every year without giving it a fallow or rotation of crops. In a rich black soil country grazing inevitably gives place to cultivation; if the cultivator can afford to leave part of his land for pasturing his cattle instead of growing a fodder crop for them, it is either evidence of his prosperity or the lightness of the rental he pays.

Statistics of Crops

171. In 1907-08 autumn or *kharīf* crops covered 1,649,101 acres or 92·7 per cent. and spring or *rabi* crops 129,143 acres or 7·3 per cent. of the gross cropped area. Since 1901-02 the relative proportion of the autumn crops has increased by nearly 108,400 acres. Cotton is the principal crop and in 1907-08 occupied 885,996 acres or about 50 per cent. of the gross cropped area. In 1905-06 it occupied 943,268 acres, the highest figure ever recorded during the last fifteen years. Fifteen years ago in 1892-93 cotton occupied 672,875 acres, so it has now gained more than 213,000 acres. Next in importance to cotton is juāri, the common staple food of the District which in 1907-08 occupied 539,282 acres or more than 30 per cent. of the gross cropped area. Twelve years ago juāri occupied between 600,000 and 700,000 acres, and it has now fallen by about one-sixth of its area, almost all of which has gone to make way for the more important and paying crop of cotton. Among *rabi* crops wheat is still of some importance. Fifteen years ago much land was devoted to wheat but it has gradually fallen off and now occupies 81,780 acres or 4.6 per cent. of the gross cropped area. The area under other crops in 1907-08 was: tūr 103,135 acres or 5.8 per cent., gram 22,891 acres or 1⅛ per cent., and linseed 10,045 acres or less than 1 per cent. Rice is not of much importance and occupies only 4260 acres. The area under sugarcane in 1894-95 was 600 acres, but it has gradually fallen to 228 acres. Orchard and garden crops occupy 1267 acres, of which 1219 acres are irrigated. There is very little irrigation in the District, the total area irrigated in 1907-08 being only 7453 acres or 4.4

per cent. of the total cropped area and this was mainly from wells.

Crops.

172. The area under cotton in 1907-08 was 888,996 acres. In 1876 cotton occupied 35.9 per cent. only of the cropped area of the District as then constituted; in 1881 36.7 per cent., in 1891 38.2 per cent., in 1901 47.7, in 1905 52 and 1907-08 50 per cent. There was thus a gradual increase in the area during the thirty years from 1876 to 1905-06, and a slight falling off in the area subsequently. In this District where the demand for fodder crops is very great owing to the very limited area available for grazing, the area under cotton has probably reached its maximum. Its cultivation was formerly restricted to the better classes of soil; but owing to the great boom in the cotton trade and the consequent rise in prices of late years, cotton is now often grown on light inferior soils. The quality of the cotton depends largely on the quality of the soil on which it is grown. On *khardī* poor soils it can only be grown profitably while high prices prevail, and any considerable fall in prices would result in the substitution of sesamum or some of the smaller millets which make less demand on the plant food of the soil. To succeed under the climatic conditions which prevail in the District the cotton grown should mature in about five months, so that at least one good picking is obtained before the cold weather.

Cotton.

173. The two indigenous varieties grown, namely *jarī* (Kāti Vilāyati) and *banī* (Hinganghāt or *Ghāt kapās*) mature in about 5 and 5½ months respectively. The *jarī (Gossypium neglectum)* is one of the coarsest and shortest stapled cottons produced in India. Its origin is not well known. It is said that the *jarī* grown thirty years ago was comparatively a superior cotton, that it spun up to 16's or even 20's and was in demand in the Bombay market for export to England. The present *jarī* falls far short of this description. Its staple is coarse and short, at its best it spins up to 10's only, and it no longer finds a market in England, not being suitable for use in the

Jari.

Lancashire mills. The introduction of the coarser strain is said to date from about the year 1873. In that year white flowered cotton, which was said to give 50 per cent. of lint, which ripened early and which was a most prolific yielder, was introduced into Berār from Khāndesh. The first cultivators of this new introduction, having observed that the seed possessed a sharp beak resembling a thorn, and having concluded that it was a foreign variety, named it Kāti Vilāyati or 'thorned English.' The Kāti Vilāyati proved to be a most vigorous grower and a big yielder, and readily adapted itself to the soil and climatic conditions. Its botanical designation is *Neglectum roseum* and *Neglectum roseum cutchica*, there being two types with white flowers but the one giving a slightly better lint than the other. The *jarī* which it has largely supplanted was most likely of the two finer-stapled types, viz. *Neglectum malvensis* and *Neglectum verum*, mixed with a fairly high percentage of *banī (Gossypium indicum)* which was the predominant cotton in those days. These are rather later in maturing than the two coarser types which now predominate. The percentage of the coarser type in this mixture has gradually increased until the *jarī* of the present days often contains from 70 to 80 of the coarser, *i.e.*, the *roseum* type. The reason would seem to be that Kāti Vilāyati is a hardy cotton with a heavy yield, which despite its coarseness finds a ready market at a good price both for export and for the use of Indian mills. It is exported mainly to Germany and Japan where it is found very suitable for mixing with wool in the manufacture of coarse woollen fabrics; in this country the existence of a large quantity of machinery especially constructed for dealing with short-stapled cotton also gives it an artificial value. The ryot, recognising that Kāti Vilāyati is a hardy cotton, that it suffers less than other varieties from the exigencies of the climate, and gives large fluffy bolls with a very high percentage of lint to seed, prefers it to the finer types which have less bulky bolls. The good cultivator, who used formerly to select and gin his own seed and still does to some extent, selected only the big fluffy bolls, i.e., bolls of the *roseum* type. The percentage of the coarser types in this mixed cotton known as *jarī* has thus gradually increased at the expense of the

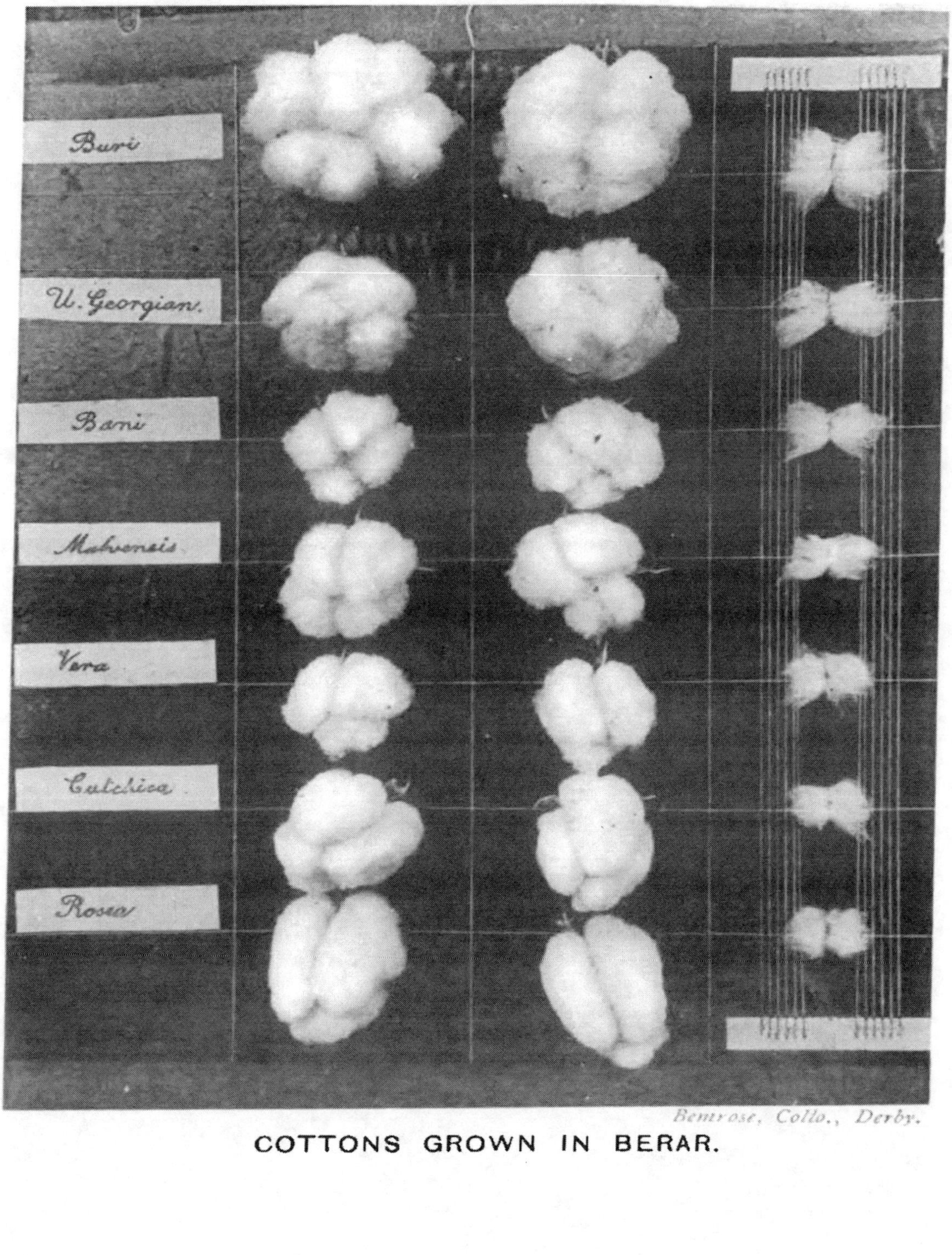

Bemrose, Collo., Derby.

COTTONS GROWN IN BERAR.

finer. Cotton buyers in Berār at the present day recognise two kinds of *jarī* cotton, *gaorāni* and *howri*. *Gaorāni* is of better staple but gives only 33 or 34 per cent. of lint; *howri* on the other hand gives 36 per cent. or even more of lint but the staple is much shorter. The difference in staple would seem to depend on the percentage of the fine-stapled types present in the mixture, which percentage varies considerably in different villages.

Banī.

174. *Banī*, Hinganghāt or *Ghāt kapās (Gossypium indicum)* is a cotton of long staple and silky fibre. The percentage of lint to seed is about 26 compared with 32 per cent. for the finer types of *jarī* and 40 per cent. for the coarser. Its staple is about 1 inch in length as compared with ½ inch for the coarser types of *jarī*. It has been almost entirely ousted from the District by the *jarī* mixture now grown, and is never grown nowadays as a pure crop. This variety formerly known as Hinganghāt or *Ghāt kapās* had earned for itself a name and was exported in large quantities to England long before power spinning and weaving had made much headway in India. When grown pure, it was suitable for spinning 40's. The price of *banī kapās* is Rs. 2 or Rs. 3 more per *khandī* than that of *jarī*, but *jarī* gives a much heavier yield than the former, more especially in years of drought or excessive rainfall. *Banī* is altogether a more delicate plant and less profitable at present prices.

Upland Georgian.

175. Upland Georgian (*Gossypium hirsutum*) is an acclimatized American variety which was introduced about thirty years ago. It is known locally as *ghoglī*. It is equal to *banī* in length of fibre and will spin up to 40's, but has deteriorated very much in strength. The total area under this variety as a pure crop is insignificant, but it can be seen growing as a mixture to the extent of one or two per cent. in every cotton field.

Burī.

176. Another exotic variety which is now being tried is *burī* (*Gossypium hirsutum*) an American Upland cotton acclimatized in Bengal. Seed of this variety was obtained nearly four years ago from the Inspector-General of Agriculture and has since been grown

successfully at the Government Experimental stations. Its lint is as good as that of *banī*; the percentage of lint to seed is 33 as compared with 26 for *banī*; it yields well and the lint is worth 50 per cent. more than that of *jarī*. This very desirable cotton is now under trial and the results so far have been distinctly promising.

Rotation.

177. Cotton being the most profitable crop grown is always recognised as the principal crop of a rotation. In *awal kāli*, *morandi* and *mali* soils it is sometimes grown continuously year after year in the same field without any rotation with another crop. Though this is contradictory to all the laws of scientific farming, there is not the least doubt that it pays the cultivator. The cotton plant is tap-rooted and being a deep but not greedy feeder, does not readily exhaust the soil. In growing cotton or any other crop continuously on the same land there is always the risk, however, of encouraging insect pests. The Berār cultivator avoids this by removing all the cotton stalks from his fields in March. Where a rotation is followed it is generally cotton-juāri; or cotton-cotton-juāri; this is a good rotation, as juāri being a shallow feeder draws its food supply from the surface soil. Cotton after *rabi* crops such as wheat, linseed, gram and cold season til is less common, except in a part of Ellichpur, Amraoti and Daryāpur tāluks. It is the practice all over the District to sow two lines of tūr to twelve or more of cotton in cotton fields. The cultivator has a hazy idea of the fact that tūr is a soil renovator, though he is ignorant of the cause. But the lines of tūr serve another purpose in so far as they divide up the field into sections of known dimensions which enable him to gauge the amount of work done by his labourers and the yield obtained from different parts of the field. The tūr also acts as a wind brake.

Manure.

178. Much of the cattle dung is used as fuel, and no attempt is made to collect cattle urine. Fields near the large towns are sometimes manured with the town sweepings; and where large herds of goats and sheep are kept, these are sometimes folded in the fields at night. Artificial manures are not in use, but

nitrate of soda has been tried and has proved a profitable manure when applied as a top-dressing.

Tillage implements and tools.

179. The tillage implements used for cotton cultivation are the country plough *(nāgar)*, *wakhar*, *dhūsa*, *daurā*, *dhundia*, *khurpī* and sickle. The heavy Berār *nāgar* is a much larger implement than the country plough of the Central Provinces. The body is commonly made of the wood of the *bābul* tree *(Acacia arabica)*, which is very tough and durable, and the beam of *bābul* or *tiwas* *(Ougenia dalbergioides)* which is also very tough, strong and durable. The plough is drawn by three pairs of bullocks and stirs the soil to a depth of 9 or 10 inches; but land in Berār is so ploughed only at intervals of ten or fifteen years. The cost of the Berār *nāgar* is Rs. 8. Some of the more enterprising cultivators are now using Ransome's turn-wrest plough, which they find to be an excellent implement for fields over-run with *kūnda* grass *(Andropogon punctatus)* and other obnoxious weeds. Its cost is Rs. 41. The *wakhar* serves the purpose both of a plough and a harrow. It is like a large scraper with a blade about 21 inches long and 4 inches deep. The blade is fixed to the body of the *wakhar* by means of pegs made of *bābul* wood. The body is about 2½ feet in length. The beam is usually made of teak *(Tectona grandis)*, *temru* *(Diospyros melanoxylon)*, or *tiwas*. The *wakhar* is guided by means of a single upright wooden stilt, is drawn by one pair of bullocks and costs Rs. 4. With one pair of bullocks a man can work from one to two acres in one day, the area depending on the state of the soil. For deeper work the driver stands upon the body of the *wakhar*. When the soil has baked very hard or when the land is infested with a thick growth of weeds, the light *wahkar* makes but little impression on it, and the cultivator will in such cases use the *moghdā* or large *wakhar*, the body and the blade of which are much larger and heavier. The *moghdā* is drawn by two pairs of bullocks and turns up the earth in clods and brings weeds to the surface. It is often used for the first *wakharing*. The cross *wakharing* is then done by the lighter *wakhar* drawn by one pair of bullocks. When turned upside down after removing the blade and worked as a clod-crusher, the *moghdā*

is called a *padhal*. The implements used for interculture are the *daurā* and *dhundia*; these are miniatures of the *wakhar*, and are used solely for interculture. The body of the *daurā* is about 16 inches long with a blade 10 inches long and 2 inches deep. Its cost is R. 1-12-0. With two *daurās* drawn by one pair of bullocks two men can hoe from 2½ to 3 acres of cotton daily. The blade of the *dhundia* is of the same depth as that of the *daurā* but is 4 inches longer. For interculture the cotton-grower therefore uses the *daurā* while the plants are small; when they have grown somewhat larger the *dhundia* is used so as to pare away the weeds growing near the rows and at the same time to ridge up earth against the plants. Cotton is generally sown in this District by the *dhūsa*. The *dhūsa* resembles a *wakhar* except that the blade and pegs have been removed and two wooden tines are substituted; these tines form the drills. Two hollow bamboos called *sartā* are attached by a string immediately in the rear of the tines; through these the seed is dropped. Two *wakhars* are usually worked behind the *dhūsa* to cover the seed with soil. With one man to drive the bullocks and two women to drop in the seed, they can sow about 4 acres of land in one day. Sowing is sometimes done with the *wakhar*, in which case only one *sartā* is used; but this method is a slow one and is only practised by the poorer cultivators. Sowing is commenced during the first break that occurs after the first good fall of rain, which is usually about the third week of June. Some of the more enterprising cultivators still follow the practice, which was once fairly common in Berār, of sowing small areas before the rains. The hand tools used are the *khurpī* and the sickle.

Seed selection.

180. There are now ginning factories within easy reach of every cotton-growing village, and factory ginned seed is commonly used for sowing. The cultivator sows about 10 lbs. of handginned seed and about 13 lbs. of the factory ginned seed per acre. The objections to the latter seed are that much of it is damaged in the process of ginning and that different varieties get mixed owing to careless handling. There is one cotton seed farm in Morsi tāluk belonging to Mr. R. S. Pethe. The aim of the farm is to propagate and distribute to cultivators new and

improved strains of cotton seed that have been selected and supplied by the Government Experiment Stations.

Insect and animal pests.

181. Less damage is done to cotton by insect pests in Berār than in most cotton-growing tracts in India. This is due (1) to the soil being almost totally bare of any vegetation that would serve the purpose of a host plant for these pests during the hot season, the cotton stalks being uprooted in February or March, (2) the area under cotton is large and compact and (3) the climate is dry and uncongenial to the healthy development of such pests for the greater part of the year. The pests that do an appreciable amount of damage are the cotton boll worm, the pink and red cotton bug, the cotton stem borer, the leaf roller, aphides, and grasshoppers. The moth of the boll worm *(Earias fabia)* lays its eggs on the leaves, stems, bracts and petals of the cotton plant; the caterpillars are hatched in two or three days and bore into the immature bolls and eat the seed; they pupate later under ground or on the plant itself. In a week the moth emerges and the pest thus repeats its life history, multiplying enormously each time. The best remedial measure that can be adopted is to uproot and destroy all cotton plants after the last picking. The pink and the red cotton bug *(lāl kīra, Dysdercus cingulatus)* lay their eggs in cracks in the soil. The bug on emerging is wingless. It moults five times, and after the third moult the wings begin to appear. The bug gradually increases in size, and is able to fly after the last moult. With its long needle-like beak it sucks the juice of the green cotton boll and immature seeds, thereby destroying the seed and lint. It may also be seen feeding on *bhindī (Hibiscus esculentus)*. The best remedial measure is to shake the bugs into a vessel containing kerosine and water. The cotton stem borer (*Sphenoptera gossypii*) is the grub of a beetle. The borer bores into the core of the cotton plant and eats its way up the stem. The plant gradually withers and dies. The borer pupates in the stem and emerges as a beetle after 10 days. The best remedial measures are to uproot and burn all affected plants and to destroy all the cotton plants after the last picking.

The moth of the cotton leaf roller (*Sylepta derogata)* lays its eggs singly on the leaves of the cotton plant. The caterpillar on emerging feeds on the leaves, rolls one up and lives inside it. They pupate within this leaf-house, emerge as moths after 10 days and couple and lay eggs. The rolled leaves containing the roller should be picked by hand and destroyed. The cotton blister beetle (*Mylabris pustulata*) eats the flowers of cotton. Grasshoppers (*naktol* of the family *Acrididiae*) and crickets (*jhingrā*) eat the leaves of cotton in its early stages. The bag method of collecting them has been tried with some degree of success.

Cotton wilt.

182. Cotton wilt (*Neocosmospora vasinfecta*) is a fungoid disease which does a certain amount of damage more especially in the rich soils where cotton is often grown year after year without a break. The fungus first enters the smaller roots, from which it spreads to the tap root and stem, filling the water ducts with its mycelia, with the result that the plant can no longer draw up its full food supply, and consequently begins to wither and die. The plant so attacked becomes dwarfed in appearance; the leaves turn yellow and shrivel up, and the main stem generally dies off. This may take a longer or a shorter period. In some cases the whole plant is dead within 50 days from the time of sowing the seed ; in other cases the plant only dies late in the season. Some plants partially recover from the disease by developing strong lateral branches after the death of the main stem. The fungus is really a parasite which enters the vascular system of the plant and feeds therein. Its reproductive bodies or "spores" on germination give rise to the fungus plants. Certain varieties of cotton are not subject to the disease, and different plants of the same variety vary very considerably in their degrees of resistance, some being readily attacked while others are altogether immune. *Burī* cotton is immune from the disease and is being introduced on the worst wilt-infested areas of this District. Rotation of crops on these areas is also desirable.

183. The cost of cultivation and profit per acre when cotton is grown after juāri is shown below :—

Cost of cultivation and profit.

Operations.	Time.	Cost per acre. Rs.	A.
Removing juāri stumps ...	March	0	3
1st *wakharing*	March or April	1	0
2nd do.	May	0	12
Sowing	2nd fortnight of June ...	0	12
Wakharing after sowing ...	Do.	0	8
Seed 12 lbs.	Do.	0	8
Tur 2 lbs	Do.	0	2
Weeding	1st fortnight of July	1	0
1st hoeing by *dawrā*	Middle or end of July ...	0	8
Hand-weeding	End of July	1	4
2nd hoeing by *dhundia* ...	Beginning of August	0	8
3rd do. do. ...	20th of August	0	8
Hoeing up to September with *dhundia*	From August to September...	3	0
Hand-weeding	October	1	4
Picking	From November to January...	3	12
Watching	From October to January ...	2	0
Government revenue		2	0
	Total ...	19	9

Outturn in lbs.	Value. Rs.	A.
Seed-cotton (*kapās*) 420 lbs. at Rs. 50 a *khandī* of 560 lbs. ...	37	8
Tur 75 at 25 lbs a rupee	3	0
Til 20 at 14 lbs. a rupee	1	7
Total ...	41	15
Deduct ...	19	9
Net profit ...	22	6

Government assessment is included under cost of cultivation ; it varies for different classes of soil. The cost of cultivation is reckoned on the supposition that all the operations are performed by hired labour, and is therefore rather misleading, as the Kunbī cultivator maintains his own establishment of bullocks and implements, and if his farm is not a large one, much of the manual labour is performed by himself and his family. Under these conditions his farming profits are higher than that shown in the statement.

Juāri.

184. Juāri (*Andropogon sorghum*) is grown on all the different classes of soils in the District. The later and heavier yielding varieties are usually grown on the deeper soils which are more retentive of moisture; while the earlier varieties, except in years of short rainfall, do fairly well on the lighter soils. The varieties may be classified, according to the time required for ripening, into early, medium and late varieties. For the heavier soils *amner* is the most commonly grown, while *rāmkel*, which matures three weeks earlier, is widely grown on medium and light soils. The varieties are more or less mixed but less so than in the case of other crops, as the cultivator almost invariably selects his seed on the threshing floor. He is not a systematic botanist, but he has fairly definite ideas as to the difference between the varieties grown. *Amner* is a late variety with fairly compact, long oval heads set with large flat seeds. The grain when well developed is the largest of all Berār varieties. The seed which is hard and yellowish in colour is considered the best among late varieties for eating. *Rāmkel* has a long loosely filled head supported on an erect stalk. The grain is large and creamy white in colour. *Rāmkel* is one of the best and most widely grown varieties in Berār, adapted to light as well as medium soils. *Gunjaoli* has a fairly compact head with red seed. The seed is well filled and round, but is considered a very inferior variety for eating; it is grown on medium soils along the foot of the hills. As a mixture, it can be seen in almost every juāri field. *Phalpalī* or *motīturā* is a loose headed variety not commonly grown. The grain is small, well filled and oval shaped, and is used for making *lāhi* (parched grain). It is not so much damaged by birds as the compact-headed varieties. Other varieties grown are *jagdhan*, an early loose-headed variety with white grain, *mānmodi*, a medium variety with compact heads, *ganerī* and *dukartondī*, late varieties with yellow grain grown on heavy soils, and several varieties known as *wānis* whose grain is roasted and eaten when green. In this state the grain known as *hurdā* is sweet and tasty. The chief *wānis* are *mohāwāni*, *bhātwāni*, *naroliwāni*, *pivlīwāni* and *chārodiwāni*.

185. The land for juāri is prepared in the same way and at the same time as that for cotton, but usually only one *wakharing* is given before the rains. Another *wakharing* to kill the weeds is given before the seed is sown which is generally about the middle of July. The seed is sown with a three-tined seed drill or *tiffan*. The body *(khar)* of the *tiffan* is from 3½ to 4 feet in length. It is set with 3 tines at distances of from 13 to 18 inches apart. The lesser width is used for poorer soils and is in common use in Morsi and Chāndur tāluks; the latter is used for the more fertile soils such as those of Daryāpur, Ellichpur and Amraoti tāluks. The drills are fixed into wooden sockets in the body and are shod with small iron shares. These drills meet in a wooden bowl at the top into which seed is fed. The seed rate varies from 2 to 6lbs. an acre. After the *tiffan* two *wakhars* are worked to level the furrows and to kill weeds. Hoeing with the *daurā* is commenced about three weeks after sowing and is repeated three or four times at intervals of a fortnight or so. In good soil where the drills are 18 inches apart the last hoeings are done with the *dhundia*. One or more hand-weedings are given. At this time the women also remove the dried leaves from the two lowest internodes. This is supposed to enable the heads to fill better by letting in more air.

Juāri cultivation.

186. In December the crop is ready for harvesting. It is reaped with small sickles, the reaper taking eight lines at a time. The stalks are laid together in bundles which are left to dry for about a week. The heads are cut off and removed to the threshing floor; the stalks are firmly bound and stacked in the field. The threshing floor is a circular piece of ground selected for the purpose within easy reach of the field. All weeds and grass are carefully removed from it, and it is made firm by pounding it with mallets or by walking cattle over it, the hardened surface being smeared with cowdung. The heads of juāri are spread in a layer about 6 inches deep in a circle round an upright post fixed in the centre of the floor. One bullock is so tied to this post that he can walk freely round it and not entangle the tying rope; other bullocks tied each neck-to-neck are arranged alongside

Harvesting and threshing juāri.

the first. They are made to march round in a line, forming the radius of the circle, treading out the grain at every step. The biblical injunction "muzzle not the ox that treadeth out the corn" is disregarded by the Indian cultivator who muzzles his bullocks very effectively by the use of a net in the form of a bag which covers the animal's mouth. Sometimes bullocks yoked to a cart are used instead, in which case the wheels help to separate the grain.

187. To winnow the grain one man stands on a stool or platform erected for the purpose, and a second man hands him baskets full of the mixed grain and chaff from the threshing floor. The grain is poured from his basket or *sūp* to the ground below. This is done when the hot winds of March are blowing. The heavy grain falls straight down; the chaff is blown beyond it. A man standing below with a broom in his hand brushes aside any bits of straw that may have fallen among the grain. The stalks *(karbī)* and chaff form the staple cattle fodder, and the grain is the staple food of the cultivator and his labourers.

Winnowing.

188. An enormous amount of damage is done every year to juāri by birds, the greatest depredator being the juāri bird *(boria)*. They come in such myriads to eat the grain that a negligent farmer is left with but little save the stalks and glumes. To protect his ripening crop the thrifty cultivator erects in each area of about 6 acres a platform ten or twelve feet high. From daylight to sunset he sits in one of these armed with a sling, and by uttering wild yells and slinging earth or stones, he scares away these unwelcome visitors. Some damage is done to the crop in its early stages by herds of blackbuck *(hiran)* and wild pig. The chief insect pest of juāri is a borer locally known as *murad* and *unni*, the only difference being that the pest is known as *murad* when it attacks the young juāri shoots of from 6 inches to 1 foot high, and as *unni* when it attacks the full-grown stems. In the first case the attacked plants often tiller freely and may give a good yield. The moth of the juāri stem borer *(Chilo simplex)* lays clusters of eggs on the leaves. In four or five days caterpillars emerge, which first feed on

Juāri pests.

the tender leaves of the juāri and then bore into the stems near the root. The caterpillar eats its way upwards through the stem, thereby damaging the plant. The stem attacked dies; but the plant if still small sends up fresh shoots from the root. The caterpillar pupates inside the stem, in which state it remains from one to two weeks. The moth emerges from the pupa, crawls outside, couples and again lays eggs. The same pest attacks sugarcane and maize. Affected plants should be uprooted and destroyed and all the juāri stubble should be removed after harvesting the crop. At long intervals the District is visited by swarms of Bombay locusts (*Acridium succintum*) which damage this and other *kharīf* crops. The female of the Bombay locust couples and lays its eggs in clusters of one or two hundred at a depth of about half an inch in light soil, burying half its abdomen in the soil while doing so. The hoppers after hatching feed on grass, juāri and other green crops. They moult seven times; after the last moult their wings develop and they fly in swarms ravenously feeding on the crops on which they alight. The locust lives about one year and then dies after laying eggs The only practical method of dealing with this pest is the bag method. The mouth of the bag is kept open by a rectangular frame work of bamboos 12 feet by 3. The bag carried by two men is swept over the field infested with the hoppers, which on being disturbed jump and fall into it where they can be killed at leisure. This method was tried in juāri fields in 1904 with some success.

Fungoid diseases and parasitic weeds.

189. Juāri is not much affected by rust. Smut (*Ustilago sorghii*) a parasitic fungus which converts the grain into a foul, dark-coloured powder is, however, very common. The damage done by it can be almost entirely prevented by steeping the seed in a ½ per cent. solution of copper sulphate. The use of this fungicide is understood by and is now practised by a few cultivators; some cultivators steep their seed in cow's urine which acts as a fungicide; they also attribute to urine the power of preventing the seed from being eaten by insects in the soil. *Tavli* or *agia* (*Striga hirsuta*), a parasitic weed, attaches itself to the roots of juāri and sugarcane, feeding on the juice of the plant

and thereby checking its growth. The crop on an area infested with *tavli* becomes yellow in appearance; frequent weeding is the only chance of saving it.

Cost of cultivation and profit.

190. The cost of cultivation and profit per acre of juāri is shown below.—

Operations.	Time.	Cost.
		Rs. A.
Wakharing twice in hot season.	April and May ...	1 12
Wakharing before sowing ...	Beginning of July ..	1 0
Sowing	2nd fortnight of July ...	1 8
Seed	Do. ..	0 4
1st hoeing	Three weeks after sowing	0 7
1st hand weeding	Fortnight after hoeing....	1 0
Two more hoeings	September to October....	0 14
2nd hand weeding	October	1 4
4th hoeing	Do. ...	0 7
Watching	November to December...	2 0
Harvesting	December	4 12
Threshing and winnowing ...	December	1 0
Government assessment ..	......	2 0
	Total ...	18 4

Outturn in lbs.	Value.
	Rs. A.
Juāri grain 640 lbs.	20 0
Juāri *karbi* 150 bundles	6 0
Mung 32 lbs.	1 4
Ambāri 4 "	0 8
Bhūsa	2 6
Total ..	30 2
Deduct	18 4
Net profit ...	11 14

Tūr.

191. Tūr *(Cajanus indicus)* is mostly grown along with cotton in the proportion of two lines of tūr to twelve or more of cotton. It is also grown at times as a pure crop. Being a leguminous crop it will give a fair outturn on land that is considered too poor for cotton, to which it is usually confined as a pure crop. There are two common varieties, a red-seeded and a white-seeded variety. Of these, the red variety is supposed to give the better pulse. There is a variety known as

rāmkati, a variety of arhar *(Cajanus bicolor)* which is sometimes grown in gardens. It has a red seed and comes to maturity in March. It grows much taller than the earlier varieties. The seed rate of tūr per acre is 6 lbs., and its outturn as an independent crop about 400 lbs. As a subordinate crop with cotton it will yield under very favourable conditions about 100 lbs. The cost of cultivation per acre is shown below :—

Operations.	Cost.
	Rs. A.
Two *wakharings* in hot season	1 12
Sowing	1 8
Seed, 6 lbs.	0 6
First hoeing in July or August	0 7
Weeding in end of August	1 0
Three more hoeings up to September	1 5
Harvesting	1 8
Threshing and winnowing	1 8
Government assessment	2 0
Total ...	11 6
	Value.
	Rs. A
Outturn 400 lbs. ...	16 0
Bhūsa ...	3 0
Total ..	19 0
Deduct ..	11 6
Net profit ..	7 10

Diseases and pests.

192. In certain patches of soil a wilt disease almost invariably attacks this crop from year to year; but the damage which it does in the District as a whole is very little. Early frost which in the north of the Central Provinces is so destructive to tūr in certain seasons, is unknown here. The tūr leaf caterpillar, *(Eucelis critica)*, which feeds on the tender upper leaves of the tūr plant, twists the leaves into a knot in which it lives. It pupates inside the twisted leaves and emerges as a tiny black moth. The twisted leaves containing the pupa should be handpicked. The tūr plume moth *(Exelastis parasita)* lays its single blue eggs on the pods of tūr. These hatch as small caterpillars, bore inside the pods and feed on the seeds. When fully fed they come out and pupate on the pods. After 4 or 5 days they emerge as moths. Handpicking is the only remedy recommended. The tūr

pod fly of the genus *Muscidæ Acalyptratæ* lays eggs in the tūr pod, by piercing the shell with her ovipositor. The maggot, after hatching, feeds upon the seed. When fully fed it pupates inside the pod and a fly emerges within a week.

193. There are two varieties of til *(Sesamum indicum)*, one with black seed and the other white seed. The former is the one widely grown; it ripens rather later than the other. On black soils rainy season til is grown mixed with cotton seed at the rate of about 5 tolas per acre; on lighter soils it is grown as an independent crop. For rainy season til the soil is prepared in the same manner as for cotton, and the seed is sown with a *tiffan* with *wakhars* working behind. Cold season til is sown either with the *tiffan* or the two-tined cotton seed drill. The seed rate is 2 lbs. an acre. To secure its equal distribution it is mixed with fine sand or earth. When the plants are about 8 inches high the crop is hoed with the *daurā* and then hand-weeded. After this two more hoeings are sufficient. The crop is ready for harvesting in October and is cut and taken to the threshing floor to dry. The oil is extracted by simple pressure in a pestle-mill. The cake is used as cattle food and the oil for human consumption, for lamps and as an ointment for the body. The stalks are mostly used for fuel.

Til.

The cost of cultivation is shown below :—

Operations.	Cost.
	Rs. A.
Two *wakharings*	1 12
Sowing	1 4
Seed 2lbs.	0 2
First hoeing	0 7
Hand weeding	1 0
Two more hoeings	0 14
Harvesting	1 4
Cleaning	1 0
Government assessment	1 8
Total ...	9 3

As it is a hardy crop and is usually grown on poor soils, the yield per acre is proportionately small. The average for poor soil may be taken as 250 lbs. which is worth about Rs. 18, giving a net profit per acre of Rs. 8-13.

194. The damage done by insect pests is not very severe; the chief being the til sphinx (*Acherontia styx*) better known as the hawk moth, the til leaf roller (*Antigastra catalaunalis*) and the til hairy caterpillar (*Diacrisia obliqua*). Handpicking and thorough cultivation after harvesting the crop to destroy the pupae underground are the only remedies known.

Insect pests.

195. Urad (*Phaseolus radiatus*) is mostly grown in the Melghāt. It is sown on the lighter soils such as *morandi* and *khardī*. It is grown alternately with cotton and juāri or grown as a subordinate crop with the latter. Being a leguminous crop it renovates the soil. In seasons of good rainfall its growth is checked by the principal crop when grown as a mixture; but in years of short rainfall it may contribute the greater proportion of the outturn. The following statement shows the cost of cultivation per acre when sown as a mixture with juāri :—

Urad.

Operations.	Time.	Cost per acre. Rs.	A.
Two *wakharings*	April and May...	1	12
Sowing with the *dhūsa* ...	June	1	4
Seed	......	0	8
1st hoeing	July	0	7
Hand weeding	do.	1	0
2nd hoeing	August beginning	0	7
Harvesting	September or October ...	1	6
Threshing and winnowing ...	October	1	8
Government assessment ...	......	1	4
Hoeing juāri after harvesting urad	November or December ...	0	7
Harvesting and threshing juāri	do. ...	1	8
	Total ...	11	7

Outturn.		Value.
		Rs. A.
Urad	300 lbs.	12 0
Bhūsa	16 *dalās*	4 0
Juāri	100 lbs.	3 2
Karbī	20 *pūlās*	0 13
	Total ...	19 15
	Deduct ...	11 7
	Net profit ...	8 8

196. On the poor soils in the Melghāt, Morsi and Chāndur tāluks, *bājra (Pennisetum typhoideum)* is sometimes grown as an independent crop. In these tāluks it is also grown as a mixture with cotton in the proportion of one line of the former to 12 or 15 of the latter; but the proper place for *bājra* is a poor light soil where cotton and juāri cannot be grown economically. Like juāri it supplies the ryot with bread for himself and fodder for his bullocks. The grain is said to be heating and to have a tendency to induce diarrhœa; but when mixed with juāri is very wholesome. Except in years in which the crop comes to grief owing to heavy rains at the time of flowering, it is more dependable than the more profitable crops.

Bājra or spiked millet.

The cost of cultivation per acre is shown below.

Operations.	Time.	Cost.
		Rs. A.
Wakharing (twice) in hot weather...	April—May	1 12
Wakharing (once) during rains ...	July	0 12
Sowing with 3 tined seed-drill ...	August	1 4
Seed, 4lbs.	August	0 4
Hoeing	August end	0 7
Hand weeding	September	1 4
2nd hoeing	September	0 7
Watching for about 25 days... ...	September and October	0 10
Harvesting	October	1 12
Threshing	October	0 8
Government assessment ...	October	1 0
	Total ...	10 0

Outturn.	Value.	
	Rs.	A.
300lbs. at 12 seers for rupee one	12	8
75 *pūlās* of fodder	3	0
Total ...	15	8
Deduct ...	10	0
Net profit ...	5	8

197. There are two varieties of tobacco (*Nicotiana tabacum*) which are locally known as *bandri* and *banī*. *Bandri* has a broad leaf with a very thick midrib and is used both for smoking and chewing. *Banī* has a long but narrow leaf and is inferior to *bandri* both in the quality and quantity of its yield. The very best soil for tobacco cultivation is *pāndhri* but *kāli*, *mali morandi* and *shorati* are also suitable where there is sufficient water available. Tobacco is grown in nearly every village in the District, but only on very small plots. The area under this crop last year (1907-08) was 1904 acres.

Tobacco.

198. Tobacco seed is first sown in a nursery in a seed bed 7 feet by 7, raised about 3 inches above the ground level. The soil is finely pulverized and manured with cattle dung and ashes. At the commencement of the rains the seed is sown broadcast and lightly worked in. If there is a long break in the rains the seedlings are watered by hand in the evening of every third day. In order to protect seedlings from the severe heat of the sun, branches of trees are spread over the bed. In the very early stages weeding is essential; otherwise, the seedlings are smothered by growing weeds. By about the 1st of August they are 6 inches high and are fit for transplanting. Tobacco is usually grown in *pāndhri* soil; in this soil tobacco followed by tobacco year after year is said to yield well, and to improve in quality. It is sometimes grown after the staple crops of the District, cotton and juāri. To prepare the ground for tobacco the land is ploughed and cross-ploughed with the country *nāgar* and then *wakhared*. The stumps of the previous crop are collected and burnt and

Cultivation.

the field manured with cattle-dung at the rate of 20 cart loads per acre and again *wakhared* before the rains. After the outbreak of the rains two more *wakharings* are given, and towards the end of July the land is levelled by means of the *wakhar* worked upside down. The young seedlings are transplanted out in rows about 21 inches apart and about 18 inches apart in the rows. This regularity in planting enables the hoe to be used lengthways and crossways in the field. If the crop is to be irrigated, and if there is no rain at the time the seedlings are ready for transplanting, the soil is raised into ridges 21 inches apart and cross ridges 7 feet apart by means of a *daurā* with a rope wound round the blade. In this way the land is divided into beds which can be easily irrigated, the water being run through the furrows. The seedlings are planted on the ridges. The crop is carefully weeded by hand at intervals of about a fortnight. In the month of October, when plants are about 3 or 4 feet high, the top shoot and the lower and coarser leaves of each plants are nipped off. This work is done by women who use their fingers for the purpose. Should there be water available the crop is irrigated once a month during the dry weather; but irrigation is not absolutely necessary and tobacco is grown to a large extent without it. When the crop is mature the plants are cut before daybreak and arranged in a line with the lower half of one plant covered by the upper half of the next so that of each plant the top portion only is exposed. After lying thus for eight or ten days and after the midrib has become sufficiently dry the plants are inverted so as to get both sides dried evenly. On the evening of the fourth day they are watered and on the following day stacked with the tops downwards. If the leaves are not sufficiently moist they are again watered. About noon next day leaves are separated from the stems by women who at the same time separate the best leaves (*dhāl*) from the inferior ones (*bhurkā*). The leaves are made into bundles which are stored in a well-ventilated room in heaps 3 feet diameter and 5 high. The heaps are taken down, the leaves examined and rotting ones removed every third day during the first month and once a week later, till the bundles are all dry. The cost of cultivation per acre is shown below:—

Operations.	Time.	Cost. Rs.	A.
Ploughing	March or April ...	12	0
Wakharing before rains	May to June	3	0
Collecting stumps of previous crop	May to June	0	4
Manure	May to June	20	0
Wakharing before transplanting	June—July	1	0
Levelling with *pathad* ...	August (beginning) ...	0	4
Cost of seedlings for an acre ...	... ...	6	0
Planting tobacco	August	5	0
Weeding	August or September ...	2	0
Hoeing 6 times	September and October ..	10	8
Nipping off suckers	October, November, and December	18	0
Curing	January to March ...	16	8
Government Assessment	.. ...	2	0
	Total ...	96	8

Outturn.	Value. Rs.	A.
640 lbs. at 4 lbs per rupee	160	0
Bhurki (from ratoon crop) 80 lbs. at As. 1-6 per lb.	7	8
Total ...	167	8
Deduct ...	96	8
Net profit ...	71	0

Wheat.

199. In this District wheat (*Triticum sativum*) is a more difficult crop to grow than cotton. In years of short rainfall it fares badly; in normal years it is much less profitable than cotton. The area under this crop last year was only 81,780 acres. As the area under cotton has increased that under wheat has decreased. *Thet kāli* is the best wheat soil. In Chānur and Morsi tāluks *hawrā* (hard white) and *kātha* (hardred) wheats are grown. In the Pūrna valley a mixture of white and red wheat locally known as *chāwal kātha* is grown. *Bansī* is also common. Wheat is a good preparation for cotton; wheat-cotton, and wheat-cotton-juāri are considered good rotations for deep black soil. The growing of wheat and gram mixed, as practised in the wheat tract, is unknown. The seed rate is only

40 lbs. per acre; it is sown with the heavy *rabi tiffan* drawn by two or three pairs of bullocks. The cost of cultivation per acre is shown below :—

Operations.	Time.	Cost.	
		Rs.	A.
Two *wakharings*...	April and May	1	12
Removing stumps of previous crop..	May	0	4
Wakharing 4 times	June to October ..	4	0
Wakharing at time of sowing ...	End of October or beginning of November ...	0	12
Sowing	......	1	10
Seed, 40 lbs. per acre	......	3	0
Harvesting	March	3	0
Threshing and winnowing ...	April	2	0
Government assessment	......	2	0
	Total ..	18	6

Outturn.	Value.	
	Rs.	A.
400 lbs. at 8 seers per rupee	25	0
Wheat *bhūsa* about 10 *dalās* at 8 *dalās* a rupee	1	4
Total ...	26	4
Deduct ...	18	6
Net profit ...	7	14

200. The area under gram (*Cicer arietinum*) last year was 22,891 acres. There are two varieties grown, one with brownish seed and the other with white seed. This crop is grown on all the different classes of soil; the cultivation required is similar to that of wheat. The seed rate is about 25 lbs. an acre. The

Gram.

cost of cultivation and profits per acre thereon are shown below :—

Operations.	Time.	Cost.
		Rs. A.
Two *wakharings*	April to May	1 12
Removing stumps of previous crop...	May	0 4
Wakharing 4 times	June to September ...	4 0
Sowing with Rabi drill	Last week of September	1 10
Seed 24 lbs per acre	......	1 8
Harvesting	February to March ...	3 0
Threshing and cleaning	March	2 0
Government assessment	... ..	2 0
	Total ...	16 2
Outturn per acre 400 lbs. at 22 lbs. a rupee		18 3
Bhūsa 12 *dalās* at 3 *dalās* for 1 Rupee		4 0
	Total ...	22 3
	Deduct ...	16 2
	Net profit ...	6 1

201. The only pest of importance is the gram pod caterpillar (*Chlorides obsoleta*). There is no practical method known of dealing with this pest.

Insect pests.

202. Of linseed (*Linum usitatissimum*) the variety grown is the red. The cultivation and soils suitable for this crop are the same as for wheat, but it is sown rather earlier. The cultivator first sows gram or lākh, then linseed and then wheat. It is generally sown about the middle of October. The seed rate is 12lbs. per acre and the outturn 300 to 320 lbs., the value of which is Rs. 22. Like wheat, linseed has had to make way for cotton and juāri ; the area grown last year was only 10,045 acres. The only disease that affects the crop is rust which is not very common. When grown too often on the same soil the crop suffers as the soil becomes linseed sick.

Linseed.

203. Masūr (*Ervum lens*) and safflower (*Carthamus tinctorius*) are only grown on a very small scale.

Masūr and Safflower.

Garden cultivation.

204. Garden cultivation is well understood and is of some importance more especially in parts of Morsi and Ellichpur tāluks. In some parts of these tāluks the water is less than 20 feet from the surface and plentiful. In 1907-08, 7453 acres were under irrigated crops, most of which were occupied by chillies, tobacco and turmeric. There were also 1219 acres of vegetables and 159 acres of orchards all of which require intensive cultivation. The area of a single vegetable garden is generally less than one acre. The land is almost continuously under crops, for when one is harvested the plot is prepared for the next crop. In the corners and on the borders of a plot sown with one crop, small quantities of other vegetables are grown so as to occupy every part of the area. The profits obtained from garden cultivation per acre are high compared with those earned by the ordinary dry-crop farmer. On the other hand the area cultivated by one man is very small and requires much more labour and capital. Garden lands irrigated from wells sunk previous to the original settlement are assessed at the highest dry crop maximum rate of the group of villages to which they belong. Lands irrigated from wells sunk during the currency of the lease are treated as dry crop lands. The fruit gardens are not so skilfully managed. They belong mostly to Mārwāris, Brāhman pleaders and other well-to-do people, who have taken to this form of gardening as a hobby. The best fruit gardens are to be found in the towns of Ellichpur and Amraoti. The general defects to be noticed everywhere are the neglect of pruning and of cultivation round the trees. For want of pruning the vitality of the tree is largely spent in producing wood rather than fruit; while by neglect to keep the surface soil round the tree well scarified, excessive evaporation and the consequent loss of soil moisture are allowed to check the growth of the tree. The fruits chiefly grown are mangoes (*Mangifera indica*), oranges (*Citrus aurentium*), guavas (*Psidium guava*), plantains (*Musa sapientum*), limes (*Citrus bargania*) and *papayās* (*Corica papaya*). Grafted mangoes are grown in the gardens in the larger towns. In the garden of Mr. Ganesh Nagesh Sahasrabudhe, Vice-Chairman of the Ellichpur Municipality, may be seen 500 of the finest grafted varieties,

including the Alphonso, Pairi and other desirable types. As these mango gardens often cover an area of several acres, difficulty is experienced in giving them sufficient water during the first two years of their growth. The common mango, groves of which may be seen everywhere in the District, being more drought resistant, fares much better in this respect. When there is cloudy weather and thunderstorms at the time of flowering, the flowers instead of developing into fruit die off, as if burnt. The failure is most likely due to the state of the weather preventing the fertilization of the flowers. There are two kinds of common mangoes : the one is rather hard and tastes of turpentine ; the other, found at Ellichpur, is more juicy. The former is used for making chutney, mango fool, etc., the latter is eaten. These mangoes are common in all parts of the District, being hardy and requiring no irrigation. When a cultivator wishes to grow mangoes he plants seeds in rows about 30 feet apart each way in the beginning of the rainy season. In the hot season the young plants are fenced with brushwood, which serves to shade them from the sun and to protect them from goats and other animals. As the plants are not irrigated they make very little progress except during the rains. The land between the rows is sown with the ordinary farm crops till such time as the mango trees shade the ground thoroughly. The first crop is obtained in the tenth year. One good mango tree will yield about 5000 mangoes which are worth from Rs. 8 to Rs. 10.

Oranges, etc.

205. In this District oranges are probably a recent introduction seeing that they are not grown by the Māli caste. *Morandi* and *kāli* are considered good soils for oranges. The young trees are planted during the rains in pits 18 inches apart each way and are liberally manured. A shallow basin about 3 inches in diameter is made round each plant and is connected with a channel running midway between the rows. The plants are irrigated at intervals of 10 or 12 days during the cold weather, and at intervals of 6 days during the hot season. They are manured with cowdung before and at the end of the rains. The trees begin to bear in five years, and are in full bearing in seven years. For the first three years the space between the rows

is cropped with vegetables or other crops. Two crops are obtained each year, one in November and December and one in February and March. The oranges of the latter crop are considered the better. One good tree yields from 500 to 1000 fruit, at which rate the trees on one acre will yield about 67,000 oranges which at Rs. 10 a thousand are worth Rs. 670; but the outturn is seldom more than half that. The chief insect pests are a caterpillar (*Virchala isocrates*) which bores the fruit, and a stem borer (*Chloridolum alcmene*). The cost of establishing an orange garden of one acre is reckoned to be about Rs. 162, and the annual upkeep on the same about Rs. 82, so that a thriving orange garden pays very well. The variety grown is the Nāgpur orange, but the taste is somewhat sharper.

Guava cultivation is understood and practised by the ordinary Māli; plantains, limes, sweet and sour, and *papayās* are also common garden fruits. In Chikaldā peaches thrive well and yield very good fruit for cooking purposes.

Implements.

206. The implements required for garden cultivation are the same as those used on the farm. The water-lift is the ordinary *mot* or leather bucket which in some places has been replaced by the Sāngli iron *mot*. There are several garden hand tools in common use, including the *kudalī*, *kulhād*, *phaurā* and *vākās*. All these are shaped more or less like an ordinary pickaxe, varying only in the breadth and slope of the head. They cost from two to eight annas and are used for digging trenches, ridging, and for uprooting such crops as onions, ground-nut and carrots.

Gardens in the District.

207. The chief gardens in the District are the Government gardens at Amraoti Camp and Chikaldā and the Municipal and Jail gardens at the former place. The Nāmdar Bāg of Ellichpur, a once famous garden, is now in ruins.

Chillies.

208. Among the crops grown in the neighbourhood of villages, chillies (*Capsicum frutescens*) hold a very important place. Two varieties are commonly grown in the District (1) *Diwāni* or *khodnea* is grown in gardens only; the plant is tall and bushy

and the fruit red and pungent. The seed is sown from November to January and usually as a subordinate crop to onions. (2) *Nowrangī* or *daryābādi*, the other variety, is less pungent and the fruit is yellowish red on ripening. The seed is sown in the end of April in a seed bed and transplanted in June or July. It is generally grown as a dry crop but chillie-growers who have facilities for irrigation irrigate from November till March.

Cultivation.

209. Well-drained black soil is considered best for chillies, but *pāndhri* fields are often used. The land is ploughed and cross-ploughed and then *wakhared* in the dry weather. Manure is applied at the rate of 30 cartloads an acre and the land again *wakhared*. The nursery beds 7 feet by 7 are prepared and manured as for tobacco and the seed is sown in May at the rate of from two to three lbs. for 20 plots. The beds are watered daily till germination takes place and every second day later. The young seedlings are covered with a layer of cotton stalks to shade them from the scorching rays of the sun. About the end of June the seedlings are transplanted in rows about 20 inches apart with the plants 20 inches apart in the rows. This permits of interculture both ways with the bullock hoes. During the rains the crop is hoed four or five times, and weeded by hand as often as necessary. The pods are ready for picking about the end of September, and the plants continue to yield for three or four months or even longer if irrigated. The crop is sometimes attacked by a green fly of the genus *Jassidae*, which cause the curling of the leaves. The cost of cultivating dry-crop chillies is about Rs. 70 per acre, and the outturn is about 500 lbs. of dry chillies worth Rs. 126; but if irrigated the outturn is increased by approximately 8 maunds and the whole crop is worth Rs. 165 an acre, leaving the grower with a clear profit of Rs. 55 in the one case and Rs. 75 in the other.

Turmeric.

210. Turmeric (*Curcuma longa*) is cultivated by the Ghāsi Mālis in the *pātasthal* lands at the foot of the Sātpurās in the Morsi tāluk. Sendurjana is the chief centre. At other places it is irrigated from wells. It is grown on well drained black soils in rotation

with ground-nut, sugarcane and sometimes even after cotton and juāri. The land is cultivated and ridged as for other irrigated crops; the sets are planted on the ridges 8 inches apart in the beginning of the rains, 50,000 being required for one acre. The crop is irrigated at intervals of ten or twelve days during the dry weather. In January the rhizomes are ready for harvesting and the shoots are cut off with a sickle. The plot is then watered and after a week the rhizomes are dug up, stored in a shady place on a layer of turmeric leaves and covered with bundles of *san* hemp or other stalks available at the time. Sets which had failed to germinate are collected separately; the inferior turmeric derived from these is used for making the red powder (*kunku*) with which women paint their foreheads. In March the heap is opened and the turmeric for seed is separated from that intended for sale, that chosen for seed being the main stock from which the side shoots have been removed. In addition to the seed there are three other marketable products derived from this crop. The sets of the previous season which are found still clinging to the roots are sold at a cheap rate to the Atāri (maker of perfumes) who uses them in the manufacture of his stock in trade. From the stocks not required for seed an inferior turmeric known as *kāp* is prepared, while turmeric proper is made from the rhizomes. These are boiled in earthen pots if the quantity is small; but if a large quantity is to be dealt with, iron pans of the same kind as are used for boiling the juice of sugarcane are used. The pan is filled with water to a depth of six inches, and the rhizomes are then put into it and heaped up above the brim. After two hours boiling the rhizomes are taken out and spread on a plastered floor in the sun to dry. Turmeric is chiefly used as a condiment; it is also used as a dye. Despite the fact that this crop is one of the most profitable grown, the area under it in this District has dwindled away to 405 acres. The local demand being in excess of the supply, turmeric is now imported from the Nizām's dominions, Betūl and the Bombay Presidency. The cost of cultivation per acre including the Government assessment of Rs. 8 for *pātasthal* land is approximately Rs. 183, and the value of the outturn of about 1600 lbs. of roots is Rs. 290, leaving the grower with a net profit of Rs. 107.

Onions (*Kānda*).

211. Onions (*Allium cepa*) are widely grown in the village garden lands. There are two varieties, white and red. The former is better for cooking, the latter for eating. Onions do well in *pāndhri*, *morandi* and *mali* soils. They are generally grown in rotation with other garden crops such as *karelā* (*Momordica charantia*), *methi* (*Trigonella faenum Graecum*), *tākot* (*Chanopodium veride*), *dhañia* (*Coriandrum sativum*), and less seldom after juāri or cotton. The land is cultivated as for other garden crops and manured at the rate of 40 cartloads per acre. The field is then ridged into plots 7½ feet by 7½, by means of a *daurā* with a rope wound round its tines ; the sides of the bed are prepared with a *phaurā*. In Amraoti and Ellichpur tāluks it is the practice to make narrow beds 7½ feet by 3½. The seed is sown in October in well-manured nursery beds 7½ feet by 7½. On the sides of the same beds a few onions are generally planted for seed production. The seedlings are irrigated at the end of every four or five days, and two months later the leaves are cut off with sickles and sold in the bazar at the rate of four or five bundles a pice. In January the bulbs are transplanted in beds about four inches apart. The crop being ready for harvesting in May the bulbs are either pulled out by hand or dug up by means of a *khurpī*. On drying the leaves are cut off and the bulbs stored in thin layers in a dry airy place. Along with the onions some other subsidiary crops are grown such as *karelā* or chillies from which a certain yield is obtained in the same year. The seed bulbs are ready in February. The tops are nipped off, dried and the seed cleaned by means of the *sūp* and sold at R. 0-8-0 a pound. The outturn per acre is about 10,000 lbs. the market value of which is Rs. 175 to which may be added Rs. 12, the value of the other vegetables grown on the same land. The cost of cultivation is about Rs. 150, leaving a net profit of Rs. 37 per acre. The onion is a favourite vegetable in this District. Its juice mixed with castor oil is valued as a remedy for ticks in cattle.

Potatoes (*ratāla*).

212. The sweet potato (*Ipomæa batatas*) is one of the common garden crops in villages which are remote from forests. Near the jungle it is hard to save the crop from wild pig. Two varieties

are grown, a white and a red. The best crops are obtained from well-drained black cotton soil but the lighter soils, *morandi* and *shorati*, give good outturns. Sweet potatoes followed by cotton or juāri are sometimes manured with *san* hemp or til ploughed in as a green manure. It is also grown after the common garden crops. The soil is ridged as for onions in beds 7½ feet by 7½ with the ridges 18 inches apart and sets each with four nodes are planted on the sides of theridges, two rows in each furrow, so that successive rows are only 9 inches apart. The sets are covered with earth and irrigated at intervals of four or five days at first and at intervals of twice that length later. The potatoes are ready for harvesting in February and according to custom some are dug up at Shivrātri as an offering for Siva. From that time till April or May the Māli continues to lift his potatoes to supply the local market. The leaves are used as a fodder for bullocks. The chief insect pest is the potato beetle. The cost of cultivation is approximately Rs. 200 and the value of the outturn about Rs. 255 per acre, leaving the cultivator with a net profit of approximately Rs. 55.

Betel vine.

213. *Pān* cultivation is carried on mainly by the Bāri caste. The important places at which *pān*-gardens are to be found are Badnerā, Dābhe and Anjangaon Bāri in the Amraoti tāluk, Mālkhed in the Chāndur tāluk, Anjangaon Surji in the Daryāpur tāluk, Ellichpur, Sirasgaon Kasbā, Ladki and Brāhmanwāda-Thadi in the Ellichpur tāluk. The area under cultivation of this crop in 1907-08 was 662 acres or 9 per cent. of the total irrigated area of the District. The maximum area under cultivation in one field seldom exceeds one acre which belongs to eight or ten different cultivators holding in common. The best loamy garden soil is selected for the *pān* garden. The preliminary cultivation is the same as for other garden crops. The land is then divided into beds with a water channel for each line, as the vines have to be irrigated at all seasons except during the rains. The row of the beds is called a *kanang* or *wāri* ; each contains 100 beds 10 feet by 3½ feet so that the area of a *kanang* is 350 feet by 10½ feet. In the beginning of the rains the seed of *sawari* (*Sesbania aegyptiaca*), is sown in the

rows, and in August the betel vine is planted at distances of 18 inches apart. The *sawari* plays the part of a support for the vine which grows up along it, and at the same time shades the vine from the sun. As a protection against strong winds a hedge of *pangra* trees (*Erythrina indica*) is grown round the garden; for still greater protection screens made of cotton or other stalks are attached to these. The whole area enclosed is known as a *tānda*. Plantains are grown all over the garden at intervals of 10 or 12 feet for purposes of shade. The betel vine cultivator generally has two *tāndas* at the same time so as to enable him to rotate his vines. He plants the one two years after the other so that he gets a crop of leaves every year. The cost of cultivating a *pān*-garden of about ⅛ acre is said to amount to Rs. 575 in the first year, and to about Rs. 260 in succeeding years. The value of the outturn is about Rs. 208 in the second year and Rs. 338 each year from the 3rd year to the 10th year, if the vines are well manured. The profits from this small area are said to be sufficient to maintain a Bāri and his family in comfort.

Melons (*Kharbūj*).

214. Water melons are grown in the beds of the Pūrna, Wardhā and other rivers. The *kharbūj wādi*, melon garden, is generally about 200 feet long and 50 feet wide. The cultivation is carried on by the Bhoi or fisherman caste. The light sandy soil of the river bed is cultivated and levelled in January. Furrows are then made with the *phaurā* at distances of 4 feet apart. In these seeds are planted and covered with cattle-dung and ashes. When the plants are about 8 inches high, they are thinned out, manured a second time and the furrows levelled. In March, manure is again applied and the plants are earthed up. The *wādi* is fenced in April to keep out jackals and pigs which are very destructive. The cost of cultivation of a *kharbūj wādi* of about 50 feet by 100 feet is Rs. 30-6-0. The value of outturn is Rs. 75, leaving a net profit of Rs. 44-10-0. Despite the fact that this is a most valuable crop, the area under melons is said to be gradually decreasing owing to the exorbitant rents charged for the *wādis* and the scarcity of labour.

Other crops.

215. Rice (*Oryza sativa*), mūng (*Phaseolus mungo*), *karelā* (*Momordica charantia*), *ambāri* (*Hibiscus cannabinus*), *san*-hemp (*Crotalaria juncea*) *sawā* (*Panicum frumentaceum*), kodon (*Paspalum scrobiculatum*), kutkī (*Panicum Psilopodium*), brinjals (*Solanum melongena*), garlic (*Allium sativum*), ground-nut (*Arachis hypogæa*), sugarcane (*Saccharum officinarum*), and other minor crops are grown. Of these rice, kodon, kutki and other inferior millets are mostly grown by the Korkūs of the Melghāt on isolated patches of the slopes and valleys of that mountainous tāluk.

Statement of crops.

216. The area under each crop for the plain tāluks and the Melghāt respectively for the year 1907-08 is shown in the statement on the opposite page.

Coffee and Tea.

217. Chikaldā is the only place in these Provinces in which coffee (*Coffea arabica*) has been tried. The area under the crop at present is about 25 acres, and is to be found mostly as small plantations in the compounds of the bungalows and on land belonging to the Order of St. Francis de Sales. The pioneer in coffee-planting was a certain Mr. Mulheran, who fifty years ago tried coffee on these hills. The plateau is in many respects suitable for coffee cultivation. The altitude is 3664 feet above the sea-level and the soil is red loam in which respects the Chikaldā plateau is very similar to the best coffee tracts in the Nīlgiris. The main drawback is that the rainfall is usually confined to four months in the year. The coffee obtained is considered to be as good as any grown in India; it requires to be matured for a year after harvest before being used. The seed is first sown in a well shaded nursery bed. The seedlings are planted out in rows 7 feet apart, with the plants 6 feet apart in the rows. As the soil is very shallow it is sometimes necessary to remove some of the stones and *muram* of the sub-soil so as to give the roots greater freedom of growth. One basket of cattle-dung and leaf mould is mixed with the earth at the roots of each seedling. Good shade is absolutely necessary. One of the best trees for this purpose is the silver oak (*Grevillea robusta*) which both shades the coffee

FIELD CROPS.

District.	Rice.	Juāri.	Wheat	Tūr.	Mūng	Gram.	Til.	Linseed.	Kardi.	Kurhal.	Cotton.	Ambāri.	San-Hemp.	Tobacco.	Kodon & Kutki	Bājra
Plain tāluks ...	94	505189	72255	97435	31255	11700	7069	9828	1024	3	851132	7778	1403	1904	...	10679
Melghāt ...	4166	34093	7528	5700	1973	11191	7128	217	...	...	34864	586	188	...	2769	..

GARDEN CROPS.

District.	Chillies.	Brinjals.	Betel vine.	Mangoes.	Ground Nuts.	Sugarcane.	Melon Pumpkins.	Bhendi.
Plain tāluks	5566	847	662	159	289	221	...	...
Melghāt	331	19	...	...	...	7	...	...

bushes from the rays of the sun and at the same time protects them from strong winds. Hand-weeding is necessary to kill weeds and to keep the surface loose and friable round the bushes, so as to prevent the excessive evaporation of soil moisture. The bushes produce berries after the third year. In their fifth year they are in full bearing and continue to yield well for at least thirty years if manured regularly. The bushes are not allowed to grow to a height of more than five feet. The yield of berries per tree in a good year is about two pounds. Most of the coffee produced is sold to officers stationed in Berār and visitors to Chikaldā ; the supply is too insignificant to create anything like a demand for it on a commercial scale. Tea (*Thea sinensis*) too has been tried but without success, as the conditions are too dry for this plant.

CHAPTER V.

LOANS, PRICES, WAGES, MANUFACTURES, TRADE AND COMMUNICATIONS.

LOANS.

Government loans.

218. Government loans, *takāvi* or *tagai*, are as elsewhere advanced to cultivators under two Acts, the Land Improvement, and the Agriculturists' Loans Act. The latter was only applied to Berār in 1891, but the former in one shape or another has been in force since 1871. Loans under it are chiefly given for the sinking of wells, the eradication of scrub and deep rooted weeds from fields and the making of embankments. In the thirty years from 1877-1907 a sum of only two lakhs of rupees was advanced, and of this Rs. 30,000 were given out in the famine years of 1896-97 and 1897-98 and almost a lakh in 1899-1900 and 1900-01. In 1908 also, as the 1907 rains were a partial failure, it was thought well to stimulate the demand for labour by this means and about Rs. 83,500 were advanced. Omitting, however, these years the average yearly amount advanced to cultivators in ordinary times was only Rs. 2631. Loans under the second Act have also been as a rule trifling. In the famine years above mentioned some eighty-four thousand rupees were distributed and in 1908 Rs. 13,375, but apart from these exceptional cases the average yearly amount is but little over Rs. 1000. Many reasons have been given for the comparative unpopularity of Government loans, the most common being perhaps the delays connected with the system. In Berār there is no record of rights in land and each separate case accordingly entails a reference to the Registration Department : procedure must always, therefore, be somewhat more lengthy than in the Central Provinces, though a recent simplification in other respects has resulted in an increased demand for the loans. It has been urged by some officers that the local conditions are unfavourable to the grant of loans in normal seasons, the

facilities and need for irrigation being small and the rich soil producing good crops without much trouble or expense. But this is contraverted by other officers, who ascribe the small demand for loans to the delays and trouble of the system of distribution and to the want of interest taken in the matter by Government officials. To this may be added a few factors which elsewhere also operate against the success of *takāvi*. Government occupies an infinitely stronger position than the ordinary creditor, and insists upon prompt repayment; the latter moreover will lend for marriages and the like ceremonies which make indebtedness a social necessity to the average cultivator, and he is naturally chary of doing so when the land is already pledged to a far stronger claimant: hence the cultivator who may need such a loan is careful not to do anything which may endanger his chance of getting it. It seems probable that, with an improved system of distribution, Government loans will increase in popularity. In the Melghāt, where cultivation is in a much more backward state, it is possible that a promising field may be found when settlement operations are complete. The Korkūs are heavily indebted and pay most extortionate interest on their scanty loans: but at present their agriculture is entirely subordinated to timber cutting. In times of scarcity of course the loan system is of immense use everywhere in enabling Government to finance the coming crop.

Private loans.

219. Private moneylending takes various forms; between bankers and men of business accommodation in one form or another is often necessary and this is given to persons of well-known financial stability. Such loans are commonly made upon note of hand only or bill of exchange payable in one case at sight (*darshanī*), in the other at 30 or 61 days from execution; and a commission of R. ¼ to Rs. 2 per cent. is charged. The ordinary rate of exchange on Bombay varies between ¼ per cent. discount in the cotton season and ¼ per cent. premium at other times. To cultivators loans are made on mortgages of land, and for these the usual rate is 1 per cent. per mensem where the security is good and the reputation of the borrower excellent; 1½ per cent. is the ordinary rate for loans to cultivators of substantial standing, and 2 per cent. or even

more will be charged in more doubtful cases. These rates are not really so high as at first sight they seem. The lenders are often persons engaged in various other trades, who may require all their capital at very short notice to meet a sudden call, and mortgages are of all forms of property the most unrealisable in an emergency. Thus it is notorious that in the recent financial crisis which swept from America throughout the world several of the local *sāhukārs* were very hard pressed to find the requisite cash, and had to sell land and mortgage rights at a loss. The great firm of Bansī Lāl will have nothing to do with this traffic, and the danger above described accounts in part for the high rates being maintained even in a District where money is comparatively plentiful. Subsequent loans on the same security must pay 2 or even 3 per cent. per mensem, though the latter rate would only be charged in the most risky transactions. Grain is sometimes advanced by *sāhukārs* on a stipulation that it will be paid back at harvest in a ratio of 5 : 4 (*laoni*) or in unfavourable cases 3 : 2 (*wādhi dīdhi*), and in the Melghāt the rates are even higher ; the system however is a vanishing one, all the larger firms having given it up. Persons who can neither show well known credit in the money market nor produce landed security must pawn valuables to the amount of their loan and will then receive the money on terms similar to those in force for mortgages. If they cannot do this, they will have no choice but to resort to the village Shylock or the Rohillā who deals in petty loans at high risk and shows but little compassion either in the rates he charges or in his method of collecting debts.

Dām Dupat.

220. Mention should be made of a rule of Hindu law which applies in Berār but not in the Central Provinces. The doctrine of *Dām Dupat* is probably the oldest existing attempt to put a check upon usury, for it does not owe its origin to the commentators but is to be found stated at length in the Institutes of Manu. In brief it declares that the amount of interest payable at any one time can never exceed the principal or balance of the principal remaining due. Thus it is both a check upon usury and a law of limitation since though it imposes no bounds to the rates which may be charged it

forces an extortionate creditor to sue promptly and prevents the accumulation of sleeping claims. It is only enforceable where both parties to the transaction are Hindus; if a Muhammadan takes up the interest or liabilities of a Hindu, the rule applies for just so long as the matter is in Hindu hands. It has been held in Bombay that the law is not applicable when there is a liability on the creditor to keep accounts as when a mortgagee having been placed in possession is accountable for profits received by him as against the interest due; but an opposite ruling has always prevailed in Berār, where in consequence the law has a much wider application than on the Bombay side.

Bankers.

221. A branch of the Bank of Bombay has been established in Amraoti since 1868 and is strongly supported. Messrs. Ralli Brothers to a large extent do their own banking. Of native firms Rājā Seth Gokuldās and Rai Bahādur Bansī Lāl both have local agents, but the chief business lies in the hands of Shrirām Sāligrām of Dhāmangaon, Shrirām Rūprām, Dhanrāj Pokarmal, and Rāmratan Ganeshdās, all of whom have extensive dealings throughout the District. In Ellichpur the best known firm is that of Lālasā Motīsā owned by Nathūsā Pachusā. Moneylending business is transacted also by a few Brāhmans, the most notable being Rāmchandra Renko Dole.

Economic condition of the cultivators.

222. It is an interesting question how far the indebtedness of the cultivator is or is not leading to a transference of the land to non-cultivating classes, but it is a question which in Berār is considerably more difficult to answer than in the Central Provinces, for the Land Records throw no light whatever on the matter and Registration records very little. It is certain that the value of land has gone up by leaps and bounds every year and is still increasing; and instances are common of fields changing hands in 1909 at prices about six times what the same fields fetched twenty years before, while even greater increase is met with in some localities. Mortgages, moreover, are commonly framed with a condition of foreclosure and not of sale, and some of the firms just mentioned have undoubtedly acquired large but scattered

estates of several thousand acres in different parts of the District. But the ryotwāri tenure, which makes it impossible to acquire a whole village by a single transaction as is done in proprietary tracts, militates against them; and as the management of a large ryotwāri estate entails infinite expenditure of time and trouble, land-grabbing is naturally confined to much smaller men and does not make great headway. It is a control of the cotton trade rather than the actual ownership of land that the moneylenders look to acquiring; and in the trade neither ryot nor moneylender can afford to do without the other and neither is completely at the mercy of the other; they fulfil different and complementary functions, the one growing the cotton, the other financing, organizing and exploiting it. Even when a mortgage is foreclosed it generally pays the creditor better to resell than to cultivate the land himself.

The prosperous and contented aspect of the villagers, their sturdy independence of manner and high standard of intelligence, all arising from their prosperity, are indeed among the first things always remarked upon by visitors from other parts of India, and the remark is borne out by numberless statistics; to take two instances the proportion of goldsmiths to the general population is large and the amount spent annually on luxuries as evidenced, *e.g.*, in the yearly Excise Bill, extremely high. Women even of the lowest castes may commonly be seen wearing heavy ornaments of silver and gold; and among the men Coimbatore scarves and coats of serge and superior cloth are common. The oldest inhabitant of a Daryāpur village put the matter somewhat quaintly when he said that in days gone by one coat was enough for a family of four or five members, that each might wear it as occasion arose but that to-day they would not be content without four or five coats to each man of them. The general wealth of the cultivating classes throughout the plain tāluks is undoubtedly very large; and is generally very evenly distributed, prosperity being evidenced rather by a generally high standard of comfort and of outward display than by large accumulations of capital in a few hands. The population is fairly dense in comparison with the system of cropping, and thrift is not a common virtue in the ryot's moral code nor are the facilities for it great. What is easily come by is easily spent, and as long as his income is sufficient for the rude plenty of the day, he takes but little thought for the morrow. Whenever, therefore, unusually high expenditure is necessary, recourse is had to the moneylender.

PRICES.

History.

223. Prior to 1853 when Berār came under British administration, the information about prices is meagre and valueless, though there is an elaborate calculation on page 254 of the old Berār Gazetteer which fixes the price of juāri (the staple food grain) in the seventeenth century at 160 to 200 lbs. for the rupee. In the same volume (page 270-271) there is a table giving the prices of various crops at three different periods since the Assignment ; this is here reproduced, the figures representing seers per rupee.

	1853-54.	1859-60.	1869-70.
Juāri	53·33	40	20
Wheat	32	26·66	10
Gram	40	32	8
Rice	40	26·66	5·71
Linseed	26·66	16	11·42

Thus juāri and wheat which together covered at settlement about 48 per cent. of the cropped area had in the interval from 1853 to 1870 risen 266 per cent. and 320 per cent. in price respectively. The next period is that from the original settlement 1869-1873 to the Revision in 1897-1900. To get a common basis of comparison for all tāluks we may take the twenty years from 1876 to 1895 and subdivide this into four quinquennial periods. The prices of juāri and wheat were as follows :—

Quantity sold per rupee in seers and decimals of a seer during the period of :—

	1876-80		1881-85		1886-90		1891-95	
	Juāri	Wheat	Juāri	Wheat	Juāri	Wheat	Juāri	Wheat
Amraoti ..	18·68	11·96		18·87	21·96	15·56	18·86	13·10
Chāndur ...	18·6	11·4	27·98	19	21·4	16·2	19·8	13 6
Morsi ..	20 8	13 4	29·2	19·2	24·4	16·4	20·8	13
Daryāpur ...	20·6	14·6	30·6	22·2	22	16·2	21	15
Ellichpur ...	20·4	15·2	29 8	18·8	20	15·6	22·2	14·4
Melghāt ...	Information not available							

Thus with an interval of cheapness from 1881-1890 the commonest food grains were selling at about the same price in 1895 as in 1876. In the next five years the District was afflicted with two severe famines, those of 1897 and 1900, in which years the prices of cereals stood as follows :—

Quantity in seers sold per rupee.

	Juāri.	Wheat.	Gram.	Rice.	Tūr.	Bājra.
1897	9·52	6 92	7·81	6·56	6 98	7·41
1900	10·82	8·89	10·7	8·26	7·81	9.3

Since 1901 the prices have been steady at between 16 21 seers of juāri and 9-12 seers wheat per rupee, except in years such as 1908 when the crops have been unusually poor. The present prices of food grains are as follows :—

Juāri ... 13—14 seers per rupee,
Wheat ... 6—7 seers per rupee,
Gram ... 9—10 seers per rupee,
Rice ... 5—7 seers per rupee,
Tūr ... 6—8 seers per rupee,
Bājra ... 11—13 seers per rupee.

A factor which has had much to do with the rise in price of food grains has been the large increase in cotton cultivation resulting not merely in a general cheapening of money (cotton being a commercial crop) but also in a special dearness of cereals which have thus been ousted from their proper place in the annual harvest. In 1907 Major Horsbrugh remarked. 'The amount of juāri sown is at present 'quite insufficient for food and fodder. Cotton-growing is the 'fashion of the day and the rotation of crops is much dis- 'regarded. Time and the land itself will teach the cultivators 'a lesson.' Perhaps the recent decrease in cotton crops may be taken as showing that the cultivators are already learning that lesson.

Prices of cotton.

224. Cotton, however, is and is likely to remain the characteristic wealth-producing industry of the District; and the price obtainable for cotton is of paramount importance to every one in the plains of Berār. There is some discrepancy between the figures furnished by the Bombay chamber and those resulting from local enquiries, but it may be assumed that the former are more correct. The difference between the price of cotton in Berār and in Bombay is about Rs. 36 per Bombay *khandī* of 784 lbs. The average Bombay price of cleaned Berār cotton from 1869 to 1878 was Rs. 230 per *khandī*, from 1878-1888 Rs. 203, and from 1888-1898 Rs. 190. The local prices for the separate tāluks gathered at the Revision settlement from shopkeepers and others are as follows :—

Period	Amraoti	Chāndur	Morsi	Ellichpur	Daryāpur
1872 to 1876 ...	175	174	116	162	141
1877 to 1886 ..	165	164	130	152	150
1887 to 1896 ...	146	145	143	149	160

The accuracy of the figures for Morsi and Daryāpur is open to considerable doubt. In the other tāluks the fall is explained in part by the general tenour of the world's markets but partly also by the gradual substitution in Berār of a coarse but prolific type of cotton for a finer but less productive. The cotton of Dhāmangaon market which is brought largely from the uplands of Yeotmāl, where the longer stapled plant is still grown, finds a ready sale in Bombay at slightly higher prices than that of Amraoti, and unscrupulous dealers have sometimes sent cotton from Amraoti to Bombay via Dhāmangaon for the sake of securing the mark of that place on the bales.

The volume on Prices and Wages in India gives the average annual wholesale prices in rupees per 10 maunds of cotton. These 10 Bengal maunds or about 820 lbs. are very roughly equivalent to a Bombay *khandī* of 784 lbs. In 1897 the price was only Rs. 145, but it fell steadily till 1900 when it suddenly rose to Rs. 187. Again in the two following years there was a decline, but in 1903 prices rose by about 20 per cent. and in 1904 they reached their highest watermark, Rs. 222. In the year 1908-1909 the price of Amraoti cotton in Bombay was Rs. 240.[1] In the local markets the cotton is sold uncleaned (in which state it is known as *kapās*) by a *kapās khandī* of 560 lbs. Prices for this in 1908-1909 show Rs. 52-53 for the first picking and Rs. 35-40 for the last.

Miscellaneous articles.

225. There is nothing of particular interest in the prices of less important produce. Ten maunds of linseed were sold for Rs. 34—Rs. 38 in 1897-98-99, but rose to Rs. 64 in 1902. Two years later there was a return to the old level, but the present price (1909) is again high (Rs. 50—52-8). Til has fluctuated between Rs. 35 and Rs. 56 per 10 maunds, standing at present at about the latter figure; while *ghī* has risen from Rs. 289 in 1897 to Rs. 380-400, the price in Amraoti in 1907-08. Owing to the *Singhast* period and the consequent falling off of demand for this commodity at marriage merry-makings the price of 1908-1909 is almost as low as in 1897. Tobacco which has been subject to considerable fluctuations stands now at a wholesale price of Rs. 200 per 10 maunds, almost the highest figure known. Salt has cheapened from 8 seers a rupee in 1870 to 16-18 seers to-day, a very satisfactory fall. *Karbī* (juāri stalks) at present sells at Rs. 5-6 and grass for As. 10—12 per 100 bundles shortly after harvest, though the prices rise very considerably in the hot weather. Oil, whether til, linseed or *kardī*, fetches As. 8 the seer, and firewood is priced at an average of R. 1-12 to Rs. 2 per cartload of roughly 20 *katchā* maunds of 28 lbs. a piece. Of live stock a cow ranges from Rs. 10 to Rs. 40 and a she-buffalo from Rs. 50 to Rs. 125.

---

[1] **Very much higher prices were reached and maintained for long periods in the current year 1909-1910.**

WAGES.

Agricultural and other unskilled labour.

226. The demand for labour, and especially unskilled labour, in Berār is large: cotton as a crop requires a great deal of care and attention, and there is a proportionate influx of casual labourers from other parts of India, chiefly the north. At the date of the former Berār Gazetteer payment for agricultural labour was almost always made in kind, and, as such a payment is entirely independent of variations in the price of money and is moreover largely based upon custom, it is not surprising to find that it remains almost unchanged at the present day.

'The cotton-picker is not paid in cash; the rate is from 'one-twentieth to one-tenth, according to the market; the 'twentieth is the old rate. If the first picking is a twentieth 'share, the second should be a tenth, the third is sometimes 'half, because one person can collect but a small quantity in 'a day at the late gathering. The Kunbīs have a supersti- 'tious predilection in favour of getting their cotton picked by 'women. As each person has completed her or his day's 'picking, she or he carries the load to the appointed place, 'where the owner is in waiting for them; as each bundle is 'received it is ranged, with the picker seated near, the Dhers 'and other outcastes apart from the others. The owner 'commences by asking for one of the loads, which is 'thrown before him; he divides it into the stipulated number 'of shares, and tells the picker to choose one, who does 'so, and takes possession of it.

'In cutting juāri a labourer's wage is one *pūla* or bundle '(sheaf) with the ears, to be chosen by himself. For 'cutting ears off the stalks two ordinary baskets for a man, 'and one for a woman, is the wage; each basket contains 'four seers (eight lbs.) of grain, value four annas. A wheat- 'cutter's wage is two sheafs, yielding about four lbs., valued 'three annas.

'A *chanā*-picker (the plants are pulled up) gets, if a man,

Bemrose, Collo., Derby.

COTTON MARKET. AMRAOTI.

'two *karaps* (heaps) and a woman one; a *karap* contains six 'lbs., worth perhaps four annas.'

It may be added that it is doubtful whether the preference for women cotton-pickers to-day is so much a superstition, as an economic hankering for cheap labour. In 1870 the rate of payment in hard cash for unskilled labour (casual) was 4 annas per diem and this remained without much fluctuation till 1900-1901. Since then it has risen till it stands to-day at about 8 annas; and the high prices prevailing for agricultural produce lately have inclined cultivators towards cash payment, a system which has its advantages for the payee also. In cotton cultivation men are paid 4 annas a day for sowing or weeding and women 2 annas. The cotton is picked from 3 to 5 times almost invariably by women. At the first picking the wage is 2 annas per diem, at the second and 3rd it is the money equivalent of a wage in kind *i.e.*, 4—4½ annas for every maund of 15 seers (30 lbs.) picked, this being a fair day's work. After this the wages fall and at the 4th and 5th pickings only 2 annas per diem are earned. Juāri is sown by men who are paid from 4 to 6 annas a day. Cutting and stocking as well as threshing are done by contract by men on a basis of 2 to 2½ *kuros* (1 *kuro*= 16 seers) for every *tiffan* (4 acres) reaped or sometimes 24 seers for every *khandī* of 320 seers harvested. The ears are separated from the stalks by women who get a basketful of ears (value about 4½ annas) per day. Similar arrangements prevail with regard to other crops. Farm-servants regularly employed got from five to eight rupees a month in the plains, seven being perhaps the commonest rate; and in the Melghāt from Rs. 2½ to Rs. 5 per month. In each case presents of clothing from their masters at Dasahra and Holi are the equivalent of a few rupees more.

The wages for unskilled labour in other professions are naturally regulated by those in agriculture. An ordinary cooly is paid 5 annas a day, a woman or a boy 3 annas: in the rains these rates are increased to 6 or 7 annas for men and 4 annas for women, that for children remaining the same. *Hammāls* for heavy work come frequently from Khāndesh; they draw 6 to 8 annas at any time of year. Watermen, chaukidārs and similar unskilled servants are paid 5 to 8 rupees a month.

Skilled labour.

227. The wages of skilled labour is of course a more complicated question : the higher kinds of agricultural labour may draw Rs. 10 to Rs. 12 per mensem, and a syce Rs. 9 or 10 per mensem : it is difficult, however, to speak of these as skilled labour. A mason gets Rs. 20 to Rs. 22, and a village carpenter or blacksmith Rs. 22 to Rs. 30. It is probably this last class of labour which is referred to in the old Berār Gazetteer (page 272) as receiving from 12 annas to 1 rupee per diem. Allowing therefore for the difference between casual and fixed labour the rate would appear to have remained almost the same. This is probably true as regards such village servants for there has been no great variation in the demand or supply during forty years : and some of the *balutedārs*, it should be remarked, continue to draw their customary *haks* at harvest though they have no legal claim to do so. In other branches, however, there has been a great rise in wages : men with a turn for mechanics command wages in the gins and factories which may commence at Rs. 28 per mensem as blacksmith and include promotion even up to Rs. 50 or higher as fitter or overseer. Good Marāthī-speaking clerks need never be without posts on Rs. 15—25 per mensem and it is very hard to get a man with a knowledge of English as well on anything less than the latter figure even when the prospects and ultimate pension of Government service are included. Even when all allowances have been made for the declining value of money this is clearly a sign of the increasing prosperity of the District.

MANUFACTURES.

Cotton spinning and pressing.

228. Though rather a process of trade than a manufacture, the ginning and pressing of cotton claims the first rank in the industries of the District. At the end of 1907

The above figures were supplied by the Executive Engineer and represent average rates. During the cotton season there is very great shortage of labour : coolies and *Hammāls* can then command from As. 8 to Re. 1¼ and women easily obtain from 4 to 6 annas daily for work in the factories. Children are not often employed and their rates of wages remain constant.

there were in existence 88 factories carrying on this business, 60 being concerned with ginning and 28 with pressing; Amraoti alone contained fifteen of the former and thirteen of the latter. The oldest is that of Messrs. Volkarts, who started pressing in 1870. No estimate can be formed of the collective capital of these concerns, though it is stated that 62 of which figures are obtainable account for some 47 lakhs; and as it is calculated that a single gin requires a little over Rs. 1200 of capital and a press Rs. 75,000 it may safely be said that the total investment is well over half a crore of rupees. In the factories which come within the scope of the Factories Act (30 only at the present day) slightly over one thousand operatives were employed in 1894: the numbers increased steadily till 1904 in which year they stood at 6000: after this the returns show a considerable falling off, due perhaps to a different interpretation being judicially placed on a word in the Act under which they are made, by which some factories have been exempted from making them. The area under cotton crop has also however slightly decreased since the same year. The monthly wages earned by unskilled labourers are about 8 rupees per mensem.

Other factories.

229. Besides the cotton gins and presses the District has only four factories, the oil presses of the New Mofussil Company and Messrs. Rāmji Kānav and Company both at Amraoti, the Berār Match Company at Ellichpur, and the Berār Manufacturing Company Limited at Badnerā, in which the principal shareholders are Kastūrchand Dāga and Sons. Of these the New Mofussil Company's Oil Mill was opened in 1872, the capital being Rs. 6,25,000, and Messrs. Rāmji Kānav's in 1894, the capital being Rs. 88,000. The oil most commonly produced is that extracted from linseed, and oil cakes are also made. Recent statistics are not available, but in 1899-1900 the total outturn of the Mills was 2,11,635 gallons of oil and 1771 tons of oil cakes. The Match Factory was started at Ellichpur in 1906. This extremely plucky enterprise has had many difficulties to contend with, being far removed from any but a purely local market, and hampered by the amount of wasteage entailed by the coarse quality of wood locally obtainable for the purpose. It has

temporarily ceased working though before doing so it had managed to produce not merely the ordinary sulphur, but very creditable safety matches. The machinery is all of the latest European pattern and the greatest care is taken to prevent any danger to the operatives from unhealthy fumes. If the project of a light railway to Ellichpur is ever fulfilled, the Match Factory may yet become a highly prosperous enterprise. But by far the most important manufacture of the District is that of cotton yarn and cloth as represented on modern lines by the Mills at Badnerā. These were opened in 1885 on an initial capital of five and a half lakhs; and at the present day contain 248 looms worked by an engine of 22 N. H. P. and 16,336 spindles by an engine of 124 N. H P. Yarn from cone 6½ to cone 32 is manufactured and all kinds of woven goods, both for Indian and European use, including *dhotīs*, *pagrīs*, *dasotīs*, napkins, handkerchiefs, and table cloths. The finish on the articles produced is not very high, but they are extremely durable and will stand any amount of rough wear. The Mills have steadily increased in prosperity since their first foundation and now dispose of their goods throughout the Central Provinces and Berār and at many stations in more distant Provinces. The latest annual outturn was of 1,286,329 lbs. yarn and 1,054,854 cotton cloth, valued at Rs. 5,42,842 and Rs. 6,21,048 respectively.

Cottage industries.

230. The most important cottage industries are the same as those practised in factories, namely the cleaning of cotton, the making of seed oils of various kinds, and weaving. The following table shows the figures in the various plain tāluks at the Revision Settlement:—

Taluk.	Oil Presses.	Cotton Looms.	Woollen Looms.	Hand Gins.
Amraoti...	76	193	72	1719
Ellichpur	162	1030	43	4123
Daryāpur	113	630	33	1311
Chāndur	48	192	59	8437
Morsi	159	378	81	3886

The oil presses turn out oil for the local market only, cotton seed, til, and linseed being used. The number of hand gins is at first sight large, but it is explained that cotton seed for sowing must be separated from the lint by hand gins, as it is damaged in the rougher usage to which the steam gins subject it.

231. Hand weaving is done in cotton, silk and wool and in a combined thread of cotton and silk. The chief centres of weaving are Ellichpur city, Anjangaon Surji in the Daryāpur tāluk and Kholāpur near Amraoti, the silk and cotton weaving being mostly done by Sālis and Koshtīs, though Khatrīs, Patwīs, Halbīs and Gadhewāls are among the castes employed; and the rougher cotton fabrics as well as those in wool are produced by Dhangars and Mahārs. The largest centre of the trade is Ellichpur, but the silk work, which is declining, is confined to Kholāpur and Anjangaon. Pure silk is rarely woven except to order, when a *sāri* costs from Rs. 20 to Rs. 50 and a *patkā* or informal turban only a slightly smaller sum. The material is not grown locally but imported, and of Rs. 25 paid for a *patkā* about Rs. 23 represents the price of the silk. The *pagrī* or full dress turban is not woven at Kholāpur. Of the mixed cotton and silk goods two kinds are distinguished, one in which the silk is pure and one in which it is an imitation, imported, it is said, from Germany. The idea may seem incongruous but the results are not unpleasing, the dull yellows and greens affected in this particular material being more soothing to the eye than the pure silks; the colours, however, are not considered to last so well. As to prices, *sāris* can be had from Rs. 5 to Rs. 10 and *patkās* at about Rs. 7. The pure cotton fabrics, chiefly *sāris* of conventional pattern, *dhotīs* and other articles of rustic wear are sold locally, and are in no way remarkable. The texture is plain though very soft, and occasionally the borders are ornamented with embroidery (in the Nāgpur style) in which case a conventional flower said to be that of the *rui* or gigantic swallow-wort is a favourite subject for presentation.

Hand Weaving.

The weaving industry and the allied craft of dyeing, particularly in *āl* for which Ellichpur was once famous, are

This is merely a superstition, but it is dying hard; machine ginned seed is now frequently sown, but in rather larger quantities per acre than the hand ginned. It is considerably cheaper.

both in a very precarious condition. Tastes have changed and the market has ebbed away from the poor Koshtī. The higher castes will no longer wear the many coloured raiment which he loves to produce and low caste folk can get their clothing cheaper elsewhere. His slow and old fashioned hand loom is at a great disadvantage in the competition with steam power, and his own position in the world so much reduced that his earnings for all his fine craftsmanship are less than those of the merest unskilled field labourer The least approach of scarcity or famine destroys his scanty livelihood at once, and Government has to step in and buy his goods, selling them again when better times return. Unless some improvement of a more permanent nature can be effected either in the style of handloom used or in suiting the pattern of goods produced to the demand of the richer classes, this once flourishing industry is bound to disappear. The coarsest forms of weaving, however, still supply a local need. Excellent small carpets produced at Ellichpur are sold all over the District, and *tadhaos*, a coarse carpet-like material used chiefly for packing unginned cotton, are turned out by Mahārs at Morsi and various other places, Woollen blankets of a very rough description are woven by the Mahārs at Kholāpur and elsewhere the ordinary size (about 3 feet by 7½ feet) selling for R. 1-4 in the cold season and R. 1-8 in the rains. Even the Mahārs who produce these goods, though not so badly off as the more highly skilled Sāli and Koshtī, are still in poor circumstances, their wages being only very slightly higher than what they might earn as village servants.

Metal working.

232. Most of the brass and copper vessels used locally are imported, though good *lotās* and very musical bullock bells are made in Amraoti, and at Karasgaon, in the Ellichpur tāluk; excellent gongs are also produced. There is a small iron industry but all the materials are imported and the results are in no way notable. Sonārs number 9589, or nearly 1 per cent. of the population—a figure which, though not so high as that of Nāgpur, still bears testimony to the general prosperity of the District; even the poorest women most frequently have some gold ornament about their persons as well as very heavy

anklets and armlets of silver. Until recently the Bank of Bombay imported annually large quantities of gold bullion for sale in the District. The goods are generally of little artistic value, being made either by hammering or hand moulding, though if a special order be received more ambitious work, including engraving and inlaying, will be undertaken.

Other industries.

233. There is no minor industry of much importance; glass beads and bangles of coarse appearance are made at Brāhmanwāda Thadi and at one or two other places. The most beautiful stone tracery was at one time produced in Ellichpur, and the Nawābs' palaces and tombs at that place, the Deshmukh's house at Daryāpur and various buildings not only in Amraoti but hidden away in villages throughout the District, give evidence of a high standard of wood-carving having once existed. It is said that there are still artificers in Ellichpur who can produce woodwork every whit as good as that of their predecessors if given an order to do so; and one occasionally, as in the new buildings of the Naubatkhāna attached to Ambā Devi's temple in Amraoti, comes across modern carving which is not unpleasing. The wood most commonly used to-day however is not the *shīsham*, and this fact in itself speaks to the decline of the industry for it means the abandonment of the most durable but also the most difficult material: and with the decline in demand the supply is also bound to go on deteriorating.

WEIGHTS AND MEASURES.

Weights.

234. The fixed basis upon which the shifting chaos of weights and measures in Berār rests is the tolā, an almost unvarying and easily ascertainable weight. It is the equivalent of one Government rupee or 180 grains troy weight. The scale of weights is :—

80 tolās = 1 seer
2½ seers = 1 *dhadā*
40 seers = 1 maund (*man*)
20 maunds = 1 *khandī*

Of these the seer alone is unvarying. Sale by weight is only the custom for sugar, cotton, *ghī*, flour, tobacco, turmeric and a few similar groceries, and even in these the

16

variations of weights are almost numberless. Thus a common term is *pāsri* which signifies 100 tolās of groceries or 120 tolās of raw sugar or 115 tolās of tobacco. If applied to cotton it may mean anything from 150 to 180 tolās, or in Daryāpur 135 tolās. Similarly the *dhadā* has variations from 200 tolās to 360 tolās according to the article purchased and the maund of 40 seers is rivalled throughout the District by a maund of 10 seers which becomes in Amraoti tāluk the commoner of the two. Goldsmiths subdivide the tolā into 12 *māshās*, each being the equivalent of 4 *wāls* or 8 *gunjās*, the last named being the seed of *Abrus precatorius*. In the cotton industry *kapās* or raw cotton and ginned cotton are dealt with according to the following scales. :—

Kapās :	38.87 tolās	=	1 lb. avoirdupois.
	7 lbs.	=	1 quarter
	4 quarters	=	1 maund
	20 maunds	=	1 *khandī* (local)
Cotton :	38.87 tolās	=	1 lb. avoirdupois.
	28 lbs.	=	1 maund
	10 maunds	=	1 *bojhā*

But cotton pressed and ready for export is dealt with by the Bombay *khandī* of 784 lbs., which is taken to be roughly the equivalent of 10 Bengal maunds slightly exceeding 82 lbs. each.

Measures.

235. The seer however, though constant as a symbol of weight, is much more commonly the term for a measure of capacity. In 1862 the officiating Commissioner, Captain Cadell, issued orders that the seer measure should contain 100 tolās by weight of water, these 100 tolās being taken as approximately the equivalent of 80 tolās of the following most common kinds of grain mixed in equal proportions : juāri, gram, lākh, rice, masūr, urad and mūng. For milk and *ghī* separate measures were prescribed, each being based on the 80 tolās weight of the article in question. The scale of measurement is :

16 chittacks	=	1 seer
2 seers	=	1 *pāili*
8 pāilis	=	1 *kuro* or maund
20 maunds	=	1 *khandī*

though in this scale there is the inevitable confusion, a *pailī* being sometimes 4 seers, and numberless other variations being introduced by local fancy. Up to 1906 in the price current returns to the Government of India the measured seer was quoted, but since that date conversions have been made to the seer by weight in common use elsewhere according to the following table :—

	Amraoti.	Chāndur.	Morsi.	Ellichpur.	Daryāpur.	Melght.
	Tolās.	Tolās.	Tolās.	Tolās.	Tolās.	Tolās.
Wheat ...	84	84	87½	84	85	83
Rice	88	85	90	87	88	85
Juāri	80	76	80	75	78	78
Gram	82	78	81	80	81	80
Til	...	...	...	66	68	66

Measures of length.

236. The English scales are in use for measures both of length and of surface : but a few native terms also survive. The depth of a well or a tank is measured by *purush* (a man), a length of about one fathom ; cloth is sold by the *hāth* of 18 inches, called also a *gaz* ; this is subdivided into 8 *girhas* and two *gaz* make a yard or *wār*. For long distances the commonest figure is a *kos* of two miles. For survey purposes the English acre is divided into 40 *gunthās*, each of which is a square chain of 33 feet. The chain is further subdivided into 16 annas. In old papers, a *bīgha* of 25 *gunthās* will be found referred to ; and in daily speech the Kunbī measures land by a *tiffan* of 4 acres.

The Calendar.

237. In this District the Saka era and calendar are generally used. This era commenced in 78 A.D. and is believed to have been founded by a Scythian King. Sālivāhan, of the Yueh-Chi tribe, who reigned in Kāthiawār. The year 1909 is 1830—31 of the Saka era and 1965—66 of the Vikrama calendar. The

Saka calendar differs from the Vikrama in common use in the Central Provinces and very often used by the Mārwāris in this District, in the fact that each month begins a fortnight later. Thus Chaitra, the first day of which month begins the new year, corresponds to the second half of the Vikrama Chait and the first half of Vaishākh. The Saka months begin with the new moon and the Vikrama months with the full moon. The first of Chaitra may fall as early as the middle of March, but more commonly comes in the last week of March or the first week of April. Consequently Chaitra may be taken roughly as corresponding to April. The names of the Saka months are practically the same as those of the Vikrama months, but they retain the correct Sanskrit form, whereas the Vikrama names are Hindī corruptions. But the Vikrama month Kunwār is called Ashvin in the Saka calendar and the month Aghan is called Mārgashir. Both eras are luni-solar and the year consists of about 355 days, but is made to correspond very nearly with the Gregorian year by the interposition of triennial inter calary months. The Faslī era observed in Berār is that of the Deccan which is ahead of the Hindustāni Faslī by two years. It begins about the 5th of June every year and corresponds roughly with the Berār agricultural year commencing on the first of April. The Faslī year 1319 commenced from the 7th of June 1909.

Fairs and Markets.

238. **Fairs.** Not counting the insignificant tombs of ascetics scattered up and down the country at almost every one of which on some particular day in the year a few score of holiday makers assemble, there are twenty-two annual or half yearly fairs in the District. These are Mārki, Ganojā and Rinmochan in the Amraoti tāluk; Kaundanyapur, Bhiltek, and Sāwangā Vithobāchā in the Chāndur tāluk; Wadner Gangāi, Yeodā, Murhā and Uprāi in the Daryāpur tāluk; Ner Pinglāi, Akhatwāda, Ridhpur, Dābheri and Sālbardī in the Morsi tāluk: Dhānorā, Jīwanpurā (in Ellichpur city), Ellichpur city (Dūlā Rahmān), Deurwāda, and Bairam in Ellichpur tāluk, and

Diwa in Melghāt. Most of these, however, are completely insignificant; one or two, such as Uprāi, Ridhpur and the annual *urs* or saint's day of "Dūlā Rahmān" at Ellichpur, being notable not so much on account of the gathering as of the peculiar sanctity attaching to the shrine venerated. Four, however, those of Sālbardī, Kaundinyapur, Bhiltek and Bairamghāt, have something more than a local celebrity. All these places are situated close to the Central Provinces border, and traders and villagers flock together to attend them not only from all over Berār but from the neighbouring Districts of Betūl, Wardhā and Nāgpur as well. The attendance at the first named is estimated at about twenty-five thousand and at each of the others at fifty thousand, probably not a very large estimate. Mārki also in the Amraoti tāluk, though not much more than a local merry-making, has an attendance of probably ten to fifteen thousand. Full particulars of each of the fairs will be found in the Gazetteer Appendix and there is no need to repeat them here. That of Bhiltek lasts for no less than two and a half months and at all of them a little religion is made the excuse for much trading and a pleasant holiday. With the increasing facility of communication, however, and the consequent spread of retail shops, the taking of an annual holiday or the purchase of such necessities as brass pots, clothing, village carts, etc., has become a less formidable affair than before, and the fairs as a whole are undoubtedly on the decline. One in particular, Wirul in Chāndur tāluk, which not very many years ago lasted for some three weeks every year and attracted many thousands of people, has now dwindled to an affair of a single day, so insignificant that it is not thought worthy of a place in the list. Even figures collected so recently as the Revision Settlement are no longer completely trustworthy, though the four great fairs already mentioned still retain their importance.

Markets.

239. The weekly markets however are numerous and important. At the Revision Settlement there were a hundred and fifty in the plains tāluks alone. This with ten in the Melghāt and a dozen or so which have come into existence since gives an average of one market to every eleven villages, or every

nine villages if the Melghāt be omitted from the count. Of these by far the most important is still Chāndur Bazār, though local residents tell one that it has lost something of its old preeminence, having remained almost stationary for the last forty years or even declined in spite of the enormous increase in wealth during that time. The sales are estimated at over half a lakh every week[1] of which some Rs. 35,000 is accounted for by grain and groceries. Chāndur also, though not an established cotton market, sees transactions in cotton during the season to a weekly value of about seven thousand rupees; about five thousand of the total is accounted for by livestock. Next to Chāndur Bazār in importance comes Ellichpur (Paratwāda), the great wood mart for this part of Berār, with weekly sales aggregating over Rs. 10,000 in value, of which about six thousand is represented by timber and bamboos. Vegetables from Khāmla and Chikaldā are also an important item. The Amraoti Sunday market (there is one also on Wednesday) and that at Badnerā rank next in importance, having an estimated turn-over of about nine and eight thousand respectively. Others in approximate order of importance are Sendurjana Buzurg, Rājurā, Anjangaon Surji, Morsi, Mangrul Dastgīr, Sendurjana (Malkāpur), Hiwarkhed, Khel Tapmālī in Ellichpur city, Wānosā (Daryāpur), Dattāpur, Ner Pinglāi. The ten in the Melghāt are of merely local importance and the same remark is true of the remainder of those in the plains. Most of the more important markets, it will be noticed, lie close to the hills and they fulfil among other useful functions that of exchanging the products of the jungles and of the fertile plateau of Khāmla and Multai against those of Berār. At every village where a bazar is held certain land is set apart for the purpose, and in three markets of the municipal towns and sixty-nine of the markets in the District Board area the traffic is regulated and cesses and stall fees collected according to the bazar rules. In both cases the right to collect the dues is put up to auction annually, market by market, and the proceeds of the auction credited to District Board or Municipal funds as the case may

[1] The Berār Gazetteer 1870 gives the figure as one lakh.

Bemrose, Collo., Derby.

THE STONE AT BAIRAM.

be. In 1908 the sum derived from these auctions was Rs. 12,000 in municipal limits and Rs. 52,970 outside. In return for this the local bodies undertake the upkeep of the bazars concerned, laying down *chabūtras* for merchants and their goods, planting trees and arranging water-supply. The bazars are controlled by patels and if the latter collect bazar cess they are paid 10 per cent. on the collections.

Cotton markets.

240. In addition to the above the District has six markets solely for cotton, namely Amraoti, Ellichpur, Morsi, Wānosā (Daryāpur), Chāndur Railway and Dattāpur. These are managed in each case by a small committee appointed by the Commissioner. The largest is Amraoti where the sales are estimated at 72 lakhs of rupees per year, Dhāmangaon which receives the Yeotmāl trade coming next with 24 lakhs per year. The smallest is Wānosā (Daryāpur) with a yearly average of 4 lakhs of rupees. At the end of the cotton season the balance in hand, if any, is credited to the District or Municipal fund to which the cotton market is subordinate. In 1907-08 the total receipts were Rs. 15,809 and the total expenditure Rs. 13,675.

TRADE.

Trade in former years.

241. 'Very few people outside the province,' says the Census Report for 1891, 'know where 'Berār is or what it is. . . Its only claim 'to fame lies in the cotton market where the name of Oomras '(or Oomrawuttees) refers in uncouth and archaic form to the 'chief product and the chief mart of the Province.'

The cotton trade is by far the most important item of Berār commerce as it is of Berār agriculture forming about half the annual crop to the detriment of the harvest in food grains and more than half the total foreign trade. Though flourishing to-day it laboured less than a century ago under almost every disadvantage and one can only wonder that it was found worth while to grow cotton at all in Berār. The miserable and depressed condition of the cultivator, his indebtedness and his uncertainty of tenure were drawbacks which operated alike against all forms of cultivation: but cotton was additionally handicapped by the distance of the market, the low prices then prevailing, and the hundred dangers and uncertainties of primitive transport through disturbed country. In the season of 1825-26 Messrs. Vikaji and Pestonji, merchants of Bombay and Hyderābād (the great revenue farmers), made what is said to have been the first exportation of Berār cotton direct to Bombay. The figures in these days sound trivial for it was only 120,000 lbs. weight valued at Rs. 25,000 but 500 bullocks were required to carry it. The same enterprising firm opened the first Cotton Press in 1836: but matters continued for a long while without much improvement, so that General Balfour, C. B., writing about 1847 says:

'Formerly the greater part of the cotton of Berār was 'taken 500 miles on bullocks to Mirzāpur on the Ganges and 'thence conveyed in boats 450 miles to Calcutta. Now the 'greater part goes to Bombay, still wholly on pack oxen, the 'distance varying from 126 to 450 miles according as the cotton 'is purchased at one market or another. The hire of a bullock 'for the journey ranges from about Rs. 5 to Rs. 16, the chief 'cause of variation being the time of year. A load is about '250 lbs. But this is not by any means the whole cost 'of conveyance, the indirect expenses are much greater. The 'cotton is eaten by the bullocks, stolen by the drivers, 'torn off by the jungles through which the road passes 'and damaged by the dust and the weather as well as 'by having to be loaded and unloaded every day often in wet 'and mud.' If the difficulties of other districts were the same, it is little wonder that "Surats," or Indian cotton, was a byeword in Lancashire for everything vile. Better days were however dawning: the suppression of the Peshwā and the pacification of the intervening country by the British had already brought Berār nearer to Bombay. The American Civil War and the Lancashire cotton famine have relieved the cultivator of his ancestral indebtedness. He has security of tenure and the arrangement by which land revenue is paid after, not before, harvest has removed at least one of the many temptations to resort to the moneylender. The railway has given him speedy transit, an improvement which coincided with the rise in prices and was so much appreciated that the first rush of cotton to the newly opened stations completely paralysed traffic. Finally the establishment of gins and presses throughout the province has enabled the cotton to be despatched in a compact and portable form instead of the loose *dokrās* or sacks formerly in vogue, and the opening of six cotton markets in this District has brought the merchant more near to the producer and has limited the functions of the middleman.

Rail-borne trade.

242. All the railway stations in the District are to some degree centres of trade, but by far the most important are Dhāmangaon (Dattāpur), Chāndur, Badnerā and Amraoti, statistics of the exports and imports of which are given in the two tables next following; these statistics do not, of course, represent accurately the total foreign commerce of the District, for they exclude the Daryāpur tāluk which is served by Murtizāpur station in Akolā District, as well as the six minor stations, and they include the Yeotmāl traffic which reaches the line at Dhāmangaon. Balancing inclusions and omissions, however, roughly against one another, the statistics give a fair general idea of the District trade.

The tables call for but little comment. Cotton is, as has already been remarked, overwhelmingly the most important export, accounting in one form or another, for three-quarters of the total value. Cotton (raw) it should be explained includes ginned and pressed cotton, for without these processes the material is too bulky for export. The export of manufactured cotton is practically confined to the Mills at Badnerā, the work of local Koshtīs and other weavers seldom spreading much beyond their own neighbourhood; and as might be expected the import of manufactured cotton is also extremely large. It is somewhat startling to find fodder included among the exports, for the grassland of the plains is certainly not in excess of local requirements: the export, however, is probably mostly *karbī* or juāri stalks. The list of imports is somewhat longer than of exports, but of a simple nature, chiefly articles of food and clothing. The small space occupied by coal in the list is probably due to the local ginning and pressing factories using *bābul* and other local wood fuel in their furnaces. Liquor furnishes the largest item of import, and may be expected to show even larger totals in future now that the Ellichpur distillery is abolished. The average annual expenditure per head of the male population judged by

EXPORTS.

FIGURES REPRESENT THOUSANDS.

Articles.	1902.		1903.		1904.		1905.		1906.		1907.	
	Quantity.	Value.	Quantity.	Value.	Quantity.	Value.	Quantity.	Value.	Quantity.	Value.	Quantity.	Value.
	Mds.	Rs.	Mds.	Rs.	Mds.	Rs.	Mds.	Rs.	Mds.	Rs.	Mds.	Rs.
Cotton, raw	1,138	1,76,42	1,222	2,12,67	1,107	2,40,86	1,599	2,77,85	1,263	2,39,17	1,206	2,20,42
Cotton, manufactured	31	12,09	30	12,02	26	10,86	30	12.18	26	10,98	27	11,30
Cotton-seed	238	7,13	430	5,37	356	4,46	594	7,43	425	5 31	299	3 73
Oil cake	22	62	29	58	53	92	77	1,53	95	2 03	102	2,61
Hay, straw and grass	6	10	4	5	14	16	13	17	23	31	9	11
Juāri	331	7,43	8	13	21	39	124	2,33	165	3,76	53	1,38
Hides and skins	14	2,10	14	2.52	12	3,24	14	3,90	20	5,63	17	4,95
Other oilseeds	484	11,88	14	59	28	95	33	1,36	10	47	20	1,04
Bones	1	4	2	8	2	8	4	14	5	16	6	22
All other articles	136	10,45	116	9,25	157	11,68	243	16,37	621	29,57	201	14,08
Total Exports ...	2,401	2,28,27	1,869	2,43,26	1,776	2,73,60	2,731	3,23,26	2,653	2,97,39	1,940	2,59,84

IMPORTS.

FIGURES REPRESENT THOUSANDS.

Articles.	1902.		1903.		1904.		1905.		1906.		1907.	
	Quantity.	Value	Quantity.	Value.	Quantity.	Value.	Quantity.	Value.	Quantity.	Value.	Quantity.	Value.
	Mds.	Rs.	Mds.	Rs.	Mds	Rs.	Mds.	Rs.	Mds.	Rs.	Mds.	Rs.
Coal and coke	324	81	273	68	329	82	387	97	382	96	430	1,07
Cotton, manufactured	51	29,97	46	27,73	55	34,29	57	35,42	59	37,15	40	25,14
Turmeric	5	38	6	35	5	35	6	52	5	65	5	64
Fresh fruits and vegetables ...	17	39	38	84	16	57	54	2,14	28	1,01	42	1,33
Gram and pulse	273	6,39	235	4,99	138	3,10	137	3,43	129	4,35	223	7,74
Rice...	300	10,13	290	10,18	373	13,51	364	13,43	339	4,39	299	13,72
Wheat	403	11,48	324	8,55	273	7,68	148	4,38	205	7,10	246	9,25
Other grain and pulse	13	31	156	2,69	153	2,87	10	19	11	26	60	1,56
Hemp	5	26	1	8	1	4	1	8	2	13	2	8
Gunny bags	35	2,93	18	1,56	18	1,79	27	2,83	24	2,73	16	1,93
Liquors	12	10,64	16	14,85	20	18,55	38	36,12	40	37,60	34	32,68
Metals	108	13,57	96	12,49	114	16,22	129	16,46	145	19,37	85	10,59
Kerosine oil	88	3,99	95	4,38	108	4,99	115	4,99	121	5 61	117	5,69
Other oils	37	4,79	30	3,73	37	4,59	51	6,55	44	5 94	38	5,19
Linseed	9	56	17	73	64	2,19	82	3,39	108	5 17	151	8,09
Til seed	10	54	4	14	3	11	2	11	6	36	3	20
Provisions...	97	11,36	123	14,42	132	15,80	94	11,62	85	10,67	57	7,39
Salt	137	5,13	150	5,03	158	5,14	161	4,54	165	4 32	164	3,90
Betel nuts	31	4,13	33	4,60	41	5,92	42	6,66	41	7,63	43	7,82
Chillies	18	1,32	11	84	11	91	11	1,23	19	2,18	37	3,20
Sugar	161	11,37	188	13,05	193	16,42	231	20,11	233	17,92	196	15,51
Tobacco	4	75	5	83	6	1,38	11	1,97	12	2,07	8	1,40
Wood	188	3,95	228	4,75	287	6,01	288	6,11	342	7,04	277	5,64
Wool, manufactured and raw...	2	82	2	53	2	1,14	3	1,06	3	1,07	2	58
All other articles	227	22,24	169	18,14	227	25,71	238	24,06	287	28,13	362	31,16
Total Imports	2,555	1,58,21	2,554	1,56,16	2,763	1,90,10	2,687	2,08,37	2,835	2,23,75	2,937	2,01,50

these figures was Rs. 2-5-4 in 1902, the year after the famines but rose to Rs. 9-1-8 in 1906. The figures are significant, even when we allow for the intemperate habits of primitive tribes such as the Korkūs, of the amount which the population manage yearly to spend on luxuries.

Railway rates.

243. The export trade in cotton from Amraoti could not be the flourishing business that it is, were it not for the specially favourable freightage rates granted by the Great Indian Peninsula Railway which enable Amraoti cotton to compete favourably in the Bombay markets with cotton from stations nearer to that capital. This is done in order to prevent the cotton going to Calcutta *via* the Bengal-Nāgpur Railway. The following table gives the comparison so far as the Berārs are concerned :—

Name of Station.		Rate per maund of 40 seers.			Distance from Bombay in miles.
		Rs.	a.	p.	
Buldāna District	Malkāpur	1	3	2	308
	Shegaon	1	4	11	340
	Khāmgaon				341
Akolā District	Akolā	1	6	2	363
	Murtizāpur	1	4	7	386
Amraoti District.	Amraoti	1	2	3	419
	Chāndur	1	0	8	430
	Dhāmangaon	1	1	1	441

The price of Berār cotton in Bombay is uniform, variations being slight and due only to quality. Dhāmangaon cotton for instance is generally considered better than that of Amraoti. Were it not for the favourable rates given for the more distant stations, the Chāndur cultivator could scarcely compete with his rivals of Khāmgaon. At present the railway rates are not merely not against but actually operate in his favour.

Classes engaged in trade.

244. Scattered over the District in the various towns and larger villages are nearly a hundred steam factories for the ginning and pressing of cotton, and a scrutiny of the owners' names proves that the trade is not by any

means entirely in the hands of a single class. True there are many Mārwāris but Muhammadans, Pārsis, Baniās, Bhātias, and Brāhmans, as well as the richer members of the local cultivating castes also take a share. All or almost all of these will be found to combine moneylending with the trade in cotton and it looks as if the two were very closely connected. The cultivator is always ready to take a loan for celebrating a marriage or some similar festivity, and once he has done so, cotton is the crop which leaves him the largest margin of profit after paying interest to his creditors. To the moneylender a double profit accrues; first from the interest on his loans, secondly from the increasing quantity of cotton brought to his gins. The system of loans for seed is also a popular one and from the creditor's point of view has all the advantages of a purchase of the yet ungrown harvest, while the borrower takes the risk of that harvest being a failure. When it is reaped, the *sāhukār* takes a quantity in payment of his loan and the remainder at cash rates; if it fails, the debt still remains. Even those few independent cultivators who bring their own cotton to market invariably place it with a broker for sale; and the broker is merely a moneylender in a different rôle. Among themselves the big merchants indulge freely in speculation on options, *sattās* as they are called, and this leads to not infrequent insolvencies. Of European firms Messrs. Volkarts and Co. and Messrs. Gaddam and Co. have agents at Amraoti, but by far the most important are Messrs. Ralli Brothers, who do business in all the six cotton markets and carry on a considerable trade also in grain and oilseed. All these deal with the brokers.

Retail sale of local goods and of imports is in the hands of Bohrās, Cutchis, Memons, Khojās, Lāds, Mālis, Koshtīs and a variety of minor castes and deserves no special mention.

Excess of exports over imports.

245. In 1870 so far as can be ascertained from the figures given in Sir Alfred Lyall's Gazetteer the imports of this District appear considerably to have exceeded the exports. Commerce was not as yet centred entirely on the railway and the services of the Berār bullock who still did much of the carrying trade both of exports and imports, were probably

largely responsible for this state of affairs. To-day however the balance is inclined very much in the other direction; in 1902 the excess of exports was valued at about 70 lakhs and it rose steadily to 114 lakhs in 1905. The figures at first sight are startling, but their explanation is to be found in the cotton trade; thus in 1906 when the harvest was a poor one the excess fell from 114 lakhs to about 73 lakhs and again in 1907 to 58 lakhs. The real market of cotton is of course Bombay, and the values given include the cost of services rendered by the Great Indian Peninsula Railway in freightage, and by Bombay firms such as Messrs. Ralli Brothers as well as the big Mārwāri firms which arrange for its transport thither. The return for these services is not made in the District and hence in part at least the extreme disproportion between the figures. There is practically nothing in the way of invisible import, for besides the whole external carrying trade being in outside hands, local rich men are very chary of distant investments. Money, however, is very cheap, and living proportionately expensive and it is therefore probable when all allowances have been made for the facts just noticed that some portion of the return for the District exports is being made in cash.

COMMUNICATIONS.

System of Communications.

246. The system of communications in Berār and in this District in particular may be roughly compared to the human anatomy. The Great Indian Peninsula Railway running the whole length of the central valley is the backbone: on it converges a network of roads, metalled and unmetalled, communicating with most of the important towns and centres of trade. There is a short arm reaching from Badnerā to Amraoti, and it is hoped that at no very distant date branch railways will bring most of the more distant tracts in touch with the main line.

Railways completed.

247. The Nāgpur branch of the Great Indian Peninsula Railway enters the District on the south-west and quits it on the south-east at the Wardhā river after a run of about 45 miles It was opened for traffic in 1866 and has now nine stations

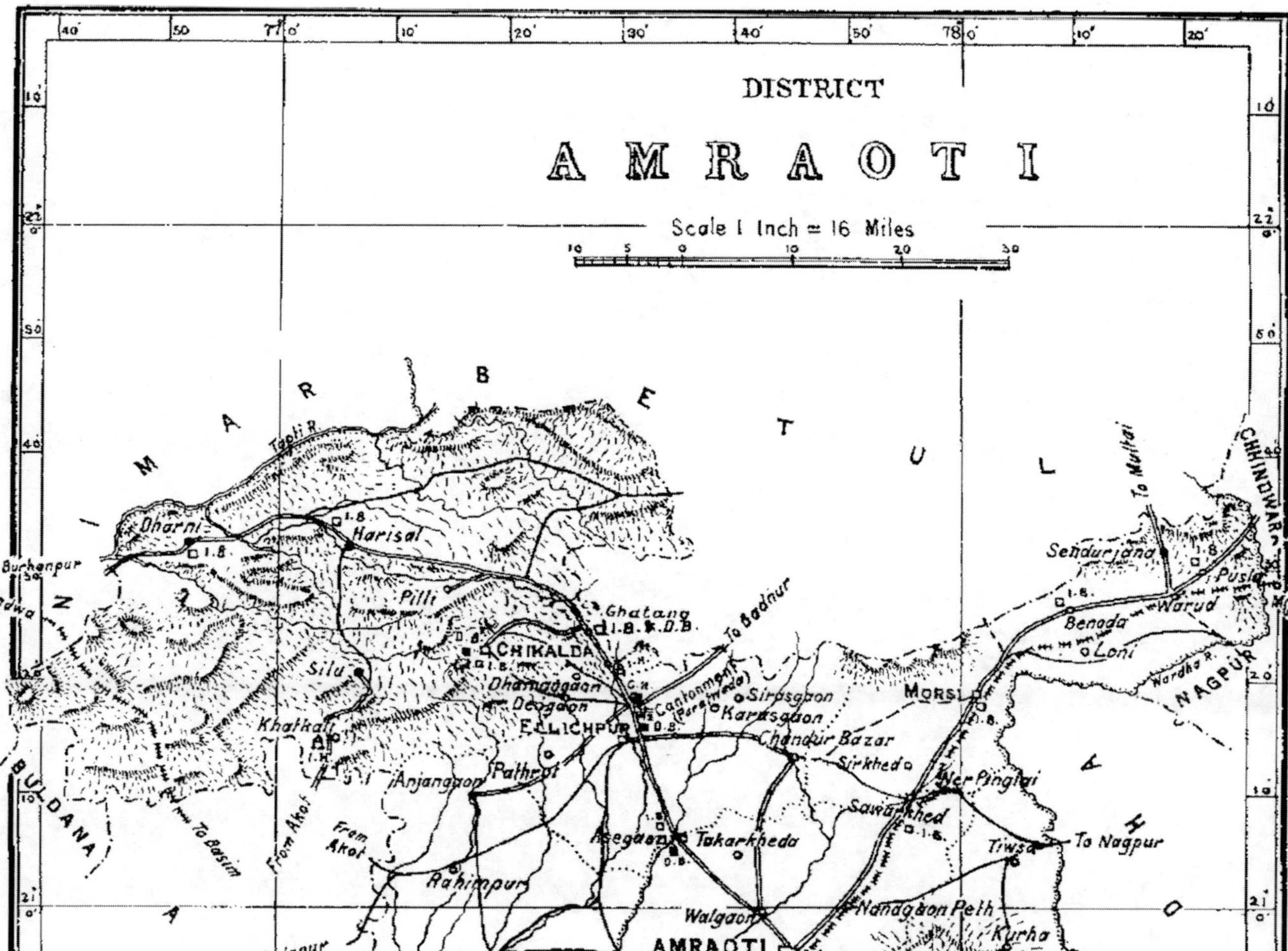

Specially prepared for the Snperintendent Gazetteer C.P. from an original supplied by him.

Reg. No. 1652 B., 09.—V.—450

in this stretch: Kuram, Tākli, Badnerā, Anjangaon Bāri, Mālkhed, Chāndur, Dipori, Dhāmangaon and Tālni. Of these Badnerā, Chāndur and Dhāmangaon are important places at which the Mail trains stop and there is a considerable goods traffic. The Amraoti branch above alluded to is a State-owned line worked by the Great Indian Peninsula Railway and was opened in 1871. Both lines are single and the heavy traffic carried over them in the cotton season leads to frequent unpunctualities and delays.

248. Main roads. From Amraoti city branch out roads which connect the north of the District with the rail. Of these the longest is that which runs through Balgaon jāgīr and Assegaon to Ellichpur and Paratwāda, and on thence into the Melghāt to Ghātang, Sembādoh and Dhārni debouching into Nimār at Dhertalai, a distance in all of 98 miles of which 21 are first-class or fully metalled road The main branches of this great artery are one from Balgaon due northwards to Chāndur Bazār, a distance of 16½ miles fully metalled; one from Ghātang to Chikaldā, winding up the hillsides for some fifteen miles on a sufficiently easy gradient for most motor cars, and others maintained by the District Board which branch east and west from Ellichpur to Chāndur Bazār and Anjangaon Surji; the first of these being continued as a fair weather road to Morsi, and the latter as a gravelled road to Daryāpur. From Ellichpur a gravelled road shortly to be raised to the first-class runs to Betūl, crossing the border at Bairamghāt about the 11th milestone. The main road is also crossed at Assegaon by a fair weather track from Chāndur Bazār to Daryāpur, and the last mentioned place is connected with Amraoti by a very good country road and with Murtizāpur, a railway station in the Akolā District, by a high road, partly metalled and partly gravelled, of 14 miles. The Morsi tāluk is served by another first-class road which runs from Amraoti by Sāwarkhed close to Ner Pinglāi and Sirkhed to Morsi and thence to Hiwarkhed, Benodā, Warūd, and Puslā to the Wardhā river which it crosses soon after the sixty-sixth milestone into the Nāgpur District. The whole length of this is now first-class road. Its only branch of importance, however,

is that from Warūd to Multâi *via* Bikatghāt, a distance of 8 miles first-class road in this District. Country roads from Nāndgaon Peth to Tiosā and thence to the Wardhā border, from Warūd to Amner and from Morsi to Chāndur Bazār (already alluded to) carry a great deal of traffic and it is proposed to make them all first-class, the two former being continued to Nāgpur.

Amraoti, on which the above system of roads converges, is connected with Badnerā not only by the railway line already mentioned but by a first-class metalled road of seven miles. Thus the arrangements connecting the north and east of the District with the outside world are, or will be when the proposed additions are made, extremely good.

It is otherwise with the south and south-east of the District. This portion derives a far greater advantage from the railway line which connects three of its most important towns (Badnerā, Chāndur and Dhāmangaon) and is not very far from any of them; but there is only one metalled road and that is rather for the convenience of Yeotmāl than of Amraoti, connecting the headquarters of the former District with the railway at Dhāmangaon. It has a length of 8 miles in the Chāndur tāluk. The lack of first-class or second-class roads, however, is not so serious a matter as might at first sight be supposed, for the country tracks, except in the rainy season, are excellent and their soft surface is probably less tiring to the bullocks' feet than a more permanent roadway would be. Of these tracks that from Nāndgaon Peth to Tiosā, as already mentioned, is to be raised to the first-class, and a second-class branch from Tiosā *via* Kūrha will connect it with the railway at Chāndur. Along the extreme south of the District runs the old Nāgpur Dāk line and a few hundred rupees yearly are still spent on keeping it in moderate repair. Its Amraoti branch is similarly maintained as far as Badnerā. Though passing by one or two large villages, it is now of little importance: its place as a through route has been taken by the railway, and the only roads of importance now are those communicating directly or indirectly with the latter. Finally mention should be made of the excellent short roads for local purposes in Amraoti Camp, Ellichpur Civil Station, Chikaldā and one or

Bemrose, Collo., Derby.

BERAR CHHAKRA AND BULLOCKS.

two other places, and of the splendid system of communications maintained by the Forest Department in the Melghāt reserves. This is chiefly useful for forest purposes; and for through traffic the tāluk depends chiefly on the P.W.D. roads already mentioned and on a road from Akot to Selu which is in charge of the Executive Engineer West Berār. In the C III tract the great local road is one which follows a semi-circular course from Jhiri in the extreme south-west through the Amner pargana into Bairāgarh.

Proposed new Railways.

249. The Great Indian Peninsula Railway propose in the course of the next few years to lay down a broad gauge line from Amraoti by Morsi and Warūd to Sāoner in the Nāgpur District, connecting with the Itārsi-Nāgpur line now under construction. This will bring the whole Morsi tāluk within easy distance of headquarters. A similar line from Khandwā to Akolā and Bāsim shortly to be constructed will also be of use to the remoter parts of the Melghāt, and it is hoped that before long it may be found possible to connect Ellichpur with the main line by a light railway.

Accommodation for Travellers.

250. For the convenience of various classes of travellers it may be well to give the accommodation available for them.

(*a*). Circuit Houses :—(1) Amraoti Camp and (2) Ellichpur Civil Station.

(*b*). Officers' Rest Houses :—(1) Amraoti Camp, (2) Chikaldā (two bungalows) and (3) Ellichpur Civil Station (for Police Officers only).

(*c*). Forest Inspection Bungalows :—

Amraoti Division :—(1) Pahorā & (2) Mehdari.

Melghāt Division (in the Bairāgarh reserve.)

Melghāt Division (in the Bairāgarh reserve.)	(1) Maklā	(2) Tāora
	(3) Chunkhari	(4) Jaridā
	(5) Rāhu	(6) Hatru
	(7) Butram	(8) Raipur
	(9) Chaurākund	(10) Kolkaz
	(11) Rangobeli	(12) Chopan

Melghāt Division (in the Gugumāl reserve)	(1) Tārubānda	(2) Rangarao
	(3) Dākhna	(4) Kotku
	(5) Dhārgarh	(6) Patuldā

(*d*) P.W.D. Inspection Bungalows :—

(1) Amraoti Camp	(2) Puslā	(3) Chikaldā
(4) Chāndur Bazār	(5) Sāwarkhed	(6) Daryāpur
(7) Morsi	(8) Khatkali (Melghāt)	(9) Benodā
(10) Sembādoh	(11) Assegaon	(12) Belkund (Melghāt)

(*e*). Combined Dāk and Inspection Bungalows :—

(1) Dhāmangaon Railway,	(2) Badnerā
(3) Chāndur Railway	(4) Ghātang

(*f*) Dāk Bungalows :—

(1) Amraoti Camp, (2) Ellichpur Civil Station, (3) Assegaon

(*g*) P.W.D. Inspection Huts :—(1) Kohāna and (2) Khatkāli (Melghāt)

(*h*) *Sarais.* The following is a list of those maintained by the District Board :—

Amraoti Tāluk	(1) Anjangaon Bāri	(2) Kholāpur	(3) Daryābād
	(4) Bhātkūli	(5) Wāthodā	(6) Ganūri
	(7) Dhānorā Fasi	(8) Māhuli	(9) Sāyat
	(10) Chichked	(11) Virul	(12) Rahatgaon
	(13) Shirāla	(14) Naothā	(15) Takerkhedā
	(16) Pusadā	(17) Badnerā	
Chāndur Tāluk	(1) Chāndur Railway	(2) Mālkhed	
	(3) Dattāpur	(4) Tālni	
	(5) Talegaon Dashāsar	(6) Mangrul Dastgīr	
	(7) Ajansingi	(8) Nāndgaon Kāzi	
	(9) Wirul	(10) Sendurjana Buzurg	
	(11) Kalāsi	(12) Kaudinyapur	(13) Dipori
Morsi Tāluk	(1) Benodā	(2) Burgaon	(3) Hiwarkhed
	(4) Jarūd	(5) Puslā	(6) Malkāpur
	(7) Barūr	(8) Ganeshpur	(9) Loni
	(10) Morsi	(11) Daryāpur	(12) Sāwarkhed
	(13) Ner Pinglāi	(14) Belūra	(15) Ridhpur
	(16) Ambāda	(17) Khānāpur	(18) Shirkhed
	(19) Rajūra.		

Tāluk			
Daryāpur Tāluk	(1) Wanosā	(1) Adūl	(3) Yeodā
	(4) Wādnergangāi	(5) Surji	(6) Kapūstaln
	(7) Khallar	(8) Pimplod	(9) Bābhli
	(10) Daryāpur	(11) Tākli	(12) Sātegaon
	(13) Borāla	(14) Anjangaon	(15) Kadatkhedā
Ellichpur Tāluk	(1) Kāndli	(2) Chāndur Bazār	(3) Konwardhā
	(4) Pāthrot	(5) Mādhān	(6) Bhūgaon
	(7) Sirasgaon Bund	(8) Karajgaon	(9) Bairam
	(10) Assegaon	(11) Kurhā	(11) Gaurkhed
	(13) Dhāmangaon	(14) Saolāpur	(15) Brāhman-wāda Thadi

In addition to these there are in various places *dharamshālās* maintained by private munificence for native travellers, and it is a point of honour with every village that can afford it to maintain a *musāfirkhāna* of some sort.

CHAPTER VI.

FORESTS AND MINERALS.

FORESTS.

Government Forests.

251. The District comprises two forest divisions, Melghāt and Amraoti. The latter contains the forest of the 5 plain tāluks of the District and the former, that of the Melghāt tāluk alone. The Amraoti Division consists of 4 ranges and the Melghāt Division of 7 ranges, as follows :—

(a) Amraoti.

(1)	Amraoti	with its headquarters at	Pahorā
(2)	Chāndur	do.	Kurhā
(3)	Morsi-Warūd	do.	Warūd
(4)	Morsi-Bairam	do.	Morsi

(b) Melghāt.

(1)	Gugumāl	with its headquarters at	Kohā
(2)	Chaurākund	do.	Harisāl
(3)	Butram	do.	Raipur
(4)	Khandu	do.	Jaridā
(5)	Sembādoh	do.	Sembādoh
(6)	Chikaldā	do.	Chikaldā
(7)	Revenue	do.	Ellichpur

The range officer of the last named has no forest actually in his charge but has control of the line of *nākas* or forest custom houses situated along the south side of the timber reserves. The total area of the District covered by forests is 1758 square miles, of which 253 square miles lie in Amraoti and the rest in Melghāt. Thus the forest of the District represents 37.15 per cent. of the total area of the District. The forests are further divided into three classes, A or timber and fuel reserve, B or fodder reserve and

C pasture grounds. The area under the three classes is shown below separately for each division :—

Area in square miles of classes.

Division	A.	B.	C.	Total
Melghāt	843	6	656	1505
Amraoti	57	18	178	253
Total	900	24	834	1758

Of the total area of the District forest, working plans have been provided for 702 square miles only, but for B and C classes are of course unnecessary. The A class forests of the Amraoti Division are worked under a plan prepared by Mr. E. E. Fernandez which has never been sanctioned. A new working plan for them is now under preparation.

The principal state forests in the Amraoti Division are :—

(i) The Chirori reserve which lies in the Amraoti range and is situated partly in the Amraoti and partly in the west of the Chāndur tāluk about 10 miles east of Amraoti town.

(ii) The Lakhara reserve
(iii) The Mehdari ,,
(iv) The Shekhdari ,,
} Situated in the north-east of the division and lying in the Morsi tāluk in the Morsi-Warūd range.

Those in the Melghāt Division are :—

(*a*) The Bairāgarh reserve
(*b*) The Gugumāl ,,
(*c*) The Chikaldā ,,
(*d*) The Kohāna ,,
} These occupy very nearly the eastern half of the Melghāt tāluk.

The area protected from fire consists of 531,405 acres (830 square miles) namely, the above reserves and the two large B class Forest Blocks near Amraoti. Thus the whole of the A class forest with the exception of the *bābul bans*, and most of the B class is thoroughly protected.

Description—Amraoti Division.

252. Of the A class forests in the Amraoti Division the most important are the *bābul bans*, small woods of a few acres apiece scattered here and there throughout the plain tāluks but amounting in all to a total of 7062 acres. They are commonly found in low-lying ground and along the banks of streams in the open country where there is an accumulation of soil washed in during the monsoons and fresh

moisture is plentiful even in the hot weather. Black cotton soil is most suitable. The *bābul* (*Acacia arabica*) is usually almost pure with a slight admixture of other *Acacias* (chiefly *A. leucophloea* and *A. eburnea*), *Dichrostachys cinerea*, *Balanites Roxburghii*, rarely *Prosopis spicigera* and *Azadirachta indica*. In very wet low situations close to nullahs containing perennial pools the wild date palm becomes invasive. The *bābul* is of great value as a furnisher of excellent timber for village purposes, of the very best fuel, of thorns for fencing and of pods as food for cattle. It is in great demand as furnace fuel for the numerous cotton ginning and pressing factories scattered throughout the country. On the rough hill sides in the reserves originally covered with *salai* (*Boswellia thurifera*) the characteristic growth is now an open, often sparse, scrub and stunted trees. Such *salai* as remains is used for fuel, and in the Shekhdari reserve teak (*Tectona grandis*) is also found yielding small timber. Even under the most conservative treatment however nothing better than low open fuel reserves interspersed with a few timber trees can be hoped for in this division.

The Melghāt Division.

253. [1] The whole Melghāt tāluk with the exception of 'Chikaldā civil station and the jāgīr lands 'is classified as forest, but in reality the 'name is only applicable to the State forests of class A and B 'which are directly under the Forest Department. These 'latter forests comprise 849 square miles or one half of the 'tāluk, and extend from the banks of the Tāpti river—here- 'about 1000 feet above the sea-level—southwards over hill 'ranges of 2000 to 3000 feet elevation (culminating in the 'Chikaldā plateau 3664 feet and Bairāt 3866) to the southern 'slopes of the Sātpurās. From the east where they border 'on the Betūl District they spread south-west to the valley of 'the Wān river. The forests are deciduous and the chief 'characteristic is the prevalence of teak and its tendency to 'grow gregariously. The best is found on the lower slopes of 'the valleys of the Sipnā, Khandu, Khapra and Kuapati 'rivers in the Bairāgarh reserve lying north of Chikaldā. 'The more recently protected and dryer Gugamāl reserve

[1] This description was supplied by Mr. H. E. Bartlett, Divisional Forest Officer, Melghāt.

Bemrose, Collo., Derby.

HOLY TEAK TREES, MELGHAT.

'west of Chikaldā contains less teak and of smaller dimen-'sions and usually restricted to the heads of valleys, *salai* 'predominating on the hills. The Chikaldā plateau (excepting 'the civil station) and the forests east and south-east form the 'small Chikaldā and Kohāna reserves, more recently constitu-'ted, and contain little but fuel. Associated with the teak is 'found the small bamboo (*Dendrocalamus strictus*) on northern 'slopes and in all sheltered valleys, but rarely on the level. 'Mixed with teak are more than a hundred common species. '*Sāj* (*Terminalia tomentosa*), *tendū* (*Diospyros Melanoxylon*), *palās* '(*Butea frondosa*) with its brilliant scarlet flowers, the fruit tree '*chār* (*Buchanania latifolia*), some mahuā (*Bassia latifolia*) are 'characteristic trees on low-lying lands. *Dhaurā* (*Anogeissus* '*latifolia*), *lendia* (*Lagerstroemia parviflora*), *tiwas* (*Ougenia dalber-*'*gioides*) and the best bamboo clumps (*Dendrocalamus strictus*) are 'noticeable on lower slopes and plateaux; but it is here also that 'the majority of indigenous species are represented. *Haldū* '(*Adina cordifolia*), often pure, grows to a large size. *Mokā* '(*Schrebera swietenioides*) which yields a manna, *mohin* (*Odina* '*Wodier*) and *bījasāl* (*Pterocarpus Marsupium*) may be mentioned, 'and on the steeper slopes the *kusum* (*Schleichera trijuga*,) whose 'early leaves show brightly on the hillsides in the hot season. 'On poor and rocky ground the *salai* (*Boswellia thurifera*) marks 'the type, associated with *ganiar* (*Cochlospermum Gossypium*) 'and *karai* (*Sterculia urens*) the latter clining to bare rock 'scarps associated with the so-called "*Cactus*," *Euphorbia nerii-*'*folia* (Linn) and the wild plantain (*Musa superba*). Creepers 'are chiefly confined to narrow moist ravines and the lower 'valleys. Of these *mahul* (*Bauhinia Vahlii*) and *gurār* '*Millettia auriculata*) the root of which is used for poisoning 'fish, are most common. On the Chikaldā plateau *Pinus* '*longifolia*, *Grevillea robusta*, *toon* (*Cedrela Toona*), a cypru and '*lantana* (a pest which spread rapidly and choked the forests 'until large sums were spent on its eradication) have been 'introduced.'

254. **System of Management.** The Forest Department was formed in Berâr in 1865 by the appointment of an Assistant Conservator working under the guidance of the Conservator of Forests, Central Provinces,

This officer, however, had little to do with the forests of the then Amraoti District, which were managed under the Waste Land Rules by the Deputy Commissioner. In 1867-68 a Darogā (Forest Ranger) was appointed in charge of these District forests under the immediate and sole orders of the Deputy Commissioner; but the forests continued to be managed exclusively on a revenue basis and were farmed out on yearly leases. The first step towards conservation of the forests was made in 1869 by dividing the forest tracts on the hills east of Amraoti into 5 blocks to be worked in rotation. People were allowed to cut and remove, free of charge, what they liked with the exception of certain specified trees: and even for these nothing more than the Tahsīldār's permission was necessary. Leases were freely given for cultivation till 1870-71, when they were stopped under orders of the Government of India.[1]

In 1880-81, the same tract, 78 square miles in all, was placed under the control of the Forest Department; but the remaining area continued under the management of the Deputy Commissioner. In 1883, the Divisional Forest Officer was put under the orders of the Deputy Commissioner for the management of the District forests; but the sole control in matters of departmental finance and organization and of the State reserves was vested in the Conservator of Forests. In 1884, the position of the Divisional Officer was made that of an assistant in all forest matters to the Deputy Commissioner. He consequently ceased to have any direct official relations with the Conservator; these however, were resumed with certain modifications in 1901.

Melghāt forest.

255. Melghāt forest history is somewhat different from that of the Amraoti Division. The Melghāt came under British rule with the rest of Berār in 1853, when there was no forest administration. Aboriginal Korkūs were scattered over the tract practising *dhyā* cultivation and selling timber in the Berār plains. The first measure of protection was taken in 1858, when under the Commisioner's orders, a red belt was painted round teak trees to prevent unlicensed cutting. In 1864-65

---

1 Revenue and Agricultural Department No. 520, 26th October, 1871.

Colonel Pearson, then Conservator of Forests of the Central Provinces, examined the forests and made proposals for their management. In 1865-66, Captain K. J. L. Mackenzie, then Assistant Commissioner Melghāt, demarcated as reserved about 400 square miles of forest (Bairāgarh reserve) and started protection and regulation of export. It was as a result of Captain Mackenzie's enthusiasm that Mr. Ballantyne who had been trained in the Edinburgh School of Forestry came out to India to take charge of this tract. In 1869 Sir Dietrich Brandis, Inspector General of Forests, inspected the Melghāt forests and drew up a scheme for their management which has formed the basis of all subsequent working. From 1866 indiscriminate felling of trees in the reserve was practically stopped, and from 1870 fire protection was started and by 1872 extended to the entire reserve. In 1874-75 Bairāgarh was divided into 40 blocks for working purposes and the experimental cutting back of unsound teak was started in the Sipnā valley. Extensive tracts of old cultivation along both banks of that river were planted with pure teak. At the same time bamboo cutting was regulated. In 1876-77 the Gugumāl reserve was demarcated and fire protected. Bamboo cutting in both reserves was regulated on a three years' rotation. The area of reserved forest in 1876 was 725 square miles and that of unreserved forest was 927 square miles. In 1880 temporary cultivation on the banks of streams and on the slopes of hills where a plough could not be used, was forbidden and the cutting of bamboos for fodder was also prohibited.

Present management of the District forest.

256. The Berār Forest Law was passed in 1886, and rules for the constitution and management of the various classes of State forests were issued in 1892. Thus according to the rules in force, the A and B class forests of both the divisions of the District are strictly under the control of the Forest Department. It is still laid down that the Divisional Forest Officer is an assistant in forest matters to the Deputy Commissioner, but the latter's authority is rather interpellatory than direct and consists of a right to be informed of measures taken or proposed. Forests of A and B class are in practice managed entirely by the Forest Department, the head of the

District being consulted on such matters as fixing rates of royalty, matters, that is to say, affecting the general population and not of a purely technical nature.

C class forest.

257. Forests of C class, however, stand on a different footing. Scientific forestry is not practised in them. There is considerable timber growth in parts of the Melghāt C class and a few patches in the plains which should have been classified as *bābul bans*: but no attempt is made to conserve or improve these and no check is put upon their wholesale destruction. In A and B class forests, grazing by camels, sheep and goats is forbidden and grazing licenses are separately issued for each particular forest: a C class grazing pass is valid throughout the District. Shooting is permitted in C class under the same rules that apply to Revenue lands; in the Reserves, a special license is required.

There are three sub-classes:—

C i. Forest outside the Melghāt reserved for pasture and ordered not to be resumed during the term of Settlement.

C ii. Do. do. and not ordered not to be resumed during the term of Settlement.

C iii. All pasture forest within the Melghāt.

In practice the difference between the three is that C i. is revenue paying pasture, C ii. (of which there is no longer any in the Amraoti District) free pasture, and C iii. a tract of 656 square miles of inhabited but backward country; the latter contains of course plentiful pasture land which is grazed under the same system as C i, but much of the land has been taken up for cultivation, a thing not generally permitted in the C class elsewhere. The tract includes the whole western portion of the Melghāt as well as the southern foothills and a small area in the pargana of Katkumbh in the east. It was originally forest in the usual sense, and though containing good culturable soil was owing to its extreme unhealthiness but sparsely populated. The policy observed was to attract settlers and open up the country with a view to a regular settlement. The result is that the land has mostly been denuded of valuable timber and an area of 165,934 acres (or 259 miles), paying Rs. 51,015 revenue to Government, has been brought under cultivation. The land is leased out yearly by the Tahsīldār, the unit of assessment being the yoke of sixteen acres. In practice the Forest Department have little or nothing to do with this tract, and preliminaries of settlement in it have recently been commenced. Both here and in the plains where the C class lands are mostly isolated survey number and small blocks of pastures, a somewhat complicated system of dual control is in vogue, which has not worked particularly well. Licenses to cut trees are issued by the Deputy Commisioner with the concurrence in case of certain trees of the Conservator. It lies with the Forest Department, however, to see that concessions are not abused and trees not cut without license. Villages lying in certain blocks of C class have free-grazing rights. Elsewhere patels issue grazing passes from pass books supplied to them by Tahsīldārs and credit the receipts as forest revenue into the sub-treasuries. The pass books are however checked not by the Tahsīldārs who issue them but by officers of the Forest Department, and a lack of systematic co-operation between the two departments has led in the past to a great deal of uncertainty, and, it is to be feared, has opened the door to occasional peculation. The best aspect of the arrangement has been that it gave to village pasture the sanctity attaching to State forests; to bring it under cultivation required the consensus of the Deputy Commissioner, Commissioner and Conservator, the sanction of the Resident and a notice in the Gazette. Even this advantage was cast aside some years ago in an attempt (which has proved fairly successful) to civilize some of the wandering criminal tribes by inducing them to take to agriculture on easy terms. The reorganization of the whole system is in progress. C iii., as already mentioned, is to be brought under settlement; of the C class lands in the plains all blocks less than 160 acres in extent, except such as are capable of being made *bābul bans*, will probably be disforested and made over to the Revenue Department as revenue pasture lands: the remainder are to be managed by the Forest Department alone.

Collection of revenue.

258. The chief sources from which forest revenue is collected are grazing, fodder, and timber; to which may be added

bamboo and other minor produce, firewood and charcoal. Timber which abounds in the Melghāt is practically absent from the Amraoti Division. The firewood, grazing and fodder, however, provided by the latter are closer at hand and more convenient for the villages of the plains. In the Amraoti Division, the *bābul bans*, the grass in pasture lands, gum, mangoes and mahuā are sold by auction, the purchaser undertaking the extraction. Grazing is allowed on annual passes issued by patels for C class forests and by the regular forest staff for A forests. The right of grass and grazing in each *bābul ban* separately is also auctioned separately and prices ranging up to Rs. 5 or Rs. 6 per acre per annum are realised: hence the great value of these apparently insignificant blocks. Other produce is sold on passes at the rates fixed by the Local Administration. The produce of this division is too limited in quantity and inferior in quality to find a way beyond its borders. Existing lines of export consequently merely serve to distribute the produce such as it is over the division itself. In the Melghāt Division timber trees are marked and sold standing to purchasers, who cut and remove the timber to forest depôts, where it is measured and passes are obtained. Bamboos are cut by purchasers in the open compartments under permits, and then exported for sale. Minor produce, as a rule, is collected by purchasers and either sold locally or removed for export to the revenue stations (*nākas*). All such produce, with the exception of certain products, consumed locally is free. Mahuā and mango trees are put up to auction in the village, and the lessee has the right to collect fruit and flowers; the right to collect lac, gum, *harrā* and other commercial products and the right to distil *rūsa* grass oil are usually leased out. Speaking of Melghāt exports Mr. Bartlett says: 'Owing to the distance 'of Bairāgarh and Gugumāl reserves from the Berār plains, 'the forest export is practically restricted to teak and *tiwas* 'timber and bamboos. Of minor produce lac, myrobalans, the 'fruit of the *hilda* and *rūsa* oil are the most important. 'Some firewood is removed from the south of the Gugumāl 'reserve and from Kohāna, but it is from the southern C iii. 'forests (pasture lands where no control is exercised over the 'felling of trees) that the bulk of fuel is exported as well as 'most of the fodder grass and *rūsa* oil. These latter forests 'also supply grazing for the cattle of the majority of the 'plain villages near the border. The demand for fodder grass 'in and around Ellichpur is met by the Hātighāt *ramnah* 'and the Kohāna reserve. The principal markets for timber 'are Ellichpur, Popatkherā and Jhiri Bazār (the latter two 'supplying Akot), and some produce is taken direct to Burhān-'pur and Khandwā. Much of the produce of the C iii. forests 'is consumed locally.'

Minor forest products.[1]

259. Two minor forest products of the Melghāt may be mentioned, lac and *rūsa* oil. Of the former there is a large quantity, but unfortunately the Korkūs regard it as unclean, and cannot be prevailed upon to touch it. The Gond has no scruples about the matter, but is unfortunately ignorant of the best methods of cultivation and gathering. It is proposed to import a few skilled lac-pickers from the north of the Central Provinces and teach them, and it is hoped that the cultivation may then prosper. *Rūsa* on the other hand is freely handled by both tribes. The oil which is used in preparing *itr* and other perfumes is obtained from a variety of the grass *Cymbopogon*[2] *Martini*, which the distillers know as *motia* (or "pearly" alluding to the value of the oil); there is an inferior quality called *sofia* (or "second rate") which yields a pungent oil, and at least two other varieties which are never used for distillation. In the plains of Berār the grass is called *tikhāri*. *Motia* is collected along the southern slopes of the Gāwīlgarh hills and also northwards on the banks of the Tāpti. *Sofia* rules in the centre and at the higher elevations; it also occurs in patches in the midst of *motia* but in no great abundance. The breadth, colour and hang of the leaves are the chief characteristics by which the eye can distinguish the two varieties; the scent is the final test. The grass flowers at the end of the rains, and this is the time for distilling. Stills are erected beside streams up and down the little valleys, and villagers collect the grass. There is then a rush to get the most out of the short time when the work can be done, for the

---

[1] For the information on *Rūsa* we are indebted to Mr I. H. Burkill, Reporter on Economic Products to the Government of India.

[2] *Vel Andropogon.*

fine scent of the grass depreciates alike if kept too long uncut or if stacked too long after cutting. The still owners attempt to compromise both by stacking and by prolonging the time over which the grass is reaped. In the beginning of October one may see a little sun-dried rick of grass ready stacked for use by the side of every still. A distillery consists of a row of cauldrons, usually three or four on a built-up range of fire places at the edge of a stream, and from the cauldrons bamboo pipes pass to receivers submerged in the stream. Two sizes of cauldron rule, one taking more than twice as great a charge as the other ; the best are made of copper, inferior ones of iron. The best receivers have long necks but many distillers work with neckless receivers. The sand and mud of the stream gets in small quantity into the oil, and makes a sediment together with soot and copper oxide from the still. The distilled oils are collected together in Ellichpur and other centres and decanted off the sediment ; thence the chief part finds its way down to Bombay for export to Europe.

Receipts and expenditure.

260. The total revenue derived from the forests of the District in 1890-1891 was Rs. 272,817. In 1900-01, however, owing to the famine it was Rs. 97,360 less than this figure. Even in that year, as the following table shows, the forests more than paid their way, ending with a substantial margin of close on three-quarters of a lakh in hand. In subsequent years, the revenue of the Amraoti Division has steadily increased, while that of Melghāt also has shown an immense improvement. By far the largest item of Amraoti revenue is, as might be expected, grazing and fodder, the largest in the Melghāt being timber.

The following table shows Forests receipts and expenditure in the Amraoti District :—

Year.	Timber.		Firewood and Charcoal.		Bamboos.		Grazing and Fodder Grass.		Minor Produce.		Total.		Total Expenditure.		Surplus.	
	Amraoti.	Melghāt.	Amraoti.	Melghāt.	Amraoti.	Melghāt.	Amraoti.	Melghāt.	Amraoti.	Melghāt.	Amraoti.	Melghāt.	Amraoti.	Melghāt.	Amraoti.	Melghāt.
	Rs.	Rs.	Rs.	Rs.	Rs.	Rs.	Rs.	Rs.	Rs.	Rs.	Rs.	Rs.	Rs.	Rs.	Rs.	Rs.
1890–91	123	1,22,757	19,643	11,397	3	47,187	48,277	14,801	4,828	3,486	72,874	1,99,628	9,824	69,183	63,050	1,30,445
1900–01 a	1,133	55,803	18,280	9,434	136	26,727	38,730	11,778	2,186	10,935	60,465	1,14,677	21,983	84,318	38,482	30,359
1901–02	527	92,740	15,669	19,882	302	36,754	52,119	17,782	4,271	11,975	72,888	1,79,133	17,664	73,611	55,224	1,05,522
1902–03	477	80,007	15,770	15,702	489	28,781	71,580	20,202	4,280	23,103	92,596	1,67,795	21,105	74,669	71,491	93,126
1903–04	758	83,315	13,858	13,616	1,241	34,896	82,292	25,122	6,259	17,794	1,04,408	1,74,743	27,649	87,326	76,759	87,417
1904–05	350	81,758	18,623	18,653	695	27,944	86,243	26,998	6,434	18,858	1,12,345	1,74,211	32,937	76,570	79,408	97,641
1905–06	58	99,821	18,638	17,664	22	32,852	93,478	26,397	7,138	17,887	1,19,334	1,94,621	36,001	74,320	83,333	1,20,301
1906–07	143	95,535	22,490	17,056	13	34,276	94,556	23,105	7,584	15,785	1,24,786	1,85,757	33,741	80,214	91,045	1,05,543
1907–08 b	50	78,907	12,957	7,355	92	31,058	96,072	32,338	6,737	15,618	1,15,908	1,65,276	38,263	86,678	77,645	78,598

(a) 1900 was a famine year. (b) Rainfall short.

261. Of the total area of 1758 square miles of the District forest, 903 square miles (69 from A forests and the whole of C forests) is open for grazing to all animals all the year round. The remaining area of 791 square miles of A forest (780 from Melghāt and 11 from Amraoti) is closed for grazing to all animals except those belonging to forest villagers which can be grazed only on an area of 774 square miles of the Melghāt A reserve. It is estimated that 389,678 head of cattle grazed in 1906-07.

Area closed and open to grazing.

262. The District does not contain any private forests. There is, however, in most villages of the five plain tāluks of the District some area—apart from that occupied by the Government forests—set aside for free grazing. Many of these so-called grazing lands are in reality dense *bābul* thickets and consequently of little use for pasture. Such area amounted to 44,275 acres in 1906-07; the whole of the former C ii. forest has been included in this area. The Melghāt jāgīrs contain some 51,032 acres of land under forest, but it is of little importance.

Private Forests.

263. Of 236 miles of road in the District controlled by the Public Works Department 99¼ have complete avenues, 46¾ miles have avenues that still contain gaps, 2¾ miles have been lately planted with young trees and 87 miles have no avenues. Parts of the Amraoti-Ellichpur and Amraoti-Morsi roads are well shaded, but as a rule, the avenues are very poor. The District Board maintains small avenues of about seven miles in all, and the Amraoti Camp Municipality has also a few miles. In Ellichpur civil station are one or two very fine avenues, especially one known as 'the Mall.' The trees most usually planted are *nīm*, mango, mahuā, tamarind and various members of the fig tribe.

Roadside Arboriculture.

MINERALS.

264. No mines are worked in the District nor is it at all likely that any of importance will be discovered. The brackish water of the Daryāpur tāluk discloses the presence of considerable

Minerals.

quantities of salt below the surface, and in former days a small amount of salt-drying was locally carried on and the product was even one of the exports of Berār. At a hill known as Gulāl Tekri, about a mile north of Dabheri (Morsi tāluk), and in the Amraoti hills iron ore of laterite origin is said to be obtainable, but is not turned to any account. Considerable masses of Gondwāna sandstone crop out along the southern face of the Gāwīlgarh hills, and the stone which is extremely fine might be much more used for building than it is. The old fort at Karasgaon, the city walls and the magnificent tombs of the Nawābs at Ellichpur are of sandstone. Besides this the trap of which both the hill ranges of the District are largely composed, makes very durable building stone as exemplified in the town walls of Amraoti as well as many of the new public buildings, and good though by no means perfect road metal. *Muram* (a softer road metal but better for light traffic), earth, sand and lime are also quarried. Some manganese ore was once found at Pimpalkhūta in the Morsi tāluk:[1] but the result of local inquiry was to show that the broken fragments of ore which had been found at a short depth beneath the surface inside the village had been brought from some unknown localities by former inhabitants. Similarly there is a block of excellent coal in the Geological Museum at Calcutta said to come from a ravine near Chikaldā: but nothing further is known about it. Its history is probably very similar. The annual outturn of minerals, chiefly trap, *muram*, etc., is insignificant and is included under the heading 'minor produce' in the Forest Accounts already given.

---

1 V. Ball Manual of the Geology of India, Part III. Economic Geology, page 331 (1881).

CHAPTER VII.

FAMINE.

265. Amraoti has no separate famine history prior to the cession in 1853, but there are various references to famines in Berār, which may be taken to include this District. In the reign of Muhammad Shāh Bahmanī (1378-1397) Berār, in common with the rest of the Deccan, was devastated by a terrible famine, and the orphanage established by that sovereign at Ellichpur is one of the earliest recorded attempts to mitigate such a disaster. It is highly improbable that the province escaped the famine of 1417, which affected the greater part of the Deccan. Again in 1472-73 Mālwā and the Deccan including Berār were wasted by a famine which lasted for 2 years and caused wholesale emigration to Bengal and Gujarāt. In 1630-31, the fourth year of the reign of Shāh Jahān, there was a terrible famine throughout Gujarāt, Khāndesh, Berār, and the Province of Daulatābād. Tradition has it that the flesh of dogs was sold by butchers as goats' flesh, crushed bones of the dead were mingled with the flour exposed for sale, and parents devoured their children. The famine of 1803 was remembered 50 years afterward and Berār did not escape the famine of 1833 which caused considerable distress. In the great famine of 1839 the distress was very great and no measures of relief were attempted by the native government. The extensive emigration, which took place at this period, must have been a powerful factor in reducing the District to its poor condition at the time of the Assignment in 1853. In 1845 there was distress caused by the high price of juāri, which rose from Rs. 5 to Rs. 20 a *khandī*, and the enraged populace of Amraoti murdered one Dhanrāj Sāhu, a wealthy trader, who had bought up large quantities of rice with a view to obtain large profits. In 1853 Amraoti with the rest of Berār came

Early famines.[1]

[1] This chapter deals with the Amraoti and Ellichpur Districts, as constituted prior to their amalgamation.

under British rule and there ensued a period of prosperity only broken by the prevalence of high prices in the year 1878 and 1879. So remote did the idea of famine seem that in 1893 the Commissioner felt justified in reporting that a programme of relief works was not required for Berār. This optimistic attitude was to receive a rude shock during the next decade.

Famine in the plain tāluks, 1896-97.

266. The season of 1895-96 had been one of scanty rainfall, only 24 inches 8 cents being recorded, but a bumper crop of cotton was reaped and except for the deficiency in the water-supply the condition of the people up to June 1896 was quite satisfactory. The rains of 1896 opened very favourably and by the beginning of August everything pointed to a bumper crop of cotton and juār. But suddenly and inexplicably the rains ceased about the 25th August and beyond a fall of 3 inches in November no rain of any value fell again till June 1897. The total rainfall of the year was 34 inches 12 cents. The result of the sudden cessation of the rains was that the *rabi* crop, owing to the lack of moisture, was almost a total failure. But the important crops of this District are cotton and juār, and these, though much below the average, shewed fair results, a rough estimate putting them at half a normal crop. Had Berār been an isolated tract dependent on its own resources, it is probable that in the plain tāluks there would have been no famine. But unfortunately the general failure of the monsoon throughout India affected Berār by causing a sudden rise of prices, which paralysed local trade for the time being. Juāri rose from 19 seers in the rupee to 12 seers in October 1896 and varied from 10 to 7 seers from November 1896 to October 1897. Wheat rose from 13 seers to 8 seers in October 1896 and remained at about 7 seers from November 1896 to October 1897. It was realized that some distress was inevitable, the Bombay Famine Code was therefore applied, and a programme of relief works was prepared. A sum of Rs. 33,000 was spent on relief works which consisted principally of stone-breaking, road-making and tank repairs, and the percentage of persons thus relieved to the total population was 0·9 only. Gratuitous relief was mainly given by means of poor-houses and

relief-centres. Ten poor-houses were maintained with a daily average attendance of 2270 and the total expenditure in connection with them was Rs. 16,238. Weekly doles were also given to a number of old and infirm persons; and the distress among the weavers of Ellichpur and Anjangaon was met in this way. The opening of cheap grain shops also afforded relief to a number of poor but respectable people. The measures of Government were largely supplemented by the efforts of private charity, which was especially active in this District. A poor-house was maintained at Amraoti by private subscriptions at a cost of over Rs. 8000. A sum of Rs. 35,000 was also raised in the District in connection with the Indian Charitable Relief Fund, and from charitable funds of all kinds the large sum of Rs. 76,000 was spent. The famine operations were complicated by a sudden inrush of paupers from the Central Provinces in July and August 1897. Many of these arrived in an emaciated condition, and there was a considerable mortality from starvation among them, though every effort was made by means of poor-houses and village relief to meet the difficulty. The death-rate of the District compared favourably with that of the previous year till April 1897, when it began to rise and in August and September it reached its highest monthly average of 8 per mille. Cholera prevailed in April and May and in the rains dysentery and diarrhœa of a severe type were common. The District death-rate for 1897 was 59.4 per mille. The cultivators were not severely affected by the distress; the high prices obtained by them for their crops enabled them to pay the land revenue with ease, 99 per cent. of the demand being paid, and the presence of a large number of labourers gave them the opportunity of making many cheap improvements in their land. The class that suffered most from the high prices was the class of agricultural labourers, who form 30 per cent. of the population; for not only did they have to pay more for their food, but their wages were reduced by the competition of workers, who flocked in from the neighbouring Provinces.

1899-1900.

267. In the season of 1897-98 the rainfall amounted to 32 inches and 18 cents or more than 8 inches below the average of the previous ten years. The *kharīf* crops were everywhere

excellent but there was not enough moisture in the soil for *rabi* crops. The juāri crop was one of the finest ever known, and the general price of the grain fell to about 20 seers for the rupee. The season of 1898-99 was also one of short rainfall, the average for the District being 21 inches 26 cents or 14 inches 3 cents less than the average of the preceding ten years. The juāri harvest was again good and the price of this grain fell to about 27 seers per rupee; as in the previous year the *rabi* crops were inferior. Thus by the spring of 1899, the stock of the chief food grain had been replenished by two good harvests in succession, and the condition of the people was generally good. The effect of four years of deficient rainfall however began to be felt on the water-supply, and the scarcity of drinking water caused much inconvenience and distress. The season of 1899-1900 opened fairly well in June, an average rainfall of 3·84 being recorded; but the average for July was 2.97 inches and for August 2.46 inches only, and the rains ceased altogether in the third week of September. The result was a complete failure of both the *kharīf* and *rabi* crops. The normal outturn of the principal food crops, juāri and wheat, for the preceding ten years, exclusive of 1896-97, had been about 35 lakhs of maunds; the actual outturn of 1899-1900 was about 14,000 maunds. The loss represented by this difference is estimated to have been about 164 lakhs of rupees. At the end of September the price of the staple food grain, juāri, went up to famine point, selling at 13 to 15 seers a rupee. It rose in October to 9½ seers and fluctuated between 11 and 8½ seers from November 1899 to May 1900, when there was a further rise, and the highest price reached was 7½ seers in July 1900. From August 1900 the price began to fall again but it did not reach the normal till some months later. But for the large imports of Bengal and Rangoon rice at the beginning of the famine the price would have gone still higher.

Relief works.

268. At the end of September 1899 the imminence of famine was realized and test works were opened at once. The test works proved the existence of famine conditions, and in November large relief works under the charge of the Public Works

Department were opened. These works mainly consisted of stone metal collections, constructions of new roads and repairs existing roads, carriage of stone metal from quarries to roadside, construction of new tanks, and cleaning of old tanks. Each work formed a separate charge under a civil officer, whose duties were administrative, while the Public Works Department supplied the technical knowledge. Altogether 44 works were opened, the maximum open at one time being 27 in July 1900. The number of workers varied from 6000 to 7000 during the quarter ending November 1899; by April the number reached 46,000, and in June the panic caused by the holding off of the rains sent the numbers up to 48,000. In July there was a rapid decrease and by the end of September there were only 1112 people on the works. The total expenditure on the works was nearly 11 lakhs of rupees, whereas their cost at normal rates would have been only 4½ lakhs. The cause of this high cost is ascribed to the necessity of employing much ineffective labour, such as children and weakly persons, and also to the existence of a minimum wage. With the exception of four roads in the Ellichpur tāluk, of which the earth work only was done, the works were all of permanent utility. The total number of units relieved was 11,593,810 and the incidence per head was 1 anna ten pies.

Village works.

269. In June 1900, when the rains set in, the policy of opening village works with a view to affording temporary employment to people near their homes until there should be labour in the fields was adopted. The work done consisted chiefly of improvement to village sites and local roads, and the collection of *kankar* (limestone nodules) for road repairs. The carrying of stone metal from the large works to roadsides was also made available for village works, and many of these works were located so as to serve circles or blocks of neighbouring villages. Such works were conducted under more or less supervision from the establishment of the Public Works Department and the District Boards; but it was difficult to exact adequate tasks, and the value of the work done was not high. The maximum number of workers was 25,000 in July 1900. The total number of units relieved was

1,086,137 and the expenditure was Rs. 1,04,608, giving an incidence of 1 anna 6 pies per head.

270. In the old Ellichpur District special measures for the relief of the weaving community were found necessary and the Nāgpur system was adopted. Advances were made to middlemen who were supposed to employ none but distressed weavers, and the cloth manufactured was purchased by Government from the middlemen at prices slightly in excess of the market rates. The total expenditure was Rs. 17,000 and out of this Rs. 13,000 were recovered by the sale of cloth.

Relief to weavers.

271. The gratuitous relief given fell under three main heads, namely:—

Gratuitous relief.

(*a*) Relief of non-working children and other dependents of relief workers on large works.

(*b*) Grain doles or cooked food given to persons eligible under the Famine Code.

(*c*) Relief in poor-houses.

(*a*) At the beginning of the famine cash allowances were paid to dependents, but, as soon as they could be organized, kitchens were attached to every large work. The number of dependents so relieved reached its maximum figure, 15,000, in May 1900; of which 86 per cent. were children. The total units of dependents relieved were 2,151,068 and the expenditure was Rs. 78,544, giving the incidence of cost per head as 7 pies.

(*b*) The gratuitous dole was given in grain to certain classes, who were incapable of working and had no means of support, and also to a certain number of the village servants who had their ordinary duties to perform. Emaciation was always accepted as proof of eligibility for the dole. The dole was distributed through the agency of the village officers assisted by local committees and in municipalities under the municipal authorities. The relief lists were strictly examined and controlled for some time, but during the hot weather and rains the expansion of such relief was inevitable. The total of units so relieved was 22,88,596 at an expenditure of Rs. 1,71,380, with an incidence of cost per unit of 1 anna 2 pies. Before the rains of 1900 there had been 30 State kitchens open in the District but during the rains the number went up to 231. Each kitchen was expected to serve an area of 2 to 3 miles. They were under the same supervision and control as the relief dole and were used principally by children. The total number of units relieved was 3,040,367 at an expenditure of Rs. 1,64,332 or an incidence of 10 pies per head.

(*c*) Fourteen poor-houses were opened in the District. They were frequented by the lower castes, the infirm, beggars and children. The inmates were so largely persons broken down by disease and wanderers brought in at a stage when no relief could save them that the poor-houses may be regarded almost as infirmaries. The poor-house population was kept down by drafting inmates to relief works, as they became fit for labour and transferring others for gratuitous relief in their villages. The total number of units relieved was 841,899 at an expenditure of Rs. 62,152, or an incidence of 8 annas 2 pies per head.

Indirect relief.

272. Instructions were issued to Tahsīldārs that the land revenue should be collected only from persons able to pay it and that nobody should be driven to borrow in order to pay the assessment. At the close of July 1900, out of a demand of about 27½ lakhs only a little over 6 lakhs remained uncollected. Of this amount about Rs. 38,000 were remitted in the ensuing year. The Famine Commission condemned the relief as altogether insufficient and also remarked that the procedure of enquiry into the circumstances of individuals should never be followed in times of famine. During the years 1899-1900 and 1900-01 loans amounting to Rs. 1,47,421 under the Land Improvement Loans Act were advanced to cultivators; also petty advances amounting to Rs. 5410 were made to poor cultivators free of interest.

Charitable relief.

273. The Famine Commission make a special reference to the remarkable degree of success which was attained in this District in the organization of private charity. Twenty-seven poor-houses were maintained by private subscriptions, and the expenditure on the village dole in the Chāndur tāluk was nearly all met from the same source. Gifts of clothing and cooked and uncooked food were also frequently made by private persons. In the

Ellichpur tāluk grain funds were organized under the supervision of village committees. A number of private gentlemen and traders also helped the poor by the distribution of cooked food and made liberal gifts to poor-houses. The missionaries as usual were active in relieving distress and spent Rs. 76,000 on various forms of relief. The Roman Catholic Mission and the Christian Missionary Alliance were at work in the old Amraoti District, the Daughters of the Cross at Amraoti visiting relief camps in all weathers, dispensing medicines and tending the sick. In the old Ellichpur District the Korku and Central India Mill Mission gave employment to a number of the distressed Ellichpur weavers, purchasing cloth from them at low rates. They also maintained an asylum at Kothāria for distressed lepers, and the number in the asylum was at one time 200. A liberal grant of Rs. 2,40,231 was made from the Indian Charitable Relief Fund; of this Rs. 21,000 were devoted to providing the inmates of poor-houses and kitchens with clothes and other necessaries, Rs. 21,000 were spent on relief to the respectable poor and Rs. 1,13,521 were devoted to assisting cultivators, who for want of security could not obtain loans from Government, with seed, bullocks, fodder, etc. This latter form of relief was of the utmost value and as a direct result of this assistance 89,500 acres of land are estimated to have been sown, which would otherwise have remained waste.

Cattle and fodder.

274. Berār cultivators formerly had an unfortunate habit in the monsoon of getting rid of the stacks of *karbī* left on their hands by burning them down after green grass had sprung up. The cattle thus had nothing to depend upon except grass until the next juāri crop was ready, and, when, as in 1899, both juāri and grass failed, heavy mortality among the cattle was inevitable. Many owners of cattle were compelled either to sell their cattle at nominal prices or to send them into the Melghāt, where fodder was ample. But the steep and stony hillsides of the Melghāt did not suit the cattle of the plains and they perished in large numbers there. Every effort was made by the Forest Department to meet the fodder difficulty. From the 8th September the Melghāt reserves covering an area of 808 square miles were thrown open to free grazing.

The 'A' and 'B' reserves of the plains were divided into a series of three blocks and opened in rotation for grazing. It is estimated that 85,427 tons of grass were removed by private exporters from the forest reserves of the District. Government grass-cutting operations were started in the Melghāt. Grass was collected to the amount of 5,437,882 lbs. and stacked at 19 sale depôts in the Melghāt, and when it was found that there was a keen demand for grass delivered in the plains, 3 more depôts were opened there. These operations, though resulting in a small financial loss, greatly helped in saving the plough cattle and also afforded useful employment in the way of famine relief to large numbers of the labouring population. But, in spite of all the efforts made to save the cattle, it is estimated that in the old Amraoti District 53 per cent. and in the old Ellichpur District 60 per cent. of the total number perished.

Public health and crime.

275. In the earlier months of the famine period the mortality per mensem was less than usual, and it increased gradually till April. From May it rose rapidly, till in August it reached the highest point, viz. 11·2 per mille in the old Amraoti District and 10·1 per mille in the old Ellichpur District. The average for the same month in the previous ten years had been 4 per mille. From September 1900 the death-rate fell gradually till it reached the normal again in January 1901. The year 1900 was unusually unhealthy apart from the famine. The severe drought made water and vegetables scarce ; when the rains broke, people drank foul water and ate too much rank green stuff. The consumption of old and unwholesome juāri, which had been stored for years in pits, also caused a great deal of sickness. Deaths from starvation were very few, and such isolated cases as there were, were found to be wandering immigrants from other Provinces. The birth-rate showed a marked decrease from 40 per mille to 31, a natural result of the disorganization of domestic life caused by the famine and of the impaired vitality of the poorer classes. At the beginning of the famine the sudden rise of prices caused a panic and several small grain riots were committed with the object of preventing the export of food grains and compelling the dealers to sell their stocks. Offences against property

naturally increased but the crime was not of a serious nature and considering the circumstances of the year may be said to have been surprisingly small.

Effects of the famine and history of succeeding years.

276. The District showed remarkable recuperative powers. At the close of the measures for famine relief it was found that the full normal area was under crop, that the labouring classes were earning high wages and that the public health was unusually good. In the year after the famine it was difficult to detect signs of the recent calamity. Two good years ensued followed by seven of no more than moderate crops, in one of which (1907-08) the harvest was not more than half the average, and detailed enquiries into the desirability of suspensions of revenue were necessitated. These enquiries showed that the loss of half the crops could be borne without any remission and without a serious increase of indebtedness. The high prices obtained for cotton have brought a great deal of wealth into the District, and it is improbable that a single bad year would cause serious distress among the mass of the cultivators. Labourers, forming the most numerous class even in this land of small farmers, have gained immensely by the rise in the rates of wages, more than compensating for the great dearness of food, but they are not accustomed to save against the chance of a failure of rains and consequent curtailment of employment, and their position would be most serious in the event of famine. The provision of fodder for cattle forms a great difficulty in years of scanty rainfall, and this is accentuated by the partial substitution of cotton for juāri which has taken place. Cultivators realize this but are only in part able to sacrifice the certainty of a good money return for their cotton to provide against a mere possibility of failure of fodder for their cattle.

Famine in the Melghāt. 1896-97.

277. The famine history of the Melghāt, differing as it does in every respect from the rest of the District, requires a separate notice. This tract is populated almost entirely by the aboriginal Korkūs and similar tribes, a people of the poorest description, shy and diffident, living from hand to mouth, with no resources and extremely averse to any work

except fitful labour in the forests. The prosperity of the tract depends on three factors in the following order of importance; first, prosperity in Berār and consequently a good demand for Melghāt forest produce; secondly, a good crop of cereals locally; and thirdly, a good season for wild fruit. It is estimated that one-fourth of the population live for a greater part of the year on the profits of converting and selling timber and other forest produce. At the close of the rains in 1896 the distress in the plain tāluks caused the demand for timber to fall considerably, and the Melghāt exporters found their income from this source reduced to one-fourth of the normal. Moreover the local harvests in the Melghāt had been bad for three or four years previously, and in 1895 there had been a partial failure of crops. In 1896 the early cessation of the rains produced a total failure of the crops on the light red shallow soils, which form the bulk of the cultivated area; though the black soil area, which principally lies in one block of eighty villages, is said to have given a 6 to 8 anna crop. There was also a rapid rise in the prices of food-grains, which by November 1896 were double the normal. Thus at the close of 1896 the Korkū with no stock of grain to draw on and with no market for his forest produce found himself face to face with starvation. Small bands of them began to appear in the plains seeking for work, a sure sign of distress. Luckily the situation was realized by the Forest Department, in whose hands the administration of the Melghāt rested, and in December 1896 measures were taken to cope with the distress.

Relief works.

278. Large relief works were not considered suitable to the peculiar condition of the Melghāt with its scattered population and defective water-supply. With a people too, who hate steady work under supervision, it was felt that the application of the strict letter of the Famine Code was inexpedient. A free hand was therefore given to the Forest Department to modify the Code to meet the requirements of the case. Small and scattered works were opened; exact tasks were not laid down, but the officers in charge by moral suasion and patience tried to exact a fair day's work from the labourers; wages in cash were paid sufficient to support the worker and his dependents,

and the workers were allowed to go away on Sundays to take the savings or the equivalent in food to their dependents in their villages. As there were no stocks of grain in the tract, food for the workers had to be imported from the plains. Baniās were assisted by the payment of carriage from Ellichpur and a small commission, and in return they guaranteed an unfailing supply at the current rates prevailing in Ellichpur weekly bazar. In anticipation of the rains, when private traders fail, Government imported and stored large quantities of grain and sold the same during the rains at the rates current in the plains. Most of the relief works consisted of road construction, but in addition wells were deepened, tanks cleaned and roads repaired. The total amount spent was Rs. 76,693 and for this sum 137 miles of forest cart roads, 6 miles of hauling roads and 2 miles of bridle roads were completed. All the works were of permanent utility, and the cost is estimated to have been about 30 per cent. above the normal. The highest number on the works was 4553 in July 1897, and 578,986 units of work-people were relieved at a cost of 2 annas 1 pie per unit relieved.

Gratuitous relief.

279. Actual relief in the home of the people was not attempted but villages were constantly inspected with a view to the discovery of the absolutely destitute. Their case was met by the establishment of about 20 relief centres consisting of depots at which food was given in the shape of uncooked grain. The people cooked their own food and the majority occupied huts on the spot. The average attendance of each centre was about 200. Only those appearing quite incapable of work were given doles.

Indirect relief.

280. The Forest Department encouraged the export of forest produce by making liberal concessions. The duty on headloads of firewood was suspended; the rates for small and inferior timber, for bamboos and for charcoal were reduced, and grazing fees were remitted except in 23 of the more prosperous villages. Cheap grain shops were opened at numerous centres, a system of tickets being adopted with a maximum amount of daily sale to one person or family. Out

of a land-revenue demand of Rs. 43,000 it was found expedient to remit Rs. 23,000.

Private charity.

281. Most valuable assistance was given by the Korkū and Central India Hill Mission, which spent upwards of Rs. 50,000, while two members of the Mission lost their lives through overwork and exposure. The Roman Catholic Mission also did good work. At the end of the famine in July 1897 a sum of Rs. 53,574 was granted from the Indian Famine Charitable Relief Fund and this sum was devoted to rehabilitating the cultivator by gifts of seed grain and plough bullocks.

General remarks.

282. It is probable that nearly 25 per cent. of the Melghāt population were being relieved in one way or another—either on works, or by cheap grain shops, or in poor-houses and mission centres. The condition of the people was very bad, and, but for the strenuous efforts of the Forest Department the mortality from starvation would have been extremely high. As no mortality returns are maintained in the Melghāt it is impossible to say what the death-rate was, but it is admitted that it was high, especially among the old and the children. This was partly due to the apathy and ignorance of a jungle people, who had never seen famine relief in operation before. Cholera of a virulent type was also prevalent for some time. The Famine Commission recognised the success of the famine operations and concluded that the mortality was probably unavoidable; but they suggested that it might be possible to achieve more success by strengthening the village inspection organization and by extending the system of gratuitous home relief.

1899-1900.

283. The harvest in 1897 was below normal in consequence of the famine of 1896-97. In 1898 the area sown and outturn were generally normal, but a portion of the tract was still suffering from the effects of the famine. In 1899 the rainfall from June to September was only 19 inches or 33 per cent. of the average, and the regular rains stopped at the end of July. The result was a complete failure of the crops. The aboriginal inhabitants were in even a worse position than in 1897, as the distress in the plain tāluks was much severer,

no field work was available and the sales of forest produce practically ceased. In September 1899 relief measures were sanctioned.

284. As in the previous famine small works distributed as equally as possible over the tract were the leading feature of the programme. The works undertaken consisted of road-making and repairing, the improvement of a few tanks and wells, and the digging of fields to take the place of ploughing for which bullocks were insufficient. When the rains drew near, the people were sent to their homes either to cultivate or to petty works. Cultivators were given grain doles while cultivating their own fields, relief of this kind being given to over 4000 families from seed-time to harvest. The grass-cutting operations, which were started by the Conservator of Forests in September 1899, also indirectly afforded considerable relief. These operations consisted of cutting and storing grass at selected depôts for sale and at cattle camps, where there was water, in and near the forests, to feed cattle in the summer of 1900 when the grazing near water would be exhausted. Grass was collected to the amount of 54,37,882 lbs. and stacked at 19 depôts in the Melghāt. By this means work for 2025 labourers was provided for 93 days.

Relief works.

285. Gratuitous relief took the form of grants of doles in villages, relief in poor-houses, and relief to dependents on works. The dole was given in money. Village relief was at its maximum in July 1900. Three poor-houses were opened in December 1899 and the highest number using them was 1773 in July 1900 ; they were all in charge of European missionaries.

Gratuitous relief.

286. To stimulate the private export of timber, grass, bamboos, etc., every facility was given in all the easily accessible forests and rates for timber and bamboos were lowered. Out of a total land-revenue demand of Rs. 34,495, the sum of Rs. 26,907 was suspended.

Indirect relief.

287. The Korkū and Central India Hill Mission again gave valuable help in men and money, and spent nearly 1½ lakhs on various forms of relief. The Indian Charitable Relief Fund gave a

Private charity.

munificent grant of Rs. 72,000; of this Rs. 8000 were spent on the purchase of clothing and other necessaries, Rs. 5000 in providing for orphans and Rs. 59,000 in assisting cultivators with seed and plough bullocks.

General remarks.

288. The maximum number on relief at one time was 13,000 or 28 per cent. of the population, the daily average number of persons relieved was 7297 or 15 per cent. of the population. The mortality was not high and was certainly lower among children than in 1897. Emaciation was far less frequently seen. The Famine Commission in their Report describe the administration of relief in the Melghāt as one of the successful episodes of the famine. They say that judged by the ultimate test of lives saved the operations, though somewhat costly, were successful, and they emphasize the importance of providing suitable work for aborigines and of employing in the relief of them officials whom they can trust.

History of succeeding years.

289. In spite of the liberal measures of relief adopted in the way of distributing seed and cattle many villages with poor soil and defective water-supply were deserted, and the revenue history of a considerable portion of the Melghāt may be said to start afresh from the years following the famine. In view of the deterioration of the tract the land revenue was reduced by half for three years (1902-1905). This wise measure of relief has been amply justified, as the subsequent history of the tract has been one of steady progress and prosperity interrupted only by slight distress in 1907-08, when it was found necessary to suspend Rs. 32,000 of the land-revenue demand. As already pointed out, the Melghāt population is only partially dependent upon its crops for its well-being and famine will not as a rule follow a failure of crops unless this is accompanied by a falling-off in the demand for forest produce in the Berār plains.

CHAPTER VIII.

LAND REVENUE ADMINISTRATION.

Early revenue administration. Pre-Muhammadan period.

290. The aboriginal unit was in Berār, as throughout India, the village. Into the vexed question of the nature of the early village community it is not necessary to enter here, complicated as that question is by the difficulty of describing in terms of civilized thought the half conscious reasonings or instincts of savages and in India by the unreliable nature of the evidence. Of the differences between the primitive Dravidian and the primitive Aryan village, of the early growth of law and the subsequent growth of a quasi-feudal society in India we really know absolutely nothing. The latter process seems to have been at least accelerated in Berār by the successive invasions, and their resulting overlordships. The Indian village has in a crystallized form survived them all, and into the successive types of rule its headman or patel has always been adopted as an integral part. Whatever the group may have been that settled the early village, whether a family or some still more formless thing, and whether it enslaved or not the aboriginals whom it may have found, certainly it had not attained to a conception either of individual property or of property in land. Cultivation was co-operative and the fruits were divided, each man receiving according to the position he bore in the village or the nature of his services to it. Thus the headman and other magnates appropriated their shares and the servants were recompensed for their service. Thus also was tribute yielded to the still greater chieftain under whose leadership they had entered the land, or under whose dominion they had fallen: a tribute which, becoming fixed by tradition at one-sixth though frequently raised by unscrupulous rulers to a higher proportion, has become the parent of modern land revenue and incidentally of the supreme rights of the State in land. As time passed the cumbrous process of sharing the harvest gave way to the expedient of dividing the soil. The more powerful

members of the village body became land-holders and because the chief village offices were connected with such holdings the Muhammadan word *watan* has acquired its peculiar local significance of heritable village office and dignity. A more complicated society supervened and the need for records and accounts produced the patwāri. Further, in each village out of those who were unable to attain the dignity of landownership, there grew up a staff of artizans, menials and servants, who became hereditary and served the villages, not for payment by the job (such a thing was of course unknown), but for a regular remuneration, paid in kind, chiefly as of old by a fixed share in the harvest. This ancient village community is the prototype of the modern Berār ryotwāri village.

Early Muhammadan period. 1294 A. D.—1596 A. D.

291. We possess no detailed information about the earliest method of Moslem revenue management, but the policy seems to have been to preserve the older village institutions. The hereditary offices of Deshmukh and Deshpāndia are supposed by some writers to owe their origin to this period, but it is a very doubtful supposition. The Deshmukh was a head patel of a circle of villages and was responsible for apportioning and collecting the land revenue, while the Deshpāndia was a head patwāri or *kānungo*, and kept the accounts. They were always Hindus, the Deshmukh generally a Kunbī and the Deshpāndia a Brāhman, and they may have been instituted by the Muhammadans to conciliate a conquered people. An interesting description of this period may be quoted from Sir A. Lyall. 'If we take the centuries between 1300 and '1600 A.D. as the period (roughly stated) of independent 'Muhammadan dominion in the Dakhan, and compare it 'with the same breadth of time in Western Europe, the 'Dakhani government will not lose much by comparison. 'We shall be struck by resemblances more than by contrasts 'in all that concerns civil policy and the use made of their 'arbitrary power by princes and lords of the land. Long 'wasting wars, bloody feuds, revolts, massacres, assassinations, 'cruel and barbarous punishments, sad stories of the death

of kings—all these things fill the chronicles of Plantagenets 'and Valois as plentifully as the annals of the Bahmanis. 'Yet, as has often been said, although these descriptions now 'startle us into horror and astonishment, it may be guessed 'that life in those times was more tolerable than it appears to 'modern readers. A majority of the people took no share at 'all in the constant fighting, or in the perilous intrigues which 'were continually exploding in violent catastrophes that shook 'or overturned the throne; while another section of the people 'enjoyed the stirring life and chances of rebellion, and staked 'their lives on the sport quite as readily as men now risk 'their limbs against a tiger. For Berār, it seems to have 'been always an agricultural country, situated off the high 'road of foreign armies, and distant from the capitals of 'royalty. It suffered like other districts from inroads and 'internal disorders, but its battle-fields are comparatively 'not numerous. Then the settled Muhammadan government 'always attempted, in the interests of revenue, to protect the 'tillers of the land, keeping the collections as much as possible 'in their own hands, except when jāgīrs were granted, and 'never formally abandoning the cultivator to the mercy of 'a feudal lord. We may conjecture that the peasantry as a 'class were much above the mediæval serfs and villeins of 'Europe; and altogether that they were at least as well off 'under the Bahmanī and Imād Shāhi rulers as the commons 'of any outlying counties of England during the great wars of 'the fourteenth and fifteenth centuries. Probably the peasants 'of France were worse off up to the end of the 17th century. 'Certainly the *sūbah* of Berār was in a high state of 'cultivation, and yielded an ample revenue when Akbar 'annexed it; and the land must have prospered still more 'under the wise administration of Malik Ambar, of whom more 'hereafter. In those ages the whole Deccan swarmed with 'adventurers from every nation in Asia, and from the 'African coast of the Indian Ocean. These men and their 'descendants settled in the towns, their chiefs occupied most 'of the high military and civil offices; but, in Berār at least, 'the Muhammadans appear to have left the Hindus in undis-

'turbed possession of the soil. And although the hereditary 'revenue authorities, the Deshmukhs and Deshpăndias who 'were chief officers of districts with much influence and profit, 'are said to have been instituted by the early Muhammadan 'kings; yet in Berăr these places and perquisites have from 'time immemorial been in the hands of Hindus.'

Mughal period, 1596 A.D. to 1720 A.D.

292. Berăr was ceded to the Emperor Akbar in 1596 A.D. and was one of the *sūbahs* which came under the famous land revenue settlement made by him and his Hindu minister Todar Mal. The early Hindu system had been one without any survey or measurement and without any records to speak of. The Mughal rulers crystallized it into more business-like permanence by measuring and recording villages, parganas and *sarkārs* with their revenue assessment. The first beginning of a change from the mere levy of a share of grain to a regularly assessed cash revenue may be traced to Akbar's settlement, and the cash rates were when possible fixed for a period of years instead of being liable to annual alteration. A more or less uniform system of revenue accounts was also established. The settlement was fixed by measuring the arable lands and making a careful estimate of their produce. The unit of land for purposes of assessment was taken to be a *bīgha*—a term used to denote a piece of land measuring a little more than two-thirds of an acre. Each *bīgha* was rated at the value of one-fourth the estimated produce, and the sum total of the demand on a village or group of villages thus calculated was termed its *tankhwā* or standard rent-roll; from this rating were omitted lands which were barren or never brought under cultivation. The average rate of assessment per *bīgha* of land was R. 1-4-0. Mr. Bullock, in his report on North Berăr for 1854-55, gives the following account of the land assessment of this province under the Mughals. It is probably taken from some old papers preserved among the kānungo records, but these are usually copies, several times repeated, of original documents. 'I may as well mention 'that under the kings of Delhi, when the mode of assessment 'was under strict regulation, the valley of Berăr was divided

'into three main descriptions of land, viz. *Ainkāli*, *Miānkalās* 'and *Kalāspati*. The *ainkāli* was the deep black soil. The '*miānkalās* was the soil where the black began to mingle with 'a lighter description. The *kalāspati* was the light soil lying 'towards the hills. The black soil is towards the centre of the 'valley. Each of these divisions had its general rate fixed 'upon each *bīgha*, but divided into various sorts with a rate on 'each, and these rates were only slightly modified by local 'circumstances. The *bīgha* of arable land was less than the '*bīgha* now in use in Khāndesh or elsewhere, which is 3600 'square yards, and the garden and *inām bīgha* was larger, viz. 'the *inām* land was measured by the *Ilāhi gaz*, equal to 7225 'square yards per *bīgha*. The garden land was measured by 'the *barā Sikandari gaz* which gave 5500$\frac{60}{100}$ square yards per '*bīgha*, and the arable land by the *chhotā Sikandari gaz*, which 'gave 2256 $\frac{25}{100}$ square yards per *bīgha*. The average rates on 'land were as follows:—1st sort, divided into two sorts—1st 'sort R. 1-3-9; 2nd sort R. 0-13-3 per *bīgha*; 2nd sort, 'subdivided into two sorts—1st sort, R. 1-1-3, 2nd sort 'R. 0-12-3 per *bīgha*; 3rd sort, subdivided into two sorts—1st 'sort R. 0-11-6, and 2nd sort R. 0-11-3 per *bīgha*. Garden 'land in two kinds—1st sort Rs. 3-11-0, 2nd sort Rs. 2-4-0. 'The whole was under *khām wasūl* and the Annual Settlement 'paper was as nearly as possible that which I have now 'introduced, but with even more exact detail. We can form 'some idea of the prosperity of the valley at that time, as the 'total revenue in the year quoted during the reign of Alamgīr 'was Rs. 27,44,750-11-0, because the land was fully cultivated, 'and the population abundant and vigorous, instead of being 'scanty, ill-fed, and weakly, as they are now.' The present Amraoti District comprised the greater part of the *sarkār* Gāwil of which the demand on account of land revenue was 21 lakhs. Another important settlement in Berār was made by Malik Ambar, a minister of the Nizām Shāhi Kings, who ruled in their name in the Deccan in the seventeenth century. Although this settlement left a great mark on the province, if the traditions of the people are to be believed, the information about it is very meagre. It is probable that his assessments varied with the crop and were not fixed like the Mughal settlement; they were also lump assessments on the village in some cases. Grant Duff states that when the assessment was in kind it was ⅗rds of the produce, and that where there was a cash assessment, it equalled in value ⅓rd of the produce. Malik Ambar is also credited with having settled the land revenue upon a recognition of private property in the land, whereas Akbar held that all land belonged to the state. Writing in 1870 Sir A. Lyall estimates that the revenue raised in Berār in the 17th century was much larger than that paid under the original settlements made after the cession and that the cultivated area was not less. His conclusion as to the view we ought to take of the history of this period is as follows:—'It is a common mistake to suppose that the normal 'state of India was that in which we English found the country 'when we conquered most of it; whereas each province usually 'fell into our hands, like a rotten pear, when it was at its 'worst, and because it was at its worst. The century that 'preceded our rule may be regarded as a catastrophe in the 'history of India's government—a dark age of misrule inter-'posed between two periods of comparative, though unequal 'light. We who are now clearing away ruins, repairing an 'utterly dilapidated revenue, may sometimes fancy that we are 'raising a new and quite original edifice, when we are only 'reconstructing upon the old foundation up to the level of 'earlier architects.'

Period of double Government (Do Amli) Marāthā and Nizām, 1720 A. D.—1803 A. D.

293. The Marāthā connection with Berār originated with the grant of *chauth* and *sardeshmukhī* by the Delhi Emperor in 1717 A.D. The Marāthās pretended to keep regular accounts with the Nizām's officers who were never openly ejected from their posts, as from a conquered country, though they were often entirely set aside for a time. Districts were called *Do Amli*, that is, jointly administered; and in all the revenue papers the collections are divided, the Marāthā share being usually sixty per cent. Of this ten per cent. was called *sardeshmukhī* and the rest *mokāsa*, which seems in Berār to have been the

technical term that included in a lump sum all the Marāthā dues except the ten per cent. above mentioned. The *mokāsa* was thus made up; *chauth*, twenty-five per cent.; *faujdār's* allowance for district administration, twenty-five per cent. This period has been described as one of barefaced plunder and fleecing without attempt at principle or stability. Whenever the Nizām appointed a collector the Marāthās appointed another, and both claimed the revenue, while foragers from each side exacted forced contributions so that the harassed cultivator often threw up his land and helped to plunder his neighbours.

Period of Nizām's Sovereignty. 1803-1853 A.D.

294. In 1803 the Nizām was placed in sole possession by the British Government and the administration became even worse than before. The system was introduced of farming out the land revenue to contractors, who adhered to no rates, but squeezed what they could out of the ryot's crop and his goods and chattels. Whole tāluks and parganas were let and sublet to speculators for sums far above the ancient standard assessment. During the ministry of Rājā Chandū Lāl (1820-1840) the land revenue of certain tracts was regularly put to auction at Hyderābād for the highest bid. It is related of that famous minister that he did not even respect these auction sales, as it was usual to do, but disposed of the same contracts simultaneously to several different buyers. Then came the opportunity of the pargana officers; he who secured them on his side kept the farm or sometimes these officers solved the complication equitably by putting all purchasers on a roster, whereby each got his turn at the collections. While this roster was known to be full, even Rājā Chandū Lāl could not persuade a fresh set of contractors to deal with him. There is a story told of one of these contractors that he rode out of Hyderābād after the auction with his face to the horse's tail. His followers approached him and asked 'why this undignified position?' 'I am on the look-out,' said he, 'for my successor to overtake me.' Some of the great farmers-general deserve mention. One Rājā Bisan Chand who held the greater part of the

Berār valley in farm about 1831 left a name alike for extortion and miserliness at which the Kunbī still grows pale; to pronounce it of a morning early is unlucky. Another by name Pūran Mal, a mighty moneylender of Hyderābād, at one time got most of Berār in farm. In 1839 he was turned out of his districts by the Nizām's minister, under pressure from the British Resident. Pūran Mal refused to quit hold of his security for advance made, and showed fight when his successors sent agents to take his place. However in the end he had to give way; but he presented to the Hyderābād government an account showing a balance due to him of two millions sterling, which the ministry altogether refused to pay, proving by a different system of book-keeping, that Pūran Mal was deeply in debt to the treasury. Pūran Mal's successors were Messrs. Pestanji and Company, enterprising Pārsi merchants, who in 1841 received large assignments of revenue in Berār for reimbursement of advances to the State. But in 1845 they were ordered to give up their Berār districts, and on their refusal their collecting agency was attacked and sixteen men killed. They were then forced to evacuate the assignments with a claim of forty lakhs of rupees against the Nizām. Messrs. Pestanji and Company had made large and liberal advances to tenants in Berār; they had thus restored cultivation over wide tracts, and rekindled the lamp in many deserted villages. Among Berār agriculturists they left a very good reputation. One result of the farming system and the disorder into which the country fell, was a great decrease in the revenue. The net revenue collected about 1815-20 was not more than half the sum which the province was estimated to yield in 1803, and the land revenue of the present Amraoti District mentioned in the treaty of 1853 was only 7 lakhs, a great fall from the 21 lakhs of Akbar's settlement. Under the farming system the government had no means of checking false revenue returns and the rough enquiries made by the British officials after the cession shewed cultivation to be concealed to an incredible extent. Thus in 1854 the Resident reported that whereas the cultivated area in North Berār was recorded at 425,000 *bīghas*, the naked eye detected by rapid survey of each village more than 1,700,000 *bīghas*. The Government simply looked to the revenue for which the contractor was answerable and did not trouble about the extension or otherwise of cultivation. In spite of this concealment of cultivation the ryots in 1853 were found to be in a very depressed and impoverished state. This was due, not so much to the severity of the assessment, for that was not found to be too heavy, but to its shameful inequality. Deshmukhs, Brāhmans, Rājputs and Musalmāns were paying an average of 7½ annas a *bīgha*, while the Marāthā Kunbī was paying as much as 1 rupee 14 annas a *bīgha*. The mode of assessment was very arbitrary and seldom had any reference to the capabilities of the soil. Thus it was found that one man was paying 10 rupees for land of the same extent and description as that for which another man was paying 100 rupees. When waste land was required by a cultivator it was apportioned out by the patwāri by guess work so that the amount allotted to any individual depended partly on the ability of the patwāri to judge area, and partly on his good will towards the cultivator.

Land tenure and the position of revenue officials prior to 1853.

295. The ordinary tenure from time immemorial had been that which permitted a man to keep possession of his fields so long as he paid to government the customary rent. Some such general principle of reciprocal convenience must have always prevailed, so long as land was more plentiful than cultivators. Malik Ambar (1612 A.D.) is stated to have recognised the ryot's private property in his land, but such rights, if ever they were conferred, cannot long have out-lasted the wear and tear of the disorders which followed his death. We may suppose that where the tenants managed to keep land for any long time in one family they acquired a sort of property adverse to all except the government; that where the land changed often by the diverse accidents of an unsettled age, in such cases occupancy never hardened into proprietary right. Good land would have been carefully preserved, bad land would be often thrown up; failure of crops or the exactions of farmers would sever many holdings; and all rights ceased with continuity of possession. When misgovern-

ment became chronic, and the country was incessantly exposed to be wasted by famine, war, or fiscal extortion, the tenant's hold on any one piece of land would be more precarious and ephemeral. But perhaps it may be said that in theory the general basis and limit of property in the land was cultivating occupancy undisturbed, except by violence or injustice, so long at the traditional standing rates of assessment were paid upon the fields taken up. It is easy to see that various rights and prescriptions might, under favouring circumstances, arise out of this sort of holding. Several terms as *mirāsi*, *mundkari*, etc., were formerly known to distinguish the class of occupants in Berār whose possession of their land was long established and by descent, but their precise privileges were never closely defined. The essence of these holdings seems to have been the privilege of paying a fixed sum without regard to cultivated area, and the right to trees. The property was also admitted usually to be heritable and transferable. Then certain advantageous tenures were created by expedients used to revive cultivation in deserted tracts; long leases were given at a rent mounting upwards very gradually year by year, or a whole ruined village was made over by what is called *pālampat*, a tenure which fixes the rental of the entire estate without taking account of the spread of cultivation. Whatever rights in the land may have grown up previously, they all disappeared under the Marāthā and Nizām's government. Under this régime the mass of cultivators held their fields on a yearly lease which was made out for them by the patel at the beginning of each season; the land was acknowledged to belong to the State, and as a general rule no absolute right to hold any particular field, except by yearly permission of the officials, was urged or allowed. A man could not always give up or transfer his holding without official authorization. Cultivators were ejected from their holdings and others put in their places, as it suited the caprice or interest of the farmer of the revenue. Under such a system all value was wrung out of property in land.

The patels, Deshmukhs and Deshpāndias who were employed to manage the collection of land revenue in villages and parganas never got beyond hereditary office nor transmuted themselves into proprietors of the land. The patel always remained the agent between the State and the village tenants for cultivation and collections. He was paid by rent-free land, money-dues and dignities, the whole being grouped under the term *watan.* The Deshmukhs and Deshpāndias had risen to great local importance under the Muhammadan dynasties. They held by virtue of office the right to take certain dues from the revenue collected in their subdivisions, but some of the more powerful families received large grants of land in jāgīr and patents for the collection of additional subsidies on condition of military or police service and the maintenance of order. Towards the decline of the Mughal power in Berār they sometimes obtained their subdivisions in farm, and some of them were probably fast developing into the status of the tālukdārs and zamīndārs of Upper India. But the Nizām and Marāthās were too powerful to let any subjects stand between them and the full demand, and in 1853 it was decided that though these officials had frequently, beside their money dues, large quantities of *inām* or revenue-free land, and they themselves advanced the most extravagant pretensions, their real position was that of hereditary officers and not that of landed proprietors.

Early British administration, 1853-1869.

296. The Amraoti District when made over in 1853 resembled a squeezed orange, as the Nizām's tālukdārs in anticipation of the cession had screwed up their demand to the highest pitch and had even in some cases extorted collections in advance. The mistake was at first made by the new administration of attempting to collect these extraordinary rates, and in 1855-56 there were heavy irrecoverable balances, and at the end of that season cultivation began rapidly to contract—a sure sign of over-assessment. The mistake was however soon corrected and the District entered upon an era of prosperity from which it never looked back. The British officials in the period from 1853 to 1869, the first year of the survey settlement in the Amraoti District, were occupied in clearing up the confusion into which the land-revenue administration had fallen and in feeling their way towards some

better system. The services of the Deshmukhs and Deshpāndias were dispensed with, pensions being granted to them in perpetuity as compensation for the loss of their emoluments.[1] The patel and the patwāri were retained. An annual *jamābandī* was made by the Deputy Commissioner through the medium of the patel and the account of each man's holding was taken from the patwāri's papers. But without accurate measurements no assessment could be satisfactory, as the officials were working in the dark. The system was fraught with the greatest inconvenience both to the Government and to the people, besides being made a fruitful source of peculation and corrupt practices. A five years' settlement was at one time ordered by the Government of India but the information on record about it is very vague and it seems that owing to the complete breakdown of the *khasrā* survey by patwāris that it was never brought to completion. The urgent need of some scientific method of assessment was felt. The question arose whether the mālguzāri system of Northern India or the ryotwāri system of Bombay should be adopted. The former was in 1860 sanctioned by the Government of India, but in 1861, in deference to the earnest protests of the local officials,[2] these orders were cancelled and sanction was given to

---

[1] The amount disbursed under this head in the Amraoti District in 1907-08 was Rs. 57,000.

[2] Colonel Meadows Taylor was one of the local officials who was most strenuous in his opposition to the introduction of the mālguzāri system. In his autobiography he writes of the question as follows. 'The Supreme Government had proposed to make a 'settlement of my province on the same system as had been adopted in 'the North-Western Provinces, and I had to fight a very hard battle 'with the authorities to gain my point. I believe I was considered '"most impracticable and obstinate" and incurred, I have little doubt, 'much ill will, but for that I care absolutely nothing. I could not up-'hold any system that I believed would be an injury and a wrong to my 'people, or become a party to a course which I considered was not 'only unjust and unpopular to the last degree, but which would abolish 'all those ancient hereditary tenures to which the people had clung 'with devoted pertinacity through all revolutions and vicissitudes for 'many centuries, and which the old Musalmān kings and rulers of the 'Deccan had continuously respected. My view of the question was very 'strenuously supported by my friend Bullock, Commissioner in Berār; 'and in the end I rejoice to say that we so far prevailed as to enlist 'the sympathies of our Chief Commissioner on our side, who 'earnestly protested against the system proposed from Bengal, and 'was successful in his opposition, insomuch as the question was 'deferred for future consideration. In writing the "Story of my Life"

the introduction of the Bombay system which is described below. The patels of Berār thus narrowly missed being promoted to the position of mālguzārs or landlords, the fate which befell their brethren in the Central Provinces. In spite of the absence of a proper system of settlement this early period of British rule was one of great prosperity, and remissions of revenue were almost unknown. Writing of it in 1870 Sir Alfred Lyall remarks that 'the land revenue increased and 'multiplied with marvellous rapidity, under the combined 'stimuli of good Government, railways and the Manchester 'cotton famine. Cultivation spread over the land like a flood 'tide' and Sir R. Temple's remarks in 1867 are also deserving of quotation. 'The condition of Berār when the province 'was assigned to British management, though weakly, and 'needing restorative measures, was not beyond the hope of 'speedy recovery. And fortunately the means of restoration 'were at hand; for the soil was famed far and wide among the 'peasantry for its fertility; and its repute, always high, was 'further enhanced by the fact of so much of it having 'remained fallow of late years, a circumstance which was 'supposed to ensure a rich return to those who reclaimed 'the waste and raised the first crops on virgin culture. The 'neighbouring districts were full of families who had emigrated 'thither from Berār, and who, with the usual attachment of the 'people to their original patrimony, were anxious to return 'on any suitable opportunity. Thus hundreds of families and 'thousands of individuals immigrated back into Berār. Many 'villages in the Nāgpur country lost many of their hands in this 'way, and were sometimes put to serious straits. Some 'apprehension was even caused to the Nāgpur officials. But of

---

'I cannot pass this question over without notice, as it was a point on 'which, firmly believing myself to be in the right, I deliberately risked 'not only the good-will of the Government of India at that time but 'my own employment as Deputy Commissioner. I would never have 'agreed to carry out the unjust measure proposed in ignorance of local 'tenures by the Government of India, and my friend Bullock and myself 'were prepared to have resigned our appointments in case stringent 'orders were issued on the subject; and there is no act of my public 'life which, to this day, gives me more pleasure and satisfaction than 'my successful resistance to the orders of Government to the settle-'ment being made according to the North-West system.'

'course the natural course of things had its way, and Eastern 'Berār became replenished. This was only one mode out of 'several, which it would be tedious to detail, whereby the 'cultivation of Berār was restored and augmented.'

Berār Survey and Settlement system

297. The basis or unit of assessment is the survey number or plot of land of a size not less than cultivable by a peasant with a pair of bullocks. The arable land, whether cultivated or waste but available for cultivation, is split up into these numbers, the area of which is accurately ascertained by survey measurement. Each field is separately measured by means of the chain and cross staff, and in the field register there is a separate map of each field complete in itself. The area of the holding is obtained by simple arithmetic and the calculations are recorded. This detailed field register obviates the necessity of having the village map on a larger scale than 8 inches to the mile. The area of each survey number does not exceed from 20 to 30 acres, and the minimum below which survey numbers cannot be divided is 5 acres in the case of dry crop land, 1 acre in the case of rice land, and ½ acre in the case of garden land. The fields are marked off from each other by a *dhurā* (a strip of land 4½ feet in breadth) being left uncultivated between them; by mounds of earth (*warli*), 10 feet in length by 5 feet in breadth, and 3 feet in height; and by stones (*gotā, khūn*) between 2½ and 3 feet in length sunk in the ground at certain angles. Besides the culturable land the *gaothān* or village site is also surveyed and allotted, and land is reserved for free grazing and other purposes. The term *pūrampok* is used for numbers that are unculturable by reason of having tombs, sites of wells, etc., on them, and the Bombay plan of allowing parts of numbers to be deducted from the culturable area as bad bits (*potkharab*) is followed. The survey being done, the classification of the soil begins. There are three classes of land, unirrigated or dry crop (*jirait*) land, rice land and garden land (*bagait*) which is called *motasthal* if irrigated by means of a well, and *pātasthal* if irrigated by a channel. For classification purposes each field is divided temporarily into parts of some two

acres each. Three tests to discover kind of soil, depth of soil and freedom from defects are made in each part. For the first test soils are divided into three classes or orders, which are described briefly as black, red and white. The full description is: 'First order—of a fine uniform texture, varying in colour 'from deep black to deep brown. Second order—of uniform 'but coarser texture than the preceding and lighter in colour, 'which is generally red. Third order—of coarse, gravelly, or 'loose friable texture and colour varying from light brown 'to grey.' For the second test, that of depth, the soil is dug up and a crowbar driven in until it is obstructed by rock or some hard substratum or until it has gone in 1¾ cubits, that is, 31½ inches. For the third test a list of eight defects has been drawn up, the chief being the presence of fragments of limestone or of excessive sand, slope, liability to flooding, excess of moisture, and clayey soil. When a classification is being made, the classer draws an outline of each field, marks the parts into which it is temporarily divided and enters in each part figures and symbols to show the results of each test. A soil to be of standard quality, a sixteen anna soil, must be black, of full depth, and free from all defects. Indeed, it may have some special advantage, such as a beneficial flooding in the rains, which raises it two or four annas more. For every detail or combination of details in which a plot falls short of standard quality so many annas are deducted according to a table which has been drawn up. Each field is finally valued as a field of so many annas according to the average value of the plots contained in it. In the case of garden land it is necessary in addition to examine the effect of the well or other means of irrigation on the soil. Rice land is classified on a scale of its own. The full details thus obtained about each field are entered in a *prate* or field book which is kept at the headquarters of the District. These operations of measurement and classification have nothing whatever to do with the pitch or amount of the assessment. They are only the methods by which the assessment is distributed over the numerous individual holdings of a ryotwāri system. The basis of the distribution of the assessment having being fixed, the next step is for the Settlement Officer to work out the rates of assessment. These rates are determined in the following manner. The area dealt with, which is the subdivision of a District known as the tāluk, is divided into groups homogeneous as to physical characteristics and economic advantage, such as climate, rainfall, general fertility of soil, communications and the like. For each of those groups uniform maximum rates are fixed. These maximum rates are the sums which would be leviable upon a field, the soil valuation of which is sixteen annas. Thus if the maximum rate be Rs. 3 per acre of a sixteen anna field, the assessment per acre upon a field the valuation of which was eight annas would be R. 1-8 and so on. By applying the maximum assessment rates to the soil valuation the rate per acre on each field is arrived at. In an original settlement the difficulty is to arrive at suitable maximum rates. This difficulty was solved for Berār by taking the rates found in the neighbouring District of Khāndesh as a basis for the early settlements. Special rates are imposed on rice and irrigated land. The settlement is made for 30 years and at the end of that period is liable to revision.

Land tenure.

298. The ordinary tenure is the ryotwāri tenure, and all land paying revenue to government under that system is known as *khālsa* land. The state is recognised as the superior landlord, and the settlement is made directly with the cultivator himself and not through middlemen. The assessment is on the land, not on the person. Subject to certain restrictions, the occupant is absolute proprietor of his holding, may sell, let or mortgage it, cultivate it or leave it waste, so long as he pays the assessment, which may be revised on general principles at the end of the fixed term. Being in arrears with the assessment at once renders the right of occupancy liable to forfeiture. No occupant is bound to hold his land more than one year if he does not like it, and provided he gives notice according to law, he is free to relinquish his holding. The occupant is free to make any improvement he likes but he must not apply the land to any other purpose than that for which it

was granted without the permission of the Deputy Commissioner. Government retains a right to all minerals in the soil. Only one occupant is recorded as the *khātedār*, to whom the government looks as responsible primarily for the revenue. Apart from this he is not necessarily a person with any rights in the soil whatever. Mutation of names is not compulsory and hence it often happens that a *khātedār*, from motives perhaps of sentiment, perhaps of sloth, prefers to keep his name on the government register long after he has parted with the land. This description requires to be qualified in the case of land given out for cultivation since 1st January 1905. From that date all unalienated assessed land is disposed of subject to the following additional condition, viz., neither the occupant, nor his heirs, executors, administrators and approved assigns, shall at any time lease, mortgage, sell, or otherwise encumber the said occupancy or any portion thereof without the previous sanction in writing of the Deputy Commissioner.

Original Settlement.

299. The original settlements were made in the Amraoti, Daryāpur and Morsi tāluks in 1869, 1870 and 1871 by Major P. A. Elphinstone, that in Chāndur in 1873 by Mr. R. R. Benyon, and the rates came into force between 1871 and 1874. The settlement dealt with 1493 Government or *khālsa* villages, which were divided into three groups in each of the Amraoti, Ellichpur and Daryāpur tāluks, and into four groups in the Morsi and Chāndur tāluks, the grouping being based upon proximity to markets, convenience of water-supply and similar considerations. The maximum rates were based upon those adopted in the tāluks already settled in other Districts, and these in their turn owed their origin to rates prevailing in the neighbouring Bombay District of Khāndesh. In the first group the maximum rate per acre was fixed at Rs. 2-4 except for the town of Amraoti, where it was Rs. 2-8, and the tāluk of Chāndur where with the exception of three villages on the railway line it was R. 1-14. In the second and third groups, except in the Chāndur tāluk, the maximum rates were Rs. 2 and R. 1-2 respectively; in the Chāndur tāluk the rates for these groups were R. 1-10 and R. 1-6 respectively. For

the fourth group in the Morsi and Chāndur tāluks the rates were R. 1-8 and R. 1-4 respectively. Lower rates were fixed for the Chāndur tāluk because of the existence there of a large amount of waste land (223,415 acres). For land irrigated by wells and watercourses a maximum rate of Rs. 6 or 7 was fixed for villages in the first group and of Rs. 3 or 4 for villages in the remaining groups. The average rate per acre in the different tāluks worked out as follows :—

	Rs.	a.	p.
Amraoti	1	5	6
Ellichpur	1	9	8
Daryāpur	1	9	6
Morsi	1	4	7
Chāndur	0	13	10

There was an increase of 32 per cent. in the land revenue for the District as a whole, the highest increase being in the Amraoti tāluk where it was 51 per cent., and the lowest in Ellichpur where it was 15 per cent.; the increase in the other three tāluks of Chāndur, Daryāpur and Morsi was respectively 43, 37 and 24 per cent. In the instructions given to the Settlement Officer great stress had been laid on the necessity of light assessments and much of the increase of land revenue was due to the discovery of large areas of concealed cultivation. The settlement was made for a period of 30 years. The effect of the settlement was that, in the words of Sir Alfred Lyall, 'The Berār cultivator passed from all the evils of rack-renting, 'personal insecurity and uncertain ownership of land to a safe 'property and a fixed assessment,' and the same writer in discussing the value and popularity of the settlement goes on to say: 'Yet we should remember that this contrast 'between the two administrations, which cannot now fail 'to strike the generation which remembers the Assignment of '1853, would not have much impressed the foregoing generation if the country had been transferred thirty years earlier. 'The Berār cultivator is lucky in that he came under British 'management at a time when our government had sown its 'wild oats, and reaped the fruits thereof; when we had drained 'the slough of fiscal blunders and blind carelessness in which 'our Collectors had been floundering, and had placed them on 'the firm and fertile ground of method and moderation. It 'would be dangerous to assert that the agriculturist under the 'rigid, irresistible, unconscious maladministration of the early 'English school was even so well off as under the conscious 'haphazard misrule of the Native government, which was kept 'elastic by the possibility of evasion or revolt. This rigid 'irresistibility is probably the prime cause of our mismanaging '(as we constantly do) the land revenue of a new province 'during the first years of our administration. Even in 1853, 'when the Nizām's tālukdārs had in North Berār made over 'to us a squeezed orange, we began by attempting to collect 'the extraordinary rates to which the land revenue demand 'had been run up by our predecessors, whence it may be guessed 'that the agriculturists did not at once discover the blessings 'of British rule. On the other hand there are some reasons 'why cession to the British should have been more popular in 'Berār than it usually is found at first to be. Peaceful culti-'vating communities, living at a dead level of humble equality 'under strong tax-collectors, got none of those compensations 'which indemnified the Rājput clansmen of Oudh for chronic 'anarchy and complete public insecurity. Rough indepen-'dence, the ups and downs of a stirring life, a skirmish over each 'revenue instalment, faction fights for land affording a good 'working title to the survivor—all these consolations were 'unknown to the Berār Kunbī, nor would they have been 'his taste had they been within his power. He had as much 'land as he wanted without quarelling with anyone; all that he 'desired was secure possession of the fruits of his labour, and 'a certain State demand. The classes which lost by the 'assignment of Berār to British administrators were those who 'had hitherto made their profit out of native administration—'the tālukdārs, the farmers of any kind of revenue, and the 'hereditary pargana officials.'

Revision Settlement.

300. The original settlement gave what has been called 'free trade in land' and this combined with the high wages prevalent attracted from the Central Provinces and from Northern India a constant

stream of immigrants. 'From the Central Provinces,' wrote Sir A. Lyall, 'came labourers and cultivators by thousands; 'from North India came artizans and the classes which take 'service in the towns.' The period of settlement was one of steady prosperity broken only by the famine of 1896-97. Revision settlement operations were started between 1896 and 1898. The settlement of Amraoti, Chāndur, Morsi and Ellichpur tāluks was carried out by Mr. Francis, and that of the Daryāpur tāluk by Major Garrett. The remeasurement and re-classification were carried out on the partial system, only 6 villages in the Daryāpur tāluk being entirely remeasured. The classification of soils of villages varying from 9 to 10 in each tāluk was tested. The work of the original survey was found to be satisfactory and was confirmed. The old system of grouping was changed, each of the tāluks of Daryāpur, Ellichpur and Amraoti constituting one group, and Morsi and Chāndur each being divided into two groups. In fixing the maximum rates an enhancement of revenue was held to be justified on four grounds :—

(*a*) That communication had greatly improved.

(*b*) That there were general indications of sustained prosperity, as for instance a large increase in population, houses, carts, wells and working cattle.

(*c*) That the culturable area was fully occupied and that land was valuable, subrents of three times the Government assessment being easily paid.

(*d*) That the first assessment had been easily paid.

The maximum dry crop rates fixed varied from Rs. 2-12 in Amraoti and Ellichpur to R. 1-12 in Chāndur. Garden land irrigated before the original settlement was assessed at the maximum dry crop rate of the group in which it was situated. Land irrigated from wells dug since the original settlement was treated as dry crop land, and no extra assessment was levied. Land irrigated by channels from stream was assessed at a combined water and soil rate of Rs. 8 and rice land was assessed at a rate of Rs. 6. By the revised settlement the revenue demand was raised by 35 per cent. in the Amraoti tāluk, by 30 per cent. in the Ellichpur tāluk, by 22 per cent. in the Daryāpur tāluk, by 25 per cent. in the Morsi tāluk and by 52 per cent. in the Chāndur tāluk. The average incidence per acre in the different tāluks worked out as follows:—

	Rs.	a.	p.
Amraoti	1	12	10
Ellichpur	2	2	10
Daryāpur	2	0	6
Morsi	1	11	4
Chāndur	1	4	2

In the case of 68 villages of the Amraoti tāluk, 3 villages of the Ellichpur tāluk and the whole of the Chāndur taluk, it was decided to levy interim rates for 15 years and the full rates for the remaining period of settlement. Owing to the famine of 1899-1900 the revised rates were not brought into force till 1903-1904 in the tāluks of Amraoti, Ellichpur, Daryāpur and Morsi, and till 1904-05 in the Chāndur tāluk. Since their introduction the new rates have been paid with ease and no remissions have been found necessary.

Land Revenue administration of the Melghāt.

301. A considerable portion of the Melghāt though nominally classed as forest, has a revenue history of its own both curious and interesting, and its classification as forest has for a long time been misleading. At the time of the cession in 1853 the whole of the Melghāt was occupied either by the persons known as the Melghāt Rājās or by villages of Korkūs and other aboriginals, who practised *dhya* cultivation and were constantly changing their village sites. Land revenue was assessed on the yoke of oxen, though the existence of *bīgha* rates in a number of villages (which have remained unaltered to the present day) proves that some advance had been made on this primitive system of assessment. The tract was divided into 12 parganas and a nominal list of 853 villages was found in the records at the cession and was maintained for a long time afterwards. What was represented by these villages is not exactly clear, as they were never verified by the new administration. Probably they never

represented separate villages with fixed village sites and definite areas; the habits of the Korkūs who were constantly changing their habitation and adopting new village names make it hardly conceivable that without demarcation of village boundaries an authentic list of villages could be maintained. The Melghāt had its golden age, though unfortunately it had no historian—for after the cession it was stated that within the memory of men then living, its hills were thickly populated and well cultivated and a proverb had been current that the villages were within a peacock's flight of each other and that the sound of the drum was to be heard from village to village. In 1860-61 Mr. James Mulheran was in charge of a topographical party which prepared maps for the whole tract on the scale of one inch to the mile, and he wrote an interesting report. The whole tract was still at that time under the administration of the revenue authorities and no alteration had been made in the system carried on under the Nizām's Government. The area under cultivation was found by Mr. Mulheran to be 97,280 acres and the land revenue did not exceed Rs. 12,000. He compiled a list of 300 inhabited and 348 deserted villages but he did not vouch for the separate existence of the latter. In 1866 the Forest Department was organized and the demarcation of the reserves began in the same year. The tract outside the reserves was known at first as the unreserved forests, then as D class forest and finally as C III forest, a name it still bears. The area of this tract, which may now be called the revenue tract of the Melghāt, has gradually decreased with the growth of the reserves. It now comprises an area of about 671 square miles and consists of a broad belt lying south of the reserves and adjoining the Berār plains, a small area on the east in the Kātkumb pargana, and the whole of the western portion of the Melghāt. The forest policy adopted with regard to this tract was to denude it of all forest growth; cutting, grazing and cultivation (subject to the payment of certain dues) being permitted practically without control. This policy was aptly described by an old conservator as an '*après moi le déluge*' policy, and though the Forest Department between 1880 and 1906 drew an income of 23 lakhs from the tract, the work of destruction has been so complete that the tract has been converted into a wilderness, the only timber of any value being now confined to the Bairāgarh block. On the revenue side the administration was conducted on paternal lines with a minimum of correspondence and up till quite recently the administration might be described as administration by the patwāri and the patel tempered by the occasional interference of the Tahsīldār. Systematic rules regulating the condition of cultivation were not framed till 1899, and if changes were from time to time made in the yoke rates they were unrecorded. The whole tract was surveyed by the Imperial Forest Survey Department between 1883 and 1886, maps on a scale of 4 inches to the mile in the more advanced parts and in the scale of 2 inches to the mile in the more backward parts being prepared. These maps were excellent but their chief value lay in the fact that they removed the confusion caused by the old list of villages referred to above; the separate villages of the C. III area were demarcated and surveyed, and at last the revenue authorities were in a position to know exactly what they were dealing with. Some internal demarcation was also done but this was rendered valueless by the failure to carry out some form of ryotwāri settlement *pari passu* with the survey. The need of some advance upon the primitive system of assessment by the yoke rate had long been felt. Mr. W. B. Jones, the Commissioner who visited the tract in 1879, described the revenue system as so unsatisfactory that no change could be made for the worse. 'It is a ryotwāri system with many of the evils of 'other systems and few of its own advantages. The government 'though nominally dealing with the ryots, leaves them really 'unprotected and exacts its revenue from patels through alien patwāris, asking no further question. The patel is thus a 'mālguzār with none of the advantages of the position, the 'cultivator a tenant of the state with few of the advantages of 'that position.' The project of a ryotwāri settlement was not raised again till 1892, and after some delay the revenue survey was actually started in 1896. It was abandoned however the same year for what now appear to be inadequate reasons.

The fugitive nature of the Korkū's cultivation and the risk of disturbing those aboriginals were continually put forward as obstacles in the way of a settlement, and it was not realized that in certain parts of the Melghāt the cultivation was as stable as in the Berār plains and that the existing system or absence of system left the aboriginal without any protection against the usurer and land grabber, who were gradually ousting him from all the best land. The question of a settlement was again raised in 1906 and a special officer was deputed to report on the tract. He found that the fugitive nature of the cultivation had been greatly exaggerated. Cultivation was permanent over a large area, a lien on fallows being retained and the idea of private property in land had fully developed. The yoke rate system in its primitive form would hardly be said to exist and the needs of the trac- had given birth to a bastard ryotwāri system. The figure of 16 acres (which had been assumed merely for statistical purposes to represent the amount of land cultivated by a single yoke of oxen) had been converted by the patwāri into a standard of measurement. Although the land was held merely on a yearly occupation tenure and every occupant was liable to ejectment at 6 months notice, the land was being dealt with exactly as if the occupier had the heritable transferable right which exists in the rest of Berār. Land was being sold, mortgaged and sublet to a great extent, and a considerable area had been taken up by outside speculators, who were waiting their chance to get it converted into a valuable property by the efforts of the aboriginals who would become their subtenants. In the centre of the Amner pargana the aboriginal had been dispossessed of his land by the money lender and the liquor seller, principally Bohrās and Kalārs from Burhānpur, and the land at the foot of the hills bordering on the Berār plains was almost entirely in possession of Berār cultivators. But elsewhere the older races still reigned supreme, over 50 per cent. of the total occupied area being held by Korkūs and Gonds. In 1906-07 there were 338 villages, 240 of which were inhabited and cultivated, 56 uninhabited but cultivated and 42 both uninhabited and uncultivated. The cropped area was 166,376 acres, of which 25 per cent. was under cotton, 14 per cent. under juāri, 8 per cent. under wheat and 4 per cent. under gram. The revenue work was done by 11 patwāris who received as remuneration 5 per cent. on collections as pay and 3 per cent. as *chillar* (writing expenses). The patels received 6 per cent. on the land revenue collections. There were 39 jāglias paid at the rate of Rs. 5 a month and each village had its village servant—generally a Balāhi, Nihāl or Korkū—who was paid at the rate of 1 *kuro* of grain for each yoke of land. The special officer recommended the introduction of a ryotwāri settlement into the greater part of the tract, the doubtful portions being parts of the Bairāgarh and Dhulghāt parganas where the conditions justifying the retention of a yoke rate system, viz., shifting cultivation and excessive unoccupied areas still to some extent existed.

Orders on the subject were issued in 1909. The Chief Commissioner decided that any large blocks of unculturable land in the tract should be demarcated and reserved as A class forest, being managed with the aid of the usual forest staff, with the objects of (1) securing a continuous supply of bamboos, small timber, fodder, etc., and (2) protecting the forest on the steep hill-sides in order to secure the continuance or improvement of existing meteorological conditions. Small patches of cultivation inside these extensive blocks would be abolished so as to secure compactness. It was also decided that the great majority of the villages were not worthy of regular settlement which will probably be confined to the tract round Dhārni and the block of black soil in the Bairāgarh pargana, together with the best of the villages on the southern border.

Special tenures in the Melghāt.

302. A full account of the Melghāt Rājās has been given in the section on leading families. According to the returns for 1906-07 the total area of the jāgīr villages held by the Melghāt Rājās was 48,572 acres, which included 15,413 acres classed as unculturable, 26,982 acres fit for cultivation but unocupied, and 6117 acres occupied with an assessment of Rs. 3,605. The two villages leased to the jāgirdār of Kalamganā

contained 2016 acres of which 1,521 were classed as unculturable, and 258 acres were occupied with an assessment of Rs. 115 of which Rs. 10, annas 4 were paid to Government. There are two *inām* villages, Kalamganā Khurd and Wazar. The former has been referred to in the section on leading families; the latter is held on behalf of the temple of Ganpati at Akot. The area of the two villages was 2520 acres, in 1906-07, of which 1050 acres were occupied with an assessment of Rs. 1481, the whole of which was enjoyed by the *ināmdārs*.

Tenures—Ryotwāri tenure.

303. The ryotwāri tenure already described is in force throughout the District except the Melghāt. Out of 1640 villages in the plain tāluks, 1615 are settled on this tenure, and are known as *khālsa* villages. The area of these villages in 1906-07 was returned as 1,968,467 acres, of this 57,668 acres were occupied by village sites, tanks, rivers and the like, 162,061 acres by forests, 56,318 acres were set apart for village purposes and for free-grazing, 7 acres were left in the Chāndur tāluk as unculturable (*pārampok*) land, and the balance of 1,692,412 acres was available for cultivation. Of the latter area 1,692,345 acres were occupied and only 67 acres remained unoccupied. The land revenue demand of the *khālsa* villages amounted to Rs. 28,02,724 in 1906-07 against Rs. 27,69,144 in 1905-06.

Jāgīr tenure.

304. Jāgīr now means any rent-free holding consisting of an integral village or villages. The history of the tenure is thus traced by Sir Alfred Lyall—'The jāgīr[1] of Berār seems to have been 'originally always, like the earliest feuds, a mere assignment of 'revenue for military service and the maintenance of order by 'armed control of certain Districts. In latter times the grant 'was occasionally made to civil officers for the maintenance of 'due state and dignity. The interest of the stipendiary did not 'ordinarily extend beyond his own life, and the jāgīr even 'determined at the pleasure of the sovereign or it was transfer- 'red, on failure of service, to another person who undertook

[1] Berār Gazetteer 1870, page 101.

'the conditions. But some of these grants when given to 'powerful families acquired an hereditary character. It would 'seem, nevertheless, that until recently these estates very 'seldom shook off the condition under which they were created. 'The assignments were withdrawn when the service ceased; 'and they were considered a far inferior kind of property 'to that of hereditary office. Probably the double government 'of the Marāthā and the Nizām kept this tenure weak and 'precarious. The Nizām would have insisted on service from 'his jāgirdārs during his incessant wars. The Marāthā treated 'the Mughal jāgirdārs very roughly, taking from them 60 per 'cent. of all the revenue assigned, wherever such demand 'could be enforced. To plunder an enemy's jāgīr was much 'the same as to sack his military chest—it disordered the army 'estimates. When this province was made over in 1853 to 'the British, some villages were under assignment to jāgirdārs 'for the maintenance of troops, and these were given up by 'their holders. Up to that date, however, the system of '*tankhwā* jāgīr or assignment for army payments by which 'whole parganas in Berār had been formerly held, had barely 'survived. The irregularities of the old practice were noto-'rious. A few followers to enable the jāgirdār to collect 'the revenue were sometimes the only armed force really 'maintained; no musters were held, and when troops were 'seriously called out the jāgirdār made hasty levies or occa-'sionally absconded altogether. There are still several personal 'jāgīrs without condition in Berār which have been confirmed 'to the holders as a heritable possession. But none of these 'were made hereditary by original grant, save only the estate 'given to pious or venerable persons—to *saiyids*, *fakīrs*, *pīrzādas*, 'and the like—and perhaps an estate which was first assigned 'as an appanage to members of the reigning family. Other 'jāgīrs have been obtained by court interest, acquired by local 'officers during their tenure of power, or allotted to them for 'maintenance of due state and dignity, and such holdings were 'often continued afterwards as a sort of pension which slided 'into inheritance. Almost every jāgīr title was given by the 'Delhi Emperor or the Nizām, one or two by the Peshwā; but 'not one full grant derives from the Bhonsla dynasty, which 'never arrogated to itself that sovereign prerogative.' Alienation of jāgīrs by sale, mortgage or otherwise is prohibited except in cases where the jāgīr on confirmation by the British was converted into a freehold. Personal jāgīrs are continued hereditarily subject to a legacy duty or succession fees graduated on a scale according to the degree of relationship of the heir. Jāgīrs for religious and charitable objects[1] such as for the support of temples, mosques, *idgāhs* or other public buildings or institutions, or for service therein are continued, so long as the buildings or institutions are maintained in an efficient state, and the service performed according to the conditions of the grant. A jāgīr for personal maintenance may be divided by inheritance, though not in any other way. But even its division by inheritance is strictly limited to the direct heirs male of the body of the original grantee. Adopted children and heirs through women are not recognized. A jāgīr for service may not be subdivided without forfeiture. The latter is a tenure in which the jāgirdār is little more than a trustee with a right to make something for himself from his trust, in the former he is a proprietor. The relations between the jāgirdār and his tenants are governed by chapter VII. of the Berār Land Revenue Code. Tenants are divided into two classes, ante-jāgīr and post-jāgīr tenants. The former are those who have held their land from a period prior to the alienation and they are entitled to continue in possession subject to the payment of the survey assessment. Post-jāgīr tenants pay rent according to agreement with the jāgirdār. The revenue courts have no cognizance over disputes between jāgirdārs and their tenants. The rights of the latter are amply protected. When the court is called upon to determine what shall be considered a reasonable rent, the enhanced value of the property due to improvement effected by the tenant is not allowed as a reason for enhancing rent. In cases of ejectment also the court can order compensation to be paid for the unexhausted improvements made by the tenant. A notice of 6 months is necessary before a landlord can

[1] Such jāgīrs may be compared with the mediæval frankalmoin.

enhance the rent of a tenant and an annual tenancy cannot be terminated by either party without 3 months notice.

The number of jāgīr villages in the plain tāluks of the District is nineteen. The total area was 22,396 acres in 1906-07 of which 969 acres were included in village sites, tanks, rivers and the like and the balance of 21,427 acres were occupied for cultivation. The land revenue of these villages enjoyed by the jāgirdārs amounted to Rs. 34,528, and the quit-rent paid to Government was Rs. 237.

Pālampat tenure.

305. The word *pālampat* means a protecting lease, and the *pālampat* tenure originally was one under which whole villages were made over at a fixed rental for a number of years, no account being taken of the subsequent spread of cultivation. It thus resembled the modern *izāra* system. Many however of the Berār *pālampats* (and those in the Amraoti District are a particularly striking instance) are well situated villages of extremely fertile land, such as even in the worst of times must always have tempted cultivation. It seems probable therefore that this tenure lost its original meaning and that it became more often than not an honorific grant for the support of personal dignity. Six villages in the Daryāpur tāluk are held on this tenure by Deshmukh and Deshpāndia families. The total area of these villages is 8716 acres, of which 8445 acres are occupied, and the revenue assessed is Rs. 17,126. Of this Rs. 11,450 are enjoyed by the *pālampatdārs* and the balance of Rs. 5676 is paid to Government. The latter payment is fixed for ever and is not liable to change at future settlements. The older tenants in *pālampat* villages are protected by the Berār Land Revenue Code in the same way as in jāgīr villages.

Inām land.

306. Under the head of *inām* are classified plots of land in *khālsa* villages held wholly and partially rent-free. They are either service or personal grants.[1] In 1907-08 the area so held was 18,489

---

[1] The word jāgīr is sometimes used for *all* personal grants and *inām* for *all* service grants; but the definitions given in the text are the correct ones.

acres, the land revenue assigned was Rs. 31,349 and the quit rent paid to Government was Rs. 3719.

Cesses.

307. When Berār came under British management in 1853, a class of village servants known as *havildārs* was found in existence. It was the *havildār's* duty to assist the patel in collecting the revenue and in other village matters, and he also occasionally acted as a *chaukidār*, patrolling the village at night. It was no part of his duty however to report crime. He was paid from a fund known as the village expenses either in money or land, receiving also contributions of grain from the villagers. After the cession the *havildār* was commuted into a police *chaukidār*, but it was found that the patel needed help and that the village required a recognised servant for watch and ward and other services. It was decided to unite the various offices in one man, where one man was capable of performing them, and the new official was termed jāglia. A cess of one anna in the rupee of land revenue was sanctioned in 1866 and was known as the jāglia cess. The practice grew up of spending the surplus of the jāglia cess on public improvements, and to mark this fact the designation of the cess was changed in 1880 to the "Jāglia and Local Cess." In 1867 a school cess was imposed at the rate of 1 per cent. on the land revenue, but the system of calculating this percentage was not uniform and great confusion resulted. In 1879 it was changed to 3 pies in the rupee, and in 1880 it was amalgamated with the Jāglia and Local Cess. The combined cesses are now being recovered in *khālsa* or unalienated villages at the rate of 15 pies per rupee of the assessment of each survey number, and at 2 per cent. of the total of the assessments of all the survey numbers in jāgīr villages. The proprietors of jāgīr villages can make their own arrangement for the maintenance of jāglias, but if the Deputy Commissioner considers these inadequate, he may levy an additional cess at the rate of one anna in the rupee on the total of the assessments of all the survey numbers. The surplus of the jāglia and local cess, after the expenses of the jāglia cess have been defrayed, is handed over to the District Board. The surplus so handed over in 1907-08 was Rs. 62,000, while

Rs. 1,11,450 were spent on the jāglia force. The school cess produces about Rs. 44,000. In 1856 a road cess was imposed at the rate of one per cent. of the land revenue, but owing to a mistake of the Settlement Department, effect was not given to the intentions of Government, and, instead of a cess being levied, this percentage of the land revenue was set aside in each District for the maintenance of roads. The road cess in jāgīr villages produces Rs. 518.

CHAPTER IX.

GENERAL ADMINISTRATION.

The Province and the Nizām's Salute.

308. Amraoti is the headquarters of the Commissioner, Berār Division; also of the Conservator of Forests, Berār Circle, the Inspector of Schools, the Chaplain of Berār and other Divisional officers. In some Departments, notably the Judicial, the Public Works and the Post Office, the Province is divided into two parts, East and West, having headquarters at Amraoti and Akolā respectively. Previous to the amalgamation with the Central Provinces in 1903, Amraoti contained in addition to the present staff a Judicial Commissioner, a Sanitary Commissioner, and Inspectors-General of Police, and Excise, etc., but these appointments have now been merged in the Central Provinces cadre. The Hyderābād Assigned Districts (to use the old name) are, however, still foreign territory, not a part of British India, though held on a lease in perpetuity. Legislation for Berār is still carried on by orders of the Executive Council; and Acts of Parliament and of the Indian Legislature have no force in the Province unless applied to it by special notification. His Highness the Nizām receives a yearly rent of twenty-five lakhs of rupees; and his sovereignty is solemnly recognised every year on his birthday, his salute of twenty-one guns being fired at Amraoti and his flag flown from sunrise to sunset.

Staff.

309. The head of the District is the Deputy Commissioner, who is also District Magistrate. He is assisted by a Subdivisional Officer and Magistrate at Ellichpur, and at headquarters by three assistants, usually members of the Provincial Service. Amraoti has also for several years past been a training ground for a newly joined member of the Indian Civil Service, and there is now an Extra Assistant Commissioner for Excise. One of

Bemrose, Collo., Derby.

PURNA BRIDGE AT ASEGAON.

the three ordinary Extra Assistants is Treasury Officer, and the post of District Registrar is also held by an Assistant. The Treasury banks with the local branch of the Bank of Bombay for currency, but there is a very large stamp store under the direct control of the Treasury officer. The subdivisional system has been introduced and the six tāluks are at present arranged as follows :

(a) Amraoti Subdivision (headquarters Amraoti) Amraoti,
(b) Chāndur Subdivision (headquarters Amraoti), Chāndur, Morsī,
(c) Ellichpur Subdivision (headquarters Ellichpur) Ellichpur, Daryāpur, Melghāt.

Previous to the 1st September 1905 the Murtizāpur tāluk now joined to Akolā was part of Amraoti, and the Ellichpur Subdivision was a separate District. Each tāluk is under a Tahsīldār aided by a Naib Tahsīldār. The former, in addition to his revenue powers, is a 2nd or 3rd class magistrate and sub-treasury officer, and a few of the latter have been invested with 3rd class magisterial powers.

There is an Honorary Magistrate of the 2nd class at Daryāpur, and benches (3rd class) at :—

Amraoti city, Kholāpur, (Amraoti tāluk),
Ellichpur city and Chāndur Bazār, (Ellichpur tāluk),
Dhāmangaon, (Chāndur tāluk),
Warūd, (Morsī tāluk),
Anjangaon Surji, (Daryāpur tāluk).

Two members of the Ellichpur bench have 2nd class powers ; and when they sit the court has second class jurisdiction. The District Superintendent of Police has an Assistant and a Deputy Superintendent at headquarters ; and either an Assistant or a Deputy Superintendent at Ellichpur. The District and Sessions Judge, and the additional District and Sessions Judge have jurisdiction also in the adjoining District of Yeotmāl. There are 4 Subordinate Judges at Amraoti, one of whom has charge of the Small Cause Court, and one each at Ellichpur, Daryāpur, and Morsi. There are also Munsiffs' courts at these three places as well as in Amraoti. The District comprises two forest divisions, Melghāt (with headquarters at Chikaldā,) and Amraoti. There is a Civil Surgeon of the Indian Medical Service with Assistant Surgeons at Amraoti and Ellichpur ; and the Executive Engineer, East Berār Division, has his headquarters at Amraoti with Subdivisional officers at Amraoti, Ellichpur and Murtizāpur, the last-named having the Daryāpur tāluk in his charge. There are Deputy Educational Inspectors at Amraoti and Ellichpur.

Village administration.

310. The unit of government in Berār is the ryotwāri village, the representative of which in all its dealings with the various departments is the patel. 'He represents,' says Sir Frederic Lely, 'both government to the people and the people to government. If he loses his influence, both suffer.' He is a *watandār*, or hereditary officer, and his chief business is to collect the land revenue of his village and to take it to the tahsīl where he is remunerated by a percentage. He also collects and is similarly remunerated for all other Government and District Board dues, including income tax from any villagers who may be liable to it, and the revenue arising from forest lands if there be any in his village. It is incumbent on him to report to the Tahsīldār any discontent or ill-feeling of which he may have knowledge, to control the village watch, and in general to assist the police in the detection and prevention of crime. His varied duties also include the maintenance of the fair-weather roads and of village sanitation and statistics of births and deaths. He is bound to report an outbreak of plague or other epidemic, to help travellers in distress, and to render information or assistance to any officer who may require it. Thus patels were recently, in the interests of plague prevention, instructed to make a census of cats in their villages. The great majority of these officers are Marāthās or Kunbīs, though there are also Mālis and members of other cultivating castes, and a few Musalmāns. Their appointment, duties and control are regulated by the Berār Patels and Patwāris Law and the rules thereunder ; and

in all large villages there are two patels, one for revenue and one for police duties. They are generally among the leading landholders, and the office, the *watan* or right to which is sometimes confined to a single family (*khel*) and sometimes shared by several, carries with it the *mānpān* or right of precedence in the village with sundry presents of a ceremonial nature on marriages and festivals. The office is highly valued, not only for its allowances, but for the honours which attach to it and for the power which it gives the holder in his village, a power which as a general rule is well used. It carries with it under orders of the Government of India an official (*not* personal) exemption under the Arms Act. Both patels and patwāris have an authorised uniform as officers of Government, an *angarkhā* or long coat, for the former of black, and for patwāris of red.

Land Records Staff.

311. The patwāris[1] are appointed under the same law and rules as the patels. They are village accountants and writers, expected to maintain the various village records in accordance with the model set forth in the Berār Patwāri's Manual. They are almost always Deshastha Brāhmans, and except in the Melghāt and at a few places in the other tāluks are *watandārs*. Like the patels, to whom they are loosely subordinate, they are paid by percentages laid down in the rules already referred to. There is ordinarily one patwāri for each village, though charges of even four or more are not unknown. In this case, if the number of villages or their distance from the one in which he is expected to reside render the work beyond the powers of one man, the *watandār* may work through subordinates appointed by the Deputy Commissioner or Subdivisional Officer. Few of the patwāris are at present trained in survey, but a class has recently been established at headquarters and is now attended by them periodically. In the few villages where patwāri *watans* do not exist, appointments are made without regard

1. Also known as *pāndyas*, a title which should be carefully distinguished from *pāndewār*. v. infra.

to claims of inheritance; but the method of appointment, remuneration and duties are the same. In the Melghāt tāluk there are patwāris only in the C—iii forest area. Of these there are eleven paid by percentages and having each a circle of thirty to forty villages in his charge; their offices are not hereditary and there is no Circle Inspector. The disafforestation and settlement of this tract are in progress, and a revision of the patwāri system will probably take place. The work of patwāris is primarily supervised by Circle Inspectors; a District Inspector of Land Records with an Assistant is attached to the Deputy Commissioner's office. Previously the work was done by *Munsarims*, who, however, differed from Circle Inspectors in being merely assistants of the Tahsīldārs. There are now four Circle Inspectors each in the Amraoti, Chāndur and Morsi tāluks and three each in Ellichpur and Daryāpur; one Circle Inspector has on an average about thirty-nine patwāris to supervise. The duties of the Land Records Staff are contained in the rules framed under section 17 of the Berār Land Revenue Code.

Registration.

312. The Judge of the Small Cause Court was formerly District Registrar, but the office is now held by one of the Deputy Commissioner's Assistants. Partly owing to the ryotwāri tenure of Berār, and partly to the very high value of land in the District, the business of registration is very much larger than in any other District in these Provinces, though in the Melghāt tāluk, especially since the commencement of the settlement, it is almost a negligible quantity for in that tract the holder of land has no right to alienate. There are sixteen sub-registrars with offices at the following places:—

Amraoti tāluk,	*Daryāpur tāluk,*	*Morsi tāluk,*
Amraoti city,	Daryāpur,	Morsi,
Kholāpur,	Anjangaon Surji,	Warūd,
Tākerkhed,		

Chāndur tāluk,
Chāndur Railway,
Dhāmangaon,
Kurhā,
Nāndgaon Kāzi,
Tiosā,

Ellichpur tāluk,
Ellichpur city,
Chāndur Bazār,
Assegaon,

Melghāt tāluk,
Chikaldā.

Of these all except the two last are special salaried sub-registrars. The Assegaon office is held by a rural Sub-registrar, and that at Chikaldā is in charge of the Tahsīldar ex officio. Towards the end of 1906 two sub-offices, Khallār and Ritpur, were abolished. In the year 1896-97, in the area now included in the Amraoti District and Murtizāpur tāluk, 14,373 documents, value (so far as stated) Rs. 47,79,592, were registered; the income was Rs. 38,136 and the expenditure Rs. 16,124. The figures for the present District in 1907 were 10,359 documents value Rs. 72,10,112, Rs. 39,459 income and Rs. 12,573 expenditure.

Excise.

313. The District cannot be said to be a temperate one, the average consumption of the various excisable articles, except *gānja*, being among the highest in the Provinces. A belief in the efficacy of opium as a protection against ague and fever is prevalent among the Kunbīs, and it is therefore very largely consumed except in the Melghāt, where the sales are almost *nil*, for the population, being Korkūs, prefer a more exhilarating febrifuge. Both there and in the other tāluks the liquor traffic is excessive, and the excise revenue for 1906-07 surpassed that of any other District. Owing to the alteration of the District a comparison with previous years has become difficult, but in that year the excise licences and revenue were as follows :—

Description.	No. of Shops.	License fees.			Duty.			Total revenue.		
		Rs.	a.	p.	Rs.	a.	p.	Rs	a.	p.
Foreign liquor ..	9	987	0	0	3,590	0	0	4,577	0	0
Country liquor ..	243	4,35,465	15	10	4,25,701	5	6	8,61,167	5	4
Sindī	217	15,454	0	0	...			15,454	0	0
Gānja, etc. ..	104	26,005	4	0	18,409 (including duty on *bhang*).	0	3	44,414	4	3
Opium	50	85,727	14	0	1,48,031	3	0	2,3. 759	1	0
Total ..	623	Total excise revenue ...						11,59,37	10	7

The Madras Contract Distillery System is in force, having been Introduced on 1st April 1899. The liquor, which is invariably that distilled from mahuā, is supplied from the distilleries at Akolā and Ellichpur to the warehouses. Of these there is one for each tāluk, that for the Melghāt being at Dhārni and the others at tāluk headquarters. The distillers pay a fee of Rs. 100 per annum to Government for each distillery; and the retail vendors buy at the Depôts, paying the price of liquor to the distillers, and Government duty. There is a Distillery Inspector in charge of the Ellichpur distillery and sixteen Sub-Inspectors, one at each of the six warehouses and the remainder on inspection circles. These are under the Excise Extra Assistant Commissioner already mentioned. The distillers (Messrs. Umrigar) also make their own arrangements at distillery and warehouses. Annual auction sales of the liquor contracts have in the past been characterised by internecine competition due to local jealousies of competitors; and the excise revenue has thus been increased much beyond its natural limits. Recent temperance agitation, however, and years of high rates, tend and will tend to make bidders more cautions and to reduce the sales to figures more nearly representing the actual value of the contracts; and consequently to curtail the revenue. But the present liquor contract system is a popular one and the scale of shops appears to supply a real demand. Cases of smuggling are very rare. The Central Provinces rules are now in force with regard to opium and *gānja* which are therefore imported from Ghāzipur and Khandwā respectively: but until 1906 Mālwā and Indore opiums were sold. Previous to 1898 *gānja* was grown locally and at the date of the Berār Gazetteer 1870, opium was largely cultivated round Badnerā. The *sindī* or *tāri* traffic (the names are used indifferently, though the former is the correct one) is small. As in the case of other excisable articles, licenses for retail vend are disposed of by annual auction: but the licensees are left to make their own arrangements with the owners of the trees. Trees growing in A and B class forest cannot be tapped without the consent of the Conservator, and a fee is charged: but those in C class and other Government waste land may be freely used. It is now proposed to introduce a tree tax. *Sindī* trees are not common except in a few parts of the District. The following table gives statistics of consumption:—

Description.	Area in square miles per shop.	Population per shop.	Consumption per 10,000 persons per annum.
Liquor ...	19·6	3,331	1706·5 proof gals.
Sindī ...	21·9	3,730	,, ,, ,,
Opium ..	45·7	7,784	79·9 seers.
Gānja ...	95	161,90	33·4 seers.

314. **Police.** The District Superintendent of Police has under his orders, besides the Gazetted Officers already mentioned, one European Reserve Inspector and one Sergeant, one Court Inspector, a City Inspector for Amraoti Town and Camp, and a Circle Inspector for each of the five tāluks of the plains, Melghāt, where the work is light, forming part of the Ellichpur circle. Previous to 1st October 1907 the force under these consisted of 822 head-constables and men, with 36 Sub-Inspectors, or Chief constables. On that day one Station-house, Badnerā Railway, with a Sub-Inspector and 30 men, was transferred to the Superintendent of Railway Police, and various changes including the abolition of beat duties, have followed. At

present there are 37 Sub-Inspectors and 115 head-constables and 630 men, this total being distributed besides the Reserve among twenty-seven first-class Station-houses, each under one or more Sub-Inspectors. The location of these and of three smaller units known as "Road Posts" is as follows:—

Amraoti circle and city.

Amraoti town,
Tākerkhed,
Kholāpur,
Badnerā,
Mahuli,
Lonī (near Badnerā),
Balgaon (*Road Post*),

Ellichpur and Melghāt circle.

Ellichpur,
Chāndur Bazār,
Shirasgaon Kasbā,
Pathrot,
Assegaon,
Chikaldā,
Dhārni,
Ghātang (*Road Post*),
Bairāgarh (*Road Post*),

Chāndur circle

Chāndur Railway,
Nāndgaon Kāzi,
Talegaon Dashāsar,
Kurhā,
Teosā,
Dattāpur,

Morsi circle.

Morsi,
Sirkhed,
Warūd,
Benodā,

Daryāpur circle.

Daryāpur,
Anjangaon,
Rahīmapur,
Khallār.

The total cost of the police in 1907 was Rs. 1,53,928 and the propor'ion was one to every 6 square miles and 1,023 persons. The men are mostly Pardesīs, or inhabitants of the Upper, particularly the United Provinces, though the term, which means "foreign," includes in Berār men from the other Divisions of the Central Provinces. There is no noticeable predominance of any one caste, Brāhmans, Rājputs, Chhatrīs and Muhammadans being equally common. They are as a rule recruited in the District, whither they come in search of a living; but the wages of labour being locally high, it is often found difficult to obtaid sufficient men; and drafts had recently to be brought in from Jubbulpore and Nimār to complete the strength. The men are armed with smooth bore muskets, and the old pattern bayonet, but there is a Special Reserve 25 strong who carry the Martini-Henry Rifle and the sword bayonet. A small band has been started with the object of smartening the drill in the Reserve.

Crime.

315. Among the twenty-two Districts of the Provinces, Amraoti is surpassed only by Nāgpur in the amount of work dealt with by the courts, showing 5504 persons accused during the year 1907 as against 7991 of the latter, while in the volume of important crime it is unsurpassed even by Nāgpur. Perhaps the most interesting figures in that year's report are those giving the number of cases compounded (2001, a total only surpassed by Nāgpur and Akolā); and those for the numbers proceeded against under the security sections of the Criminal Procedure Code, no less than 256 persons having either furnished such security or been sent to jail in default of it. This total, which is only sixty less than that for the whole of the Central Provinces, is no doubt abnormal. There was a large influx of nomadic criminal tribes from Hyderābād and elsewhere during the year. Many such tribes,[1] however, are indigenous to Berār, and the wealth of its peaceable inhabitants must always prove a tempting bait. It is probable, therefore, that such action will remain frequent. Of more specific charges, cases of dacoity, cattle-theft, and house-breaking fluctuate much in numbers with the state of the season. The high value of land and the lack of a record of rights, such as exists in other Provinces, combine to make both preventive and punitive action against rioting and similar agricultural offences extremely frequent. The Melghāt, despite its enormous yearly drink bill, is a peaceful area, providing but little occupation for either criminal or civil courts.

Village Servants.
A.—Jāglias.

316. The village watch and ward is in the hands of jāglias and mahārs. The former, known also and perhaps more commonly as havildārs or chaukidārs, are a force

[1] No less than thirteen different thieves' jargons are known to be in common use among criminal tribes in Berār.

appointed by Government, the 'village police' of older records: and the chaukidāri is probably the only post in the village which is not hereditary. Their numbers vary from village to village according to a scale laid down in Rule 413 Berār Land Revenue Manual: they are appointed by the patel, subject to confirmation by the Tahsīldār: and they are paid quarterly at a rate which varies at present between Rs. 3-2-8 and Rs. 5 per mensem, and may be determined from time to time by the Chief Commissioner. Their principal duty, it is laid down, is the maintenance of the peace in their villages: but they are also in practice the patel's chuprāssis and servants in the multitude of different duties he is called upon to perform. They are under his orders in collecting the revenue; they attend on him at the *chāwri* and when he comes to headquarters or goes to meet an officer arriving in his village: they carry District officers' post and purvey their supplies when on tour. The uniform supplied to them—a belt and badge, blue *pagrī* and coat edged with yellow—bears a distant resemblance to a police constable's: and a jāglia vain of his personal appearance will sometimes try to heighten the likeness by adding breeches and gaiters of the same colour.

B.—The Mahār.

317. The jāglia is the servant of the patel; the mahār is, through the patel, the hereditary servant of the whole village. The former is an orderly, the latter a menial: the one is usually an impecunious member of one of the higher castes in his village—a Kunbī or a Musalmān: the other belongs to the outcaste race known as Dheds: the very name mahār, indeed, is strictly that of the caste, and the village servants should be distinguished as the *kāmdar* mahārs or *pāndewārs* from other Mahār families who may happen to reside there. Their duties are to be found enumerated in Rule 437 of the Land Revenue Manual; and include not only all those to which the jāglia is liable but the less honourable duties as well. They are the village scavengers: they remove dead cattle from the houses: repair fair weather roads and are supposed to keep clean the public buildings of the village, the *chāwri*, *musāfir-*

khāna, and so forth. They are the village undertakers and remove corpses under the orders of the police for inquest. They are also incidentally the village band, and their music is in great request at marriages and other festivals. The mahārs are appointed by the patel subject to the approval of the Tahsīldār. Their pay is given in kind by the cultivators at harvest, and varies according to the custom of the village: certain crops, *e.g.* cotton are frequently exempt, and the rate of the *haks* may be altered by the Deputy Commissioner or Subdivisional Officer, if a change in the village crops necessitates this course. As a matter of custom, the mahārs also get the skins and carcases of dead animals. In alienated villages the jāgirdār is responsible for the up-keep both of the jāglia force and the menials, and in the Melghāt jāglias are appointed on a different system and the Mahārs replaced by Balāhis, Nihāls, Pardhāns and other low caste tribes, and even occasionally by Korkūs themselves. From the point of view of police, the effectiveness of the village watch and ward has recently been the subject of much criticism and discussion and the reorganisation of the jāglia force is now being considered. Without entering upon debatable ground it may be said to be generally admitted that the excuse is to be found in the extreme smallness of the pay of jāglias and the mahārs' *haks*. The latter, moreover, are in the first instance village servants, not watchmen, in which capacity they are merely auxiliary to the jāglias. As *watandārs* too they have in the past been admitted to office without much inquiry into their characters. However this may be, there are some matters is which their probity is universally admitted. Neither jāglia nor *pandewār* draws more than the barest living wage, sometimes they draw considerably less. Both are most frequently landless men who would have no difficulty in disappearing. Yet they are daily trusted with hundreds and even thousands of rupees, sums amounting to many times their yearly pay, to take to the tahsīlīs; and it is almost if not quite an unknown thing in the history of Berār for them to fail in their trust.

Civil justice and litigation.

318. The Civil District of East Berār is second only to Nāgpur for the dubious distinction of being the most litigious in the Provinces. According to the latest figures 9749 suits were filed in 1907 as compared with 11,660 in the latter District. The District Court, however, considered 659 appeals in that year, while that of Nāgpur had only 390; figures which suggest that the amount spent in litigation must be higher in Berār. The commonest suits are those connected directly or indirectly with land; with questions of the right to be considered a member of Deshmukh or Deshpānde, Patelkí or Patwāri families; and with cotton, which is the staple industry of the District. Land is held under the ryotwāri tenure and as it is of very great value and fertility, suits regarding it are taken to the highest courts regardless of expense; mortgages with a condition of foreclosure are common, those with a condition of sale rare; and the right of pre-emption is also a frequent source of discord. Further, as the revenue law makes no provision for a compulsory mutation of names in village registers when a field changes hands, it commonly happens that the *khātedār* or registered occupant is a person with no tangible right in the soil save that of paying the revenue on it: and thus many suits are filed for a declaration in favour of mutation. The titles of the village and ex-pargana officers are used in Berār as family surnames conveying a certain amount of distinction. The allowance, (*rusūm* or *lawāzimā*) made to the latter is a matter to be divided among members of the family. Hence there are always a number of claimants to be declared members of Deshmukh or Deshpānde families. Suits for partition of ancestral property are also not uncommon, while a decree of the civil court in favour of an applicant's claim to patel or patwāri family has always this additional attraction, that it may some day be found useful when the revenue court is deciding the right to the office itself. Finally, the ginning and pressing of cotton in partnership leads to suits for dissolution of partnership and rendition of account: and the *sattā* system of speculation on the coming crop gives rise to

suits upon losses so incurred which provide the courts with a considerable amount of work. There are two barristers-at-law, both Europeans, practising in this District, seven advocates of the High Court and 60 District vakīls: this does not include those resident in Yeotmāl.

Guardians and Wards.

319. The Court of Wards does not exist in Berār, the system in force in its place being that of the Guardians and Wards Act VIII of 1890. Responsible persons are appointed by the District Judge to be guardians of minors' estates: they give substantial security for the proper performance of their duties: and in important matters they cannot act without first consulting the court. The system is believed to work satisfactorily. In 1907 there were 63 estates so managed in this District with a total value, though many of them were small in size, of over eight lakhs of rupees.

Public Works.

320. There are 236 miles of road in charge of the Public Works Department, of which 114½ miles are class 1, or fully metalled. A road from Sembādoh to Dhārni (24 miles) is under construction, and it is proposed to make over to the Department the road from Morsi by Chāndur Bazār and Ellichpur to Paratwāda. The road from Amraoti to Ellichpur has two fine bridges at Balgaon and Assegaon. The total value of buildings under the Department reaches the large figure of Rs. 23,71,159, of which Rs. 19,79,687 is represented by civil buildings, Rs. 2,63,473 by the military buildings formerly belonging to the Hyderābād Contingent, Rs. 49,668 by Ecclesiastical, and Rs. 78,331 by the Postal and Telegraph Departments. The annual cost of upkeep is Rs. 17,929. Among the more notable structures are the Deputy Commissioner's office at Amraoti (Rs. 1,80,993), the Commissioner's office (Rs. 37,213), and the Conservator's (Rs, 27,246): the two latter have been recently built. The Law Courts cost Rs. 1,37,726, the Church, Rs. 14,204, and the District Jail Rs. 4,02,010. There is a fine Circuit House with Officer's Rest House attached (total cost Rs. 57,946) and a

Circuit House at Ellichpur (Rs. 16,663). At the latter place, besides the former military quarters, there are the usual buildings of a civil station, the most important being the former Deputy Commissioner's office, now used as a court house (Rs. 1,32,850) and a Church (Rs. 16,197). These high figures are of course partly accounted for by the higher cost of building and especially of labour in Berār as compared with the Central Provinces. The two tanks at Amraoti are under the control of the Department; and the dâk bungalows throughout the District have recently been made over to it by the District and Municipal Boards.

Jail.

321. The former District Jail at Ellichpur has been abandoned, the buildings being made over to the Police Department; and the Central Jail at Amraoti was reduced on the 16th April 1908, to the status of a first class District Jail. The building has accommodation for 633 prisoners, including 48 in the women's ward. The daily average number of prisoners for the last five years of its maintenance as a Central Jail were as follows :—

1903	290
1904	271
1905	260
1906	224
1907	244

and the cost of maintenance per head was in 1906, Rs. 91-14-10 and in 1907, Rs. 85-5 0. The chief industries were formerly stone-breaking and lithography, but the latter has now, with the transference of the long-term prisoners, been transferred to the Central Jail at Nāgpur. The lithography was done solely for Government departments, and the forms supplied to these in 1907 brought in Rs. 43,630. In the garden attached to the jail and worked by prison labour, vegetables for prison use and aloes. (*Agave cantala*) are grown. The leaves of the latter are smashed by beating and yield an excellent long fibre, from which coarse rope and twine are prepared : this work is given as an alternative to stone-breaking to some of the prisoners.

Hospitals.

322. The Civil Surgeon of Amraoti has hospitals at Amraoti Camp and Ellichpur Civil Station each in charge of an Assistant Surgeon, and smaller ones (maintained by Government) at Chikaldā and Dhārni in the Melghāt. There are also dispensaries (most of which have wards attached) at the following places. They are supported by subscriptions from private persons and local bodies, and are managed by committees of local residents under the guidance of the Civil Surgeon.

Amraoti tāluk.	*Chāndur tāluk.*	*Daryāpur tāluk.*
Amraoti City,	Chāndur Railway,	Dāryapur,
Badnerā,	Tālegaon,	Anjangaon,
Kholāpur,	*Ellichpur tāluk.*	*Morsi tāluk.*
	Ellichpur City,	Morsi,
	Chāndur Bazār,	Warūd.

These, together with the two in the Melghāt, are in charge of hospital assistants. In the State institutions the total accommodation is for sixty-seven men and eight women, at the dispensaries for forty men and ten women. There is also a Dufferin Hospital in Amraoti City with accommodation for 20 in-patients. This is in charge of a fully qualified Lady practitioner, and is managed by a committee of which the Commissioner is president. At Kothāria, near Ellichpur, an asylum for lepers is maintained by the Korkū Mission on behalf of the Mission to Lepers in India. This has recently been accorded a Government grant-in-aid; the buildings include a church and a dispensary and accommodate about twenty-seven lepers. In 1906 the number of outdoor patients treated in the District was 109,776, and in 1907 95,113; such treatment may therefore be looked upon as fairly popular. Indoor patients in these two years have numbered 1371 and 1183; and when Government servants, paupers and cases brought in by the police are deducted from these totals, it cannot be said that the hospital wards except perhaps that at Amraoti, are used by the public to any great extent. Probably the cause of this is the publicity of the ward system; for when in India a man comes to hospital, he generally brings his wife with him. The extension of family wards therefore is the policy now being pursued.

Vaccination.

323. The District is divided into circles for purposes of vaccination, two in each tāluk. In the four municipalities, vaccination is compulsory under the Act; but in the villages much depends on the co-operation of the village officers, who as a rule support it energetically. Previous to 1894 vaccination was carried on by the hospital assistants: the experiment of having special vaccinators was tried and abandoned in 1904, since when there has been some falling-off in the numbers of persons vaccinated. The last quinquennium for which statistics are available (1898-1903) shows a small-pox death-rate of 0.15 per thousand. Further information may be had from the interesting reports of Lieutenant-Colonel Little.

Education.

324. Prior to the Assignment there were no schools supported expressly by the State Private schools existed in which Sanskrit was taught to Brāhman boys and Marāthī to Hindus of lower castes. Mahārs, Māngs, Chamārs and other degraded tribes were not allowed to enter any school. *Munshis* taught the Arabic of the Korān, Persian and Urdū, and in the old Muhammadan city of Ellichpur the traditional Muhammadan culture was (and to a very limited extent still is) maintained. 'But up to 1861,' (writes Mr. J. H. Burn) 'when education became the concern 'of the State, the occupation of teaching was looked upon as 'derogatory, and metaphorically designated grazing (cattle). 'Thus it never got beyond mere rudiments with most of the 'pupils. We have nevertheless a stock of good writers and 'excellent accountants raised by the few indigenous schools or 'by private household tuition. The village writers, several 'literary deshmukhs and patels among the Hindus, many 'well-to-do traders, the kāzis and other Muhammadans all 'represent the results of private education.'[1] Scattered

---

[1] *Berār Gazetteer* (1870), p. 273.

schools were organised by Government in 1861 and succeeding years, and the Educational Department was introduced in 1866; middle and lower class schools were opened, and on the 1st November in that year the High School at Amraoti was established. At the present day Amraoti shows a higher proportion of children under instruction to children of school-going age than any other District in the Central Provinces or Berār. The High School at Amraoti has an attendance of 400 boys, of whom 40 are boarders; and extra boarding accommodation is being built. The Anglo-Marāthī middle school has an average attendance, of 273, and the Anglo-Urdū school[1] 57. The High School, prior to the amalgamation of Provinces, prepared for the examinations of the Bombay University, but now for those of Allahābād. Besides these there are 6 other Anglo-vernacular schools in the District, and English classes supported by voluntary contributions in many of the District Board schools. A small Government industrial school at Amraoti has been merged in the Victoria Technical Institute. The total of 273 schools for boys and 22 for girls in the District, with an attendance (out of a population of 809,499 and an estimated child population of 121,000) of over eighteen thousand, is a fairly creditable one. The large majority of boys' schools are owned and managed by the District Board and Municipalities, and the system of grants-in-aid to privately owned schools has in recent years been almost entirely discontinued, only ten such remaining; all these, together with several unaided schools, teach the ordinary curriculum and are inspected by Government officers. Three only are completely independent, and the teaching given in these is entirely of a religious character, two being maintained at Horderngan j and Tiosā respectively by wealthy Mārwāri merchants for the teaching of Sanskrit, and one at the village of Kakada being held in a mosque for the inculcation of the Korān. As in other parts of India, female education lags far behind. Government has recently taken over from the local bodies the twenty girls' schools maintained by

[1] Since raised to the status of a High School.

them, and there are two unaided schools belonging to Mission bodies. The female normal school for the training of teachers was transferred from Nāgpur to Amraoti in 1905. One Urdū and four Marāthī newspapers are published in Amraoti, and one Marāthī periodical in Ellichpur. Their names are as follows:—Safir-i-Berār, Pramod Sindhu, Kartavya, Vyāpār Samāchār, Mahārāshtra Vāgvilās, Prabhāt (Ellichpur).

District Board.

325. The Amraoti District Board came into existence in 1890, and now controls, except in the Municipalities and in the backward tract of the Melghāt, the primary schools and a variety of other matters. Minor public buildings, and all but the most important roads and bridges are in its charge; it regulates bazars and fairs and attends to village sanitation and water-supply; it supports with large contributions the dispensaries throughout the District and the Dufferin Fund: it pays the expenses of vaccination, and it maintains the veterinary establishment and the pounds. In years of scarcity or plague it also takes up large measures of relief or prevention. Under it are the Tāluk Boards, one for each of the five tāluks in the plains, which act as its advisers with regard to the needs of their charges, and its agents in carrying out the work ordered. They have no authority of their own, though the question of investing them with powers similar to those possessed by Local Boards in the Central Provinces is now under consideration. The District Fund reaches a total of from two to three lakhs of rupees, and its chief items as laid down in section 22 of the Rural Boards Law are the various cesses, grants-in-aid from Government for general purposes and for education, some minor receipts such as pound fees, and fees levied in the schools. By far the largest heads of expenditure are education and public works, dispensaries and hospitals ranking third. As at present arranged, the constitution of the Board is somewhat complicated. A limited electorate chooses twelve members for each of the Tāluk Boards and six (including the Tahsīldār, who is usually chairman) are nominated by Government; the Tāluk Boards then elect two members each

yearly for a term of 3 years and to the thirty thus obtained are added eight nominated on behalf of Government, including the five Tahsīldārs and the Deputy Commissioner who is ex-officio chairman. The vice-chairman is elected by the members. The Board has a sub-committee for finance and audit, and another, on which some non-members sit, for education. It has a paid Secretary who conducts the office work, and a Public Works Department under a Local Fund Supervisor, which carries out all works of less than Rs. 1000 estimated value.

Minor Excluded Local Funds.

A. The Melghāt Fund.

326. Two minor excluded local funds deserve some mention, namely, the Melghāt, and the cotton market funds. As already mentioned, the Melghāt is exempt from the operation of the Berār Rural Boards Law, and sends no representatives to the District Board. Its school cess is paid to and its schools managed by that body, but for all other local purposes its funds are separate under the immediate control of the Deputy Commissioner. These purposes include the maintenance of the Chikaldā sanitarium to which the ground rent of bungalows in Chikaldā, as well as a fixed Provincial grant (in supersession of the former District grants) are applied.

B. Cotton Market Fund.

327. There are six cotton market committees in the District, one at each of the tāluk head-quarters, and one at Dhāmangaon-Dattāpur, the most important town in the Chāndur tāluk. The committees are concerned with the maintenance and improvement of the market and its surroundings, the construction of *chabūtras* and other necessary buildings, and in general with the health, safety and convenience of persons using the market. Thus they license weighmen and enforce the use of standard weights. Fees are levied by the committee from persons using the markets, and at the end of each year the balances are credited to District Board or Municipal funds according to the situation of the market.

328. The work of sanitation in non-municipal areas is, as already stated, attended to by the District Board, and by the patels. A peculiarity of the District is to be found in the number of very large villages, such as Badnerā, Karasgaon, Shirasgaon Kasbā, or accumulations of villages such as Anjangaon Surji and Dhāmangaon-Horderngan j-Dattāpur, which present peculiar difficulties in the way of sanitation, but have no organisation to meet them. In some there are village sanitation committees, which are supposed to work under the District and Tāluk Boards, and to offer suggestions. They have no source of income and no independent standing; in general, the members show little or no interest in their work preferring to leave it in the hands of the patel; the District Board, on the other hand, is not unnaturally chary of favouring selected places in the matter of expenditure, with a result that real sanitation is but little attended to. However, it is only fair to recognise the help village authorities generally have given in preventing the extension of epidemic disease such as plague and cholera. The question of extending the Central Provinces Village Sanitation Act to Berār is now under consideration; and it is hoped that this may provide a means of improving at any rate the more advanced of the towns in question. There is nothing in Berār to correspond with the Central Provinces system of Notified areas.

Sanitation.

329. There are four Municipalities, all constituted under the Berār Municipal Law of 1886, namely, Amraoti town and camp, Ellichpur city and civil station. The largest, Amraoti town, has 18 elected members and 6 nominated by the Chief Commissioner; but in the others the membership is entirely by nomination; all employ paid secretaries. The Deputy Commissioner is ex-officio chairman of the two headquarters committees; and it is usual for the Subdivisional Officer to fill the same post in the two at Ellichpur. The taxes, with the exception of a small toll on carts coming into Amraoti town (this is let to farm), are all direct, the main

Municipalities.

imposts being on professions and trades (except in Amraoti camp) and on houses and lands (except in Ellichpur civil station). Considerable difficulty is experienced, especially in Amraoti town, in collection, as the rate-payers have acquired the habit of delaying payment as long as possible; and though the burden is not heavy, appeals to the magistrate for aid in collection are very numerous; and in general the committees may be said to be in straitened circumstances. The following table gives the position of the Municipalities according to latest reports, those for year ending March 31st 1908:—

Municipality.	Population Census 1901.	Members.	Income.			Expenditure.	Incidence per head.					
			Tax and Cesses.	Others.	Total.		Tax.			Income.		
			Rs.	Rs.	Rs.	Rs.	Rs.	a.	p.	Rs.	a.	p.
1 Amraoti Town.	34,219	24	53,410	14,418	67,828	67,285	1	9	0	1	14	7
2 Amraoti Camp.	5,295	10	8,196	9,811	18,007	14,003	1	8	9	3	5	7
3 Ellichpur City.	26,822	22	14,083	6,715	20,798	30,256	0	8	8	0	12	8
4 Ellichpur Civil Station ..	8,132	12	5,377	13,098	18,475	14,898	0	10	7	2	4	3

At the date of Sir A. Lyall's Gazetteer, 1870, Ellichpur city had 27,782 inhabitants, while Amraoti could not boast of more than 23,410. It has recently been proposed to introduce the electoral system into Ellichpur, but the proposal was abandoned owing to the lack of interest displayed. Even in Amraoti town at the last election, when party feeling ran unusually high, little over 20 per cent. of the electors could be induced to register their votes. The chief problems before the Municipalities, besides that of finance, are water-supply and sanitation. The latter is good in the two civil stations, but poor in the two cities, particularly in Amraoti, where various schemes proposed from time to time have had to be abandoned owing to lack of funds. The problem is intimately associated with that of street widening and providing open spaces, and the high value of land in Municipal limits has been one of many stumbling blocks. Water is drawn in the two Ellichpurs from wells only, though in the city there is an ancient conduit now no longer fit for use. In Amraoti camp the Wadāli tank and filtering station supply excellent water to the various bungalows and public offices ; but the tank leaks considerably, and as its storage capacity is small, it cannot be relied upon in a shortage of rainfall. Two subsidiary tanks which were constructed during the famine of 1899-1900 gave way before a flood in 1903, and have not since been repaired. The wells in camp are both numerous and excellent, and may generally be relied upon except in seasons of extreme drought. The case is different in Amraoti town, where the wells contain only brackish water and are constantly being fouled. The Kālapāni tank, four miles away, gives a fair supply of water, but even in good years is inadequate for the rapidly increasing population, and has always to be supplemented by pumping operations at Rājāpeth waterworks about a mile from the city. Even this source is insufficient in times of scarcity and, if the town is to develop in the future as it has done in the immediate past, a large addition to the water-supply is a necessity. A scheme was mooted a few years ago for the construction of a large tank at Indla, some miles away, which, it was thought, would not only give a sufficient supply for the two Municipalities but even perhaps leave a surplus for irrigation ; the project, however, would be a very costly one, and nothing has as yet been done. A general scheme for a sufficient water-supply has been and is still under consideration. Further details as to the separate municipal towns will be found under the separate headings in the Gazetteer Appendix.

330. The following table gives statistics of revenue in recent years:—

Statistics of Revenue.

Year.	District.	Land Revenue and Cesses.	Forests.	Stamps.	Excise.	Registration.	Town Fund Tax.	Income Tax.	Other receipts.	Total Revenue.
		Rs.	Rs.	Rs.	Rs.	Rs.	Rs.	Rs.	Rs.	Rs.
1890-91	Amraoti ...	14,76,230	72,942	92,329	3,79,675	19,331	12,973	...	25,856	20,79,336
	Ellichpur ...	9,54,808	1,99,875	41,404	2,20,465	9,437	Not available	...	7,912	a 14,33,901
1900-01	Amraoti ..	16,87,996	61,248	79,085	2,85,586	22,048	29,403	...	25,453	21,90,819
	Ellichpur ...	9,47,114	1,15,931	28,238	1,43,993	9,505	12,886	...	12,821	12,70,488
1901-02	Amraoti ...	17,08,588	73,931	2,96,371	3,11,218	24,008	31,568	..	32,007	24,77,691
	Ellichpur ...	9,00,084	1,80,137	1,37,316	1,97,239	15,515	12,098	...	23,913	15,56,302
1902-03	Amraoti ...	17,10,337	95,353	2,74,445	3,94,468	24,529	29,251	...	35,926	25,64,309
	Ellichpur ...	9,79,042	1,70,544	1,23,108	2,32,235	13,967	12,285	...	33,008	15,64,189
1903-04	Amraoti ...	20,81,704	1,07,216	2,46,402	4,57,659	25,485	28,625	...	38,532	29,85,623
	Ellichpur ...	12,38,993	1,76,102	1,04,339	2,70,993	14,076	12,448	...	16,232	18,33,183
1904-05	Amraoti ..	22,19,780	1,14,628	2,69,578	5,29,108	28,094	...	65,602	37,689	32,64,479
	Ellichpur ...	12,42,009	1,75,569	1,21,387	3,59,572	14,539	...	31,867	18,215	19,63,158
1905-06	Amraoti ...	30,44,723	1,21,500	3,61,372	10,94,257	29,829	...	79,574	57,156	49,84,28
	Melghat ...		1,95,876							
1906-07	Amraoti ...	30,50.347	1,27,484	3,29,850	11,61,209	41,274	...	73,910	41,123	50,12,353
	Melghat ...		1,87,156							
1907-08 (b)	Amraoti ...	30,18,409	1,26,459	3,78,208	10,93,616	39,459	...	70,990	44,798	49,63,770
	Melghat ...		1,91,731							

(a) Excludes Town Fund Tax.

(b) The figures are in some cases for slightly different periods from those in the succeeding table.

Receipts and charges.

331. The District balance sheet for the year ending March 31st 1908 is as follows :—

Receipts.					Charges.				
Heads.		Amount.			Heads.		Amount.		
		Rs.	A.	P.			Rs.	A.	P.
I.	Land Revenue ...	28,41,851	15	11	1.	Refunds and drawbacks...	10,783	2	7
II.	Opium ...	51,535	8	0	2.	Assignments and compensation	2 390	2	7
IV.	Stamps ..	3,78,878	4	0	3.	Land Revenue	5,15,244	1	7
V.	Excise ..	10,42,081	6	8	6.	Stamps ...	9,824	4	5
VI.	Provincial rates ...	2,30,514	3	0	7.	Excise ...	17,230	1	11
VII.	Customs ...	21,105	3	2	10.	Assessed taxes	3.704	15	7
VIII.	Assessed taxes ..	82,012	12	7	12.	Registration.	15,299	9	4
X.	Registration	44,139	14	9	18.	General Administration ..	56,420	4	8
XII.	Interest ...	2,289	11	5	19A	Law and Justice. Courts of Law ...	1,24,519	12	1
XVIA.	Law and Justice. Courts of Law ...	17,614	3	5	19B.	Law and Justice. Jails ..	21,520	15	5
XVIB.	Law and Justice. Jails ..	2,827	7	4	20.	Police ...	3,18,339	2	9
					22.	Education ...	1,18,132	8	2
					23.	Ecclesiastical.	11,234	2	0
XVII.	Police ...	21,322	13	8	24.	Medical ..	43,466	6	6
XIX.	Education...	17,527	13	5	26.	Scientific ...	6,627	8	9
XX.	Medical ...	155	6	0	27.	Territorial and Political ...	768	6	5
XXII.	Receipts in aid of superannuation ..	3,330	13	9	29.	Superannuation allowances and pensions ...	80,802	10	8
XXIII.	Stationery and Printing ...	2,662	3	7	30.	Stationery and Printing ..	12,504	15	6
					32.	Miscellaneous	13,649	15	0
XXV.	Miscellaneous ...	85,781	5	9	45.	Civil Works...	1,63 347	10	5
	TOTAL ...	48,45,334	5	5		TOTAL ...	15,25,812	11	6

To this may be added the following:—

	Income.
	Rs.
Forest, Amraoti Division	1,26.459
,, Melghāt Division	1,91.731
TOTAL	3,18,190
P. W. D. Communications &c. ...	276
,, Irrigation	nil
Badnerā Government Book Depot ...	46,374

The income and expenditure of local bodies is following table. The excess of expenditure o some cases is due to temporary reasons and comment.

	Income.
	Rs.
District Board	294,700
Amraoti Town Municipal Committee.	67.828
Amraoti Camp Municipal Committee.	18,007
Ellichpur City Municipal Committee.	20,798
Ellichpur Civil Station Municipal C.	18,475
TOTAL MUNICIPAL FUND	1,25,108
Melghāt Fund	3,761
Amraoti Cotton Market	9 412
Ellichpur ,, ,, ...	1,204
Daryāpur ,, ...	1,206
Morsi ,, ,, ...	972
Chāndur ,, ,, ...	1,102
Dattāpur ,, ,, ...	1,913
TOTAL COTTON MARKET FUND ...	15,809
Dispensary Fund	20,166
TOTAL ALL LOCAL FUNDS	45,9,544

These total receipts however include grants ment and payments from one local fund to anot

APPENDIX.

GAZETTEER OF TALUKS, TOWNS, IMPORTANT VILLAGES, RIVERS AND HILLS.

APPENDIX.

GAZETTEER OF TALUKS, TOWNS, IMPORTANT VILLAGES, RIVERS AND HILLS.

Ambada.—Tāluk Morsi[1]: houses 701. Population 3,242. A large but unimportant village in the Morsi tāluk, having a combined post office and Marāthī school and also an Urdū school. The weekly bazar is held on Fridays. The watandār Patel is a Muhammadan.

Amla.—Tāluk Chāndur: houses 640. Population 2,438. A fair is held here for a single day on Shivrātr in the month of Māgh (February) and is attended by about 2,000 persons. There is a modern temple of Visheswar (Mahādeo) managed by a village *panch* on the profits of a few fields privately set apart for the purpose.

Amner.—Once the headquarters of the Amner pargana, Melghāt tāluk: the village is deserted, but 'the little fort of 'Amner, often called Jilpi Amner, has had some fame in 'recent wars. It occupies an elevated position immediately 'overlooking the waters of the Gargā and Tāpti at their 'junction. It is a compact-looking quadrangular building of 'brick and mud pointed with mortar. The walls are flanked 'by four round bastions of the same material, and enclose 'about an acre of ground. The west angle is occupied by a 'mosque, which, with its minarets towering about the rest of 'the fort, presents rather a picturesque object. There is only 'one approach, that from the north-west, on a level with the 'left bank of the Tāpti, which, though entirely of earth, is 'very steep and lofty. The gateway and a portion of the 'ramparts were destroyed in 1858. At the same time the

[1] In this Appendix the words "gin" and "press" are used throughout as equivalents for steam ginning and pressing factory irrespective of the number of gins or presses at work in the factory.

Berar Gazetteer 1870.

'guns, four or five in number,' were removed.' It lay in the line of Tantia Topi's retreat at the close of the Mutiny and subsequently when Tantia Bhīl was harassing the surrounding country with his raids a police watch was established here under the command of the late Rājā Khumān Singh, without however very much effect.

Amner.—Tāluk Morsi houses 329. Population 1,522. A village on the Wardhā opposite the town of Jalālkhed in Nāgpur District. Formerly a place of much importance, it has to-day been left in a corner and can only be reached by country roads from Nāgpur or Warud; but the ruins of the town walls as well as of many temples, mosques and tombs bear witness to its former glories. It is said to have had manufactures of laces and silk and a fair to which elephants, horses, jewellery, and other outward signs of wealth were brought. There was a great fight here between the Bhonsla and the Nizām when the latter was marching to the reduction of Nawāb Ismail Khān, and the tombs of the slain are still shown. In 1826, the Muharram and the Hindu festival Ganesh Chaturthī coinciding, a serious faction fight took place. To-day the population is chiefly Muhammadan. There is an old temple to Mahādeo, on the banks of the river, and, about 30 paces off, a pool, the depth of which is unknown; at the bottom of it there is said to be a temple which can be seen when the river is clear. Tradition has it that the place is presided over by the gods, and that at one time any Brāhman by asking for cooking vessels over-night would find them near this hole in the morning; he was, however, bound to return them, when used, into the water: one day a Brāhman prayed for a large number, and, instead of returning them, sold them, since when they have never been supplied. Perhaps the most striking of the ruins, though it is little over two hundred years old, is the *makbarā* of Lāl Khān Pathān, a large domed building in white stucco, with small spires at the four corners. Over the gateway is an inscription in Persian as follows:—

'For the service of the throne of the Emperor Alamgir, his 'servant Rājā Kisn Sing, with great exertions and in purity of 'heart and soul laid the foundation of a beautiful tomb, a 'mosque, a cistern and a garden as well constructed as 'Paradise itself. It was on the felicitous day the fourth of 'Ramzān that Lāl Khān Bazlaman passed from this world. 'Though his body be placed in the earth of Amner, yet his 'pure soul is entrusted to the Hari. O God! Ever preserve 'this matchless resting-place that his holy tomb and the dome 'of light may always shine. When I sought of the unseen one 'the year of his death, I was told "Lal Khān achieved martyr-'dom at Badnūr." The building of the mausoleum was 'accomplished between the 34th and 36th years of the Emperor's 'reign at Delhi, Hijri 1100.' The chronogram '*Lāl Khān yāft 'shahâdat bamakān Badnūr*,' gives not only the place but the date of his death. Perhaps the most notable feature of the tomb is that it should have been built by a Hindu Rājā.

Amraoti Taluk.—The headquarters tāluk of the Amraoti District lying between 20°41′ and 21°12′ N. and 77°32′ and 78°2′ E. with an area of 672 square miles, or 14 per cent. of that of the District. The tāluk contains 330 villages and towns; of which 9 are jāgir. It lies in the fertile valley of Berār but the almost uniform characteristics of this valley are broken by a low range of stony and barren hills which, cropping up in the immediate vicinity of Amraoti camp, extends over the eastern border of the tāluk. The tāluk is bounded on the north by the Ellichpur and Morsi tāluks, on the west by the Daryāpur tāluk and the Murtizāpur tāluk of Akolā District, and in the east and south it borders upon the Chāndur tāluk, almost touching with its north-eastern extremity, the river Wardhā which forms the line of division between Berār and the Central Provinces. The tāluk is compact in shape though it narrows towards the north; it has a length of 30 miles and an average breadth of some 23 miles. The tract contains no large forest; but *bābul* and mango are plentiful everywhere, though the latter tree does not attain to any very great size. The tāluk has a great variety of soils ranging from the prevalent black argillaceous mould to the worst of rocky soils. Inferior in appearance though the latter are, however, they are tolerably fertile owing to the iron felspar they contain, and in favourable seasons they produce excellent crops, but require periodical manuring. The black soil, however, except in the western part of the tāluk where it contains an excess of saline matter, is very fertile, requiring little or no manure nor even heavy ploughing, for the production of the prolific cotton for which this part of Berār is so justly renowned. The soil is deep and in the hot weather great fissures form in it sometimes several feet deep. When the rains come, the surface matter is washed well below and the soil turned as effectually as it would be by the best ploughs.[1] The climate is on the whole healthy, though trying in the months of April, May and June on account of the extreme heat. The only rivers of any importance are the Pūrna and the Pedhī; the former separates Amraoti from Daryāpur on the western border and contains a supply of water throughout the year. The Pedhī running through the centre of the tāluk also has a perennial supply. Many of the villages are dependent on wells for their drinking water. The same salt bed, however, which underlies parts of the Akolā District and Daryāpur tāluk, infects Amraoti; and well water accordingly is frequently very brackish especially in the western towns and villages. Two large tanks have been constructed near Amraoti to supply the Civil Station and the city, but in years of short rainfall the supply is precarious. There are also tanks at Pohorā, Anjangaon Bāri, and one or two other places.

Population.

The population of the tāluk in 1901 was 175,557 persons, or about 22 per cent. of that of the District. In 1891 the population was 183,508 and in 1881, 163,456. The increase between 1881 and 1891 was 12.3 per cent. as against the District figure of 9.2 per cent., and the decrease between 1891 and 1901 was 4.3 per cent, as against the District figure of 4.7 per cent. As usual, the decrease in the last decade may be attributed to the series of bad years and the famines. The density of population is 261 souls per square mile, and excluding towns the density of rural population is 170 persons per square mile. The tāluk contains 5 towns and 325

[1] This is the popular theory.

villages, of which 67 are uninhabited [1] according to village lists. The towns in the tāluk are Amraoti, Amraoti Camp, Badnerā, Kholāpur and Balgaon Jāgir. Of the population 34.76 per cent. live in towns and 65.24 per cent. live in villages. Besides the above towns the following 11 villages contained a population of more than 2,000 persons in 1901 :—Anjangaon Bāri, Tākarkhedā, Thugaon Kasbā, Nāndgaon Peth, Pusdā, Bhātkuli, Māhuli Jāgīr, Yaoli, Wathodā, Sahur, and Siralā. There were also 15 villages whose population exceeded 1,000 persons.

Agriculture.

Formerly the principal crop was juāri, which forms almost entirely the food of the people. At the original settlement it occupied 36 per cent. of the cultivated land. Second in importance then stood wheat which occupied 22 per cent., and though partly consumed in the District was chiefly exported. Cotton came next, and the area occupied by it was 68,660 acres or 21 per cent. of the entire land under cultivation. This proportion was considered reasonable and it was expected that the cultivation of cotton would not be much further extended here—at least not in undue proportion to the other crops—as it would bring about a still greater scarcity of food than already existed. At revision settlement the figures based on the average for the settlement period (1893-1897) show that the area under cotton annually was 122,804 acres or about 35 per cent., and that juār was second though not far behind with 111,896 acres or 32.5 per cent. of the cultivated and. Wheat then came next in importance with 57,918 acres or 16.3 per cent., whilst linseed with 26,485 acres or 7.5 per cent. covered less than half this area. In 1906-07 the total village area excluding State forests but including the area of jāgirs was 399,445 acres ; of this 372,861 acres or 93 per cent. were occupied for cultivation. The total cropped area including double cropped (200 acres only) was 360,880 acres. The continued demand and the consequent high prices have greatly

[1] An uninhabited village is one whose inhabitants in the Pindári times betook themselves to live in some more strongly fortified place, generally the *Kasba* or Pargana Town, but continued their separate village organization and the cultivation of their old fields,

stimulated the cultivation of cotton; the area under it being 172,472 acres or about 48 per cent. of the total. The area under juāri had declined, being 97,561 acres or 27 per cent. Wheat occupied 44,026 acres or 12.2 per cent. and linseed 5,276 acres or 1.4 per cent. The area irrigated was only 1,674 acres, chiefly from wells, there being no *pātasthal bagait* land.

Land Revenue.

At the original settlement the 330 Government villages were divided into 4 groups and assessed with a dry crop maximum acreage rate of Rs. 2-8-0. The average rates per cultivated acre, however, varied from R. 1-2-4 to R. 1-8-9. As in other tāluks the grouping of villages was made from a consideration of their proximity or otherwise to the large bazar towns and the railway stations. At revision settlement, considering the excellence of communications in the tāluk both by road and rail it was thought unnecessary to tone down assessments by division of villages into separate groups. Hence all villages of the tāluk were included in one settlement group and a maximum dry crop standard acreage rate of Rs. 2-12-0 was fixed. The demand at the time of revision settlement on Government occupied land of 349,905 acres according to the former survey was Rs. 4,66,057 giving an incidence of R. 1-5-4 per acre; while at the revision settlement the assessment on Government occupied land of 349,893 acres according to revision survey was increased to Rs. 6,30,144, the incidence per acre falling at R. 1-12-10. The increase in revenue thus amounted to Rs. 1,64,087, being 35.2 per cent. in excess of the previous demand. In 1907-08 the land revenue demand including cesses was Rs. 6,71,559 while the actual collections according to Treasury figures were Rs. 6,76,662 including however some amount on account of arrear collections. For purposes of land records the tāluk has been divided into three Circle Inspectors' circles with headquarters at Badnerā, Dhamoni and Nāndgaon.

Miscellaneous.

It contains 6 Police Station-houses, of which the one at Amraoti is under the Amraoti City Inspector, while the others at Tākarkhedā, Kholāpur, Badnerā, Māhuli and Loni, each under a Sub-

Inspector, constitute a single police circle under the Amraoti Tāluk Inspector. The Chirodi Forest Reserve lies partly in this tāluk and partly in that of Chāndur.

Amraoti Town.—The chief town of the province of Berār and of the Amraoti District and headquarters of the tāluk of the same name. It stands about 1,118 feet above sea-level in 20°56′ N. and 77°47′ E., and is distant by railway about 113 miles to the south-west of Nāgpur, 419 miles to the north-east of Bombay and 814 miles to the south-west of Calcutta viâ Nagpur. Hyderābād, Deccan, the Resident of which place formerly administered Berār, is not connected with it by any direct line of rail or road but lies about 250 miles to the south as the crow flies. Amraoti suffers from the disadvantage of not being on the main line of the Great Indian Peninsula Railway, but is connected with it at Badnerā 6 miles away by a branch line of State Railway. The town includes portions of the villages of Tarkhed, Rājāpeth, Gambhīrpur and Mahājanpur, and is bounded roughly speaking by the Amba Nāla on the south and a smaller watercourse (called Dalelpuri after a bygone Gosāwi) on the north. To the west lie the cultivated fields of Gambhīrpur and Mahājanpur and to the east the civil station. The area of the town is 361 acres and 38 *gunthās*.

Population.

At the census taken in 1867 the population of the town was 23,410: it was 23,550 in 1881, 28,946 in 1891 and 34,216 in 1901; an increase of 46 per cent. in 35 years. Since then however it has three times been visited by plague, and it is probable, even when we allow for large immigrations from elsewhere, that the figure of population has been little more than stationary. It now stands 5th among the towns of the Central Provinces being the most populous in Berār, though 40 years ago it was surpassed by Ellichpur. Of the total population 26,773 are Hindus, 6,295 Musalmāns, 781 Jains, 186 Animists, 112 Christians, 38 Pārsis and 31 Sikhs.

History and Antiquities.

Amraoti contains a large number of Hindu and two Jain temples as well as several mosques. One of the latter, that of Bade Nāl Sāhib, is still supported by *inām* land, and the Jāmi Masjid is said to be 300 years old but none of them is of any interest. The Jain temples are small and call for no particular comment. Among the Hindus the most important are the temples of Ambā Devī and of Bālajī, next in order after which come those of Ekirra Devī, Someshwar, and Narāyaṇ and the Dattā Mandir. The Bālajī temple and pilgrims' *math* attached to it are supported from the revenues of the *inām* village of Jamgaon in Amraoti tāluk. The Ambā temple is said to be the oldest in Amraoti and lays claim to a respectable antiquity of 1000 years, though how much of the present building can be of that age it is impossible to say, since pious hands have covered the whole with plaster and ornament. It was from hence, we are told [1] that Krishna carried off Rukmini, who had come to the temple with her brother Rukmaya to pay her vows before her marriage with Shishupāl. With them to witness the ceremony came a number of persons called Warhādis or Warhāris, who settling here gave their name to the country "Warhār" corrupted into "Berār." Rukmaya after Rukmini's *enlèvement*, tried the chances of a battle with Krishna, but was defeated and only spared at the urgent entreaties of his sister. He then settled at Bhātkuli a village 14 miles to the westward, where his name has been perpetuated by a temple erected in his honour. The name of the town is even said to be derived from the goddess, though the derivation is almost as doubtful as that just given for the name of the province, and the etymology "The Eternal City" or "City of the Immortals" is far more likely (vide Chapter I, para. I). The deity is held in great reverence by the Hindu community and on every occasion of a marriage or thread-ceremony invitation is invariably offered first to this deity. The most important days when the visitors come in great numbers are the 8th, 9th and 10th days of the first fortnight of Ashwin (October). The annual income, derived mainly from the offerings made to the deity and from the *dharma* fund collected by the traders, amounts to Rs. 6,000 and the main heads of expenditure are *sadāvarta* (alms-giving) and other charitable

[1] *Vide* also Kaundinyapur.

purposes. The management of the temple is in the hands of a local committee composed of bankers and influential citizens. The income and expenditure of the temple during the year 1907-1908 were Rs. 6,000 and 5,000 respectively, and doles were given to some nineteen thousand persons Apart from the temple the town is certainly a modern one, and is not even the headquarters of the pargana in which it lies, that distinction being held by Badnerā. Amraoti is said to have been founded by Raghujī Bhonsla, and its fortunes commenced from the close of the eighteenth century when the tyranny of the Akolā tālukdār drove a number of the inhabitants of that place to settle here; but its early years were by no means uniformly prosperous. Both the Nāgpur and Hyderābād rulers were represented here, the former taking 60 per cent. and the latter 40 per cent. of the revenues, and both oppressing the people. Amraoti contains two interesting relics of those days, one the Havelī or office of the notorious Rājā Bisen Chanda (see Ridhpur), a building which possesses some creditable carving and is now used as a primary school; and the other the great wall of the town. Readers of Meadows Taylor's "Confessions of a Thug" will doubtless recollect his vivid description of the famous raid of Chitu the Pindāri leader on Amraoti; it was to protect the town from calamities such as this that the wall was begun in A. D. 1804 by the Nizām's Government and was completed seventeen years later at a cost of over four lakhs of rupees. The wall, which is two and a quarter miles in circumference and from twenty to twenty-six feet in height, is neither architecturally beautiful nor strategically noteworthy. But it is so strongly built as to look almost new to-day, and is a subject of much local pride and patriotism. There are five large gates (Ambā, Bhusari, Nāgpur, Kholāpur, and Mahājanwais) and four smaller ones called *khirkis* (the Khunāri, Chatrapuri, Māta and Patel's *khirkis*). The Khunāri Khirki derives its name from a faction fight during the Muharram of A. D. 1816 in which no less than 700 persons are said to have been killed. The civil and military station of former days, which was occupied by Messrs. Pestonji and Vikaji's agents and by the early British administrators, lies just outside the wall to the north-west. Nothing now remains save the butts of the old rifle range, a large garden well, a small unenclosed cemetery with a few broken-down graves, and one large octagonal tomb surmounted by a cross. It is possible that this may belong to Wellesley's army which halted here for some time after the fall of Gāwīlgarh. The town contains nothing else of antiquarian interest, though here and there may be seen scraps of blackwood carving in verandahs and balconies and semi-fortified houses dating from before the town wall was built.

Description.

The town of Amraoti is divided into two very distinct portions the old city within and the new suburbs outside the walls; but in recent years, in addition to the gates already mentioned two new passages have been made, namely in Kāngarpurā and Sābanpurā. Within the walls lie the *muhallās* and quarters called (1) Dhanrāj street, (2) Machhisāt, (3) Dahisāt, (4) Bhusāra street, (5) Bohorisāt, (6) Shakarsāt, (7) Sarāfa, (8) Bajāja, (9) Kathadā, (10) Baripurā, (11) Patwīpurā, (12) Mālipurā, (13) Budhwāra, (14) Kumbhārpurā, (15) Bhāji Bazār. The streets are mostly narrow and crooked and the drainage is very unsystematic. Houses are closely crowded and encroachments taking up land valuable either for drainage or ventilation have been in the past only too common.

Sanitation however is by no means so bad as one would be inclined at first sight to suppose, for the houses are almost all well built upon solid plinths, which except in the case of the poorer houses are usually of stone. Outside the wall lie the weekly market and cotton market with the gins and factories, a quarter which is usually sanitary and clean; and Namuna, the best portion of the town, where are some of the Government offices and the houses of well-to-do pleaders and other leading citizens. This quarter contains two considerable open spaces, Nicoletts Park lying between the Municipal office and the railway station, and Jog square opposite the Tahsīli; and is generally the most modern and best cared-for portion of the town. In other directions lie the slum suburbs of Hamālpurā, Masānganj, Ratanganj, etc. in which live the poorest classes whom recent prosperity has brought as frequent immigrants to Berār. The best that can be said for these *bastīs* is that being outside the wall they are somewhat more freely ventilated than similar spots inside: on the other hand the houses are worse built. The question of improving these localities is being taken up as funds permit. A scientific drainage scheme is now before the Committee, as also the issue of land for building purposes to the north of the cotton market and opposite the Khunāri Khirki in order to relieve the congestion on some parts of the town.

Municipality.

The municipality was created here in 1869. It now consists of 24 members—18 elected by the ratepayers and 6 nominated by Government. The average annual receipts and expenditure from 1891-92 to 1906-07 were Rs. 58,724 and Rs. 58,628 respectively. The income in 1907-08 was Rs. 65,408, of which Rs. 48,968 was derived from taxes, Rs. 4,442 from cesses, Rs. 9,185 from fees and municipal property, Rs. 2,099 from grants and Rs. 714 from miscellaneous items. The expenditure amounted to Rs. 64,716 during the same year, the principal heads of expenditure being as follows:—

	Rs.
General administration and collection charges ...	5,673
Public safety	3,032
Public health	45,231
Public instruction	7,163

The incidence of income and taxation per head of population in 1907-08 was R. 1-14-7 and R. 1-9-0 respectively.

Municipal buildings.

Of the municipal buildings the clock tower, the Municipal Hall and the boys' school No. 3 are alone important. The five cattle pounds in charge of the municipality yield an income of Rs. 1,300 to Rs. 1,400 per annum. The weekly market is provided with sheds where the bazar is held twice a week on Sunday and Wednesday. The right to collect bazar cess for the year

1909-10 was sold for Rs. 5,500. A *sarai* has been built for native travellers, the annual charges of maintaining which are estimated at Rs. 200. The Bench Magistrates hold their court in an old building belonging to Government.

Public buildings.

Among the Government buildings in the town the Small Cause Court is the oldest, having been erected in 1868 at a cost of Rs. 54,183; beside it and in the same compound stands the Tahsīl building erected two years later for Rs. 34,447. The Telegraph Office (Rs. 16,871) and General Post Office which also face into Jog square were constructed about the same time. Postal receipts and expenditure in 1907-08 were Rs. 30,95,216, and Rs. 8,69,663 respectively. The High School was built in October 1873, the total expenditure on it up to the close of 1907-08 being Rs. 72,352. The average daily attendance of students in the High School was 206 during the year 1907-08. The receipts and expenditure for the same period were Rs. 3,681 and Rs. 16,258 respectively. The other buildings are the Anglo-vernacular school, the Anglo-Hindustāni school, the girls' school, the Urdu girls school and the normal school for women teachers. An Urdu High School has now been established. In addition the town contains a charitable dispensary and two police stations, the gate lodges of the town wall being also utilized as police *chaukīs*.

Besides Government buildings, there is the fine edifice recently erected to house the Victoria Technical Institute; this has a hall, now the largest in Amraoti. used for darbārs, examinations, and other functions. The Lady Dufferin Hospital, the Catholic Dispensary and Convent school intended for purdah ladies, a Free Library and a Theosophical Hall are perhaps the most important charities of the town.

Places of recreation.

Amraoti contains two theatres, the Indra Bhawan in the old town and the Ganesh outside the walls. There is a small club with twenty-five or thirty members which possesses two tennis courts. In Nicoletts Park travelling circuses occasionally take up their quarters; it is also used for various games.

Factories and Presses.

The number of ginning factories and that of cotton presses which fell within the scope of the Factories Act stood as 13 and 9 respectively at the close of 1908. The oldest cotton ginning factory is owned by the New Mofussil Company Limited which was started in 1872 along with the cotton and oil presses with a capital of a little over 2 lakhs of rupees. Amongst the cotton presses that belonging to Messrs. Volkarts is the oldest. It was opened in 1870 with a capital of Rs. 25,000. The two oil presses now working here belong one to the New Mofussil Company and the other to Messrs. Rāmji Kanao & Co.

Trade.

Amraoti has long been known as the principal cotton mart of Berār. The number of carts loaded with cotton brought for sale in the cotton market during the cotton season is about 100,000. The income derived from the cotton market in 1907-80 was Rs. 9,412 and the expenditure Rs. 8,281. The cotton is ginned, pressed and despatched in bales in large quantities to Bombay every year from this station. During the year 1908 ginned cotton weighing 373,626 maunds, of the value of about 60 lakhs of rupees, was exported. The other exports consisted chiefly of cotton seed (156,559 maunds), oilseed (such as linseed, linseed oil, &c.) weighing about 25,481 maunds, and hides and skins (5,663 maunds). The imports were wheat (59,382 maunds), rice (92,862 maunds,) sugar and jagree (14,319 maunds), salt (8,273 maunds) and piece-goods and twist (11,312 maunds).

Amraoti Camp.—The headquarters civil station of the Berārs is situated on rising ground to the east of Amraoti Town and about 1,283 feet above sea-level. The area is 12 square miles; the population in 1901, 5,295 persons as compared with 4,709 in the previous census. Of the total population 4,039 are Hindus, 708 Muhammadans, 461 Christians and 87 followers of other religions. The station is well laid out, the climate dry and salubrious, and the mortality rates exceptionally low.

Municipality, Station and Purās.

The municipality here was created in 1889, affairs having previously been managed by a Civil Station Committee. There are 10 nominated members of whom the Deputy Commissioner is ex-officio chairman, and the income in the year 1907-08 was Rs. 17,726; the expenditure being Rs. 12,862. There were windfalls in the course of the year, but even when allowance has been made for these the figures indicate a much healthier state of affairs than had previously been the case, for in the sixteen years preceding the average expenditure had been about 300 rupees in excess of the income. The incidence of income per head in 1908 was Rs. 3-8-7 and the incidence of taxation R. 1-8-9. The principal through roads are maintained by the District Board. The town has not been definitely marked out into wards, but falls naturally into three or four divisions. Of these the first is the civil station containing the bungalows of officers and clerks and the Government offices, and distinguished by the large amount of open space. To the east lies the purely agricultural village of Wadali included by reason of its proximity to the waterworks in municipal limits, and to the south lies Chuprāsipurā, a hamlet intended originally as its name signifies for habitation by peons and orderlies, but containing now several houses of a better class inhabited by clerks and subordinate officers. Beyond this to the southward again and separated from it by a small nullah lie the hamlets of Fraserpurā and Waddarpurā inhabited by menials and stonemasons respectively. Part of the Hamālpurā of Amraoti town also lies in camp limits.

Water-supply.

There are excellent wells throughout the whole area, but for Government offices and the civil station water is supplied from Wadali tank. This has a catchment area of about 2 square miles, and a capacity of over fifteen million cubic feet. It was designed for a daily supply of thirty gallons a head to a population of 2,000 persons, but there is unfortunately considerable leakage and pumping operations from a well just below the tank have often to be resorted to. In good years, however, the supply is just sufficient; and, as the water passes through excellent filter beds before entering the main, absolutely reliable. In the season a certain amount of shooting and fishing is to be had on the tank but this is strictly regulated.

Public buildings.

Amraoti Camp contains the headquarters offices both of the Division and District, chief among which are the Commissioner's, Deputy Commissioner's and Conservator's offices, the Civil and Sessions Courts, a fine circuit house and a well equipped civil hospital. The post and telegraph office is a branch controlled from the head office in Amraoti town. The police reserve lines have recently been completed. The District Board has a fine office built throughout of trap, the hall of which has been commonly used for darbārs etc., though it is now superseded by the larger one of the Victoria Technical Institute at Amraoti. There is no municipal building but the committee meets in a room rented from the District Board.

Antiquities.

Amraoti Camp is essentially a modern place, with but little in the way of history. Tradition has it that the hill known as 'Mal Tekri' which commands the town, and incidentally serves as a butt to the Rifle Range, contains buried treasure placed there by the wealthy *sāhukārs* of Amraoti in the old Pindāri times. The guns from which His Highness the Nizām's salute is fired were cast in the 'forties and are now of little use except for saluting purposes. To the east of the civil station lies a small shrine known as Chilam Shāh Wali, and chuprāsis and servants both Hindu and Muhammadan generally ask for an evening's leave early in the hot weather to attend the *Urs*.

Miscellaneous.

Amraoti Camp is the headquarters of a company of the Nāgpur Volunteer Rifles formerly the Berār Volunteer Rifles, who have an institute, a parade ground, a magazine and a rifle range. The Officers' Club is housed in an extremely comfortable building having two tennis courts and overlooking the public garden. There is a passable 9 hole golf course and cricket and hockey are played on the parade ground during the season. On a stretch of grazing land managed by the municipality a race-course has been laid out.

Anjangaon Bari.—Amraoti tāluk: 781 houses: population 2,979, is about 4 miles from Badnerā, being the next station on the railway line to Nāgpur, and has an eighth standard school and post office. The majority of the inhabitants are Baris and the town has extensive garden cultivation (*mota-sthal*), the two chief products being betel and plantains. The place, like Badnerā, was at one time in the Peshwa's Jāgir, and there are the usual rumours of bygone fighting in the neighbourhood, with a crumbling mud fort to bear witness to their truth. The *samādhi* of one Sādhu Rāmgir Bāwa about a mile away attracts a small fair annually in the month of December. A tank was built in the neighbouring Chāndur-Amraoti hills during the famine of 1899-1900 about 3 miles from Anjangaon.

Anjangaon Surji.—Houses 2,833. Population 11,881. Two large villages (Anjangaon 8,783 inhabitants, Surji 3,098) lying contiguously to one another in the north of the Daryāpur tāluk and usually spoken of as a single town; though for revenue purposes Anjangaon is divided into eight *khels* each with a patel and Surji is also separate. Legend connects the name of Anjangaon with Krishna's triumph over Rukmaya; and Surji, also known as Peth Muhammad Nagar after a bygone Musalmān *fakir*, is said to be a corruption of *suranji* a tree with which the place was formerly overgrown. The public buildings of the town include a police station, a sub-registry, a dispensary, a Marāthī and an Urdū boys' school and girls' schools both Marāthī and Urdū. A Bench of Honorary Magistrates has been established here to try petty cases. Betel is largely grown and sold in the neighbourhood and the weekly bazar brings in a bazar cess of about Rs. 3,500 a year. Weavers in large numbers live here and produce *sāris*, *cholkh-ānas*, *dhotis*, *khādis*, and turbans; four cotton gins have also been established. The town is connected with both Daryāpur and Ellichpur by District Board roads, being about 17 miles rom either place. The road to Ellichpur is *muram*-surfaced and partially bridged. Anjangaon holds an important position in Anglo Indian history for it was here that the second Marāthā war was concluded, the treaty with the Nāgpur Rāja being signed on the 23rd December 1803. On the same day the negotiations with Sindhia commenced, the British being represented by no less distinguished a trio than Sir A. Wellesley, Sir J. Malcolm, and Mountstuart Elphinstone, and the Marāthā by Wattel Punt, 'Old Brag' as Malcolm called him. It was he to whom Wellington afterwards compared Talleyrand, saying that the great Frenchman was like the Brāhman 'but not so clever.' (See Kaye's "Life of Malcolm," Vol. I. pp. 240 and 241). The treaty was concluded on the 30th December and was described by Lord Wellesley in a private letter to his brother as 'a glorious and brilliant termination to the war and equal to the lustre of the campaign.'

The Deshpānde family were presented with a copy of the treaty in recognition of their hospitality: but this was unfortunately destroyed in 1850 by the Rohilla troops of Ghulām Hasan Khān, Nawāb of Ellichpur. This worthy was at open war with the Munsiff of Akot, Saiyid Sirāj-ud-dīn Hasan.[1] The armies met at Anjangaon and the Nawāb was almost beaten. His adversaries however turned to plunder and in a plucky rally he won the day. 'Hundreds of Rājputs,' says the local historian, 'were killed by the gun of Thomas Brown,' an adventurer in the service of the Nawāb. Such was the state of Berār three years before the Assignment. Sheonāth Rangopant the great Marāthā poet and the religious teacher was born at Anjangaon, but his fame was acquired elsewhere.

Asadpur.—Ellichpur tāluk; houses 442. Population 2,355. A village lying a few miles west of Assegaon, consists of the four hamlets of Shāhpur, Raipur, Asadpur and Wasin, the whole being sometimes known as Rangaswasni. Nizām Ali Khān, Nizām-us-Sāni made a grant of most of the land in these villages to one Mehtāb Khān in 1763 A. D. for maintenance, and the Inām Commissioner in 1874 continued Raipur and Shāhpur as jāgir to his descendants with 100 *bīghas* of land in Asadpur, *inām*. In 1889, owing to family quarrels, the

[1] **Afterwards *Sadr us Sadūr* or Sessions Judge under British rule.**

management of the jāgīr villages was taken out of the jāgīrdār's hand and the land became therefore separate *inām* survey numbers; Riāsat Alī, one of the principal sharers in the jāgīr, lives at Asadpur. There is a vernacular school and post office, and a weekly bazar on Thursdays.

Assegaon.—A village on the Amraoti-Ellichpur road 18 miles from the former place and just within the borders of the Ellichpur tāluk. The river Pūrna is crossed here by a strong bridge of four large spans. The village has 145 houses and 758 inhabitants, and owing partly to its position as a half-way house between the two cities, and partly to the energies of Raibhān Patel, the public buildings, which include a dāk bungalow, an inspection bungalow, a 1st class police station, a *sarai*, a sub-registry and a school as well as the usual *chāwri* and pound, are for so small a village unusually good. The sub-registry is at present a rural one and is held by Raibhān's grandson. The patel's house is a old semi-fortified building of red brick.

Babhli.—See Daryāpur.

Badnera.—Town in the Amraoti tāluk, lying in 20° 52′ N. and 77° 46′ E. is situated at a distance of 6 miles to the south of Amraoti about 1,093 feet above the sea-level. It is on the Nāgpur branch of the Great Indian Peninsula Railway line, 413 miles from Bombay and 107 miles from Nāgpur. It is connected with Amraoti by a branch of State railway 6 miles long.

Position.

In 1901 the population was 10,859 against 9,916 in 1891, 6,460 in 1881 and 6,876 in 1867, a rise of 58 per cent. during 34 years. There are 2,544 houses. Hindus number 8,187, Musalmāns 2,159, Jains 119, Christians 167 and miscellaneous sects 227. It is stated that the town was in a flourishing condition at the close of the eighteenth century; and its subsequent decadence in the early years of last century is said to be due to an imposition of Rs. 60,000 laid upon its patel (who was in the service of the Bhonsla), which, though he himself evaded it by flight, the inhabitants had to pay. To-day it is prosperous and flourishing and from its convenient situation on the railway

Population.

may be expected to attract many who might otherwise settle in Amraoti.

History.

It is mentioned in the 'Ain-i-Akbarī' as the headquarters of a pargana in the 'Sarkār' of Gāwīl. It is known as Badnerā Bībi as it formed with Kāranjā part of the dowry of Daulat Shāh Begam, daughter of Daryā Imād Shāh of Berār, who was given in marriage to Husain Nizām Shāh of Ahmadnagar. Tradition however has identified the eponymous Bībi with the heroic Chānd Sultāna and a small *chunam* shrine in the fort is dedicated to that lady. The only piece of information locally obtainable about her is that "after her death her jāgīr lapsed to the Mughals." From 1151 Fasli (1741 A.D.) Badnerā was in the possession of the Nizām till 1182 Fasli (1772 A.D.), when it came into the possession of the Peshwā as a jāgīr. In 1227 Fasli (1817 A.D.) it was restored to the Nizām. It was plundered in 1822 by Rājarām Sūbah, who partly demolished the fort and town walls. These had been built by Salābat Khān and Bahlol Khān of Ellichpur, and the fort, though outwardly only a mud *garhī*, is really something more, having subterranean chambers in it vaulted with brick, and a house, now ruined, on the summit, the residence of the former Naib Tālukdārs. The revenue was divided between the Nizām and the Bhonsla in the proportion of 2 to 1.

Description.

The old town differs but little from any other in the District except in the large amount of garden land with which it is surrounded, a feature said to be due historically to a former Patel and Chaudhri, Mahināji who in 1640 brought gardeners here at his own expense from Jālna, dug wells and induced the inhabitants to take up wet cultivation. *Pān* is grown to-day in considerable quantities and in 1870 opium was still cultivated. To the south and clustered round the railway lies the new town, of which the junction with its small colony of railway officials is the nucleus. A company of the 2nd Battalion G. I. P. Rly. Volunteers has its headquarters here, and there are a rifle range, a railway dispensary and institute. The Roman Catholics have a church with a priest in residence and the Anglican chaplain also visits the place. A Christian cemetery was laid out in 1869 at a cost of Rs. 5,834 and close beside it is a Pārsi cemetery; at a distance of about a mile from the town is also a Tower of Silence. Government and District Board buildings include a post office, a dispensary, a dāk bungalow and a *sarai* within easy reach of the railway, also an Urdū and two Marāthī schools, a pound and a *chāwri.* Previous to 1905 an Assistant or Extra Assistant Commissioner was stationed here, who combined the functions of first-class Magistrate, Subordinate Judge, and Judge of Small Causes; but this post has been abolished: the Court-house is occupied by the Government Central Book Depot and the Magistrate's former quarters have been made over to the police, Badnerā being a first-class station under a Sub-Inspector.

The land revenue assessment is Rs. 5,700. There is a weekly market held on Mondays at which vegetables, betel leaves, plantains etc., are sold. The town contains two ginning factories and a spinning and weaving mill; of the former one is owned by the Badnerā Ginning Company and the other together with the mills by the Berār Manufacturing Company. A full description of this enterprise is given in chapter V., 'Manufactures,' and it is only necessary here to state that the annual outturn is valued at over eleven and a half lakhs, and that the number of hands employed in 1908 was 940.

Bairagarh.—Houses 109. Population 517. A village in the Bairāgarh pargana of the Melghāt tāluk, inhabited chiefly by Korkūs; Muhammadans coming next in numbers and various low caste tribes being also represented. It is 50 miles distant from Chikaldā viâ Sembādoh and 18 miles from Dhārni, and has a small and unimportant weekly bazar held on Mondays. Under the old arrangements, there was a second-class police Station-house here with a head-constable and three constables: this is now ranked as a 'road post' but the change is merely an administrative one. The village lies in centre of a small but fertile plateau of black cotton soil, which is one of the tracts selected for Settlement under the orders recently issued.

Bairam Ghat.—A shrine in the Ellichpur tāluk frequented by the lower classes both of Muhammadans and Hindus. 'Although no town, the place is worthy of mention, on 'account of the great fair held there in October each year, 'and on account of its sanctity. It is situated about 14 miles 'east of Ellichpur. During the night of the fair more than '50,000 persons from all parts assemble, and sacrifices are 'offered before a rock, the Hindus on one side and Musalmāns 'on the other. This rock is approached by a long flight of 'steps. It is a curious and authentic fact that, although 'thousands of animals are sacrificed in front of the rock, and 'the place is several inches deep in blood, there is not a fly to 'be seen. There is a tank said to contain water only every 'third year, which it is believed then comes from Benāres. 'The water is exceedingly dirty, but a dip in it has potent 'effects'. The description given forty years ago holds good to-day; but the popularity of the fair has if anything increased. It now lasts not for a single night but for thirty days. Cattle are brought from the neighbouring hills for sale and lacquer work all the way from Northern India. More than 500 booths are erected by neighbouring Baniās and shop-keepers and a brisk trade is done. The rock is situated within the lands of the little village of Kāranjā, and hard by are two well built tanks of stone and mortar. It is 11 miles from Paratwāda on the road to Betūl and is on the boundary of the District.

Bairat—The highest mountain in the Melghāt division of the Sātpurās is situated some six miles from Chikaldā, and attains to a height of 3,866 feet above sea-level. Former surveys gave the height at 4,200 and 3,989 respectively. On the hill is an old temple of Mahādeo Vairāteshwar which is said to be connected subterraneously with a temple of Devī somewhat nearer to Chikaldā.

Balgaon Jagir or Walgaon.—Amraoti tāluk, houses 1,156, population 5,284, a town on the Ellichpur road about 6 miles from Amraoti Town and 5 from Amraoti Camp by the District Board road known as the Red Road. The metalled road to Chāndur Bazār branches off here. Balgaon is the largest alienated village in the District, having been granted in 1842 and 1850 by Mahārāja Chandūlāl Bahādur minister and Rājā Rāmbax for the upkeep of the temple of Sri Sītarām Mahārāj at Hyderābād. The area is 5,893 acres 31 *gunthās* and the estimated rental at Government assessment Rs. 11,135-8, but there are a number of anti-jāgīr tenants whose rights to their holdings are protected as against the jāgirdār:the latter cannot evict them except for non-payment of rent nor can he enhance the payment above Government rates. The old *garhī* at Balgaon has been converted into a temple of Bālajī, and the public buildings include a police road post, a District Board *chāwri* and *sarai*, and a Marāthī school to which a post office is attached.

Barur.—See Warud.

Belura.—Tāluk Morsi. Population 2,056. Houses 341. There is an old Dīwānkhāna or cutcherry here dating from Musalmān times. The tomb of Sādhu Punjāji Māli has an *utsawa* celebrated annually on Mārgshīrsh Paurnimā when about eight thousand people collect here. A small sect called 'Satya Shodhak Samāj' has been started among the Kunbīs locally under the leadership of Yeshwantrao Khushālrao Patel. Its object is stated to be to encourage education among the backward classes including Mahārs and Māngs and to throw off Brāhman influence. The members of the sect do not employ Brāhmans at their domestic ceremonies.

Bemla River.—A river having its source near Kāranjā in the Murtizāpur tāluk of the Akolā District. It flows in a north-easterly direction as far as Chakorā on the border between Chāndur and Murtizāpur tāluks and, forming a boundary for a little distance as far as Pipalgaon, enters the south-western corner of the Chāndur tāluk. It then, flowing in a south-easterly course two miles south of Nāndgaon Kāzi and Damak, leaves the tāluk after the confluence with the Kholat from the north. The united streams form a fair-sized river which, following the same course past Nandurā in Yeotmāl tāluk, meets the Wardhā river about 5 miles north of Naigaon.

The water is very bitter and during the hot weather is only met with in pools.

Benoda.—Houses 67, population 3,430, lies in the Morsi tāluk fourteen miles east of the town on the road to Puslā, and has an inspection bungalow. The weekly bazar is held on Saturdays. The only cotton gin in the place is owned by a Mārwāri. There is a first-class police station under a Sub-Inspector.

Bhatkuli.—Houses 558. Population 2,767. A village about eight miles west of Amraoti on the banks of the Pedhī (a tributary of the Pūrna), and connected with Amraoti and Kholāpur by a fair weather road. It has the usual weekly bazar, combined school and post office, also a *masjid*, a large proportion of the inhabitants being Muhammadans. A few Mārwāris have become possessed of some land here through foreclosure of mortgages. Bhātkuli has a temple to Rukmaya who it is said settled in the village after his sister's *enlèvement* and his defeat by Krishna (see Amraoti): but it is not much frequented as Hindus consider it polluted by the proximity of the Jain temple built about 200 years ago. In this is a figure of the Saint Pārasnāth said to have been found buried in the village *garhī*.

Bhiltek.—An insignificant village in the Chāndur tāluk with 54 houses and 230 inhabitants; its sole claim to notoriety is the fair which is held annually in honour of the god Nāgoba, and lasts from Paush shuddh pratipadā (about the end of December or beginning of January) for nearly two and a half months. On the first Sunday the attendance is about 1,000, but this increases to as many as 60,000 on the fifth Sunday, after which the attendance gradually falls off. The fair is however yearly dwindling in importance. Cloth merchants and traders in copper, brass, and iron, attend it, and country carts and cart-wheels are also sold. The temple of the god is a plain *chabūtra* or platform with no superstructure whatever, and it is believed that if a person who has been bitten by a snake burns incense on this, with the appropriate prayers, and swallows a little of the ashes, he will recover. Probably but few of those who survive to reach the shrine and perform this ceremonial have much reason to be afraid.

Brahmanwada Thadi.—Houses 764. Population 4,515. A village in the north-east of the Ellichpur tāluk situated on the banks of the river Pūrna with a perennial water-supply. There is some garden cultivation ; and black glass bangles of rude make are produced. The Marāthī school teaches up to the sixth standard. A bazar is held on Thursdays. Brāhmanwāda Pāthak close by is a small village with some five hundred inhabitants.

Chandrabhaga River.—A river rising at the foot of the Gāwīlgarh Fort, flows in a southerly direction a few miles to the west of Ellichpur town, draining the western portion of the Ellichpur tāluk as far as its southern boundary. It then enters the Daryāpur tāluk near its confluence with its tributary the Sarpan, and flowing in a south-westerly course past Bemli, Māhuli, Daryāpur and Wānosa, joins the the Pūrna river at Dhamnā khurd. It contains scarcely any water except in the monsoon when it becomes a torrent, and is of little use to the country except in the capacity of a channel for draining the land. Its principal tributary is the Sarpan, which flowing past the city of Ellichpur and Nizāmpur meets the Chandrabhāga near the boundary between Daryāpur and Ellichpur tāluks. The water of the Sarpan was utilized in the old covered conduit which formerly supplied the city.

Chandur Taluk.—The south-eastern tāluk of the Amraoti District lying between 20°31′ and 21°13′ N. and 77°40′ and 78°18′ E., with an area of 855 square miles or about 18 per cent. of that of the District. It was formerly designated the Talegaon tāluk from the old tahsīl town of that name which is most inconveniently situated at the extreme south of the tāluk. On the completion of the railway Chāndur was selected as being on the line and the name of the tāluk was altered accordingly ; some of the southern villages were at the same time transferred to Yeotmāl. The tāluk at present contains 395 villages

Physical features.

and towns, including one jāgīr village and two villages which are wholly included in Government forest. The tāluk is bounded on the west by the Amraoti tāluk and Murtizāpur tāluk of Akolā District, on the south by Dārwha and Yeotmāl tāluks of Yeotmāl District, on the east by the Wardhā District and on the north by the Morsi tāluk. It lies in the Pāyanghāt or central valley of Berār and in the valley of the Wardhā river which bounds it on the east, but the uniform fertility of these two tracts is varied by the aridity of a low range of rocky hills which rises in the vicinity of Amraoti and extends eastward along the line of railway some distance beyond Chāndur station. These hills and a smaller range in the extreme south-west are of a rocky and barren nature forming a sharp contrast to the general fertility of the tāluk; and the villages in the vicinity where the soil is shallow are very dependent on timely rainfall for the production of good crops. The tāluk consists of an undulating plain sloping from west to east covered for the most part with black alluvial soil varying in depth from a few inches on the tops of the ridges to many feet in low lying situations. The eastern portion lying in the valley of the Wardhā river is by far the richest. The drainage of the country is from west to east in the direction of the Wardhā, the only river of importance, which forms the eastern boundary of the tāluk. The tāluk is not traversed by a single stream of any magnitude, the only rivers being the Bemlā and the Kholat. They are not perennial and although they form a fair sized river after their confluence, still during the hot weather water is only met with in pools. These rivers after entering the tāluk flow in a south-easterly direction and leave it at their confluence a few miles to the south of Talegaon; the combined stream under the single name of Bemlā following its course in the same direction in the Yeotmāl tāluk empties itself in the Wardhā river.

Population.

The population of the tāluk in 1901 was 192,805 persons or about one-fifth of that of the District. In 1891 the population was 198,106 and in 1881, 171,611. The increase between 1881 and 1891 was nearly 15½ per cent., as against the District figure of 9 and the decrease between 1891 and 1901 was nearly 3 per cent. as against nearly 5 for the District as a whole. During the last decade there were a series of bad years which culminated in the famines of 1896 and 1899, and this for the most part is responsible for the decrease in the population of this as well as of the other tāluks of the District. The density of population is 226 persons per square mile. Excluding towns the density of rural population is 198 per square mile. The bulk of the population is purely agricultural, even the tradespeople and artizans to a large extent supplement their earnings by cultivating fields. The tāluk contains 4 towns, Mangrūl Dastagīr, Talegaon Dashāsar, Chāndur and Dattāpur, and 391 villages of which 86 are uninhabited[1] according to village lists; 12.29 per cent. of the total population live in towns and 87·71 live in villages. Besides the above towns the following 12 villages contained more than 2,000 persons in 1901:—Amlā, Ghuikhed, Talegaon Thākur, Teosā, Dhāmangaon, Nāndgaon Kāzi, Palāskhed, Mālkhed, Mojhri, Warhā, Wirul and Kurhā. There are also 37 villages in the tāluk whose population exceeds 1,000 persons.

Agriculture.

Cotton and juār are by far the most important crops. At revision settlement[2] (1895-99) the total of the occupied assessed area comprised 459,150 acres, according to revision survey; of this cotton covered an area of 193,395 acres or about 41½ per cent. and juār 159,517 acres or 34 per cent. *Rabi* cultivation is not of importance here being only 1-10th of the whole. Wheat then occupied 30,253 acres or 6·5 per cent. and the remaining *rabi* crops are insignificant in area. The irrigated crops occupied 6,500 acres or about 1½ per cent. of the total occupied assessed area. In 1906-07 of the 503,374 acres of village area, excluding the area under State forests, 467,409 acres or about 93 per cent. were occupied for cultivation. Of this the

---

[1] See footnote, p. 353.

[2] These figures are the average annual figures for the settlement period 1895-99.

total cropped area including double cropped area (only 106 acres) was 446,061 acres. The area under cotton[1] has largely increased since revision settlement and in this year it occupied 243,256 acres or 54½ per cent. of the total. The area under juāri was 135,767 acres or 30·4 per cent., while the area under wheat had much decreased, there now being only 18,113 acres under it or about 4 per cent. of the cropped area. There is practically no *pātasthal* irrigation, whether from stream or tanks and even that from wells (*motasthal*) has declined, only 1,776 acres being now cultivated by this method as against 6,500 acres at revision settlement.

Land Revenue.

At the original settlement the 394 villages of the Chāndur tāluk were settled in five groups with maximum dry crop standard acreage rates varying from R. 1-3-0 to Rs. 2. The average rate per acre cultivated however varied from annas 10 to R. 1-3-1. In grouping the villages with various acreage rates the main idea of the original settlement was to divide the tāluk into three portions; the first to consist of the villages in the valley of the Wardhā river containing the richest soils; the second to include the villages, in the vicinity of the railway, whilst the remaining villages in the southern portion of the tāluk constituted the third division. At the revision settlement (1895-1899) the villages of the tāluk were divided into 2 groups, the first group consisting of 301 villages and the second 93 villages, with the maximum dry crop rates of Rs. 2-10-0 and Rs. 2-4-0 respectively. The average rate per acre cultivated is for the first group R. 1-7-10 and the second group R. 1-10-11. The demand at the time of revision settlement on the Government occupied area of 459,229 acres according to the former survey was Rs. 3,79,562, giving an incidence of R. 0-13-3 per acre, while at the revision settlement, the assessment on the occupied area of 459,150 acres according to revision survey was increased to Rs. 5,79,280, giving an incidence of R. 1-4-2 per acre. The increase thus amounted to Rs. 1,99,178, being

[1] Though land under cotton is single cropped, yet the harvest lasts from November to March.

52·6 per cent. in excess of the existing demand. In 1907-08 the demand on account of land revenue and cesses was Rs. 5,45,209, while the actual collections according to treasury figures amounted to Rs. 5,46,828, the increase in the actual collections being explained as due to arrear collections.

Miscellaneous.

For purposes of land records the tāluk has been divided into three Circle Inspectors' circles with headquarters at Dhāmangaon, Nāndgaon Kāzi, and Kurhā. It constitutes a single police circle under an Inspector and contains 6 police Station-houses each under a Sub-Inspector at Chāndur, Nāndgaon Kāzi, Talegaon Dashāsar, Kurhā, Teosā, and Dattāpur. The Chirodi forest reserve lies partly in this tāluk and partly in Amraoti.

Chandur Town.—Or Railway Chāndur, as it is generally called in distinction from Chāndur Bazār, is the headquarters of the tāluk bearing the same name. In addition to the tahsīli and police station, a sub-registry, a post and telegraph office, a dispensary and a Marāthī school are located here. There is also a District Board veterinary dispensary and a Government bonded warehouse for country liquor has recently been built. The dâk bungalow is an old building, having been used as a *sarai* before the present *sarai* was built. The cotton market was established in 1895, under the control of a committee of which the Tahsīldār is chairman and has an income of about Rs. 2,000. Five cotton gins and three presses with a petroleum depôt complete the commercial aspect of the place and the weekly bazar is held on Sundays. Good oranges are grown in the gardens. The old town, which lies about a mile to the north of the railway station, is unhealthy, being situated on low ground close to a stream and frequently visited by cholera and plague. The importance of the place has increased since its selection as tāluk headquarters and it now boasts of a population of 5,700. A public library has been opened and named after the King-Emperor. There is a branch of the Alliance Mission here whose head, Mr. Ramsey, did good work in the famine. There is nothing in the town to suggest antiquity; but it has been identified with a "Chandrapur" which is mentioned in an inscription of the Vākātaka kings about the sixth century of the Christian era. Such identifications must always be open to the gravest doubt, but there are several circumstances which tend to show that the theory in this case is at least plausible.

Chandur Bazar.—Ellichpur tāluk. Houses 1,094, population 5,208. A town 22 miles north of Amraoti by a fully metalled P. W. D. road and 14 miles east of Ellichpur by District Board road. The bazar for which it is famous was established by Nāmdar Khān, Nawāb of Ellichpur, in whose jāgir it was, some ninety years ago; and though it has lost much of its relative importance owing to the competition of Morsi and Hiwarkhed bazars and to the practice of wholesale firms in buying direct from the villagers instead of through intermediaries is still the largest in Berār, the annual bazar cess being over five thousand rupees. The C.P. border is only eight miles away and large quantities of *jāgri*, *gur*, wheat, gum, etc., are brought in from the fertile highlands of Khāmla Multai and Betūl; it is also a market for cattle. The market-place is well laid out with lanterns and water troughs and large sheds for the storage of merchandise, and is planted with *nīm* trees. There are several apparently prosperous shops owned and managed by Bohrās; also two cotton ginning factories. The public buildings include a Marāthī school teaching up to the sixth standard, with an English class attached; a first-class police station under a Sub-Inspector, a sub-registrar's office, and a dispensary with small hospital accommodation; also a P. W. D. inspection bungalow. Speculation among the merchants leads to frequent insolvencies and there is now not a single trader of twenty years standing. The bazar is held on Sundays. Close to Chāndur is the large village of Shirasgaon Band. (Houses 631, population 3,266). It has a combined school and post office with a boarding house attached. The Brāhman family of Ganorkar own considerable property here, and one of their number, Mr. M. B. Ganorkar, pleader of Amraoti, has kindly supplied much of the information in this paragraph.

Chendkapur.—Daryāpur tāluk, 500 houses, 2,371 inhabitants. Much of the land is *inām* in the hands of the Ellichpur Deshpānde family. There are a few gardens in which sugarcane is grown.

Chikalda.—The sanitarium of Berār is situated 3664 above sea-level[1] in latitude 21°24′ N. and longitude 77°22′ E. The plateau occupied by the Civil Station is only about three-quarters of a mile broad and about a mile in length; but it has easy access to the spacious tableland surrounding it and to many picturesque valleys, and there is ample room for expansion. A mile and a half to the south-west lies the fortress of Gāwīlgarh; and Ellichpur, the nearest town of any importance, is reached by a variety of roads and foot-paths, the best of which, available even for motor-cars, winds up through Ghatāng and Silonā amid fascinating scenery a distance of 31 miles. There is a travellers' bungalow at Ghatāng, which makes a convenient halfway halting place Arrangements for tongās have to be made in Ellichpur. A surface road *viâ* Dhāmangaon and Motā 21 miles, marking the track followed by a section of Wellesley's force in 1803, is available for cart traffic; but this is not used in the rainy season. It is probable, however, that at no very great cost it might be made into an excellent thoroughfare. Travellers in haste generally ride by the precipitous bridle-track which passes near Wastāpur and through the fort, and a small stable has been built for their convenience at the foot of the hill. By this the distance is reduced to fifteen miles and the post runners have one or two foot-paths leading up the cliff side through the fort which lessen it still further. Apart from the fort, of which it commands several splendid views, Chikaldā has little or no history. It was discovered, according to the *Nur-ul-Berār*, by Captain Robinson of the Hyderābād Contingent Battery in A.D. 1823, the very year in which regular troops were first stationed at Ellichpur, but bungalows were not built there, it seems, till 1839. Its

[1] This is the most recent calculation of the Forest Survey; the figure formerly given by Mr. Mulherran was 3,777.

popularity was very soon established and Meadows Taylor mentions its delights as early as 1840 when he was here with the troops; he visited Ellichpur again as Deputy Commissioner on the 9th December 1857 and notes 'How welcome 'were the large baskets of delicious peaches from Captain 'Hamilton's garden at Chikaldā; and I wished I could go 'up there again and revisit the old scenes.' The peach is still cultivated in a few gardens at Chikaldā though it has degenerated very considerably since Meadows Taylor's time. Coffee of the very finest quality, however, is still grown in private gardens especially on land belonging to the Roman Catholic Mission. At one time a great future was anticipated from coffee and tea plantations in Chikaldā, some European planters being attracted by the prospects of success, but the tea has entirely disappeared and coffee is now only grown in small gardens. There is a Government garden known locally as the *Company bagīcha* in which various European and tropical trees and shrubs, fruits and flowers are grown, the great difficulty being the scarcity of water. In a wild state roses, clematis, orchids, ferns and lilies succeed each other with the changing seasons, and balsams, zinnias, wild ginger and orchids also abound. The scenery is magnificent; and the eight 'points' of the station (see Map) command in turn distant views of the Nimār and Mahādeo hills to the west and north with wooded valleys lying closer at hand and to the south a broad outlook across the open plains of Berār to the Bālā ghāt beyond. Footpaths, cut in the hill sides, afford pleasant walks on the lower ridges, such as that which leads to the Devil's Punch Bowl or Andherā Khorā (the valley of darkness), a splendid deep chasm walled in by a circle of cliffs two to three hundred feet high, down one side of which in the rains tumbles a water-fall. Close by is a fine triple echo. Mountaineers can exert themselves over many precipitous pathways and can even climb a miniature Matterhorn though one has to go more down than up hill to reach it. Two miles away at the bottom of a secluded valley, lies the Roman Catholic village of Mariampur.

The native village.

In 1901 Chikaldā had attained to 961 inhabitants and was thus the most populous village in the whole Melghāt; it is possible, however, that the figures are swelled by some early arrivals for the hot weather from Ellichpur and elsewhere. Even the indigenous population is largely dependent on its popularity as a health resort, and consists mainly of Gaolīs, Musalmāns, Mahārs and Gonds, Korkūs forming a comparatively small section. The village is divided into four quarters or *purās*, and a weekly bazar of groceries and vegetables is held on Sundays. Between it and the Civil Station lie the police station and a Government school, the female orphanage and Mission house of the Korkū Mission, a *sarai* and quarters provided by Government for the Tahsīldār and other officials.

The Civil Station.

The European community is accommodated partly in the old Civil Station and partly in a smaller settlement which has grown up on a lower level round the Bīr tank. There are about a dozen bungalows of which two are owned by the Rājā of Maklā, one being used as his residence. The order of St. Francis de Sales owns several bungalows which are let during the season. For visitors making only a short stay, Chikaldā has an Officers' Rest house, recently enlarged, and a Public Works Department inspection bungalow. In the Civil Station lie the Tahsīli, the hospital and observatory, the post and telegraph office, the veterinary dispensary and the Divisional Forest Office. The only Gazetted officers who have Government bungalows in Chikaldā are the Conservator and Deputy Conservator, but the place is usually visited in the hot weather by the Commissioner of Berār and other officers. The sanitarium is supported by an annual grant of Rs. 5,000 from provincial revenues. The climate has been fully discussed in Chapter I.

Amusements.

In days gone by when Chikaldā was the summer head-quarters not only of the heads of departments of the Berār Administration but also of the Military from Ellichpur, Hingoli and elsewhere, it was a place of considerable gaiety. The band of one or other of the corps stationed at Ellichpur used to play every evening at Band Point, and the camping ground would be covered with tents. To-day the greatest charm of the place is its quiet peacefulness, and the station has not inappropriately been compared to a small village in England. It is a fairly cool retreat from the burning heat of the Berār plain during the summer, but is at its best in October, when the hill-sides are clothed in white clematis and there is a crisp coolness in the air. Its wildest distractions do not run beyond tennis and golf; there are two excellent tennis courts in the Government garden, both of which dry very quickly after rains, and on the lower plateau is a golf course. Besides the tennis courts is a trellis work summer house used during the week as a pavilion and on Sundays as a Church. The plateau and neighbouring valleys for a distance of three miles form a sanctuary in which the shooting of birds or of horned game is forbidden. Carnivora and destructive animals of course are unprotected, and, as panthers and bears are fairly common even within the Civil station, good sport is fairly easily obtained.

Water-supply.

The great difficulty of Chikaldā which will prevent its ever becoming a large hill station is the scarcity of water. There are six tanks (Shakar, Kālapāni, Dhobi, Machchhi, Nāgjhirā and Bīr Talao), but the majority of these are a considerable distance from the Station on the road to Gāwilgarh, and are not therefore of much use except to Dhobis. Such attempts as have been made to provide tanks in the Civil Station, have been failures. The Bīr Talao which is situated on the small plateau close to the Convent just beneath the Civil Station, contains water throughout the year, but not of very good quality for drinking purposes. An arrangment has been made by which a limited supply of excellent drinking water is obtainable, an underground reservoir holding 102,400 gallons constructed in the Tahsīli compound, into which after the first showers have been allowed to wash the dust away, the rain water from the Tahsīli roof is drained. An additional reservoir is shortly to be constructed with a capacity of about 50,000 gallons.

Mr. J. Mulheran in his report on the Melghāt in 1861 discusses the difficulty and expresses the opinion that by sinking wells to a depth of 40 or 50 feet, water might easily be found 'in great abundance throughout the year, but attempts in this direction have not been successful.

Dabheri.—A small village of 265 inhabitants, not far from Ridhpur in the Morsi tāluk; its chief claim to mention being its tank, a stretch of water covering nearly 90 acres on which excellent duck shooting may be obtained in the season. Situated beside the tank is a temple of Dabheshwar held in reverence by the Mānbhaos. A member of the sect making the pilgrimage to Ridhpur is supposed to visit Dabheri also; and a fair held on Chaitra Paurnimā is attended by about fifteen hundred people. At Akhatwāda, a small village close by, is a similar temple of Rokdeshwar: which is also a Mānbhao shrine.

Daryapur Taluk.—The western tāluk of the Amraoti District, lying between 20°49′ and 21°20′ N. and 77°11′ and 77°38′ E. with an area 505 square miles or 10·6 per cent. of that of the District. Daryāpur was formerly a tāluk of the Ellichpur District but was with the rest of that District incorporated in Amraoti in August 1905. The tāluk contains 273 villages including one town, of which 266 are *khālsa*, 6 *pālampat*, and 1 *jāgīr*. It lies in the fertile Pāyanghāt valley, being bounded on the west and the south by the Akot, Akolā and Murtizāpur tāluks of Akolā District, on the east by the Amraoti tāluk, and on the north partly by the extensive jungles of the Melghāt tāluk and partly by the Ellichpur tāluk. From the Melghāt border to the Pūrna river north to south Daryāpur is some 28 miles. Its greatest breadth from west to east is 26 miles but this diminishes both northward and southward, especially in the former direction where the breadth of the tāluk on the Melghāt boundary is only some 10 miles. Daryāpur presents to the eye an almost perfectly level plain with only a slight inclination towards the south unbroken by hills. In consequence of the very gentle fall southwards in the direction of the Pūrna river the soil is able to retain the monsoon showers for a longer

Physical features.

Bemrose, Collo., Derby.

GENERAL VIEW OF HILL FROM CHIKALDA, GAWILGARH.

time than if the surface had been more undulating or the slope greater, and the effect is an increased amount of fertility. Some parts of the tāluk contain large mango groves, and there are several valuable *bābul bans.* The Pūrna, Chandrabhāga, Shāhnur and Bordi rivers flow from north to south. The supply in the first named is perennial, and in the others there is flowing water until late in the hot weather, large pools remaining till the break of the rains. These streams are of great importance to the tāluk, for the wells are generally very brackish, and river water is accordingly preferred by the inhabitants for drinking purposes. They are of little use agriculturally except in the capacity of channels for draining the land. This important office is fulfilled by them most effectually for no stagnant water or marshes are to be found anywhere, notwithstanding the almost dead level of the country. Except in the immediate proximity of the larger rivers where the surface soil is much cut up and is mixed with gravel and otherwise impoverished by the yearly monsoon floods, the soils of the tāluk are of a very superior quality. They are somewhat friable yet very retentive of moisture, and are capable of producing rich crops for a succession of years without any artificial assistance.

Population.

The population of the tāluk in 1901 was 114,698 persons, or 14 per cent. of that of the District. In 1891 the population was 122,552 and in 1881, 123,109. During the two decades between 1881 and 1901 there was a decrease in the population; in the first decade it was nearly ½ per cent., and in the second decade when there was a general decrease in all the tāluks it was nearly 6½ per cent. as against nearly 5 for the District as a whole. This decrease is the largest of all the tāluks in the District except the Melghāt, which shows a falling-off of about 22 per cent. Bad seasons and the two famines together with immigration to less fully cultivated places account sufficiently for this decrease. The density of population is 227 persons per square mile, as against 170 for the District as a whole. The density of rural population is 210 per square mile, the highest figure of all the tāluks in the District. Of the land available for cultivation only 12 acres remain uncropped, and the limit of extensive cultivation has been practically reached. There are very few important landholders, holdings of one or two acres being the general rule, while even smaller ones are common. The tāluk contains one town (Anjangaon) and 272 villages of which 22 are uninhabited[1] according to village lists. About 8 per cent. of the population live in the town and 98 per cent. live in villages. Besides the one town the tāluk contained the following 8 villages which had more than 2,000 persons in 1901:—Kāpustalni, Chendkāpur, Daryāpur, Babhāli, Yeodā, Wadner, Sātegaon and Peth Muhammadnagar, better known as Surji, the last a suburb of Anjangaon, There were also 15 villages whose population exceeds 1,000 persons.

Agriculture.

The crops found here are cotton, juāri, wheat, linseed, tūr and the betel creeper. This latter crop is grown successfully in the villages of Anjangaon, Aiwajpur and Shābpur, and the betel leaves of these places have some local reputation. By far the most important crops are the cotton and juāri. At the former settlement juāri occupied 38 per cent. of the cultivated land, cotton 31 per cent. wheat 14 per cent., linseed 4 per cent., and gram and tūr each 3 per cent. At revision settlement (1892-96) the Government occupied land was 285,414 acres according to revision survey. Of this cotton occupied 112,519 acres or 40·2 per cent. showing an increase of 8 per cent. since former settlement, juāri occupied 75,075 acres or 26·2 per cent. showing a decrease of about 12 per cent. Thus a large proportion of the area under jūari cultivation had given way to that of the far more remunerative cotton crop; 42,724 acres or about 15 per cent. of the cultivated area were devoted to wheat, practically the same as that at former settlement, while the area under linseed had doubled, being about 10 per cent. The area under all other crops together was no more than 9·8 per cent. of the total. In 1906-07 of the 320,112 acres of village area (excluding the area under State forests but including that of *pālampat* villages,) 303,251 acres or about 94

[1] See note on p. 353.

per cent. were occupied for cultivation. Of this the total cropped area was 296,535 acres, the double-cropped area included in it being only 10 acres. The area under cotton has much increased since revision settlement, and in 1906-07 it occupied 161,074 acres or more than 54 per cent. of the total. The area under juāri has fallen to 73,731 acres being about 25 per cent., while wheat covers an area of 31,948 acres or about 11 per cent., and linseed 6,144 acres or 2 per cent. of the cropped area. The area irrigated is insignificant, being only 585 acres.

Land Revenue.

The 266 *khālsa* villages of the tāluk were at the original settlement divided into three groups and settled as follows :—group I. consisting of 99 villages with a maximum dry crop standard acreage rate of Rs. 2-4; group II. of 135 villages with a rate of Rs. 2; and group III. 32 villages with a rate of R. 1-12-0. The average rate per acre cultivated, however, varied from R. 1 to R. 1-7-3. The first group comprises the large bazar towns and the villages adjoining them as well as villages lying in a peculiarly fertile tract of land, the second small bazar towns, the villages adjoining them and all villages within a convenient distance of the large bazar towns; and the third a few villages which are either inconveniently far from the bazars or are badly supplied with water. At the revison settlement all these villages without exception were included in one group and a maximum dry crop standard acreage rate of Rs. 2-10 was proposed, but the rate subsequently sanctioned by the Government of India was Rs. 2-12-0 for the whole tāluk. The demand at the time of revision settlement on the Government occupied area of 285,409 acres according to the former survey was Rs. 4,74,347 giving an incidence of R. 1-10-6 per acre, while at the revision settlement, the assessment[1] on the occupied area of 285,414 acres according to revision survey, was increased to Rs. 5,79,183 which gives an incidence of Rs. 2-0-1 per acre. The increase thus amounted to Rs. 1,04,836 being 22·1 per cent. in excess of

[1] This assessment was according to the proposed maximum dry crop rate of Rs. 2-10-0.

the present demand. The revision settlement took place in the years 1892-96 and the final announcement was made in 1903-04 and during this period there were some changes in the revenue demand due partly to the raising of the dry crop rate from Rs. 2-10 to Rs. 2-12 subsequent to the revision settlement and partly to the application of revised acreage rates to the 69 villages which were originally received from Akot tāluk and to which the revised rates were not applied at the revision settlement. Therefore the demand of the tāluk in the subsequent years has increased. The land-revenue demand for 1907-08 including cesses was Rs. 6,53,113 while the actual collection according to the treasury figures was Rs. 6,63,094, including arrears. The land-revenue demand of the 6 *pālampat* villages in 1907-08 was Rs. 6,120.

Miscellaneous.

For purposes of land records the tāluk has been divided into three Circle Inspectors' circles with headquarters at Khallār, Daryāpur and Anjangaon. It constitutes a single police circle under an Inspector and contains 4 Station-houses, each under a Sub-Inspector, at Daryāpur, Anjangaon, Rahimāpur and Khallār.

Daryapur.—Houses 980, population 4,389. The headquarters of the tāluk bearing its name, is situated on the Chandrabhāga river, and is reached by a fully metalled road of eighteen miles from Murtizāpur; also by a broad fair weather road from Amraoti through Kholāpur. Within half a mile of it lies the large trading suburb of Wānosa with a population of 915 and close by is also the large village of Babhāli with 2,707 inhabitants; a total for the three places of 7,111 persons. Daryāpur though not classed at the census as a town is a centre of the cotton trade, having 5 gins and 3 presses; its cotton market is controlled by a local committee of which the Tahsīldār is chairman and has an annual revenue varying from two to four thousand rupees. Its weekly bazar has a cess income of Rs. 3,600. The public buildings of Daryāpur include besides the Tahsīli, a Subordinate Judge's and a Munsif's Court, a police station, a sub-registry, a dispensary,

Anglo-vernacular school, Urdu and Marāthi primary schools. a girls' school and a post office. There are temples to Rāma and Vithobā and two *masjids*. A short distance out of the town on the Murtizāpur road a hall has been erected in honour of the King-Emperor's accession, which contains the local library. R. B. Bhagwantrao Shankarrao Deshmukh, who is a second-class special Magistrate, has a large house containing some very handsome carving. The town derives its name from Daryā Imād Shāh, the third of the independent Kings of Berār (A. D. 1529-1560), who was its founder.

Dattapur Dhamangaon.—In the Chāndur tāluk is a town of great and increasing importance. Formerly the two villages were separate, one lying to the south and one north of the railway, but a large commercial suburb known as Horderngauj after a former Deputy Commissioner has grown up joining them together. The total population is 9,035 and the number of houses 1,951 and a bench of magistrates with third-class powers has been established. A first-class police station, a sub-registry and a combined dâk and inspection bungalow may be mentioned among the public buildings, and the railway station is now being enlarged to keep pace with the increase of traffic. The cotton market which was established in 1885 is managed by a committee and has an annual income varying from two to four thousand rupees. The Burma Oil Co., Standard Oil Co., and Asiatic Petroleum Co. have branches here and there are seven gins and four cotton presses. A weekly bazar is held on Sundays and trade in cloth, grain and other articles is also carried on. The supply of water is good, and the neighbourhood noted for its toddy, *sindī* trees growing in abundance. The dâk line for Yeotmāl starts from here, and the station is therefore the outlet for the commerce of that District. The leading inhabitants are mostly Mārwāris including Seth Fatehlāl Shāligrām a representative of the great firm of Srirām Shāligrām. The late Seth Rāmchandra Rāmpratāp established a Rāma Mandir at a cost of Rs. 40,000 and endowed it with property for its upkeep. Some of the leading merchants maintain a private school in which the Sanskrit sacred books are taught.

Deogaon.—A small and insignificant village at the foot of the hills through which the so-called Wastāpur short-cut from Ellichpur to Chikaldā runs ; between it and the fort a small stable has been established at the foot of the hill to accommodate ponies for travellers using the path. The sole claim to distinction which Deogaon possesses is that preliminaries of peace between the East India Company and the Bhonsla (or "Bouncello" as the English chronicles of the day called him) were signed here on the 19th December 1803, four days after the capture of Gāwīlgarh by Wellesley of *Langra Wasli* as he is known in Berar.

Dewalwara or **Deurwada.**—Ellichpur tāluk, houses 262, population 1,515. A village on the Pūrna, about 14 miles from Ellichpur, was 110 years ago a town of much importance, containing some 5,000 houses, and a large Brāhman population ; and the tāluk authorities used to reside there. Now it has become an insignificant village, but is worthy of notice on account of its ancient buildings. Dewālwāra is, according to Hindu mythology, the place where Narsinha, after killing Hiranya Kasipu, was able, after failing everywhere else, to wash the blood-stains from his hands. There is a temple and idol of Narsinha which has been there from time immemorial, with steps to the river, and a *ghāt*. Near this is a place now called Kar Shuddhi Tirth or the holy place of cleaning hands. There is a temple to Vitthal Rukmaya built in the time of Salābat Khān by one Mahādeo Rao Lakshman of Nāgpur, at a cost of Rs. 15,000, also a *masjid* built some three hundred years ago.

Dhamangaon.—Ellichpur tāluk, houses 410, population 1,826. A village on the shorter Ellichpur-Chikaldā road, from which the ascent of the hill begins. It lies about 6 miles from Paratwāda and has a weekly bazar on Wednesdays which serves the neighbouring tracts of the Melghāt. Has a considerable cultivation of chillies.

Dhamangaon.—See Dattapur.

Dhamantri.—A small village of 343 inhabitants situated on the banks of the river Wardhā just north of Kaundinyapur. On rising ground in a small *bābul ban* to the south of it is a very ancient temple of Mahādeo. The original structure was to all appearances Hemādpanthī, but it has been repaired at various subsequent periods in different styles. At present some Bairāgis from Benāres have taken possession of it and are putting it in order; they have built themselves a small house close by. Hemād Pant, who appears in reality to have been minister to one of the Chalukyan kings, is the putative architect of almost all the temples in this part of India of which the origin is obscured by time, though the true Hemādpanthī or Chalukyan building is one of large blocks of stone carefully dressed and adjusted without apparently any cement, or at least with very little of it. The style is that of primitive builders, who distrusted the arch and laid massive stone lintels over monolithic pillars. Legend declares that Hemād Pant was a mighty wizard who was compelled by the devil to find employment for a crew of demons during a whole night. To build temples without mortar seemed an interminable kind of job, but these ghostly engineers had finished before cock-crow. Readers of the "Lay of the Last Minstrel" will recollect that Michael Scott when faced with a similar difficulty was more successful; he outwitted the foul fiend by setting his devils to make ropes of sand.

Dhanora.—Houses 70, population 242. A small village on the banks of the river Pūrna, in the Ellichpur tāluk, has an old temple dedicated to Sundar Nārāyan, at which a fair is held every year in the month of January or February. The place is otherwise of no importance.

Dharni.—Houses 142, population 731. The largest village in the Melghāt is situated in the Amner pargana, and forms the present terminus of what will shortly be the high road through the hills from Ellichpur to Burhānpur. It is 68 miles from the former, and 60 from the latter town. A weekly bazar is held every Friday. The population is a mixed one, the Korkū element being the most numerous; the Korkū and Central India Hill Mission has succeeded in gathering together a small congregation. Foreigners are represented by a few Bohrā moneylenders from Burhānpur, who have settled in the place. Government buildings include a first-class police station in charge of a Sub-Inspector, a

P. W. D. inspection bungalow, a branch post office and a school. There is also a bonded warehouse for the sale of country liquor, built by Government and placed under the control of a Sub-Inspector of Excise. The soil is very fertile and with improved communications, and the advantages of the forthcoming settlement, it may well develop into a place of some importance. Its climate has a very bad reputation for malaria; but is said to have improved somewhat of late years owing to the clearing of the land for cultivation.

Ellichpur Subdivision.—Area 2,605 square miles, population 297,403, land revenue Rs. 12,77,502, consisting of the Ellichpur, Daryāpur and Melghāt tāluks, was from 1867 to 1905 a separate District of the Berār administration. It is now held by a Subdivisional Officer and Magistrate who has full control over the magisterial and revenue staff; there are also a Subdivisional Assistant or Deputy Superintendent of Police, and Public Works and Medical Subdivisional officers, the latter having charge of a civil hospital. A Subordinate Judge and two munsiffs are stationed at Ellichpur, and a Subordinate Judge and a munsiff at Daryāpur; there is also a joint Deputy Educational Inspector. The Subdivision contains two Municipalities (Ellichpur City 26,082 and Ellichpur Civil Station 10,410) and 5 other towns namely Anjangaon (8,783 with Surji 11,881), Shirasgaon Kasbā (6,537), Karasgaon (7,456), Chāndur Bazār (5,208) and Daryāpur (4,389 or with Wanosā 5,304). The headquarters of the Subdivision are at Ellichpur Civil Station. For further detail reference should be made to the sections on Ellichpur, Daryāpur and Melghāt tāluks.

Physical features.

Ellichpur Taluk.—Formerly the headquarters tāluk of the Ellichpur District but since August 1905 a tāluk of the Amraoti District lying between 21°9′ and 21°24′ N. and 77°23′ and 77°53′ E. with an area of 469 square miles. The tāluk contains 311 villages and towns of which 7 are jāgīr. It lies in the Pāyanghāt at the foot of the Sātpurā hills and is bounded on the north by the Melghāt tāluk and the Betūl District of the Central Provinces; on the west by the Daryāpur tāluk, the Amraoti and Morsi tāluks form the boundary on the south and east. The tāluk is compact in shape, averaging 24 miles from

Bemrose, Collo., Derby.

CHAUK MASJID, ELLICHPUR CITY.

east to west by about 16 miles from north to south and is the smallest of all the tāluks in point of size. The face of the country is perfectly level, although here and there deeply indented by the rivers and freshets that find their way down from the Sātpurā hills. The best camping grounds in the District are here. The soils here are very fertile, quite equal to those in Akot and Daryāpur. In spite of the great demand for wood fuel of recent years, many parts of the tāluk are still well wooded, and the prospect for instance in the neighbourhood of Pathrot or of Brāhmanwāda is an extremely pleasing one. There is scarcely a village which cannot boast its grove of trees, and the general prosperity and high standard of cultivation prevailing afford a satisfaction to the eye which verges on monotony. Water in many places lies close to the surface and maintains a certain amount of moisture in the soil, by which the country has been enabled to weather the severe famines of the last decade with comparative success. The climate in the greater part of the tāluk is healthy throughout the year, though the heat is very trying in April and May; the villages in the north of the tāluk lying under the hills are feverish during the last three months of the year. The principal rivers which drain the tāluk are the Chandrabhāga and the Pūrna. The banks of both are too high to make irrigation practicable unless very large works were erected for which again the supply of water would not suffice. Such as they are, however, they are a great boon to the country as the water is good and lasts throughout the hot season. The Sarpan, a tributary of the Chandrabhāga, flows past the city of Ellichpur and formerly supplied the city with water by an aqueduct. There is an old and ruined drain of similar construction known as the "Sātbudki," or seven wells, near the village of Datura, which was formerly used for the irrigation of garden lands in the neighbourhood. Legend connects its origin with the supply of water to the now empty tank of the Hauz Katorā.

Population.

The population of the tāluk in 1901 was 146,035 persons or 18 per cent. of that of the District. In 1891, the population was 146,215, and in 1881, 148,041. Thus for the twenty years ending 1901 there has been a steady but slight falling-off in the population; in the first census period it was 1.2 per cent. and in the second only 0.1 per cent. Thus between 1891 and 1901 the decrease was not only less than in any other tāluk but less than in Ellichpur itself during the previous decade, a striking proof of the richness of the country, and of its power of resistance in bad times. In the original Settlement Report it was pointed out that the population was more than the land could fairly bear, and emigration to less cultivated tracts was predicted. Though we need not agree with the Settlement Officer that Ellichpur is incapable of supporting a larger population than it had forty years ago, yet it is obvious that with the pressure of population on the soil so much greater than it is in neighbouring tracts scarcely less fertile, the opening up of communications was bound to bring a decrease; and such has been the case both in Ellichpur and Daryāpur. The density of the population is 311 per square mile, being the highest figure of all the tāluks in Berār; the density of the rural population is 193 persons to a square mile. Cultivation has practically reached its utmost extent, only 113 acres remaining available for the purpose and not yet taken up. The tāluk contains the 5 towns of Ellichpur, Paratwāda, Sirasgaon, Chāndur Bāzar and Karasgaon, and 306 villages of which 77 are uninhabited[1] according to village lists; 38.14 per cent. of the population live in towns and 61.86 per cent. live in villages. Besides the above towns the tāluk contained three villages which had more than 2,000 persons in 1901: Āsadpur, Brāhmanwāda Thādi and Sirasgaon Bund. There were also 16 villages whose population exceeds 1,000 persons.

Agriculture.

The culture of the ground is carried on somewhat more carefully here than in Amraoti, in consequence perhaps of the greater value of the land, but the area under irrigation is none the less small in extent. The principal crops grown are juāri, cotton, tūr and wheat. At the original settlement juāri occupied 39 per cent., cotton 40 per cent., tūr 7 per cent. and wheat 3 per cent. of the cultivated area. At the revision settlement (1893-97) the total Government occupied land was 241,327 acres. Of this juāri occupied 96,009 acres or 38.1 per cent, cotton 107,101 acres or 42.4 per cent, wheat 11,568 acres

[1] See note, p. 353.

or 4.6 per cent, and tūr 9,584 acres or 3.8 per cent. As usual in the black soil plains the chief crop cultivated is cotton and it had gained by about 2½ per cent, while juāri, the staple food grain of the people, had lost by about 1 per cent. These two crops account for four-fifths of the total area leaving one-fifth for other crops. The area devoted to *rabi* cultivation was only 9 per cent., more than half of this being occupied by wheat. In a large extent of land bordering on the hilly country to the north, cotton and juāri are the only crops grown, the soil being too shallow to retain sufficient moisture for *rabi* cultivation. In 1906-07 the total village area excluding State forest was 279,383 acres. Of this 257,479 acres or 92 per cent. were occupied for cultivation. Out of this the total cropped area was 248,296 acres, there being no area under double crop. The area under cotton has much increased since revision settlement, and in this year it occupied 145,851 acres or about 59 per cent. of the total cropped area. The area under juāri has fallen, being only 64,035 acres or about 26 per cent., while the area under wheat was 9,585 acres or about 4 per cent., and tūr 16,395 acres or about 7 per cent. of the cropped area. The irrigated area was only 1,638 acres during the year.

Land Revenue.

The 304 Government villages which form the Ellichpur tāluk were, at the original settlement, divided into three groups and settled with maximum dry crop standard acreage rates varying from R. 1-12 to Rs. 2-4-0 The average rate per acre cultivated however varied from R. 1-7-3 to R. 1-14-3. The principles adopted in grouping the villages depended upon their proximity to the large bazar towns and villages for the first and second class groups, while in the third class were placed the more remote villages and some lying within the spurs of the hills and having a bad climate, although within easy reach of the small bazars. At the revision settlement the facilities for communication were found to have rendered the villages independent of the larger market towns and hence the whole of the villages of the tāluk were thrown into one group as had been done with the Daryāpur tāluk, and the rate sanctioned and imposed on Daryāpur, viz. Rs. 2-12, was fixed,

At the time of the revision settlement the demand on the Government area of 241,262 acres according to former survey was Rs. 4,05,217, giving an incidence of R. 1-10-10 per acre, while at the revision settlement the assessment on the occupied area of 241,327 acres according to revision survey was increased to Rs. 5,28,486 giving an incidence of Rs. 2-3-1 per acre. The increase in revenue thus amounts to Rs. 1,23,269 being 30.4 per cent. in excess of the previous demand. The demand on account of land revenue including cesses in 1907-08 was Rs. 5,59,131 while the amount actually collected according to treasury figures during the year was Rs. 5,43,347.

Miscellaneous.

For purposes of land records the tāluk has been divided into three Circle Inspectors' circles with headquarters at Sirasgaon Kasbā, Pathrot and Ellichpur. It constitutes with the Melghāt a single police circle under one Inspector and contains 5 Station-houses, each under a Sub-Inspector at Ellichpur, Chāndur Bazār, Pathrot, Sirasgaon Kasbā and Assegaon.

Ellichpur City.—The headquarters of the Ellichpur tāluk and former capital of Berār, is situated in 21° 16′ N. and 77° 33′ E. about 1200 feet above sea-level. It lies rather more than 30 miles to the north-west of Amraoti and has an area of 8 square miles and a population of 26,082 persons. In 1891 the figure was 26,636; in 1881, 26,728, and in 1867, 27,782, so that there has been a fall of 6 per cent. in 34 years, and the city, which formerly took the first place in Berār now stands only third on the list. Further decadence only a radical change in the economic conditions, such as the introduction of a railway (which has been mooted,) can hinder, and even in that event it is possible that the Civil station with its timber market, rather than the city would reap the chief benefit.

Municipality.

Ellichpur City Municipality was created in July 1869 and the Committee to-day has twenty-four members, all nominated by Government. The average annual receipts and expenditure for the sixteen years ending 1906-07 were respectively Rs. 20,174 and Rs. 19,748. In 1907-08 the income was Rs. 20,647 derived mainly from taxes (Rs. 14,083), from fees and municipal property (Rs. 5,315) and from grants (Rs. 1,117). The incidence of income per head of population was R. 0-12-8, and of taxation R. 0-8-8. The expenditure during the same year amounted to Rs. 29,029, the principal heads being drainage, sanitation, roads, conservancy, public instruction, and establishment charges. The taxes are direct and, as elsewhere in Berār, the Committee appears to find very great difficulty in its collections. There is a Bench of Magistrates with second and third class powers.

Water-supply.

No works have been undertaken in modern times for the supply of water which is obtained by the people from wells and from the rivers Sirpan and Bichan, which flow through the town. There is still in existence though no longer in working order an underground conduit of earthen pipes by which the oldest quarter of the town (that between the Dulla Darwāza and the Barkul gate) was formerly supplied with water from the Bichan, that river having been dammed at a spot above the city in order to make a reservoir. It is thought that these waterworks which were constructed in the reign of Ahmad Shāh Wali Bāhmani (A.H. 829, A.D. 1425) could be restored at small cost, and the question is now under discussion in the municipality.

Trade and manufactures.

In the high day of its prosperity, with a lavish court in its midst, Ellichpur was the important centre of cotton and silk manufactures, and had a reputation also for woodcarving and stone work which is borne out by the remains. To-day the latter industry is almost extinct, and those of weaving and dyeing, though their followers are still numerous, are steadily on the decline. The carpets made here though rough are of a strong texture and find a ready sale all over the District ; *khādis, rumāls, pagrīs* and *patkās, sāris* with silk borders and *susīs* are also produced, but the trade is in a bad way, for the earnings of a Koshtī do not exceed those of an unskilled workman, and his goods are being steadily ousted from the market by those of the power-loom. The *āl* dyeing of Ellichpur was formerly famous, but this also is on the wane. The castes connected with these industries are the first to exhibit signs of distress in times of scarcity and require the promptest attention. To-day the most important industry as elsewhere in Berār is that of raw cotton, the income and expenditure of the cotton market in 1907-08 being Rs. 1,204 and Rs. 672 respectively. Sooner or later almost all the cotton finds its way to Amraoti, and the traffic over the high road to that place during the season is enormous, for, though there are 3 ginning and one pressing factory in Ellichpur employing in all some 380 persons, most of the cotton is taken to Amraoti in the raw state, and dealt with there.

Public buildings.

In the village lists and settlement papers Ellichpur appears as divided into eleven *khels* or *munds*, each of which bears a Hindu name, being that of the family holding the patelkī, *e.g.* Khel Japmali, Khel Trimbak Narāyan, and the like. The history however of Ellichpur is distinctly Muhammadan, and this is reflected as one might expect in the nomenclature of the place. The town was at one time surrounded by 54 *puräs* or suburbs, of which about 35 exist at the present day, and the names of nearly all are of Musalmān origin. Some are within and some outside municipal limits; a few of the most important are Shamastpurā formed by Shamast Khān in 1724, Sultānpurā by Sultān Khān about the same time, Anwarpurā named after Anwar Khatūn, Salābat Khān's wife, Nāmdār Ganj, Nasībpurā, Abbāspurā, Jīvanpurā, and Rikabah, the last-named being the headquarters of a bazar formed by Salābat Khān to accompany him on his military expeditions. There is no doubt that Ellichpur was in the past a very large and prosperous city, and it is said at one time to have contained 40,000 houses. Its prosperity depended upon two things, the presence of the court and the position of the city at one end of what must always have been a considerable, if not one of the most important, trade routes through the hills to Northern India. The court has vanished and the railway has diverted all trade elsewhere: the importance of Ellichpur is daily declining and its interests are mainly of the past.

Antiquities.

The history of the city is the history of Berār. It is given in full in Chapter II., and there is no need to repeat it here.[1] The town is

[1] Since that chapter was written R. B. Hiralal has found in Betul district a copper plate inscription in which the town of Achalpur (identified by him as Ellichpur) is mentioned, and a similar reference occurs in the Prakrit literature of the Jains; see Chapter II. section 28,

full of old buildings of greater or less importance, which bear testimony to its fortunes under different rulers. Its earliest Muhammadan invaders are commemorated fitly enough in the bare but stately Idgāh of Sultān Imād-ul-Mulk (A.D. 1347), the nephew of Muhammad Tughlak,[1] in the Jāmi Masjid dating from the same era (but subsequently restored by Ali Mardān Khān in the time of Aurangzeb), and in the Bharkul gate. This is a massive erection of stone divided into outer and inner wards and leading into the still older mud fort which dates from Hindu times. The gate has many carved stones in it, taken perhaps from some pillaged temple, and from its situation in the middle of the city is a favourite 'coldharbour' in the hot weather. From about the same period must date the Hauz Katorā, a ruined octagonal tower of brick, mortar and sandstone, about two miles to the west of Ellichpur. The architecture of it is in the style known as Pathān, and the tower stands in the midst of a circular tank whose diameter is about 100 yards and depth about 15 feet. The tower stands 81 feet in height and has three stories; it is said that a fourth and fifth were removed by one of the Nawābs to provide materials for his own palace. The *minārs* were in ruins in the time of Akbar. To-day the tank is nearly empty and the whole edifice long past repair.

The Bahman Shāh dynasty and their *tarafdārs* of Berār have left but little in the way of memorial. To the Bahmanis we owe the water-course already mentioned, the Darus Shafā Masjid (A.D. 1340) and one or two unimportant minor buildings. From the same period dates the most famous of all the Ellichpur antiquities, the tomb of Dulha Shāh Abdul Rahmān Ghāzi Ghaznavi. The legend tells of a wandering Muhammadan *fakīr* who was maltreated by Rājā Il of Ellichpur and fled to Ghazni to appeal for help. The great Mahmūd's nephew was celebrating his bridal when the holy man arrived: but he left the feast to lead a *jihād* from beyond the Himālayas to the punishment of the blasphemous king and died fighting as a good Muslim should amid untold

---

[1] So says local tradition which has dignified him with the title of "Sultan."

slaughter of the infidel; cutting off, we are even told, his own head to make the victory secure. To-day Hindus as well as Muhammadans pay homage at his tomb, and it would be little short of atheism in Ellichpur to hint a doubt of his ever having existed. The buildings are picturesquely situated on the north-easterly bank of the Bichan about one mile from the city and from a distance look almost imposing with the two great archways, the small lantern window overhanging the river and a cluster of white domes behind. On closer scrutiny they are very disappointing: the apparent stone lace work is merely a mass of bricks and tiles placed edgeways and whitewashed; the arches have been daubed over in a variety of hideous colours by the illiterate and filthy *mujawirs* who attend the place; and the whole effect is indescribably petty. Passing in through the large gate one finds a spacious courtyard containing the graves of many forgotten worthies small and great. There is one in particular which has some very creditable stone tracery. Close at hand on the right lie the houses of the attendants and on the left a small *masjid* built originally by Sūbahdār Miyān Manzūr, two hundred years ago, but restored by Ghulām Husain the last of the Nawābs. Through this one enters the holy of holies, the innermost court wherein are the resting places of the Ghāzi himself and of his mother Malikā-i-Jahān. These are said to have been erected by Safdar Khān Sīstāni, the lieutenant of Alā-ud-dīn Hasan, the first Bahmani Shāh. They are covered with a mass of tawdry colours and are in no way interesting; the silver doors which they possessed forty years ago have been stolen, and though on one occasion recovered by the police have since vanished. The largest enclosure of all is surrounded by a sandstone wall built by the brothers Raghujī and Madhujī Bhonsla of Nāgpur in alternate thankoffering for their successes over one another. The east gate built by Madhujī is the only erection in the whole crowd of buildings with any pretension to architectural beauty. It has a flight of stone steps on either side leading to a broad *bārahdari* on top. Half way up each flight is a small domed halting place. The *bārahdari* has six windows and two doors and is surmounted by four small *minārs*. Each gate of the wall has a Persian inscription commemorating its builder.

Bemrose, Collo., Derby.

IDGAH OF SULTAN IMADUL MULK. ELLICHPUR CITY. A.D. 1347.

Just outside the Dargāh two hundred yards from the west bank of the Bichan lies a small but elegant cylindrical sandstone dome supported upon white marble pillars: it is commonly known as the Moni Joni Gumbaz and commemorates the infant daughters of Ahmad Shāh Walī's Vazīr who died here.

After the fall of the Bahmani dynasty, the architectural history of Ellichpur is a blank for several hundred years. The Imād Shāhi rulers, though they hold the proud position of having been the only independent kings of Berār, were in truth but insecurely seated on a tottering throne. Gāwīlgarh, with its strong walls and precipitous approaches, was a capital far more to their liking than the ill-defended Ellichpur, and they have left no memorial. The Nizām Shāhs were busy elsewhere, and the stir and turmoil of the Mughal invasions of the Deccan left but little time for building. A few relics remain of the reigns of Akbar and Alamgir; of the former is the well or low-level reservoir known as Mamdal Shāh and said to have been built by Mān Singh, Rājā of Jaipur. It has a platform where its princely owner could sit and be cool in the hot weather and niches opposite for the musicians to make him merry: but the water is so infested with mosquitoes that it is difficult to believe anyone can really have found pleasure in such an entertainment. Alamgir is represented by the Chauk Masjid and a smaller mosque both built by Shayastā Khān or Mirzā Beg Khān as he is also called, by the municipal office formerly a Dīwān Khāna, and by the restoration of the Jāmi Masjid. But the domes of the last-named edifice have long since fallen in and it looks again for the pious patron to renew it. Khān-i-Zamān Khān's aspirations are mentioned elsewhere (v. Khānzamānagar).

But the most princely of all the dynasties that have ruled in Ellichpur was that of the Nawābs of Sultān Khān's house, and though they were themselves the subordinates of the Nizām of Hyderābād they have done more to beautify the city than all previous dynasties combined. In their time too private munificence, whether that of other rulers such as Madhujī Bhonsla or of private persons, seems to have been turned to building and to such efforts we owe the Hindu temples of Bālajī and Rāmchandra and the dome of Shāh

Ismail Fakir. Sultān Khān, the first of this dynasty, built about 1754 the fort at Sultānpurā, a strong edifice of sandstone on the south bank of the Sarpan river. The approach is covered by a flanking wall and the outer gate stands at the head of a steep approach. The fort was used in the early days of British administration as a jail, and is still though much dilapidated a place of considerable strength. Sultān Khān's son was Ismail Khān, the greatest of the Nawābs, whose lofty ideas are clearly expressed in the strong sandstone wall which he built round the city. To-day much of it has crumbled away but enough remains to show that the prince regarded beauty as well as strength. The wall is studded with carved stones (said to have been taken from the ruined Jain temples of Rājā Il though their new appearance gives the lie to this), its gates are richly ornamented, and one at least of its *khirkīs* or foot-gates, that just north of the Dulha Darwāza, is extremely graceful. To the same ruler and his sons Bahlol and Salābat Khān we owe the commencement of the Nawāb Mahāl. It consists of a multiplicity of buildings of which many have fallen into decay. The four great courtyards with their deep verandahs and beautiful carving both in wood and stone remain. Two of them are still used as dwelling houses by the representatives of the family, and two are lent to Government for schools. Ghulām Hasain Khān, the last of the line, built a large Imāmbāra; but the most beautiful of all the buildings in Ellichpur is the cemetery of the Nawābs in Sharmastpurā which contains a stately dome of Ismail Khān and various small buildings, and some very fine *jāli* stone lattice work. The whole is surrounded by a strong wall with two lofty gateways. Close by is a small mosque and cemetery, dating from older times which also contains one or two handsome tombs. All the Nawābs were fond of gardening, and Ellichpur is surrounded by the relics of many handsome gardens. Perhaps the finest is the Nāmdār Bāg, not far from Dulha Rahmān's Dargāh: it is surrounded by a wall and has a magnificent well for irrigation while one or two fine trees are still standing. Probably it could still be restored at small cost, and it would be worth restoration: at present the ground is occupied by a cotton gin. Finally, mention should be made of the graves of bygone English soldiers at Ellichpur. Just outside the north wall a marble slab commemorates Thomas Drew, "who for many years commanded a Brigade in the service of Salābut Khān Bahādur, Nawāb of Ellichpur." He died in 1815. Close to the Municipal office are buried Lieut.-Colonel Kenny and another who died in Wellesley's assault on Gāwilgarh, and beside the Idgāh lie Major Lane and Captain Grant, who succeeded Major Drew in the command just mentioned; the marble slabs of these last four have long since been filched from the masonry and are probably being used as curry stones in some frugal cultivator's home.

Ellichpur Civil Station.—Also called *Paratwāda* and *Ellichpur Cantonment*, is situated at a height of 1268 feet above sea-level, in 21°18′ N. and 77°34′ E. and lies 32 miles north-west of Amraoti and two miles north of Ellichpur City. It is connected with Amraoti by a metalled high road, and with Chikaldā and the Betūl border by *muram* roads. There is a District Board *muram* road to Anjangaon Surji (16 miles) and another to Chāndur Bazār (14 miles). The area within municipal limits is 112 acres 6½ *gunthās*, or roughly two square miles, and the population in 1901, when there were still troops stationed here, was 10,410 as against 9003 in 1891, 9445 in 1881, and 11,269 in 1867. The figures for 1901 include 7,125 Hindus, 3,055 Musalmāns, 52 Jains, 124 Christians and 54 others. Probably the total population to-day is about eight thousand. Paratwāda is the headquarters of the Ellichpur Subdivision.

Municipality.

The municipality was established here in 1893, and the committee consists of 10 members all nominated by Government with the Subdivisional Officer for Chairman. During the fourteen years ending 1906-07, the average annual receipts and expenditure were Rs. 14,087 and Rs. 13,314 respectively; and in 1907-08, Rs. 18,405 and Rs. 14,843; the main sources of income being taxes Rs. 5,377, fees and municipal property Rs. 10,538, and grants Rs. 2,306. The incidence of income per head of population was Rs. 2-4-3, and of taxation R. 0-10-7. The chief heads of expenditure have been sanitation and conservancy; there is no regular system of water-supply, but water is drawn from wells which are many and good.

Trade.

Timber brought in from the Melghāt to the bazar on Thursdays is by far the most important article of trade, and the weekly sales have an estimated value of Rs. 6,000, cattle being the next most important item in the bazar and being calculated at Rs. 3,000 weekly. The right to collect cess in the bazar in 1909-1910 was sold for Rs. 5,350. Paratwāda contains two ginning factories and one cotton press; it also contained a match factory. The latter unfortunately had to suspend work, but has found a new field in the manufacture of fireworks.

History.

Paratwāda is quite a modern town, its existence being due to its selection as a military station when Salābat Khān's Reformed Troops were converted into the Ellichpur Brigade and made a part of the Hyderābād Contingent. It was in 1823 according to the *Nurul Berār* that the cantonment was formed, Captain Sayer being at that time Commandant, and the station at Jaipur Kothli was in the same year abandoned. At one time, a whole brigade with cavalry, artillery and infantry was stationed here, and Meadows Taylor in 1840 notes that it was particularly the Brigadier's privilege to spend his summers at Chikaldā, but on various occasions since the Assignment the numbers were reduced, and in 1903 only one battalion of infantry was left to evacuate the place. The old military buildings which are valued at Rs. 2,11,782, consist of infantry and artillery lines with a military hospital and are now lying vacant.

Description.

Paratwāda is divided by the river Bichan into two parts. To the north-east lies the *basti* and to the south-west the Civil Station or Cantonment, the two being joined by bridges, one near the post office on the Chikaldā road, and the other close to the Khūni Bungalow" as the Subdivisional Officer's bungalow for some unknown reason is called. The Circuit House or Lāl Bungalow lies in an open space a few hundred yards to the north of the town. The *basti* is divided into seven *purās* or quarters named 'Chhotā Bazār,' 'Mothā Bazar,' 'Moglai Bazār,' 'Gatarmālpurā,' 'Brāhman line' and 'Pensionpurā. Its chief buildings are a native club with a tennis court and a billiard table, a town hall containing the municipal offices and a library, Anglo-Marāthī and Urdū schools, and a Marāthī girls' school, four *sarais,* and the civil and former military hospitals. There are also two temples to Shri Dattā and Shri Vitthal and a small theatre owned by Kisanlāl Motīlāl. On the north side of the town is an open space provided with *chabūtras* for the weekly bazar, and beyond this lies the parade ground. The Civil Station is a well-laid out area with broad roads and excellent bungalows and public offices. Though now wearing a somewhat deserted appearance since its reduction at one stroke from the headquarters of a District and a military centre to the suburb of a second class provincial town, it is still a picturesque place, being well shaded with splendid trees, and stocked with flower gardens and greenery. No statistics exist as to the climate, but it is generally held to be somewhat cooler than Amraoti in the cold weather, and warmer in the summer, both on account of its proximity to the hills and of the trees which prevent the wind. In the rains the same causes, together with the proximity of the river, make it very damp and unpleasant. In this portion of the town lie, besides the military lines, the site of the weekly bazar and the former District Offices, including the buildings now occupied by the Subdivisional Officer, and the Subordinate Judge, a police cutcherry now used as a rest house and the old District jail, part of which is in occupation by the police. The station has both an Anglican church and a Roman Catholic church; there is a joint cemetery. Paratwāda is the headquarters of the Roman Catholic Mission to the Dheds and of the Korkū and Central India Hill Mission. The latter body manages an orphanage and industrial school at Khudāwandpur, and a leper asylum at Kotharia three miles away, and both of these institutions are supported by Government.

Garga River.—A stream which rises under Bairat. It runs nearly north-west throughout its course passing near the villages of Daknā, Daoni and Sirpur, and unites with the

Tāpti immediately under the southern face of the fort of Amner.

Ganoja.—Tāluk Amraoti, houses 326, population 1,421, has a small fair held on the bright 15th of Mārgashīrsh (December) in honour of Devī and attended by four to five thousand persons, chiefly Brāhmans, who come here to perform their family rites. The more devout spend three nights at the shrine.

Gawilgarh.—A full description of this grand old fortress will be found in the chapter on History and Antiquities; and it is needless to repeat it here. To-day the pastoral Gaolis from whose forefathers, centuries gone by, it took its name, are its only inhabitants save an occasional panther; and their herds alone drink at the tanks which once supplied water to a stately court and a strong garrison. In the monsoon the water overflows in a torrent down the precipitous hillside. The darbār steps on which princes have held audience are a favourite resort for picnics from Chikaldā in the hot weather, the great banyan tree which has spread its boughs across them affording a delightful shade; while another class of sightseer has scribbled its names and its vulgarities in three languages on the walls of the lesser mosque. The Archæological Department has decided that it is impossible to do anything to restore the ruins; and though money is spent from time to time in removing rank vegetation from the walls, they are bound as years go by to lapse into greater decay.

Ghatang.—Is not mentioned in the village list of the Melghāt though a small colony of Korkūs lives there. The place is important only as a half-way house on the road from Ellichpur, being 15 miles from the latter place and the same distance from Chikaldā, which is reached by a branch from the main road about a mile out of the village. A combined dâk and inspection bungalow has been established here for the convenience of officers and travellers; the Korkū Mission have a station not far from the village and there is a police road-post.

Ghuikhed.—Tâluk Chāndur, houses 496, population 2,542, lies on the old Bombay-Nāgpur dâk line twelve miles south of Chāndur railway station, and is a large but uninteresting village with the usual school and post office. The patels of

Bemrose, Collo., Derby.

GARGA RIVER SCENE, MELGHAT.

Ghuikhed are very well-to-do and have steadily refused an entry to the village to Mārwāris, preferring to keep the moneylending business in their own hands.

Harisal.—A Korkū village on the banks of the river Sipna and situated 46 miles from Ellichpur on the Dharni-Burhānpur road. Houses 24, population 119. A P. W. D. inspection bungalow and a forest *nāka* are its only public buildings; it is a forest village and the headquarters of a forest range.

Hiwarkhed.—Tāluk Morsi, houses 831, population 3528, is a village on the Morsi-Warud road about 6 miles from the former town, having the usual school, post office and *sarai*, and a weekly bazar held on Mondays. Shrirām Rūprām Mārwāri, who is a large local moneylender, owns a cotton gin and press, and there is another cotton gin also owned by a Mārwāri. Jaggery from the Multai tahsīl is a great article of trade at the bazar, and in former times a considerable amount of salt was brought here from various parts of Berār for sale to traders coming from the Central Provinces. Outside the village are four temples, very old but not particularly notable for size or workmanship; a modern temple to Mahādeo has been built by subscription at a cost of Rs. 15,000. In days gone by, Hiwarkhed was the headquarters of a Naib and a Risāla of the Nizām's cavalry was stationed here; a tomb is shown by the villagers as that of Turk or Trak Sāhib who was an officer in it. It is surmounted by a cross and is therefore probably the grave of some early European adventurer. Before British rule Hiwarkhed was the scene of a great hookswinging festival in honour of the deity Meghnāth. Meghnāthis, that is men whose prayers had been answered by the god, would fix themselves to the hook and turn eight times, afterwards making an offering of money according to their means.

Jarud.—Tāluk Morsi, houses 984, population 4698. A large village on the banks of the Soki river paying Government land revenue of Rs. 10,500. It has a weekly bazar and a school, a Jain temple and temples of Māroti and Bālaji. Rao Sāhib Anand Rao Tukārām is Deshmukh of Jarud, and is patron of a moneylending firm here which spends part of its profits in charitable works connected with a temple. There are no Mārwāris.

Kapustalni.—Houses 614, population 2796. A large village in the Daryāpur tāluk with a small weekly bazar, bringing in about Rs. 250 bazar cess annually. It has both Urdū and Marāthī schools and a large camping ground for troops, being a day's march from Ellichpur.

Karasgaon.—Houses 1645, population 7456. A town about 8 miles north-east of Ellichpur in the tāluk of the same name and six miles from Paratwāda; was formerly in Nāmdār Khān's jāgīr and was the headquarters of the tālukdārs, one of whom by name Vitthal Bhāgdeo in 1806 built a fort of fine sandstone at a cost of Rs. 25,000; but it is now in too ruined a condition to be of any use. About the town is very extensive garden cultivation by wells in consequence of which it has considerable staying power in time of famine or short harvest. Karasgaon produces good country brass and copper-ware, such as gongs, *lotās* and household pots. The former police station has been abolished. There is a combined school and post office and a weekly bazar on Mondays. The village has two *khels*, Chaudhri and Mohal.

Kaundinyapur.—A village situated on the banks of the Wardhā in the Chāndur tāluk, which is of little importance nowadays having only 413 inhabitants. It boasts of an annual fair however in honour of the hero Vitthal Rukmaya, held on Kārtik Paurnimā (November) and said to be attended by some fifty thousand persons. This however is a very rough estimate. A modern temple of Mahādeo about 90 years old and three stories in height succeeds an ancient building of which, as of the Ambā Devī temple in Amraoti, the story of Krishna's carrying off Rukmini is told. The latter's father was Rājā of an ancient kingdom which had its capital here and his city Dewalwāda is said to be buried beneath the present village.

Khallar.—Daryāpur tāluk; houses 292, population 1292, has a first class police station and a school. The sub-registrar's office here has been abolished.

Khanzamanagar.—A small village in the Ellichpur tāluk Houses 115, population 431. It takes its name from that Khān-i-Zamān of the Emperor Aurangzeb who became

Nāzim of Berār in 1675 A. D. The village has a very old mosque in a half ruinous condition, said to have been founded by Khān-i-Zamān. There are other ruins also and it is said that the founder wished to make the place a rival to Ellichpur.

Khar-Talegaon.—See Talegaon-Khar.

Kholapur.—Houses 1192, population 5373, lies eighteen miles to the west of Amraoti on the borders of the tāluk of that name, part of its land lying across the Pūrna in Daryāpur. A bench of Honorary Magistrates has been established here for the trial of petty offences; and the town has a police station, a sub-registry, a dispensary, Hindustāni and Marāthī schools, a girls' school and a post office. Its silk weavers have almost disappeared; but a large number of Sālis still produce cotton *sāris* and *cholis*, and some Mahārs weave woollen blankets and cotton *khādīs*. This trade however is also languishing. The land revenue of the place is Rs. 11,269-12-0. There is a cotton ginning factory; a bazar is held on Wednesdays and Saturdays; and a yearly fair in the month of August. Formerly Kholāpur was a place of much importance. In 1809 Vitthal Bhāgdeo, Sūbahdār of Ellichpur, levied a contribution of one lakh. The inhabitants refused to pay. The Sūbahdār accordingly besieged the town which was then protected by walls, for two months, when the inhabitants gave in. The town was looted by the troops, and has never recovered its former prosperity. Its rapid decadence may also be attributed to the annual fights between the Musalmāns and the Rājputs, when the victorious party always took occasion to loot at least part of the town.

Kondeshwar.—An old black stone temple of Kondeshwar (Mahādeo) about three miles distant from Badnerā and two from Anjangaon Bāri in the Amraoti tāluk. It is said to be Hemādpanthī and may at one time have been a fine structure though now much dilapidated; the former stone dome has fallen in and has been replaced by a modern erection of white chunam. The temple is largely visited by Hindus from Amraoti and elsewhere on Mondays during the month of Shrāwan (July-August).

Kurha.—A village of 818 houses in the Chāndur tāluk having a mixed population of Bāris, Muhammadans, Kunbīs, Mālis and Rājputs numbering 3746 persons. A police station under a Sub-Inspector, a sub-registry, an Urdū and a combined Marāthī school and post office are its only public buildings. The *masjid* is supported by an *inām* grant of 150 acres. The tank at Kūrha is a good one. The place is situated half-way between Chāndur and Tiosā on the road connecting these places which was built in the famine of 1900. The famous dacoits Nandū Rājput and Pandū Patel of Tembhurni were surrounded here in a temple by the Nizām's troops in 1843, but after a three days' fight succeeded in cutting their way out. Their depredations had extended far into the Central Provinces. Nandū lived to be a very old man and died some few years ago.

Lasura.—A small village in the Daryāpur tāluk, having an old temple of Mahādeo said to be Hemādpanthī. The stones of it are carved with figures of gods and demi-gods; but the building is rapidly falling into ruin.

Loni.—Tāluk Morsi, houses 769, population 3464, commonly called Loni-Warud to distinguish it from the other Loni near Badnerā. One Ganesh Shivāji has recently built a temple to Mahādeo here at a cost of Rs. 15,000.

Mahimapur—An insignificant village in the Daryāpur tāluk. It has an old well said to have been built during the Mughal period, in which is a small chamber or grotto suitable for relaxation in the hot weather. Even the name of the sybarite for whose pleasure it was made is now forgotten, and the water is used for the ordinary village supply.

Mahuli Jagir.—Amraoti tāluk, lies 16 miles from Amraoti on the Morsi road, and contains 540 houses with a population of 2242 persons. It was granted in jāgīr in 1859 to the lineal descendants of the late Mīr Dilāwar Husain in consideration of faithful service rendered to Her Majesty. The area of the village lands is 2618 acres and 23 *gunthās*, and the estimated rental according to settlement rates Rs. 4720-8-0 per annum.

Malkapur.—See Sendurjana (Morsi).

Malkhed.—Talūk Chāndur; 541 houses, 2377 inhabitants. The village is situated about half a mile from the railway station named after it, and lies on the edge of the Chirodi forest reserve, grass cutting in which employs many of its inhabitants for several months of the year. Mālkhed has a Marāthī school and post office and the *masjid* and two Hindū temples are supported by *inām* land.

Mangrul Dastgir.—Chāndur tāluk, houses 1508, population 6588, is not an integral village but consists of eight "Munds" lying close together. The second name Dastgīr is given to distinguish it from several other towns and villages called "Mangrūl" in Berār and is derived from a Musalmān *fakīr* who lived here and is buried in the *garhi*. Mangrūl is about three miles from Tālni railway station, and has a small trade in cotton and grain to the Dattāpur market. It has one old and ruinous temple of Māroti and modern shrines of Bālajī and Ganpati. At Raina close by are a small tank and a big temple built by Wāsudeopant Deshpānde, the ancestor of Bhagwant Krishna Deshpānde the present patel. There are Marāthī and Urdū schools and a girls' school. The weekly bazar which is a large one is held on Wednesdays.

Marki.—Amraoti tāluk, houses 105, population 475, a small village remarkable for its fair which is held annually for three days at the end of the bright half of Chaitra (March) in honour of Shri Markināth and attracts from ten to fifteen thousand people. About 200 booths are erected and, it is said, not less than thirty thousand rupees worth of goods sold; but the great attraction of the fair is religious and consists of a *hom* or fire-worship performed in front of the shrine in which thousands of cocoanuts are offered to the fire. *Bhajan melās* or parties of ten or twenty persons wander over the fair singing religious songs of a somewhat enthusiastic type to the accompaniment of tomtoms, cymbals, and similar music.

Melghat Taluk.—The northern tāluk of Berār formerly part of the Ellichpur District, but since August 1905 incorporated in the Amraoti District, lying between 21°10′ and 21°47′ N. and 76°38′ and 77°40′ E., with an estimated area of 1,609 square miles. Previous to the transfer of the Ambābārwa

Physical features.

State forest to the Buldāna District the area of the tāluk was 1,631 square miles. The tāluk is also sometimes called Gāngra and consists of that portion of the Sātpurā range situated between the Khāmla plateau on the east and Jeitgarh on the west with the rich valleys and low plateaus lying between the mountains. Its extreme breadth north and south is thirty-eight miles, and its extreme length east and west sixty miles. On the north it is bounded by a portion of the Betūl District and the Tāpti river dividing it from Nimār, on the west by the Tāpti river and a portion of the Nimār District, on the south by the tāluks of Jalgaon (Buldāna District) and Akot (Akolā District) and the tāluks of Daryāpur and Ellichpur, and on the east by the Betūl District. The whole tāluk with the exception of the alienated lands and the civil station of Chikaldā, which has been disforested, is nominally State forest. In reality, however, the only tracts which merit the name of forest are the A and B class reserves. The area known as C—III forest has long since been abandoned by the Forest Department, so far as any system of conservancy is concerned, but though it has a long and interesting revenue history, cultivation having been carried on from time immemorial, it has for various reasons never been brought under the ordinary revenue law. It is this tract, which constitutes the Melghāt revenue tāluk. It comprises an area of about 671 square miles, and consists of a broad belt lying south of the reserves and adjoining the Berār plains, a small area on the east in the Kātkūmb pargana and the whole of the western portion of the Melghāt. The country is extremely rugged and broken into a succession of hills and valleys. In the more advanced portions, such as the neighbourhood of Dharni, and Bairāgarh when the *rabi* crops are on the ground, the green fields afford a pleasing and restful view to the eye. But the typical Melghāt country consists of barren hills, scrub jungle and stony ground, and is of a most dreary and desolate description. The villages are collections of hovels without any shade, as the Korkū prefers cutting trees to planting them, and one can well understand the feelings of the subordinate officials who regard the tract as *kālapāni* and whose health requires frequent visits to the Berār plains. There are no navigable rivers in the tāluk unless the Tāpti which forms a portion of the boundary may be considered such during the rainy season. The streams that drain the northern face of the range and fall into the Tāpti are the following:—The Sipnā and the Kundu both have their rise close to the village of Khāmla in Betūl District, the former running south of Mākhla plateau for 8 or 10 miles takes a north-westerly course and passing through the villages of Harisāl and Dūni unites with the Tāpti to the north-east of Amner; the latter passing through the Kātkūmb and Saolīgarh parganas falls into the Tāpti. The Gargā rises under Bairat, the highest summit of the Gāwīlgarh hills and running nearly north-west throughout its course unites with the Tāpti immediately under the southern face of the fort of Amner. The Kapra, the Majri and the Dewan are the other minor streams which fall into the Tāpti.

The climate of the tract has a very evil reputation, corresponding in this respect to the Dindorī tahsīl of Mandlā and the Baihar tahsil of Bālāghāt. A severe type of malaria prevails at the end of the rains and the beginning of the cold weather, and it has usually been considered unsafe to camp in the Melghāt before the 1st January. In the hot weather the heat in the valleys is intense and the absence of shade, the difficulties of water-supply, and the general lack of all the comforts of the plains, make the tract one of the most unpleasant for touring purposes that it is possible to imagine.

Population.

The Melghāt tāluk is the largest of all the tāluks of the District in point of size, but the smallest of all in point of population, the density being only 22 per square mile. The population of the tāluk in 1901 was 36,670 or 4½ per cent. of the total population of the District. In 1891 the population was 46,849 persons and in 1881, 42,262. The increase between 1881-1891 was 10.8 per cent. as against the District figure of 9.2 per cent. During the last decade the population declined by about 22 per cent. being the largest decrease of all the tāluks in the District. Various causes were assigned for this decrease such as famine, emigration to Nimār District and the plains of Berār. It was said that in spite of the liberal measures of relief during the famines in the way of distributing seed and cattle, many villages with poor soil and defective water-supply were deserted. Part of the decrease in population is attributed to the constant extension of the Melghāt reserves; the Korkū who dislikes being bound down to a settled habitation has gone elsewhere. The Melghāt is still, however, an aboriginal stronghold. Of the total population in 1901, 76 per cent. were aboriginals, 60 per cent. being Korkūs. There are 338 villages in the C—III tract, 240 of which are inhabited and cultivated, 56 uninhabited but cultivated and 42 both uninhabited and uncultivated. The aboriginals are still in possession of more than half the land at present occupied, and the impression that the Korkūs and other aboriginals have gone to the wall before the tide of immigration from beyond the Tāpti and from Berār is not entirely justified. It is true that in the centre of the Amner pargana the aboriginal has been to a great extent ousted by the moneylender and the liquor seller, who are immigrants from Burhānpur, and it is generally assumed—perhaps without sufficient authority—that the land at the foot of the hills bordering the Berār plains which is almost entirely in possession of Berār cultivators, has also been filched from them. The tāluk contains no town or village with more than 1,000 persons. The sanitarium of Chikaldā, the headquarters of the tāluk, boasts of 969 persons. The census, however, was taken early in the hot weather and this figure includes a considerable official population of clerks and attendants as well as Europeans temporarily resident there. The only other villages having over 500 inhabitants are Kalamkhar, Kasamkot Kalān and Bairāgarh. The largest village is Dharni with 731 inhabitants. The average population of a Melghat village is 111. Weekly bazars are held at Dharni, Popatkherā, Kātkūmb, Kalamkhar, Raipur, Dūni, Bairāgarh, Titamba and Chikaldā.

Agriculture.

In the valleys of the Tāpti, Sātpurā and Gāngra, especially in the neighbourhood of Dharni or Bairāgarh, rich stretches of black soil are to be found, and a visitor to either of these places who sees spread out before him an unbroken expanse of wheat and gram, is liable to get a very misleading impression of the tract as a whole. The remainder of the tract is of a very hilly and rugged description, though here and there pockets of black soil are met with in the valleys. The soils have never been thoroughly classified but in 1897 Colonel Garret's party classified a few typical fields in each village and worked out the average value of the soil for each village. The soil as a whole is of the poorest description. Of the 338 villages 3 were valued at 12 annas per acre, 11 villages at 11 annas, 117 at values varying from 6 annas to 9 annas, and the remaining 193 fell below 6 annas. In 1860-61 Mr. J. Mulheran in his statistical report on Gāngra stated that 'Rice 'and gram are the principal productions of Gāngra and are 'grown expressly for export. The former is much prized by 'the people of Berār and Burhānpur, particularly the finest 'kind which resembles that grown in the Pilibhīt District. 'Gram is exported principally to Burhānpur though large 'quantities are brought into Berār through all the passes by 'the people from Jalgaon, Hiwarkhed, Anjangaon, Ellichpur 'and other places south of the range. Juāri grows very 'luxuriantly near Kalamkhar and other places in the Sipnā 'and Garga valleys also upon some of the lower plateaus. '*Bardi*, *vala*, *margi*, kodon kutkī and one or two other hill 'grains are grown upon more elevated slopes and plateaus and 'are used chiefly if not entirely by the Gonḍs. Potatoes are 'not cultivated by the Korkūs of Gāngra although that veget-'able would pay them better than any other. That sold at 'Chikaldā and Ellichpur is grown by the Gaolīs located at 'Motā, Chikaldā, Shāpur and Bori and by the Hindu inhabi-'tants of the fort of Gāwīlgarh.' At this time the area under cultivation obtained by outlining and subsequent computation was 97,280 acres. In 1864 Captain Pearson refers to the rich soil and good cultivation of the plains near the Tāpti and the Gāngra, and the Gazetteer of 1870 states that thirteen different kinds of grain were produced in the Melghāt of which the most valuable were the finest wheat and rice, grown in large quantities. In 1906-07 the returns shewed that out of a total of 1,663,376 acres occupied for cultivation 142,334 acres were under crop. Of this cotton occupied 42,392 acres or 25 per cent., juāri 23,749 acres or 14 per cent., gram 14,193 acres or 8 per cent., and wheat 8,254 acres or 4 per cent. The area under rice was only 3,256 acres and the total irrigated area was 50 acres. These figures do not include those for *inām*, leased and jāgīr villages, and it is to be noted that they are not the results of accurate measurement but are derived from the statistical calculation of 16 acres per plough.

Land Revenue.

The tract has a curious and interesting revenue history, for which the Chapter on Land Revenue may be consulted. Cultivation is permitted by the Tahsīldār on a yearly tenure subject to certain conditions and land revenue is assessed on the yoke of oxen, the rates differing in different villages. For statistical purposes only, the area cultivated by one plough is taken to be 16 acres and to obtain the total acreage under cultivation, the number of ploughs should be multiplied by 16. The yoke rate system is a cheap and simple method of colonizing a backward tract but it is no longer suitable for a considerable portion of the Melghāt and the introduction of a regular and scientific assessment is urgently required. Proposals for settlement have been made at various times but have always proved abortive. A special enquiry was made in 1907 and orders regarding the settlement of the most advanced portion of the tract have recently been issued. In 1907-08 the land-revenue demand including cesses was Rs. 57,227.

Miscellaneous.

It goes without saying that the complicated systems of land records, vital statistics and the like in force in the plains do not exist in the Melghāt. There are no Circle Inspectors but eleven patwāris are in existence, each with a circle of villages, and they carry on such land record work as is necessary. Local Government likewise has not yet been found possible in such a backward tract, and it is accordingly excluded from the operation of the Rural Boards Law. The Melghāt Fund is formed of various cesses and of a contribution from provincial funds and its primary object is the upkeep of Chikaldā but certain expenditure in the C III tract such as the upkeep of village *chauris*, cattle pounds, and a few roads is also debited to it. The tāluk forms part of the Ellichpur police circle under an Inspector and contains 2 station-houses each under a Sub-Inspector at Chikaldā and Dharni. There are also two road posts at Bairāgarh and Ghātang. It is a separate forest division, the Divisional Officer having 7 range officers under his orders. A great change has taken place since 1870 when Sir A. Lyall wrote that none of the passes from the Melghāt were practicable for wheeled traffic and that there were no made roads in the Melghāt. The opening out of the Melghāt was begun in 1874 and has continued ever since with the result that especially in the reserves a most excellent system of communication has been established. The P. W. D. maintains roads from Ghātang to Chikaldā, the Gugumāl forest road (Akot to Selu) and the Sambadoh to Dharni road. These are second-class roads surfaced with *muram* partially bridged and drained. There will also ultimately be first-class communications between Burhānpur and Ghātang via Dhertalāi and Harisāl. There are 8 different roads maintained by the Forest Department and 5 by the Melghāt Fund. Perhaps the most important of these is the road running from Bairāgarh to Jhiri, 56 miles in length, which was constructed in the famine. Its cost of upkeep is only about Rs. 560 per annum, but as it is the principal line of export for the western portion of the Melghāt, its claims for improvement deserve consideration. With a few exceptions every village in the Melghāt is in cart communication with some main road; the tracts are rough and stony but they serve their purpose sufficiently well. There is no railway in the *tahsīl* but the proposed Khandwā-Akolā line will pass through the south-western corner of it.

Mojhri.—(Tāluk Melghāt) or as the Berār Gazetteer of 1870 has it, Manjira, is a small village reached from Chikaldā by a precipitous track through the fort. It has two small artificial caves, cut in the natural rock. One of these is completely choked with rubbish so that it is very difficult to discover, but the other which is about 8 feet high and 16 feet square contains in its inner part a shrine of Mahādeo. This is divided from the outer portion by a small mud wall. Beside is a spring of water dry during the greater part of the year and a cut basin. The whole is most rudely cut in the rock without any trace of carving, and is probably the work of bygone hermit ascetics, though all traditions of its origin have long since been lost.

Mojhri.—Tāluk Chāndur, houses 684, population 2906, has a combined Marāthī school and post office, and a weekly bazar held on Saturdays. The patel, Thākur Chandrabhān Raoji Deshmukh, has an orange garden and is the owner of a cotton gin.

Morsi Taluk.—A tāluk of the Amraoti District lying between 21°12′ and 21°34′ N. and 77°48′ and 78°29′ E. with an area of 622 square miles. It contains 332 villages and towns, one of these the little village of Deothāna being alienated; proceedings for its resumption are at present before the courts. The lands of the village of Ambhori are entirely absorbed in State forests. The tāluk is a prolongation of the rich alluvial plain which occupies the valley of Berār and its capabilities for the production of cotton and cereals are considerable, although a slight falling-off is perceptible from an agricultural point of view both in the formation of surface and the nature of the soils. The former is more undulating than that presented by the Ellichpur plain, and the latter are more shallow and more varied in quality than the soils of Ellichpur. The tāluk lies in the fertile valley of the Wardhā river which bounds it on the east and south-east, but a narrow strip along its north-western border occupies the lower slopes of the Sātpurā hills. The Amraoti and Ellichpur tāluks bound it on the south and west, respectively. On the north lies the Betūl district; to the east and south the Chhindwārā, Nāgpur and Wardhā districts. The Wardhā river has been taken as the boundary between the Central Provinces and Berār. It is to this fact that the tāluk owes its peculiar shape, the river approaching so near to the hills in the vicinity of Morsi as almost to cut it into two portions. Some parts of the country are fairly well wooded, and the only considerable forest reserves of the Amraoti Division (if we except Chirodi), are in the eastern half of this tāluk. The western part is bare and very dreary, and in respect of scenery the tāluk compares unfavourably with Ellichpur. The climate is good, although of course exceedingly hot in the hot weather. In the eastern portion of the tāluk water is near the surface and can be raised without much difficulty for purposes of irrigation. Of the river system which drains the tāluk the Wardhā is the main channel, and it supplies water to villagers along the border for a distance of upwards of 50 miles. Among rivers of less importance are the Charged and the Mandu in the western portion of the tāluk and the Chundāmani, Kūmbhi and Bel in the east. These rivers though of no great length contain

Bemrose, Collo., Derby.

MELGHAT FOREST ROAD.

considerable supplies of water for a large part of the year. Streams in the neighbourhood of the hills hardly worthy of the name of rivers are much used for irrigation, the rapid fall of the beds of these streams affording facilities for drawing off the water on erection of temporary dams. In no other part of Berār is the water from streams utilized as it is in Morsi and the supply here is in some cases perennial, admitting of the cultivation of sugarcane and turmeric without the assistance of well water. It is probable that there is room for a very large extension of wet cultivation in this tāluk. The possibility of artesian wells has also been mooted.

Population.

The total population of the tāluk in 1901 was 143,734 persons or about 18 per cent. of that of the District. In 1891 the population was 152,374 and in 1881, 129,688. The increase between 1881 and 1891 was 17½ per cent. as against the District figure of 9 and the decrease between 1891 and 1901 was about 6 per cent. as against nearly 5 for the District as a whole. As usual the decrease is attributed to the series of bad years and the famines during the decade. The density of population is 231 souls to a square mile. Excluding towns the density of rural population is 186 per square mile. As in other tāluks throughout Berār the population in general is purely agricultural. The tāluk contains the 4 towns of Morsi, Warud, Sendurjanā and Ner Pinglai, and 328 villages, of which 100 are uninhabited[1] according to village lists. Besides the above towns the following 9 villages contained more than 2000 persons in 1901 :—Ambāda, Jarud, Puslā, Benodā, Belura, Rajura, Rithpur, Loni and Hīwarkhed. There were also 19 villages whose population exceeded 1000 persons.

Agriculture.

Cotton, juāri, wheat and tūr are the principal crops grown. At the original settlement juāri occupied 42 per cent., cotton about 36 per cent., and wheat about 10 per cent. 'That cotton,' it was said, 'should 'still bear a proportion of more than one-third to all the other 'crops notwithstanding the low prices that have ruled during 'the last few years would be surprising, were it not that these 'prices are still remunerative and the speculative spirit 'roused during the cotton mania has not yet quite died out

[1] See note, p. 353

'even amongst the cultivators.' At the revision settlement (1894-98) the total occupied and assessed area was 311,229 acres. Of this 127,460 acres or 40.2 per cent. were occupied by juāri and 117,208 acres or 37 per cent by cotton, the cultivation of these crops having practically remained stable since the original settlement. Wheat occupied 20,034 acres or 6.3 per cent. showing a decline of about 4 per cent. over that of the original settlement. The area under tūr was 15,764 acres or 5 per cent. of the total occupied assessed area. *Haldi (Cucuma longa)* or turmeric thrives here particularly well in irrigated land. The area occupied by irrigated crops was 9,818 acres or more than 5 per cent. The irrigation by channels from streams or *pātasthal bagait* is of some importance in Morsi though almost unknown in the remainder of the District. The construction of temporary dams across the streams at the close of the monsoon rains is easily and cheaply effected, and in some cases a perennial supply of water can be turned on to the garden lands and valuable crops can be grown at a minimum of labour and cost. In 1906-07, of the 334,115 acres of village area 320,169 acres or about 96 per cent. were occupied for cultivation. Of this the total cropped area was 309,560 acres including the double-cropped area (only 187 acres). The area under juāri was 88,401 acres or 28½ per cent. of the cropped area, and under wheat 7,920 acres or 2½ per cent., while that under cotton was 171,751 acres or more than 55 per cent., having gained by 18 per cent. since revision settlement. The area under *tūr* is also on the increase, being 22,929 acres or more than 7 per cent. of the cropped area. The irrigated area has much declined being only 1,801 acres.

Land Revenue.

At the original settlement the 331 *khālsa* villages were divided into four groups, and assessed with maximum dry crop standard acreage rates varying from R. 1-8-0 to Rs. 2-4-0. The average rate per acre cultivated however varied from 8 annas 11 pies to R. 1-8-5. The grouping of the villages and the settlements were based entirely on the proximity to market towns; and the rates applied to these groups were introduced from the Ellichpur tâluk, Morsi being similarly situated as regards distance from the line of rail. At the revision settlement (1894-98) the tāluk was divided into two groups, making a distinction between the eastern and western portions and taking the river Mandu as the dividing line. The first group consisted of 174 villages and was rated at Rs. 2-12-0, and the second 157 villages at Rs. 2-8 per acre, the average rate however falling at R. 1-13-8 for the first group and R. 1-8-10 for the second group. The demand at the time of revision settlement on the Government occupied area of 311,418 acres according to the former survey was Rs. 4,25,596 giving an incidence of R. 1-5-9 per acre, while at the revision settlement the assessment on the occupied area of 311,229 acres according to revision survey was increased to Rs. 5,31,959, giving an incidence of R. 1-11-4 per acre. The increase thus amounted to Rs. 1,06,363 or 25 per cent. on the existing demand. In 1907-08 the demand on account of land revenue and cesses was Rs. 5,58,339, while the actual collections according to treasury figures amounted to Rs. 5,47,071.

Miscellaneous.

For purposes of land records the tāluk has been divided into three Circle Inspectors' circles with headquarters at Morsi, Warud and Sirkhed. It constitutes a single police circle under an Inspector and contains 4 Station-houses, each under a Sub-Inspector at Morsi, Sirkhed, Warud and Benoda. The Morsi-Warud forest range lies wholly and the Morsi-Bairam range partly in this tāluk which includes the Shekdari, Mehdari and Lakhāda State forests and the large Puslā grazing reserve. In the matter of communications the tāluk is extremely well served, the Amraoti-Wardhā-river road running along its whole length.

Morsi Town.—The headquarters of the tāluk of that name contains 1714 houses with 8313 inhabitants and is situated 34 miles north-east of Amraoti with which place it is at present connected by a first-class metalled road and is soon to be joined by a railway. The same road continues to Warud whence a branch of it is taken over the Central Provinces border to Multai and one branch goes on to the river Wardhā at the extreme east of the tāluk. To Ellichpur there is a country road, parts of which were metalled during the last famine. The public buildings include besides the tahsili (in which the police station and sub-registry are also located), a civil court for the Sub-Judge and munsiff, a post and telegraph office, and a veterinary dispensary. On the site of the old *garhī* are a Hindustāni school and a charitable dispensary. The town also possesses a Marāthī school, and a girls' school, an inspection and dâk bungalow, a *sarai* and a public library. The Lady Dufferin fund maintains a trained midwife here. A river runs by the town and the place is damp and malarious; it is however commercially important and has a cotton market established in 1900 with an income of about Rs. 1,400. Three cotton gins and two presses are at work here, and *tadhaos*, blankets, and coarse *dhotīs* are also made by hand looms. The weekly bazar is held on Tuesdays. Mālis, Kunbīs and Musalmāns are the most numerous classes among the population; and there are two patels and one patwāri.

Mota.—A village in the Killa pargana of the Melghāt situated just where the Dhāmangaon-Motā road to Chikaldā reaches the tops of the hills. "Mackenzie's Ride" from Chikaldā ends here. The present patel (1908) is a retired soldier, a great *shikāri*, and a character whose acquaintance is well worth cultivating. The village has 65 houses with 252 inhabitants; there are several families of Gaolīs who own large herds of cattle.

Nandgaon Peth.—Amraoti tāluk, is almost 7 miles from Amraoti on the Morsi road, and is inhabited by a large number of Muhammadans, the chief of whom is Syed Kāsim, the jāgirdār of the neighbouring villages of Kathorā and Tākli. The population is 4575. A bazar is held on Tuesday, Friday and Sunday. Two Hindu temples, a *masjid* and the tomb of a Muhammadan saint are supported by service *ināms*.

Nandgaon Kazi.—Tāluk Chāndur: houses 794, population 3435, has a first-class police station, sub-registry, Marāthī school, and post office, a public *sarai* and a cattle pound. The village has one police patel but is divided into eight *munds* or *khels*, each with a separate revenue patel. One Hāji Ghāzi Aolia is buried here, and there is also a combined temple of Khandeshwar, Devī and Narsinh with a common *sabhā mandap* situated ona hillock on the outskirts of the village. This is said to be Hemādpanthī, a common tradition of any old temple; as a matter of fact it is probably not more than 200 years old. In modern times a *pīrzāda* known as Māti Mile Miyan lived here. The words mean "mixed with dirt" and are a term of abuse among women locally. The name was doubtless descriptive of the *pīr*, though one may suppose it was assumed with some suggestion of "Ashes to ashes, dust to dust." A tomb has been built over his remains, and an *urs* is held annually which is largely frequented. His son at present lives in the village. Nāndgaon is situated in the rocky portion of Chāndur tāluk and in time of scarcity is one of the places to be attended to first.

Ner Pinglai.—Tāluk Morsi: houses 1252, population 5408. The second name has been given to distinguish it from Ner Parsopant in the Yeotmāl District, and is taken from a temple of Pinglai Devī situated on a small hill on the borders of Ner and Sāwarkhed. The temple, though not as sometimes said Hemādpanthī, is an old one, and is the scene of two fairs in the year, one at Dasahra and one at Chaitra Paurnimā, at which about five thousand people collect. Beside it is a small tank. A *math* for the accommodation of pilgrims has been built by the late Guru Gangādhar at a cost of about Rs. 20,000 and is supported by an *inām* of Rs. 150. Bāris, Mālis, Wānis and a few Musalmāns reside in the town, which has, in addition to the usual Marāthī school and post office, and Urdū school. The weekly bazar is held on Thursday, and there is a *sarai* at Ner. Sāwarkhed, the neighbouring village, which is 21 miles from Amrāoti by the Morsi high road, has a dâk bungalow. The proposed new railway line will have a station near here.

Palaskhed.—A large but unimportant village in the Chāndur tāluk. Houses 559, population 2581.

Paratwada.—See Ellichpur Civil Station.

Pathrot.—Houses 1081, population 4510. A large centre of garden cultivation situated in the west of the Ellichpur tāluk twelve miles from Paratwāda and six from Anjangaon Surji by the District Board road. A bazar is held on Thursdays; and in addition to the gardens there is a considerable dry crop of chillies. It has a sixth standard vernacular school and post office and a first-class police station under a Sub-Inspector.

Pedhi River.—A river rising in the southern portion of the Morsi tāluk; runs through the centre of the Amraoti tāluk roughly parallel to the Pūrna river in a south-westerly direction. It flows through Balgaon and Bhātkuli and leaves the tāluk at Bapori; and from thence taking a bend towards the west meets the Pūrna. The supply of water is small but perennial.

Peth Muhammad Nagar.—See Anjangaon Surji.

Purna River.—(Said to be the ancient Payoshni).—A river of Berār having its source in the Gāwīlgarh hills in 21°36′ N., and 77°36′ E. near Bhainsdehi in the Betūl District of the Central Provinces. The river takes a south-westerly course and flowing through the Ellichpur tāluk as far as Assegaon, forms the boundary between the Amraoti tāluk and the Ellichpur and Daryāpur tāluks up to the northern border of the Murtizāpur tāluk, thus traversing a distance of about 50 miles; it then takes a bend towards the west and flows about midway between the Gāwīlgarh and Bālāghāt hills draining the central valley of the Berārs. From the point at which it turns towards the west it forms the District boundary between Amraoti and Akolā Districts as far as Dahihandā. Then leaving Amraoti and following the same westerly course through the north-western portion of the Akolā District it enters Buldāna near Wanjargaon, from thence separating the Jalgaon tāluk from the Malkāpur aud Khāmgaon tāluks, it flows on till it leaves the Buldāna District at Dādhalgaon and after some distance meets the Tāpti in Khāndesh. The river is not navigable by boats. The banks though soft resist to a great extent serious inroads by the channel water. On the banks of the Pūrna water can be always had by sinking wells; but owing to the peculiarity of the sub-soil, the water is sometimes very brackish and except for washing can be little used. For irrigation the Pūrna is unsuitable in consequence of its high banks and the scanty supply of water. The tributaries on its right bank within the District are the Chandrabhāga and Shāhnur. The total length of the river roughly measured from the map is about 155 miles, of which about 75 miles lie within the District.

Pusda.—Amraoti tāluk, 12 miles to the north of Amraoti, and about 3 miles to the east of the Chāndur Bazār road. The population is 2,158. There is a vernacular school with a branch post office. The District Board has provided a *sarai* for native travellers. A bazar is held on Saturdays.

Pusla.—Houses 1,080, inhabitants 4,837, a large but poor village in the north-east of the Morsi tāluk. The population includes a large number of Koshtīs, who weave coarse cloth for the local market, and are in times of scarcity hard pressed to find a living. The soil of the village moreover is poor and not suited for high cultivation. Thus on the approach of famine Puslā is one of the first villages to require attention. It has a Public Works Department inspection bungalow in connection with the road from Amraoti to the Wardhā river; and the neighbouring Puslā grazing reserve is the largest block of C class forest in the Amraoti Division. Puslā is 60 miles from Amraoti and the projected railway line may be expected to bring some increase of prosperity.

Rajura.—Tāluk Morsi, houses 400, population 2,111, has a weekly bazar held on Thursdays at which grain and cattle as well as silk and silk-bordered cotton cloth are sold. It is otherwise unimportant.

Railway Chandur.—See Chandur Town.

Ridhpur or Ritpur.—Tāluk Morsi, 508 houses, 2,412 inhabitants, a village about 6 miles east of Chāndur Bazār on the Ellichpur-Chāndur-Morsi road, is famous chiefly as the headquarters of the Mānbhao sect (see Chapter III. page 121. It belonged to Salābat Khān having been given to him as *tankhā jāgīr*, and was a place of much importance. Eighty years ago, it was surrounded by a stone wall which has now almost disappeared, and contained two thousand houses and some twelve thousand inhabitants. In the time of Nāmdār Khān however the notorious Rājā Bisn Chand was tālukdār there. He is remembered alike for his oppression and miserliness, and has left a name at which the Kunbī still grows pale. To pronounce it of a morning is to incur the risk of having to do without food all day. The people fled from his neighbourhood and Ridhpur has since borne that deserted [1] appearance which characterises it to-day. In addition to the Mānbhao buildings here of which the Rāj *Math* and Krishna *Mandir* are the most important, the Hindus have a temple of Rāmchandra and the Muhammadans two *dargāhs* and a *masjid*. The latter is in the midst of the Mānbhao buildings, and till lately the only approach to it lay through them. Local tradition declares that it was built by Aurangzeb, who knocked down the original *Rāj Math* for the purpose: and the story, whether true or not, is typical of the bigoted Emperor. In addition to the weekly bazar on Tuesday, two fairs are held here yearly at Chaitra Paurnimā and Ashād Paurnimā, which though primarily Mānbhao festivals are attended by about 5,000 people of all castes. A well, known as Lāla's well, supplies excellent drinking water to about half the village. The neighbouring soil is rocky and poor.

Rinmochan.—Amraoti tāluk, houses 7, population 57, a jāgīr village granted along with Dhanorā in the Daryāpur tāluk in A. D. 1840 for the service of Muezzin at Kholāpur and personal maintenance in heredity. The present holder is Shaikh Gulām Murtazā son of Shaikh Gulām Mustafā; the acreage of Rinmochan is 295 acres 6 *gunthās*, and the estimated amount of land revenue remitted to the jāgirdār Rs. 583 per annum. The place is considered holy by Hindus, being one of the sacred places on the river Pūrna, and boasts of an annual fair held on the four Sundays in the month of Pausha with an attendance of one to ten thousand. The word *Rin-mochan* literally means 'release from debts,' and it is believed that those who attend the fair and bathe in the river attain this blissful state.

Salbardi.—Houses 36, population 163, is an insignificant village about 5 miles north of Morsi and lying partly in the tāluk of that name and partly in the Betūl District, but holds an important position in Hindu mythology. It is here that Sīta is said to have come when she was deserted by Rāma, and to have given birth to her two sons Lava and Kusha; these were taught by Vālmīk after he had been reformed by Nārad, who released him from his entombment at Sālbardī.

[1] *Rit* in Marāthī, means deserted; *pur*=village.

The twins are said to have caught the horse Shyāmkarna let loose by their father. On this a great fight occurred in which the god with his three brothers was defeated and left unconscious. Their clothes and ornaments were recognised by Sīta and they were restored to life by Vālmīk. Sīta and the sons were then acknowledged by Rāma, and were taken by him to Oudh. Sālbardī is situated on the Māru river, and is celebrated on account of two springs—one very cold, and the other hot, or decidedly tepid. The springs flow into a small stone cistern which was formerly divided into compartments for the hot and cold water but has now been made one. Some of the water was recently analysed, and reported on as containing sulphates and phosphates in small quantity; unfit for drinking but probably useful as a wash for skin diseases. Colonel Meadows Taylor records bathing here in 1857 and says that the waters gave his malaria temporary relief. As might be expected, the place contains several spots of mythological interest, particularly the bath or *Nihāni* of Sīta and an underground temple of Mahādeo in a natural cave; also some images cut in the natural rock. A hill close by is crowned with a rough stone fort known as Bābū Khān's *kilā* after a famous Pindāri who occupied it. Near this place R. B. Hira Lāl has recently discovered two Buddhist *vihāras* or monasteries consisting of spacious halls and rooms all cut out of rock. One of them contains a headless image of Buddha, now worshipped as a Devī with vermilion and water. Hence the story given in the Betūl Gazetteer from which the following is extracted.

'A small village in the Multai tahsīl on the Berār border, 'about 44 miles south of Badnūr on the Māru river, with a 'population of about 300 persons. A cave in a hill by the 'village, approached through a long narrow passage, contains 'an idol of Mahādeo. It is popularly supposed that an 'underground passage leads from this cave to Mahādeo's hill 'at Pachmarhī, and it is said that Mahādeo put two thousand 'goats into the passage at Pachmarhī, and only one came 'out of Sālbardī. It is said also that a hole in the hill leads 'down to the cave and that this hole was made by Bhīmsen 'so that he might see Mahādeo better. There were also hot 'and cold water springs here, but they have now become 'mixed. A temple on the hill contains a headless image of 'Devī and a pool of reddish-coloured water in front of the 'temple is supposed to be tinged by the blood that fell from 'the image when its head was cut off. An annual fair is 'held here in March, lasting for three days, and is attended 'by about 5,000 persons, nearly a hundred temporary shops 'being opened for the sale of goods. In the village is a 'quarry of hard stone from which mortars, cups and cooking 'slabs are made. There is also a quarry of limestone. The 'proprietor is a Khatrī.'

Sālbardī is named from its abundance of *sāl* trees and the stony character of its soil.

Sategaon.—499 houses, 2,258 inhabitants, a rich but unimportant village in the Daryāpur *tāluk*; it has a Marāthī school.

Satpura Hills.—A range of hills in the centre of India.

Geographical position.

The name, which is modern, originally belonged to the hills which divide the Nerbudda and Tāpti valleys in Nimār, Central Provinces, and were styled the Sāt putra or seven sons of the Vindhyan mountains. Another derivation is from Satpura (sevenfolds) referring to the numerous parallel ridges of the range. The local interpretation placed on the Sātpurā refers the word to the seven distinct ridges that a traveller from the Berār valley has to cross before he reaches the Nerbudda. Taking Amarkantak in Rewah, Central India (20° 40′ N. and 81° 46′ E.) as the eastern boundary, the Sātpurās extend from east to west for about 600 miles and in their greatest depth exceed 100 miles from north to south. The shape of the range is almost triangular. The western prolongation of the Sātpurā hills, which walls in the northern frontier of Berār, lies chiefly in Amraoti District and is sometimes spoken of as the Gāwīlgarh range, from the fort of that name which stands on one of its highest buttresses directly overlooking the plain. The range is almost coterminous with the Melghāt *tāluk*, so called not from *ghāt* a mountain but from Melghāt a small village and ford on its northern side; and forms the watershed between the Tāpti on the north and the Pūrna and Wardhā rivers on the south. Its greatest length through the Betūl, Amraoti and Nimār Districts is probably about 160 miles. The hills rise abruptly from the plains of Berār on one side and from the banks of the Tāpti on the other, the summits reaching an elevation of two to four thousand feet. Plateaux rather than isolated peaks are the rule, interspersed with precipitous ravines.

Heights.

The most notable elevations locally are Khāmla (3,700 feet) and Bhainsdehi (2,609 feet) in Betūl, Bairat (3,866 feet), Chikaldā (3,664 feet) in Amraoti and the two great fortresses of Gāwīlgarh (3,513 feet) in Amraoti and Narnāla (3,052 feet) in Akolā. The last-named though geographically part of the Melghāt tāluk was handed over to Akolā apparently with the idea that it should be a hill station for that District. Its inaccessibility, however, has largely prevented its use. For further details reference may be made to the article on the Melghāt tāluk.

Saur.—In the Amraoti tāluk, 417 houses, population 2,162 It is 18 miles from Amraoti by road and about 4 miles to the west of the *pakkā* road to Chāndur Bazār. There is a vernacular school, with a branch post office. A bāzar is held on Saturdays.

Sawanga.—Pargana Mālkhed, tāluk Chāndur, a small village with 664 inhabitants. A fair in honour of Vithobā commences on Chaitra Sudi Pratipadā (March) and lasts for 10 days, being attended by about 2,000 people. There is no temple or other building of any importance.

Sawalpur.—Houses 268, population 1,147, in the Ellichpur tāluk, on the borders of Amraoti tāluk adjoining Assegaon, is situated on the banks of the Pūrna. Its only claim to be noticed is a fairly executed image ot Keshaorāj which was unearthed here in 1884.

Sembadoh.—Melghāt tāluk, a forest village 30 miles from Ellichpur, on the Dharni road ; the population, 342 in number, is entirely Korkū. It is the headquarters of a forest range, and has a Public Works Department inspection bungalow.

Sendurjana.—A village in Morsi tāluk about 60 miles east of Ellichpur with 1,463 houses and 6,860 population. The contiguous village of Malkāpur has 1,946 inhabitants. Sendurjanā formerly belonged in jāgīr to an agent of the Nāgpur Rājā called Gaikwār who lived there and made the village one of considerable importance. He built a splendid well about a mile distant which goes by his name and cost, it is said, some 20,000 rupees. There are also ruins of a small mosque, and a temple of Bālajī for the support of which seven *inām* fields are assigned. Some tombs also exist of early European adventurers. A big weekly bazar is held on Fridays at which timber and jaggery are sold. Now that the police station here has been suppressed a Marāthī and an Urdū school and post office are the only public buildings. Mālis are the chief element in the population, Kunbīs and Musalmāns coming next. The place is well known for the manufacture of *kunku*, a red powder, used by women. Rai Sāhib Sunder Lāl has a cotton gin here.

Sendurjana.—Pargana Talegaon, tāluk Chāndur, houses 438, population 1,926, like its namesake is noteworthy chiefly for its large weekly bazar and cattle market.

Sendurjana Buzruk.—Pargana Kurha, tāluk Chāndur, houses 302, population 1,429, has a *musāfir khāna*, a District Board *chaodi*, and a school. The weekly bazar which is held on Tuesdays is a very large one, and cattle are sold. There is also a Sendurjana Khurd with a population of 260 in the same pargana.

Shahnur River.—A river which, taking its rise near the Gāwilgarh fort, flows through the length of the Daryāpur tāluk from the north southward. The name is said to be derived from the Shaha Neera or "javelin thrown" by Rāmachandra: and the river to have sprung up where the javelin struck the ground. It is met by its tributary the river Bordī close to Adul and thence taking a westerly course leaves the Daryāpur tāluk at Dahihandā, and flowing in the same direction effects a junction with the river Pūrna near Pilakwāri in the Akot tāluk. At one point, about a quarter mile north of the little hamlets Malkāpur and Wāgdeo, which form part of the Ellichpur tāluk and lie at the foot of the Sātpurā hills, it is possible that a fine reservoir might be constructed. The banks of the river here are very high and precipitous, and approach each other so closely that by means of a small embankment a large valley can be easily enclosed. In the monsoon a large body of water rushes down this channel only to disappear, however, as rapidly as it collects, and it has been is suggested that this amount of water could be saved by a reservoir for purposes of irrigation.

Shirala.—Amraoti tāluk, about 15 miles north of Amraoti, is about 2 miles to the east of the Chāndur Bazār road, and has a population of 3,546. Like other villages of its class it has a vernacular school with a branch post office attached, a pound and a *sarai*. The weekly bazar is held on Wednesdays. A Marāthī school for girls teaches 3 standards, and the Hindustāni school contains 4 classes. Good *tadhaos*, a coarse cotton cloth like canvas, used as carpets etc., are made here on handlooms by Dhangars.

Shirasgaon Band.—See Chāndur Bazār.

Shirasgaon Kasba.—A large and rich village with 1,289 houses and a population of 6,537, situated on the banks of the river Meghā about 14 miles from Ellichpur. A large area of garden land belongs to the village. The bazar day is Wednesday; and the village has a first-class police station and a combined post office and vernacular school teaching up to the sixth standard. There is nothing else of note. The yearly land revenue is about Rs. 17,000.

Sipna River.—This stream in the northern portion of the Melghāt tāluk rises near Khāmla and Kukru in the Betūl District of the Central Provinces, and runs south of the Mākhla plateau for eight or 10 miles. Passing under the villages of Harisāl and Dūni, it then meets the Tāpti about 4 miles north of Dharni. Otters (*Lutra nain*) are found in the Sipna.

Surji.—See Anjangaon Surji.

Takerkhera.—Amraoti tāluk, is about 14 miles from Amraoti and about 3 miles to the west of the *pakkā* road to Chāndur Bazār, population 2,260, houses 472. It has a police station in charge of Sub-Inspector, a sub-registry, a vernacular school and a branch post office. A bazar is held on Tuesdays.

Talegaon Dashasar.—A corruption of the Sanskrit Dasha Sahasra. Houses 1,511, population 6,220, at one time the largest town in the Chāndur tāluk, formerly contained the tahsīli which has been removed to Chāndur on account of the latter being on the line of railway. Talegaon is now greatly decayed but the ruins of many fine houses and temples attest its former prosperity, one of the best known of its relics being the *dargāh* of Fakīr Shāh Abdul Latīf which is supported by a grant of land from the Emperor Shāh Jahān.

"The origin of its nickname, Dasha Sahasra (Talegaon of "the pumpkin, it might be called), is peculiar, but not very "credible. The legend runs thus:—The wife of the jāgirdār "and the wife of a wealthy merchant went to market one day. "Now it happened on this particular day that an uncommonly "fine pumpkin was exposed for sale. It attracts the notice "of both simultaneously. Their mouths water. They both "admire it, both desire it, and finally both try to outbid each "other for it. The merchant's wife, in all the pride of wealth, "determines to have it at any price; the dignity of the jāgirdār's "wife forbids *her* giving way. The price rises rapidly. One "hundred is a trifle. So is five. A thousand is reached, and the "pair get warm to their work. So they quickly bid up to five "thousand, and from that to ten thousand, at which price it is "ultimately knocked down. The legend unfortunately leaves us "in the dark as to who carried off the prize, but it is currently "believed that the merchant's wife was the victor." In memory of this exciting but bloodless contest the town was dubbed "Dasha Sahasra," which being translated (from the Sanskrit) means ten thousand. A more probable derivation is from the numbers of inhabitants in the time of its prosperity. To-day Talegaon has a cotton gin, and hand-worked spinning and weaving frames which produce rough yarn and cloth used by the poorer classes. It contains a police station, post office, dispensary, and Government Anglo-Marāthī and Hindustāni schools.

Talegaon Khar.—Amraoti tāluk, houses 398, population 1,932, a village lying between Balgaon Jāgīr and Kholāpur, with a combined post office and Marāthī school to which an English class supported by local subscriptions has been added.

The water is very brackish, and the distinguishing name "Khar" is taken from the old salt wells which used formerly to be worked here. In the patel's house, a small building not otherwise noticeable, is some handsome old blackwood carving.

Talegaon Thakur.—Tāluk Chāndur, houses 700, population 2,859, is only mentioned to distinguish it from the more important town of the same name Tālegaon Dashasar. The name Thākur is taken from a Rājput family who hold the *patelki* of this and a few neighbouring villages (v. Mojhari). They are very well-to-do and have considerable influence locally.

Tapti River.[1]—One of the great rivers of Western India.

Course in the Central Provinces.

The name is derived from *tāp*, heat, and the Tāpti is said by the Brāhmans to have been created by the sun to protect himself from his own warmth. The Tāpti is believed to rise in the sacred tank of Multai (*mūl-tāpi*, the source of the Tāpti) on the Sātpurā plateau, but its real source is two miles distant (21°48′ N. and 78°15′ E). It flows in a westerly direction through the Betūl District, at first traversing an open and partially cultivated plain, and then plunging into a rocky gorge of the Sātpurā hills between the Kālibhīt range in Hoshangābād and Chikaldā in Berār. It touches the northern boundary of the Melghāt tāluk, 3 miles to the east of Melghāt ferry and runs along the border for about 30 miles. During this course it receives the Kapra, Sipnā and Gargā rivers which take their rise in the Gāwīlgarh hills. Its bed here is rocky, overhung by steep banks, and bordered by forests. At a distance of 120 miles from its source it enters the Nimār District, and for 30 miles more is still confined in a comparatively narrow valley. A few miles above Burhānpur, the valley opens out, the Sātpurā hills receding north and south, and opposite that town the river valley has become a fine rich basin of alluvial soil about 20 miles wide. In the centre of this tract the Tāpti flows between the towns of Burhānpur and Zaināбād, and then passes into the Khāndesh District of Bombay. In

[1] The article on the Tāpti river is a reprint from the draft article for the Imperial Gazetteer.

its upper valley are several basins of exceedingly rich soil, but they have long been covered by forest, and it is only lately that the process of clearing them for cultivation has been undertaken.

In Bombay.

Shortly after entering the Khāndesh District the Tāpti receives on the left bank the Pūrna from the hills of Berār, and then flows for about 150 miles through a broad and fertile valley, bounded on the north by the Sātpurās, and on the south by the Sātmālas. Further on the hills close in, and the river descends through wild and wooded country for about 80 miles, after which it sweeps southwards to the sea through the alluvial plain of Surat, and is a tidal river for the last 30 miles of its course. The banks (30 to 60 feet) are too high for irrigation, and the bed is crossed at several places by ridges of rock ; hence the river is only navigable for about 20 miles from the sea. The Tāpti runs so near the foot of the Sātpurās, that its tributaries on the right bank are small, but on the left bank after its junction with the Pūrna, it receives through the Gīrna (150 miles long) the drainage of the hills of Bāglān, and through the Bori, the Pānjhra and the Borai, that of the northern buttress of the Western Ghāts. The waters of the Gīrna and Pānjhra are dammed up in several places and used for irrigation. On the lower course of the Tāpti, floods are not uncommon, and have at times done much damage to the city of Surat. The river is crossed at Bhusāwal by the Jubbulpore branch of the Great Indian Peninsula Railway, at Savaldā by the Bombay-Agra road, and at Surat by the Bombay-Baroda and Central India Railway. The Tāpti has a local reputation for sanctity, the chief *tīrthas* or holy places being Chāngdev, at the confluence with the Pūrna, and Bodhān above Surat. The Fort of Tālner and the city of Surat are the places of most historic note on its course, the total length of which is 436 miles. The port of Swally (Suwali), famous in early European commerce with India, and the scene of a sea-fight between the British and the Portuguese lay at the mouth of the river, but is now deserted, its approaches having been silted up.

Thugaon.—Amraoti tāluk, population 3,384, houses 696, 14 miles from Amraoti, about a mile to the west of the Ellichpur road. There are country liquor, opium and *gānja* shops, a pound, a vernacular school, and a branch post office. The bazar day is Friday.

Tiosa.—Tāluk Chāndur, 111 houses and 1,182 inhabitants. Rāmratan Ganeshdās Mārwāri, who has a house here and is a member of the Amraoti Bench of Magistrates, has built a temple to Bālajī, at a cost of about fifteen thousand rupees. In the famine he gave a thousand rupees to local relief. He has a large moneylending business in the neighbourhood. The soil of Tiosā is very rich, and had tempted the people to disregard rotation; cotton being sown every year, as yet without any perceptible deterioration in the crop. The place has a police station and a sub-registrar's office.

Uprai.—Houses 138, inhabitants 572, in the Daryāpur tāluk, is only mentioned as being the headquarters of the cult of Shāh Dāwal whose tomb is situated here. A full description of the cult will be found in Chapter III.

Wadali.—See Amraoti Camp.

Wadner Gangai.—Daryāpur tāluk, houses 711, population 3,071, a village of no particular importance with a Hindu and Muhammadan school. The land revenue is Rs. 19,605-7-3. A story is current that Aurangzeb in his march through Berār halted at this village at midday, and being thirsty called for milk, which, after much trouble and many threats of the Emperor's displeasure, his followers succeeded in obtaining. The "Lord of the Earth" drank it and was not only much refreshed, but noticed that a small spot of white leprosy on his leg was healed. He enquired the cause of the miracle, and was told that the milk was mother's milk, and has been given to the King's messengers by two old women Sitai and Gangai both over a hundred years of age, whom they found near the temple of Māroti. Henceforth the village was given its second name, though why Gangai and not Sitai should have been selected is not clear. The village is also known as Wadner Zāgajī Bāwa, after a Kunbī ascetic whose shrine here has an *inām* of 140 acres.

Walgaon Jagir.—See Balgaon Jāgir.

Wanosa.—See Daryāpur.

Wardha River. [1]—A river in the Central Provinces which rises on the Multai plateau of the Betūl District (at 21°50′ N. and 78°24′ E.), some 70 miles north-west of the town of Nāgpur, and flowing south and south-east, separates the Nāgpur, Wardhā and Chānda Districts of the Central Provinces from Berār and the Nizām's Dominions. For over fifty miles of its course it forms the boundary of the Morsi tāluk and for a similar distance of that of Chāndur. After a course of 290 miles from its source, the Wardhā meets the Waingangā river at Seonī in the Chānda District, and the united stream under the name of the Prānhita flows on to join the Godāvari. The bed of the Wardhā, from its source to its junction with the Pengangā at Jugad in the south-east corner of Yeotmāl is deep and rocky, changing from a swift torrent in the monsoon months to a succession of nearly stagnant pools in the summer. For the last hundred miles of its course below Chānda it flows in a clear channel, broken only by a barrier of rocks commencing above the confluence of the Waingangā and extending into the Prānhita. The project entertained in the years 1866-1871 for rendering the Godāvari and Wardhā fit for navigation, included the excavation of a channel through this expanse of rock, which was known as the Third Barrier. The scheme proved impracticable, and except that timber is sometimes floated up from the Ahiri forests in the monsoon months no use is now made of the river for navigation. The area drained by the Wardhā includes the Wardhā District, with parts of Nāgpur and Chānda in the Central Provinces and the eastern parts of Amrāoti and Yeotmāl districts in Berār. On the eastern or Central Provinces side, it is a rich tract of country confined between the river and a range of hills to the north, and widening to the south as the hills recede. The valley is covered with light black soil, and is a well-known cotton growing tract. In the Chānda District, the Wardhā valley coalfield extends for a long distance in the

1. The article on the Wardhā river is a reprint from the draft article for the Imperial Gazetteer.

vicinity of the Wardhā, Prānhita, and Godāvari rivers. The coal is worked by a Government colliery at Warorā, and fresh seams are now being exploited in other localities. The principal tributaries of the Wardhā are the Wunnā and Erai from the Central Provinces, and the Bemblā and Pengangā which drain the southern and eastern portions of the plain of Berār. The banks of the river are in several places picturesquely crowned by small temples and tombs, and numerous ruined forts in the background recall the wild period through which the valley passed, during the Marāthā wars and the Pindāri raids. Kaundinyapur (Dewalwāda) on the Berār bank in Amraoti District, is believed to represent the site of a buried city, celebrated in the Bhāgavat as the metropolis of the kingdom of *Vidarbha* (Berār). A large religious fair is held there. At Ballālpur near Chānda are the ruins of a palace of the Gond kings and a curious temple on an islet in the river which for some months in the year is several feet under water. The Wardhā is crossed by the Great Indian Peninsula Railway at Pulgaon.

Warha—A prosperous but unimportant village in the Chāndur tāluk, of 655 houses and 2,958 inhabitants, the greater part of whom are Ghasmālis. The temple of Māroti was built by subscription at a cost of Rs. 6,000. A bazar is held on Fridays.

Warud Bagaji—A small village of about 500 people on the banks of the Wardhā river in the Chāndur tāluk, about three miles distant from Mangrūl Dastagīr. The second name is derived from the *samādhi*, or tomb, of a Hindu ascetic named Bagāji Bāba, in whose honour a fair is held annually on the 6th day of Phālgun *Wadya* (March). Formerly the fair lasted for a month or so, and carts, cart wheels, cloth, copper and brass vessels were sold. For the last fifteen years, however, it has dwindled to an affair of a single day.

Warud or Barur.—Houses 1609, population 7179 formerly the headquarters of the Morsi tāluk, the tahsīli having been moved some 30 years ago to Morsi. It is situated on the Chandra Chūdāman river about 56 miles east of Ellichpur and 53 miles from Amraoti, and is so far as communications are concerned the most important town in the tāluk, having a first-class metalled road through Morsi to Amraoti, another to Multai by Bikatghāt, and roads to Nāgpur via the Wardhā river and Kātol, and viâ Amner. Of these that by Amner is a country road, but the former is *muram* surfaced and is shortly to be fully metalled. The proposed railway will also run by here. Warud however has neither dâk nor inspection bungalow, the nearest being that at Benodā. Turmeric is sold here, but the chief trade is in cotton, the two gins being owned respectively by Srirām Rūprām and Srirām Sāligrām. A Bench of Magistrates tries petty cases and the public buildings include a police station, a sub-registry, dispensary, post office, Anglo-Marāthī and Urdū schools. It is the headquarters of the Morsi-Warud forest range. There are several old temples and two new and small but very creditable mosques.

Wathoda.—About 4 miles north of Kholāpur on the Pūrna, has a population of 2121. It has a vernacular school and a branch post office, an opium and a country liquor shop. A temple of Sukleshwar has for its maintenance a field of 21 acres and 28 *gunthās* rent free.

Wirud.—Tāluk Chāndur, houses 481, population 2163, is situated to the north of Chāndur four miles from the railway. The village is an unimportant one in spite of its size, having the usual school and post office and a weekly bazar on Fridays. Four small temples are supported by a grant of *inām* land, and it is said that before the British Administration a peculiarly painful vow was regularly performed before them. The devotee would take a length of coarse string and pass it under the skin on both sides of his body. Two friends would then hold the ends and he would walk to and fro along it in front of the temples, the string sawing his flesh as he did so.

Yoli.—Amraoti tāluk, 16 miles from Amraoti and 4 miles from Māhuli on the Morsi road. The land around the village is boggy and communication is difficult during the rains. The population is 2059. The teacher of the vernacular school is in charge of a branch post office and the patel manages a cattle pound.

Yeoda.—Daryāpur tāluk, houses 832, population 3419, a large village having 11,556 acres of land under cultivation and paying Rs. 30,000 land revenue; totals only surpassed in Berār by Shegaon in the Buldāna District. Under the Nizām, a Naib Peshkār or Mahālkari named Ukadsing was stationed here for a considerable time and built the temple of Rāmchandra, still in existence. Marāthī and Urdū schools are established here. The village is occasionally spoken of as Yeodā Ukadsing.

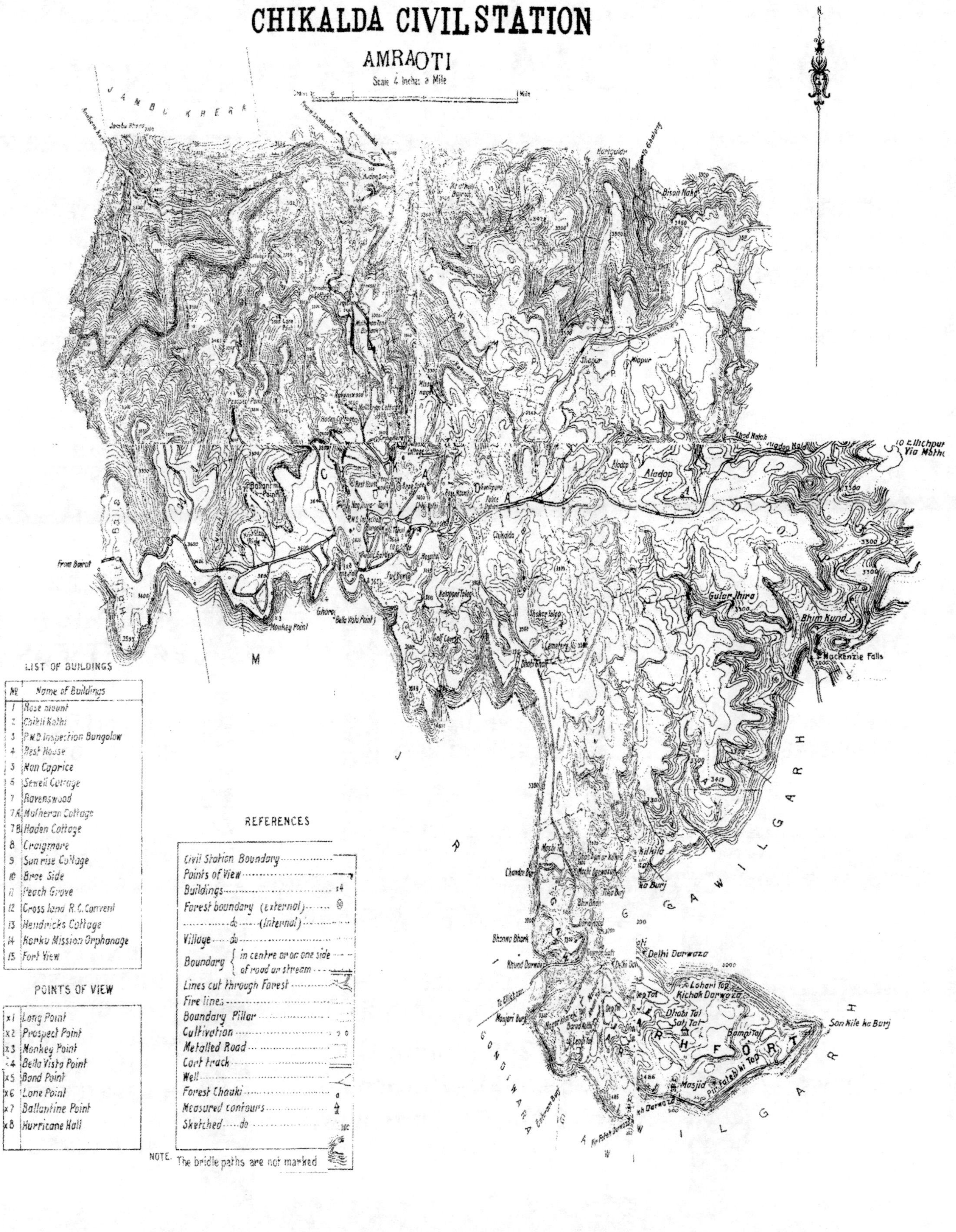
CHIKALDA CIVIL STATION
AMRAOTI
Scale 4 Inches a Mile
LIST OF BUILDINGS
No. Name of Buildings
1 Rose mount
2 Chikli Kothi
3 P.W.D Inspection Bungalow
4 Rest House
5 Mon Caprice
6 Sewell Cottage
7 Ravenswood
7A Matheran Cottage
7B Haden Cottage
8 Craigmore
9 Sun rise Cottage
10 Brae Side
11 Peach Grove
12 Cross land R.C. Convent
13 Hendricks Cottage
14 Korku Mission Orphanage
15 Fort View
POINTS OF VIEW
x1 Long Point
x2 Prospect Point
x3 Monkey Point
x4 Bella Vista Point
x5 Band Point
x6 Lone Point
x7 Ballantine Point
x8 Hurricane Hall
REFERENCES
Civil Station Boundary
Points of View
Buildings
Forest boundary (external)
do (internal)
Village do
Boundary { in centre or on one side of road or stream
Lines cut through Forest
Fire lines
Boundary Pillar
Cultivation
Metalled Road
Cart track
Well
Forest Chauki
Measured contours
Sketched do
NOTE. The bridle paths are not marked
Bisan Naka
Shapur
Alladoh
Aladoh
Chikalda
Gular Jhira
Bhim Kund
Mackenzie Falls
From Bairat
Monkey Point
Bella Vista Point
Prospect Point
Delhi Darwaza
Lohari Tap
Kichak Darwaza
Dhobi Tal
Masjid
Son Kile ka Burj
To Ellichpur Via Mothe
GAWILGARH
GAWILGARH FORT